World History
FOR
DUMMIES®
2ND EDITION

by Peter Haugen

WILEY

Wiley Publishing, Inc.

World History For Dummies,® 2nd Edition

Published by
Wiley Publishing, Inc.
111 River St.
Hoboken, NJ 07030-5774
www.wiley.com

For general information on our other products and services, please contact our Customer Care Department within the U.S. at 877-762-2974, outside the U.S. at 317-572-3993, or fax 317-572-4002.

For technical support, please visit www.wiley.com/techsupport.

Wiley also publishes its books in a variety of electronic formats. Some content that appears in print may not be available in electronic books.

Library of Congress Control Number: 2009926358

ISBN: 978-0-470-44654-6

Manufactured in the United States of America

C10003121_080118

WILEY

About the Author

Peter Haugen is the author of *Was Napoleon Poisoned? And Other Unsolved Mysteries of Royal History* (Wiley). A graduate of the University of California, Berkeley, he has been a frequent contributor to *History* magazine and is among the co-writers of *The Armchair Reader Amazing Book of History, mental_floss Presents Condensed Knowledge,* and *mental_floss Presents Forbidden Knowledge*. A veteran journalist and critic, he was a staff member at several U.S. newspapers, including *The St. Petersburg Times* and *The Sacramento Bee,* and has written about topics ranging from the fine arts to molecular genetics. Haugen was an adjunct instructor at the University of Wisconsin-Madison and California State University-Fresno and is a proud veteran of the U.S. Army. He lives in Wisconsin.

Author's Acknowledgments

Thanks to my editors at Wiley — Project Editor Tim Gallan, Acquisitions Editor Lindsay Lefevere, and Copy Editor Elizabeth Rea — all of whom helped make the process of writing this second edition remarkably painless. Thanks, too, to all my family, especially my wife, Deborah Blum, for her constant support. I'd like to thank historian David McDonald, again, for his invaluable help with the first edition of this book, and all the wonderful history writers whose works I have combed through, pored through, and compared one against the other while once again skimming over the surface of the wonderful body of scholarship that is world history.

Publisher's Acknowledgments

We're proud of this book; please send us your comments through our Dummies online registration form located at `http://dummies.custhelp.com`. For other comments, please contact our Customer Care Department within the U.S. at 877-762-2974, outside the U.S. at 317-572-3993, or fax 317-572-4002.

Some of the people who helped bring this book to market include the following:

Acquisitions, Editorial, and Media Development

Senior Project Editor: Tim Gallan

(Previous Edition: Kathleen A. Dobie)

Acquisitions Editor: Lindsay Lefevere

Senior Copy Editor: Elizabeth Rea

(Previous Edition: Esmeralda St. Clair)

Technical Reviewer: Amy Bielot

Editorial Program Coordinator: Joe Niesen

Editorial Manager: Michelle Hacker

Editorial Assistants: Jennette ElNaggar, David Lutton

Art Coordinator: Alicia B. South

Cover Photos: © liquidlibrary

Cartoons: Rich Tennant (`www.the5thwave.com`)

Composition Services

Project Coordinator: Katie Crocker

Layout and Graphics: Carl Byers, Reuben W. Davis, Christin Swinford, Christine Williams

Proofreaders: ConText Editorial Services, Inc., Nancy L. Reinhardt

Indexer: Potomac Indexing, LLC

Publishing and Editorial for Consumer Dummies

    Diane Graves Steele, Vice President and Publisher, Consumer Dummies

    Kristin Ferguson-Wagstaffe, Product Development Director, Consumer Dummies

    Ensley Eikenburg, Associate Publisher, Travel

    Kelly Regan, Editorial Director, Travel

Publishing for Technology Dummies

    Andy Cummings, Vice President and Publisher, Dummies Technology/General User

Composition Services

    Debbie Stailey, Director of Composition Services

Contents at a Glance

Table of Contents

Introduction

The complete history of the world boiled down to 400-some pages and crammed between paperback covers? The idea is preposterous. It's outrageous. I'd be crazy to attempt it. So here goes.

No, wait. This book doesn't claim to be complete. It can't. Hundreds of other volumes are devoted to a measly decade or two — the World War II era comes to mind. To plumb thousands of years in one little book would be impossible. To skim across the surface, however, is another matter. If, while reading the following chapters, you hit upon an era, a personality, or a civilization that you'd like to know more about, there's no lack of places to find out more. You can turn to many far more complete accounts of the history of specific countries, such as the United States; continents, such as Europe; and events, such as the U.S. Civil War. You can find books about all these topics and more in this excellent *For Dummies* series. But if you want a simplified overview consisting of a collection of easy-to-read glimpses into major players and events that have made the world what it is today, then I'm your guide and *World History For Dummies,* 2nd Edition is your first-stop reference.

About This Book

The history of the world is like a soap opera that has been running ever since the invention of writing. The show is lurid, full of dirty tricks and murder, romances and sexual deceptions, adventures, and wars and revolutions. (And, yes, treaties and dates.) Or maybe a better analogy is that history is like hundreds of soap operas with thousands of crossover characters jumping out of one story and into another — too many for even the most devoted fan to keep straight. All the more reason for an easy-to-use overview.

The most important thing to remember when paging through this book is that history is fun — or should be. It's not as if this is life-and-death stuff. . . . no, wait. It *is* life-and-death — on a ginormous scale. It's just that so many of the lives and deaths happened long ago. And that's good, because I can pry into private affairs without getting sued. History is full of vintage gossip and antique scandal, peppered heavily with high adventure (swords and spears and canons and stuff). The more you get into it, the better you'll do when the neighbors drag out the home version of *Jeopardy.* Renaissance Italy for $500, please.

Conventions Used in This Book

Every field from brain surgery to refuse collection has a special vocabulary. History is no exception, but I tried to steer clear of historians-only words in this book. When such a word is unavoidable, I explain it in reader-friendly terms. As for other technical terms, I italicize them and then follow up with definitions and explanations. If you still think you may get lost amid the dates, facts, quotes, and other details, this section guides you through the conventions I use in order to help you better understand the book and access the information you want or need.

What do I mean by "history"?

This isn't a stupid question. People apply the term *history* to fields other than, well, history. For example, scientists talk about geological history, and physicians talk about your medical history. There's also archeological history, in which experts use physical evidence to piece together the story of humankind before anybody wrote anything down. Even though historians often disagree about the details, history must be true or at least reasonably close to what really happened. Historians use educated guesses, too. I get into some of that in this book, but for the most part, I stick to documented human events.

History is also a written account (or at least on film or video). It often starts as *oral history,* but until the tale is set down in some permanent form, it's too easy for facts to get lost or changed. Things written down aren't immune to exaggeration, but there's something about the spoken word that invites outlandish embellishment. (Think about fishing stories or campaign speeches.) That's how history gets mangled and myths get made (that and cable news shows).

Some of the first stories ever written down were passed on by word of mouth for centuries before they ever were etched in mud or stone or on papyrus. They got pretty wild over the years; for example, Homer, a blind Greek poet, passed down a tale of the Trojan War based on a real military campaign, but many of his details are obviously myth. That stuff about Achilles' mom being a water nymph, for example, and the way she supposedly dipped him in the River Styx to make him invulnerable — forgive me if I don't buy that as exactly the way things went down. (Now, if Homer had told us Achilles was an alien from the planet Krypton. . . .)

Positively post-historic

Because history needs to be set down in some kind of permanent record, it dates back only about as far as the written word, which some scholars say the Sumerians invented, at least in *pictograph* (or picture-writing) form, around 3500 BC. Among the best early record keepers were the Egyptians, who invented their own form of writing (called *hieroglyphics*) around 3000 BC. Before written history, it was *prehistoric* times.

Making sense of AD, BC, CE, and BCE

The years 1492, when Columbus sailed, and 1620, when the *Mayflower* Pilgrims arrived in Massachusetts, are AD, just like this year. AD stands for *Anno Domini.* That's Latin for "Year of Our Lord," referring to the Christian era, or the time since Jesus was born. Before that, I designate years as BC, or Before Christ. Historians now prefer CE, for "Common Era," instead of AD; and BCE, for "Before the Common Era," instead of BC. The new initials aren't tied into just one religion. AD and BC, however, are what most people are used to. They're widely understood and deeply ingrained, so I stick with them throughout this book.

The years BC are figured by counting backwards. That's why the year that Alexander the Great died, 323 BC, is a smaller number than the year that he was born, 356 BC.

Yet Alexander didn't think of himself as living in backward-counting years three centuries before Christ any more than Augustus Caesar of Rome wrote the date 1 AD on his checks. This system of dating years came about a lot later when scholars superimposed their calendar on earlier times. Given that Jesus actually may have been born a little earlier than 1 AD — perhaps in about 6 BC — the system isn't even particularly accurate. As the twentieth century came to a close, some self-proclaimed prophets thought the world would come to an end when the calendar turned over to year 2000. Obviously, it didn't happen then or in any of the years since. As for next year or the year after that, I make no guarantees.

In this book, you can safely assume that a four-digit year without two capital letters following it is AD. For example, William the Conqueror invaded England in 1066. For the years 1–999 AD, I use the AD; for example, Norsemen invaded Ireland and began building the city of Dublin around 831 AD. I also include the initials for all the BC years. For examples, Saul was anointed the first king of the Israelites in about 1050 BC, and the Roman general Marc Antony died in 30 BC.

The reason I say "around" and "about" when giving the dates of Dublin's founding and King Saul's coronation is that nobody knows the dates for sure.

Another thing that confuses some people when reading history is the way centuries are named and numbered. When you see a reference to the 1900s, it doesn't mean the same thing as the nineteenth century. The 1900s are the twentieth century. The twentieth century was the one in which four-digit year numbers started with 19. The nineteenth century was the one in which years started with 18, and so on. Why isn't this century, the one with the 20 starting every year, the twentieth? Because the first century began in the year 1. When the numbers got up to 100 (or technically, 101), it became the second century, and so on. Figuring the centuries BC works the same way (in reverse, of course): The twenty-first century BC is the one with years starting with 20, just like the twenty-first century AD.

Pardon my French, I mean Latin

For Dummies books are intended to make complex topics easier to understand, and a large part of achieving that goal is avoiding hard-to-understand, experts-only language, especially if it's not in English. But like so many things in life, there are exceptions.

You'll find a very small number of Latin and other foreign words and phrases sprinkled throughout this book. I have to include them because I tell you about cultures and countries where English was unknown. With Latin, in particular, it's not just that this book's subjects include the important, influential Roman Empire, where everybody spoke Latin. I also cover Europe in the Middle Ages, when Latin was the international language. Finally, I can't write about world history without covering the enormous influence of the Roman Catholic Church, an institution that for many centuries clung to Latin as its official means of expression. But don't worry. I promise not to use many such terms, and when I do, I'll explain what they mean.

Perceiving and avoiding biases

Some intellectuals question the very concept of history. "Whose history are we talking about?" they ask. If the victors write history, why do we accept those big bullies' tainted point of view as true? What about the victims? What about the indigenous peoples, such as American Indians and Australian Aborigines? What about the women? Doesn't it stink that so much of history is so overwhelmingly about white men?

Yes, it does. And it's true that history is slanted. It's people writing about people, so prejudice is built-in. You have to factor in the biases of the time in which events happened, the biases of the time when they were written down, and the prejudices of the scholars who turn them over and over again decades and often centuries later. I can't change the fact that so many conquerors, monarchs, politicians, soldiers, explorers and yes, historians, have been men. It's just as true that conventionally taught world history still spends a fair amount of time on Europe — how it was shaped and how it shaped other parts of the world, including the Americas.

Are there other stories worth telling, other points of view, other truths? You bet. You find some of them in this book, lightly touched upon, just like everything else here. But to be honest, the tilt is toward a male-centered history of what has been called *western civilization*. Why? Because that view is built on well-documented, widely disseminated tales of how the world became what it is.

You may want to change the world, and that's often a noble ambition. You may just want to change the history books. Either way, it helps to know what you're up against.

Where I can, I nod toward the realities of the twenty-first century, as non-Western countries — notably China and India — have grown into major forces in both the global economy and global politics, and where developing nations such as resource-rich Brazil seem poised to play ever larger roles in shaping the world's history.

What You're Not to Read

Although this book focuses on what you need to know about world history, I also deal with topics that, though useful, are less essential, at least during your first read-through. This skippable material includes:

- **Text in sidebars.** Sidebars are shaded boxes that pop up here and there in the chapters. They deal with interesting subjects related to the chapter, but they aren't necessary reading in order for you to understand major topics.

- **Anything with a Technical Stuff icon.** You may find this information interesting, but you won't miss out on anything critical if you pass over it.

Foolish Assumptions

As I wrote this book, I made some assumptions about you. They may be foolish, but here they are:

- You've studied at least some history in school. You may even know quite a lot about certain historical topics, but you'd like to find out more about how it all fits together.

- You've seen movies or read novels set in various historical eras, and you suspect they'd be more enjoyable if you were better informed about the time periods and the historical peoples featured.

✔ At least once in your life you've encountered an obnoxious history know-it-all, one of those people who spews random facts about ancient Rome or the French Revolution. In the event that it happens again, you want the satisfaction of telling Ms. Smartypants she's wrong.

How This Book Is Organized

I haven't laid out history in chronological order in *World History For Dummies,* 2nd Edition. Not quite. I try to tell stories in the order that they happened, but as I explain in Chapter 1, many different threads run through history, and they crisscross and influence each other. But if you sort out the some of the many approaches you can take to history and some of the many topics within it, the threads are easier to understand and follow. With this in mind, I've divided the book as follows:

✔ Each part is based on a broad topic such as civilizations throughout history, warfare throughout history, or the impact of religions and philosophies upon history.

✔ Each chapter looks at a particular aspect or time period within the broad subject of the part.

✔ Headings and subheadings isolate specific points within each chapter so that you can more easily get in and out of chapters and access just the information you need or want.

What follows is a breakdown of each part.

Part 1: Getting into History

This part includes perspective to help you connect with the past. Your ancestors of decades, centuries, and millennia past were essentially the same as you. True, they dressed differently and didn't have iPhones and cars and such. They may not have showered as often as you do, either, but they can still reveal things about you and how your world came to be as it is.

Part II: Finding Strength in Numbers

How did human society get to be a worldwide, interconnected network of cultures? What makes a civilization, and how does one succeed or fail? How does a civilization influence those that follow? This part of the book traces the growth from the earliest civilizations to today's global community.

Part III: Seeking Answers

People act upon what they think and what they believe. In this part you can
glimpse the ways that thoughts, ideas, and feelings — and the way people
express and explore them in religion and philosophy — have always been a
fundamental part of history.

Part IV: Fighting, Fighting, Fighting

History isn't all conflict between nations — or between governments and the
governed — but violent clashes and upheavals have immediate, often widespread, and sometimes long-lasting global consequences. This part examines
historical battles of all scales as well as developments in warfare throughout
the centuries of human conflict.

Part V: Meeting the Movers and Shakers

This part includes an extremely incomplete collection of capsule biographies
of people who changed history, along with a few who were changed by it.

Part VI: The Part of Tens

In the grand tradition of *For Dummies* books, this part contains easy-to-digest
lists of history's unforgettable dates, indelible documents, and indispensible
discoveries.

Icons Used in this Book

The margins of this book contain picture road signs that clue you into what's
going on in that particular portion of text. Some warn you of what you can
skip, while others may help you find just what you're interested in. I use the
following icons:

This icon clues you in to an event, decision, or discovery that changed the
world — whether at the time it happened or at a later date.

Screenwriters, perpetually hungry for plots, are always mining history for story ideas. This icon alerts you to film (and some TV) versions of real stories. Movies rarely get the facts right, but they can get you thinking about history.

This icon marks memorable sayings that you may have heard before but didn't know who said them or in what context. When you know the stories behind these famous words, you're qualified to toss them out over coffee or cocktails.

This icon marks major historical concepts to keep in mind as you read. They're also points that you may want or need to refer back to as you work your way through the book.

This icon clues you in to more technical information — usually when, where, and/or how things were made and how things got done. For example, this icon marks paragraphs that tell you what society invented paper and who came up with a more accurate compass.

Where to Go from Here

A great thing about this book is that you can start with Chapter 1 and read to the end, but that's not required. The parts are organized so that you can jump in any place you want. As you page through and browse, note that you can look at the same era from different perspectives. Part III, for example, tells you how philosophy and religion shaped history, and there you can find the religious wars that followed the Protestant Reformation. But if you're more interested in the weaponry and strategies of war, jump to Part IV. And if you just want to browse through some historical all-stars, check out Part V. Not sure what you're looking for? Part I is a good place to get a general feel for history. The table of contents and index, along with the part summaries in the earlier section "How This Book Is Organized," should get you to the page you need.

Part I
Getting into History

The 5th Wave   By Rich Tennant

"Oh, Will — such passion, such pathos,
such despair and redemption. I've
never read a more moving grocery list."

In this part . . .

Browsing through history can be like looking at the stars. Even if you don't know a planet from a supernova or the name of a single constellation, the first thing you're likely to get from gazing at the night sky is a sense of how small you are. That's a good place to begin in astronomy, and it's not a bad place to find yourself when peering into world history.

It's easy to think of 100 years as a long time and 1,000 years as a long, long time. The modern habit is to chop up history and social trends into little decade-sized chunks — *the 1980s, the 1990s,* and so on. But if you step back a bit and consider how long human beings have been doing a lot of the same things people do today — buying, selling, cooking, falling in love, traveling, and fighting wars — you can gain a broader perspective. That's both humbling and enriching.

Whether you define *now* as a day, a year, or a decade, it's both a minuscule sliver of history and *part* of the larger thing. One of the best parts of being human is that you have more than your own experience to rely on. Language, lore, reading, writing, and, more recently, microchips, DVDs, and a few other technological tricks help people build on what their ancestors discovered generations, centuries, and millennia ago. History is a big part of what defines humanity; some may say it's the biggest part. It led to the present. It led to you. You might as well get comfortable with it.

Chapter 1

Tracing a Path to the Present

- -

In This Chapter

▶ Pondering how the past shaped the present

▶ Thinking about humankind's remarkable journey

▶ Following an intricate tapestry of historical threads

- -

During the first decade of the twenty-first century, a lot of news stories on American TV and in print addressed the question: "How did we get here?" For several years, those stories were about U.S. wars abroad, especially a war in Iraq that went on much longer than the U.S. officials who started the conflict had foreseen.

"What series of events led the United States to this predicament?" asked the journalists. "How did decisions made by American leaders take us down this path?" pondered the pundits. "Why the heck didn't anybody see this coming?" screamed bloggers.

Then, in 2008, the American economy unraveled. Huge financial institutions teetered on the edge of failure. Congress and the White House threw these firms a rope by pledging many hundreds of billions of dollars in public money to save private businesses — banks and investment companies so big that, to let them die, the taxpayers were told, would mean absolute disaster for the nation and the world.

"What was the series of events?" asked the journalists. "How did leaders' decisions take us down this path?" puffed the pundits. "How could we be so stupid!" thundered the bloggers.

This book isn't about a twenty-first century war in Iraq any more than it's about first-century BC wars in Greece. It isn't about modern economics, either. (That's a subject I know way too little about.) It's about the broader questions of "How did things get to be like this?" and "Why is the world as it is?"

I can't answer those questions in detail because there have been too many years of human activity on this planet, too many lives lived, too many migrations, wars, murders, weddings, coronations, inventions, revolutions, recessions, natural disasters, and financial meltdowns. Too many historians have interpreted events in too many contradictory ways. But what I hope you find in this book is a general view of how human history has gotten you and the world you live in to current reality. To now.

Firing Up the WABAC Machine

If you're old enough to remember or are a fanatic about classic TV cartoons, you may have heard of the WABAC machine. Pronounced "way back," it was a fictional time-traveling device built and operated by a genius dog named Mr. Peabody. In every episode of a 1960s animated show called *Rocky and His Friends* (later repackaged under other titles including *The Bullwinkle Show*), the professorial pooch and his pet boy, Sherman, would transport themselves to some historical setting — say, ancient Rome, revolutionary America, or medieval England — where they would interact with famous people from history and usually solve whatever ridiculously absurd dilemma was troubling Julius Caesar, George Washington, or King Arthur. Thus, Mr. Peabody and Sherman allowed the events we all know as history to take their proper course.

Filled with outrageous puns and deadpan humor (if a cartoon can be deadpan), these episodes were a goofy variation on a classic science fiction premise. Imaginative storytellers have often used time travel as a plot device. American novelist Mark Twain did it in 1889 with *A Connecticut Yankee in King Arthur's Court*. England's H.G. Wells followed suit in 1895 with *The Time Machine*. More recent examples include the *Terminator* films, British TV's various incarnations of *Doctor Who,* and innumerable episodes from the *Star Trek* television and feature film franchise.

Often these stories involve someone or something going back in time in order to change something in the present or to prevent the present from being changed in some disastrous fashion. One tiny interference in the "time continuum," as it's often called, can lead to a monumentally altered chain of events.

Of course nobody can really do that. Not now. Maybe not ever. It's a realm of possibility — or impossibility — that modern science has hardly begun to address, except in theoretical terms.

You can, however, understand a heck of a lot more about the present if you time travel in your head — that is, think about the ways that yesterday's events shaped today. Ponder how what happened a decade ago shapes this year and how a single change somewhere in the past could have shaped a different present. Historians scoff at the "what if" game, but there may be no better tool for getting your head into history.

What if John McCain had won the 2008 U.S. presidential election instead of Barack Obama? Would anything be different? How about Al Gore over George W. Bush back in 2000? That election's results were so close, and the outcome so hotly contested, that it could easily have turned out the other way.

What if the terrorists who crashed airliners into the World Trade Center and the Pentagon on September 11, 2001, had been stopped before they could board those planes? Think about the lives saved, the grief avoided. Imagine the years since. What would have been different? U.S. troops wouldn't have been sent to Afghanistan, for one thing. Would you have ever heard of Osama Bin Laden? Would there have been that next U.S. war in the Middle East, the one in Iraq? Would you still be exactly where you are, doing the same thing you're doing now? For many people worldwide, the answer to all those questions is "no."

From Footpath to Freeway: Humanity Built on Humble Beginnings

The earliest human beings were hunter-gatherers. There may be a slim chance that you're still living that way — spending all your time and energy intent on getting food from the natural world around you. But I very much doubt it. Instead you're a student, an office worker, a homemaker, a cable TV installer, or you perform any of thousands of occupations unimagined by early humankind. You use tools like cellphones and laptop computers — things hardly dreamed of when I was born in the middle of the twentieth century, let alone back at the dawn of civilization. Yet here I am, clacking away on a computer keyboard, checking my meager investments online, and listening to my iPod, just like a modern human being. And in a way, here too are the people of 30,000 years ago, my ancestors and yours.

They may have thought a lot about root plants, berries, seeds, probably insects and grubs, shellfish in season, meat when it was available, and calorie-rich bone marrow from fresh or scavenged kills. They literally had to scrounge to get what they needed to stay alive. In the warm climates where early members of the species lived, survival may not have been terribly difficult. They were endowed with the same basic mental equipment we have today. They were big-brained, tool-using animals, and after many tens of thousands of years living hand-to-mouth off of what they could find or kill, some of them decided there had to be a better way.

Either pushed by circumstance (climate change, for example) or somehow inspired by the thought of new possibilities, they traveled from the lush forests, savannahs, and seacoasts of Africa to face the harsh challenges of virtually every environment on Earth — mountains, deserts, frozen steppes, and remote islands. Eventually, they traded in their stone spearheads and scrapers for tools and weapons made of copper, then bronze, then iron . . . and ultimately things like microcircuits and NASA Mars rovers. Those people traveled and adapted and innovated all the way to today. They are you and me. In a weird way, then is now.

At some point around 10,000 years ago, not very long after the last Ice Age ended, some people whose technology still consisted largely of sticks and rocks settled down. They were discovering that if they put seeds in the ground, plants would come up there. It worked even better if they stuck around and tended the plants. This realization led to farming.

Historians point to an area they call the *Fertile Crescent* as a hotbed of early farming. Shaped like a slightly mangled croissant with a big bite taken out of it, the Fertile Crescent stretched from what is now western Iran and the Persian Gulf, up through the river valleys of today's Iraq, into western Turkey and then hooked south along the Mediterranean coast and the Jordan River through Syria, Lebanon, Jordan, Israel and the Palestinian Territories, into northern Africa and the Nile Valley of Egypt. In my flaky croissant analogy, the eastern Mediterranean is the missing bite.

The crescent is also where archeologists have found some of the oldest cities in the world. The mantra for the beginnings of civilization goes something like this: Agriculture means a reliable source of food. People stay put and grow food. Ample food enables population growth. Ample food also gives the growing population commodities to trade. Trade leads to more trade, which leads to more goods and wealth. Not everybody has to work in the fields. Some folks can specialize in shipping goods, for example. Others can specialize in building — whether as paid laborers or slaves — or perhaps concentrate on using weapons, either to protect their own wealth or take away that of others. Artisans create jewelry and turn mundane objects (weapons, pots, baskets) into aesthetic statements. Society gets more multilayered. Buildings rise. Cities rise. Trade necessitates keeping track of quantities and values, which necessitates a way to record information. Number systems get invented. Writing follows. Books get written. Ideas blossom. More trade results, cross-cultural influences appear, and so on.

Next thing you know, a English-speaking woman in Los Angeles, whose various ancestors spoke Spanish, Celtic, and Japanese, is sitting in her South Korean-made car, stuck in traffic on the freeway, a style of limited-access road invented in Germany. She's sipping a cup of coffee harvested in El Salvador, brewed in the Italian style with a machine manufactured in China to Swiss specifications. On her car's satellite radio, a voice beamed from Toronto is introducing news stories filed by reporters in India, Afghanistan, and Ukraine. She reaches over and switches to a station that features a style of music invented in Jamaica by English-speaking people of African descent.

War! What Is It Good For? Material for History Books, That's What

A view of history that sees only progress — as in, this advance leads to that terrific advance, which leads to another incredible breakthrough, and so on — doesn't account for the fact that people are imperfect, even awful. Some are ruthless, some destructive, some just plain stupid. Not you, of course. You're capable of some pretty great things, I know. Even I, on a good day, may contribute something positive toward history. And we all know or at least know *about* somebody whose ability to make this a better world is off the charts. But the human race also produces bad characters. Sometimes really bad.

Much of this book deals with war. I wish that weren't so, but for reasons that anthropologists, psychologists, historians, politicians, and many more have never been quite able to illuminate, there always seems to be somebody willing and even eager to skewer, shoot, blast, or even vaporize somebody else. And history is too often an account of how one group of people, under the banner of Persia or France or Japan or wherever, decided to overrun another group of people. Many such efforts succeeded, if success can be defined as killing other people and stealing their land, resources, wealth, wives, children, and so on.

One of my favorite quotations about war is this one from the historian Barbara Tuchman: "War is the unfolding of miscalculations." It underscores the fact that so many decisions made in war turn out to be wrong and so many successful wartime strategies have turned out to be the result of dumb luck.

Historians cite the twentieth century as perhaps the worst ever in terms of war and its toll — not because people were necessarily more warlike but because the weapons had grown so much deadlier and transportation (including that of weapons and troops) so much faster. In World War I (1914–1918) and then even more so in World War II (1939–1945), the machines of destruction reached farther and did much more damage than ever before.

Luckily, the wars since WWII have been limited wars in that they were contained to a particular region and didn't spread too widely, or they were fought with an understanding that neither side was going to escalate the weaponry or the tactics too far. The Vietnam War, a conflict between communist North Vietnam and the anticommunist government of South Vietnam, fits both categories.

Each side had allies with deep pockets and big guns. The Soviet Union and China provided supplies and arms to the North Vietnamese, while the U.S. sent military advisors and then, starting in 1965, active troops to fight for South Vietnam. Yet the conflict was somewhat contained. It spread to neighboring Cambodia and Thailand, yes, but not much beyond. The Americans, though deeply suspicious of and armed against both the Chinese and the Soviets, avoided a shooting war with either power. Some say that was a mistake, that the limited tactics employed by U.S. leaders caused the failure of the South Vietnamese effort. Others say that avoiding a larger war was well worth any disadvantage, even worth humiliation.

Were an all-out war to occur in the twenty-first century, humankind has far more than enough destructive power at hand to kill everybody on the planet. So, remember that there's progress as in trade, peaceful innovation, cultural exchange — and then there's *progress* as in thermonuclear weapons.

Human advances also have been disrupted and forestalled by natural disasters such as volcanic eruptions, massive storms, floods, droughts, and disease. For example, the Black Death of the fourteenth century, an epidemic of plague that swept through Europe, changed history because it so drastically reduced the continent's population. Fewer people meant labor was worth more and there was more wealth. More wealth meant more demand for goods, which spurred a search for better trade routes, which led Europeans to places like India, China, and the Americas. The results were great for Europeans but not so great for the Indians, Chinese, and Native Americans.

Appreciating History's Tapestry

A standard history book analogy is that human events over the centuries are a "rich tapestry." Whoever originated the tapestry image deserves credit, because it's not a bad conceit. Yet many readers and students aren't all that familiar with *tapestries,* which are decorative fabrics usually hung on a wall or draped over a side table to show off their craftsmanship. Made from weaving threads together in such a way that the colors of the thread form recognizable shapes and scenes, a tapestry may be called "rich" so often because, through much of history, you had to be rich to own one.

The classic tapestry is hand-woven and takes a lot of time and skill to produce. That makes it expensive. It's complex. Each thread contributes a tiny percentage of the finished image.

History is like that, even if the threads interweave somewhat randomly and the picture is often hard to figure out. Yet with history, you can follow a thread and see where it crisscrosses and crosscrisses (if you will) other threads to get an idea of how the picture formed into what you recognize as the historical present.

Threading backward

History usually gets told in chronological order, which makes sense. Much of this book is in chronological order, but not all of it. That's because I thought it would be a good idea to break out some of the big influences on how people behave — things like philosophy and religion, styles of warfare, and even individual personalities. Giving them their own parts of the book (Parts III, IV, and V) allows you to come at the same events and eras from different perspectives.

Even when I tell you things in the order they happened, though, I sometimes refer to latter-day developments that have resulted from long ago events, or I use modern examples of how things now can still work pretty much as they did then, whenever then was.

In studying history, it can also help to start at the now and work back, asking the questions that the journalists, pundits, and bloggers did earlier in this chapter — questions about how things came to be.

Take the war in Iraq, for instance. I mean the one that began in March 2003, when U.S. planes bombed a bunker where Iraqi president Saddam Hussein was thought to be meeting with top staff. (They didn't get Saddam then but followed up with an invasion that led to his eventual capture and execution.) To trace every thread from that war through time would be too ambitious for this book (and this writer), but you can follow a few of them. Warm up the WABAC, Sherman.

U.S. President George W. Bush and his advisors citied a number of reasons for invading Iraq, among them the need to free Iraqis from the brutal dictator Saddam Hussein. Hussein came to power in 1979 when his cousin and predecessor Ahmed Hassan al-Bakr stepped down, or — as many believe — was forced from office by Saddam. Al-Bakr's career included ousting two previous Iraqi military dictators and helping to overthrow Iraq's monarchy in 1958.

The monarchy dated to the 1920s when Great Britain, which ruled Iraq as a colony, installed King Faisal I without really giving him any power. The king, a descendant of the family of the Prophet Mohammed, wasn't from Iraq but rather from Mecca Province in what's now Saudi Arabia. Yet he helped secure Iraq's independence from Britain before he died.

The League of Nations, a short-lived predecessor to the United Nations, cobbled together what you think of as Iraq in the 1920s. The body put Britain in charge of Baghdad and Basra, two adjacent parts of the old Ottoman Empire (which fell apart in WWI), and then a few years later threw in Mosul to the north.

The Ottomans, based in Istanbul (today in Turkey), had first conquered Baghdad in 1535. It had previously been part of the Mongol Empire and was a center of the Islamic world after Arabs conquered the region in the seventh century. Before that, it was a province of the Persian Empire for 900 years. Before that, a people called the Parthians were in charge, and before that, Alexander the Great conquered Baghdad.

In fact, when Alexander died in 323 BC, he was in Babylon, one of the most famous cities of the ancient world and one of those early cities that arose in the Fertile Crescent after agriculture took hold. Babylon had been the capital of a kingdom established by a people called the Amorites in the nineteenth century BC. Archeologists think the city, whose ruins lie about 50 miles south of present-day Baghdad, was a much older town that grew to city size by 2400 BC, more than 4,400 years ago.

Crossing threads

Okay, so the preceding section has a highly superficial tracing of a thread I'll call "what was Iraq before, and who ruled it?" It's so superficial that I kind of skipped over some parts when different conquerors fought over the territory and rule shifted back and forth. For example, a famous Turkish-Mongol conqueror called Tamerlane took over for a while in the fourteenth century. His thread would take you back to his ancestor Genghis Khan, a great Mongol warrior and ruler. And *his* thread would take you to Genghis Khan's grandson, Kublai Khan, thirteenth-century emperor of China.

But in tracing that one thread back from twenty-first century Iraq, I crossed a number of other threads. At one intersection was WWI, which was triggered by a Serbian nationalist rebellion against Austrian rule of Bosnia. That war redrew the map of Europe and brought down not just the Ottoman Empire but also the Russian, German, and Austro-Hungarian empires.

The overthrow of the Russian Empire led to the establishment of the Soviet Union — a military superpower and arch rival to the U.S. through much of the late twentieth century. Then there's the fact that WWI ended with the 1919 Treaty of Versailles, whose harsh terms imposed upon Germany have been blamed in part for the rise of Adolf Hitler and WWII. The war also led to the establishment of the League of Nations, which lumped together the group of territories known today as Iraq.

Weaving home

The German Empire (another of those that fell in WWI) was a successor to the Holy Roman Empire, a union of Central European territories dating back to Otto the Great in 962 AD. It was considered a successor of the Frankish

Empire, established in 800 AD, when Pope Leo III crowned Charlemagne as Emperor of the West — essentially naming him the successor to the Roman Emperors, going back to Augustus, whose rule began in 27 BC.

Follow Leo's popish thread and you'll get to Pope Urban II, who in 1095 called upon Europe's Christians to join together in a war against the Turks, especially the Seljuk Dynasty of Turks who controlled the city of Jerusalem and the land surrounding it, considered the Christian Holy Land.

Urban's war became the First Crusade, followed by at least nine more crusades over several centuries in which Christians from Europe traveled east with the express purpose to kill Muslims in western Asia. Not surprisingly, these incursions contributed to enduring hard-feelings by many Muslims against the West and Christians.

Some people may find a thread between the Crusades and latter-day anti-U.S. sentiments, such as those held by the terrorist group Al Qaeda. However, that thread also crosses the one in which the United Nations partitioned what had been British Palestine (another post-WWI territory) into Arab and Jewish areas to make way for a modern nation of Israel.

Al Qaeda attacked the U.S. on September 11, 2001. The American response to Al Qaeda's aggression was a War on Terror(ism) that included the invasion of Iraq, whose leader was thought to be aiding terrorist groups. And I'm back where I started.

Making the Connections

If you're not thrilled with the tapestry analogy of the previous section, how about the game called Six Degrees of Kevin Bacon? In it, you try to link any actor or movie to the veteran screen star Bacon by associating somebody who appeared in such-and-such film, who worked with so-and-so, who was married to what's-his-face, who directed the TV series that starred the actress who had a cameo role in a movie in which Bacon also starred. You get the idea.

The game calls for you to make the connection in six people or less. So let's see if I can do that with Alexander the Great, mentioned earlier in this chapter as having died in Babylon, and the Iraq War that started in 2003.

1. Alexander's conquests spread Greek influence around the Mediterranean Sea.

2. Romans embraced aspects of Greek religion and philosophy.

3. The Roman Empire switched to Christianity.

4. The Roman Catholic Church preserved ancient writings containing classical (Greek and Roman) ideas through the Middle Ages.

5. Christian scholars rediscovered Greek philosophy, sparking the Renaissance.

Oops. I'm not there yet.

So historical connections aren't as easy as Kevin Bacon connections, but I almost did it. See, the Renaissance led to the Enlightenment, when ideas such as government by consent of the governed took hold. That led to the American Revolution and modern democracies — the style of government that George W. Bush said he would establish in the Middle East after getting rid of Saddam Hussein by invading Iraq. A few more than six steps, but not bad.

If you fill in enough steps and make enough connections, you'll begin to see the interconnectedness of virtually everything people do on Earth. Maybe once upon a time, a band of hunter-gatherers in what would later be Yemen or Thailand could live for a thousand or even ten thousand years in blissful ignorance of the rest of the world. And no other band of hunter-gatherers anywhere would have the slightest clue that those prehistoric Yemeni or Thai people existed.

But if it was ever really so, that moment is long gone. Pull on any little piece of humankind now and you tug loose a thread that reaches far beyond whatever city or village you reached for. And each one of those threads tugs not just on other threads that together reach around the world; it also tugs through time to what came before. Every thing that ever happened, somebody once said, is still happening. History is now.

Last man standing

How long ago was WWI? I can tell you that it started in 1914 and ended in 1918, but not everybody is good at visualizing when that was. What if I told you that of the millions of Americans mobilized in that war, only one man is still alive as I write this: 108-year-old Frank Buckles of West Virginia.

Buckles, originally from Missouri, managed to enlist in the U.S. Army in 1917, when he was 16 years old. Many accounts of his service say he lied about his age. He denies it, and maybe the recruiter didn't ask. Regardless, Buckles served as an ambulance driver and motorcycle courier in France and escorted prisoners of war back to Germany after the war. Among his distinctions, he reportedly met Adolf Hitler in the 1930s, before WWII.

Given his age, I can only hope that Frank Buckles is still alive as you read this. Perhaps you can think of him and his service as a teenager and remember that WWI happened a lifetime ago, a very long lifetime.

Tracking the Centuries

Before 12000 BC: The Pleistocene Epoch, also known today as the last major Ice Age, ends after ice sheets recede northward.

Perhaps 10000 BC: Agricultural societies develop in an area called the Fertile Crescent, in the Middle East.

About 2400 BC: The town of Babylon, between the Tigris and Euphrates Rivers, has grown into a city.

About 323 BC: Alexander the Great dies of a fever in the ancient city of Babylon.

27 BC: Augustus becomes the first Roman emperor.

962 AD: Otto the Great is crowned Holy Roman Emperor in Aix-la-Chapelle, Germany.

1535: Ottoman Turks conquer Baghdad.

1919: The Treaty of Versailles sets out terms of peace to officially end WWII.

1932: The Kingdom of Iraq wins its independence from British rule.

1947: The United Nations partitions what had been British Palestine into Jewish and Arab areas.

1965: The U.S. escalates its involvement in the Vietnam War by sending troops to fight on the side of the South Vietnamese government.

2001: Nineteen suicide terrorists hijack four commercial airlines and succeed at crashing two of them into New York's World Trade Center and a third into the Pentagon. The fourth plane crashes in Pennsylvania.

2003: The U.S. and Great Britain, along with small contingents of troops from other allied countries, invade Iraq.

2009: Barack Obama takes the oath of office as the forty-fourth president of the United States.

Chapter 2

Digging Up Reality

· ·

In This Chapter

▶ Unearthing long-lost legendary cities

▶ Spawning myth or reality: Plato's Atlantis

▶ Connecting with the past in the form of preserved bodies

· ·

*I*f you think of history as lists of facts, dates, battles, and key civilizations, you may discover a lot, but you'll never experience the thrill of the past. If, on the other hand, you're able to make the leap to identify with people who are long dead and to imagine what living their lives must have been like, you may be among those for whom the past becomes a passion and perhaps even an addiction.

Some people have no trouble making that connection; they read history and their imaginations go to work. Other people need help. Hard evidence often works, the kind of evidence you can examine at historic sites or in museums. Seeing what the people of the past left behind — what they made and built and even their exquisitely preserved bodies — can bridge the gap between then and now. These things are reminders that real people walked the earth long ago, carrying within them dreams and fears not so unlike yours. In this chapter, I look at two legendary "lost" cities and discuss evidence for their actual existence. I also look at various kinds of mummies and discuss the ways they can bring history alive.

Homing In on Homer

The Iliad and *The Odyssey,* epic poems passed down from the ancient Greek singer Homer, tell fantastic stories about a war between Greeks and Trojans and the journey home from that war. They're *so* fantastic — full of vengeful gods and supernatural peril — that it's hard for modern people to credit any part of them as true.

Yet history is in these poems, history that became more tantalizing in the late nineteenth century when an eccentric German businessman dug up the city of Troy, revealing that it had been a real place, one of many ancient Troys built in just the place Homer described. Each rose and fell and another rose on top of it while the old one was forgotten.

The Troy story

Greeks attacked Troy more than 3,200 years ago, in the thirteenth century BC. The stories about that war were already ancient by the time of the philosopher Aristotle and Alexander the Great in the fourth century BC. Nobody knows for sure who Homer was or when he lived (although the ninth century BC is likely — more than 2,800 years ago). As centuries and millennia went by, the real Trojan War faded so far into the past that the legends were all that was left.

That was until Germany's Heinrich Schliemann, a wealthy amateur archeologist, decided to find Troy. With little to go on except his faith in Homer, he dug up not just one but a stack of nine Troys built one on top of another. Then he went to Greece and discovered the mighty civilization of Mycenae, which also figures in Homer's saga.

Sure that *The Iliad*'s account of the Trojan War was true, Schliemann fixed on an ancient mound at a place called Hissarlik that's close enough to the Aegean Sea for the invading Greeks to have jogged back and forth between it and their camp on the shore, just as Homer's story says they did.

Schliemann hired workers and started digging at the mound. Ironically, he hardly slowed down as he passed through what later archeologists identified as the probable Troy of the Trojan War (about 1250 BC), only three levels down. Schliemann's workers burrowed to an earlier layer of the ancient city, one from before 2000 BC — maybe 700 years earlier than the Troy in Homer's stories. In 1874, Schliemann found priceless gold artifacts that he erroneously thought had belonged to Priam, the Trojan king in *The Iliad*.

Not satisfied with his Trojan findings, Schliemann went back to Greece to look for the palace of King Agamemnon, the leader of the Greeks in *The Iliad*. Unbelievably, he not only found evidence of another legendary civilization, but he again came up with golden treasure, this time dating from 1550 BC.

Inspired archaeological finds

Schliemann paved the way for later scientists such as Arthur Evans (1851–1941), an Englishman who uncovered the remains of the great Minoan civilization. (The Minoans were a vigorous, powerful people who thrived on Crete and other Aegean Islands between 3000 and 1450 BC.) Such finds reminded professional archeologists that ancient stories — even those that sound fantastical — often contained important clues and that tales of lost cities weren't necessarily make-believe.

Raising Atlantis

Archeologists have found many forgotten cities. Does that mean that *every* lost civilization was for real? Does it mean, for example, that scientists or explorers will someday find the sunken nation of Atlantis? Oops. Did I just mention Atlantis? There isn't room in this book to delve into even a small fraction of the theories about where and what was Atlantis — if it ever existed — but this section gives you an idea of what all the fuss is about.

The story of the lost continent of Atlantis describes a land of peace and plenty that was destroyed in an overnight cataclysm. The story traces back to the writings of Greek philosopher Plato (about 428–347 BC), who used Atlantis to make a point about social order and good government. But Plato's descriptions leave room for interpretation, and people have been interpreting wildly for more than 2,000 years.

If Atlantis wasn't in the Atlantic Ocean, just past Gibraltar on your way out of the Mediterranean (and geology seems to dictate that it couldn't have been there), then where was it? Historians, archeologists, mystics, and self-appointed prophets have argued vociferously over the site. Dueling proponents put the lost continent everywhere from Britain to Bermuda to Bolivia, from Colorado to the China Sea. One theory claims it was on another planet. And then there are comic books that depict Atlantis thriving in a giant plexiglass bubble on the ocean floor. Virtually every theory has to make allowances for Plato getting the story of Atlantis indirectly from an Athenian statesman, Solon, who supposedly got it from scholar-priests on a visit to Egypt in about 590 BC. Because Plato wrote his version almost two centuries later, in about 360 BC, details may have changed along the way, or so many Atlantis-seekers have rationalized.

One of the least outrageous theories is that the story of Atlantis is an interpretation of the volcanic disaster that destroyed Santorini, an island in the Mediterranean. Modern archeologists and geologists have studied the way the Santorini cataclysm caused a monstrous tsunami followed by sky-darkening ashfall that devastated Minoan civilization on nearby Crete.

Santorini (also known as Thera) lies about 45 miles north of Crete, which was the center of the Minoan culture. Minoan ruins are plentiful on what's left of Santorini, but that's only a small remnant of what the island was until about 1500 BC, when the 5,000-foot volcano in its middle exploded and collapsed into the sea. Ever since, the island has been a crescent surrounding a volcanic-crater lagoon. The volcanic eruptions continued for 30 years, building up to a devastating climax: an enormous tidal wave. It knocked down buildings on islands throughout the region.

The tsunami decimated the population, and the subsequent rain of volcanic ash probably finished off the Minoan civilization. Nobody knows for sure whether the sinking of Santorini had anything to do with launching a lasting legend of a capsized civilization, but news of such a catastrophic event surely spread around the Mediterranean and, in time, became legend.

Reading the Body Language of the Dead

Some people who lived hundreds and thousands of years ago left more than just their images in sculpture and paintings on stone. Preserved bodies are flesh-and-blood evidence of a long-ago reality. The mere fact that a human body from thousands of years past is still more or less intact and still recognizably the same as this year's model can help open your mind to the connection between then and now. There's something about a mummy that helps your imagination bridge all the generations since that puckered flesh was taut, upright, and dancing.

In history books that cover big expanses of time, you have to adjust your perspective so that a century becomes a relatively small unit of history. In this book, you can breeze through a thousand years here and a thousand years there. Thinking of the Byzantine Empire as one civilization, a single station on the history train, is easy to do. Yet, it grew and receded, changed governments, and restructured policies over a stretch of centuries more than five times longer than the United States has been a nation.

When you back up far enough to take that in, you may lose sight of individual lives. They flicker past so quickly. I find that contemplating mummies is a helpful tool for hooking into the perspective of a single life span, a single individual, so long ago. Strangely, you may be able to easily identify with a mummy, if you don't find that too macabre.

Mummies have turned up all over the world. Some were preserved naturally by something in the environment where the body came to rest. Others, as in the celebrated tombs of ancient Egypt, were artfully prepared for their voyage into death.

Frozen in the Alps

In the summer of 1991, German tourists hiking in the Ötzal Alps on the border between Austria and Italy spotted a human body lodged in high-altitude ice. A few days later, a rescue team cut free the corpse of a bearded man dressed in leather. Perhaps he had been a back-to-nature hippie whose 1960s wanderings went tragically awry? No. Other curious details made that unlikely — the man's flint-bladed knife, flint-tipped arrows, and copper-bladed ax.

Researchers at the University of Innsbruck in Austria first estimated the freeze-dried body's age at 4,000 years. Further examination moved the date of death back by 1,300 years, meaning that "Ötzi," as scientists nicknamed him, was journeying over the mountains around 3300 BC when he died and was covered by falling snow.

Ötzi, who resides in Italy's Museo Archologico dell'Alto Adige in Bolzano, is a natural mummy in that his body was preserved by nature. Scientists find out all kinds of things about the ways people lived and died from mummies, especially those preserved whole. Ötzi was between age 40 and 50 when he died, and he suffered from a number of chronic illnesses; his medicine pouch contained herbal prescriptions for what ailed him. Researchers even probed the mummy's stomach to learn that he'd eaten the meat of chamois (a kind of European mountain goat) and deer, as well as grain (possibly in the form of bread) and some plum-like fruit called sloes on the day he died.

Ötzi's mummified body and the things found with it prompted scholars to rethink some assumptions about the roots of European civilization. His copper ax showed that the transition from stone technology to metal happened earlier than archeologists had previously believed. The rest of his gear — a bow, a quiver of arrows, a waterproof cape woven of grass, even his well-made shoes — show that Ötzi was well equipped for his trek across the mountains. The stress patterns in his leg bones suggested he took such journeys routinely. At first, scientists theorized that he may have been a shepherd, but further research showed that he had been shot with an arrow and involved in a physical struggle with other men. A blow to the head and blood loss from the arrow wound probably killed him. This man could have been a soldier, perhaps part of a raiding party.

Salted away in Asia

In the dry climate of Chinese Turkestan (between Russia and Mongolia), bodies buried in the salty soil near the towns of Cherchen and Loulan as long as 4,000 years ago turned into mummies rather than rotting away.

Some of the Turkestan mummies have well-preserved blond hair and many appear to be of Caucasian ancestry, a fact that challenges latter-day assumptions about the range of ancient ethnic groups. Based on their well-made, colorful clothing, they may have been related to the Celts, whose culture would later flourish all over Europe and whose descendants include the Irish, Scots, and Welsh. The fabrics show weaving techniques similar to those still practiced in rural Ireland in the twenty-first century AD. DNA analysis of the bodies has suggested genetic links ranging from Western European to East Asia, which may mean that their home, the Taklimakan Desert basin, was an ancient crossroads between diverse cultures.

Bogged down in northern Europe

The watery peat bogs of northern Europe also made many mummies. Tannins in the *peat* (partially decayed plant matter) and the cold water preserved bodies in such startlingly good condition that Danish villagers have sometimes mistaken a 2,500-year-old body for that of someone they knew only decades before.

The bodies, though discolored by the tannins, look much as they did when the people died. Some people fell into the bogs, but many were killed and dumped there, perhaps as ritual sacrifices or as victims of another kind of execution. Mummies of young women wear blindfolds, and some appear to have been drowned alive. Some mummies have ropes around their necks, and others' throats were slit.

Most of these peat bog mummies have skin, hair, fingernails, and even facial expressions intact. And their jewelry and clothing sometimes look unsettlingly like something that could hang in your twenty-first-century closet.

Dried and well preserved in the Andes

The 500-year-old bodies of Inca children in the Argentine Andes that archeologist Johan Reinhard and a team from the National Geographic Society discovered in the 1990s atop Mount Llullaillaco are among the best-preserved mummies ever found. Apparently killed in a religious ritual sacrifice, the boy and two girls — aged between 8 and 15 — were so perfectly frozen that the scientist said they looked as if they had just drawn their last breaths.

The Argentine discoveries are more than fascinating and informative; they're also terribly sad. The idea of killing an 8-year-old is so repellent to people today that you may recoil in horror. What could possibly possess a culture to worship gods that must have the blood of innocents? Yet that's another reason why the three preserved bodies are so compelling: They draw you into the past as you struggle to comprehend how these people who were so startlingly similar to people today in some ways could have understood the world so differently.

Preserved pharaohs in Egypt

Perhaps nobody devoted quite so much thought and energy to death and the afterlife as the ancient Egyptians. After burying their dead with great care and ceremony since perhaps 4000 BC (Chapter 4 has more on ancient Egypt), the Egyptians began artfully mummifying their pharaohs sometime before the twenty-fourth century BC.

By the year 2300 BC, the practice had spread beyond royalty. Any Egyptian who could afford it was dried and fortified for the trip into the afterlife. The mummy was buried with possessions and even servants for the next world.

Egyptian mummies differ from many others in that researchers actually can figure out who some of these people were in life. Egypt's King Tutankhamen's identity is intact thanks to ancient Egyptian writings, called *hieroglyphics*. British Egyptologist Howard Carter discovered fabulously preserved artifacts in his tomb in 1922. The discovery made Tutankhamen the most famous pharaoh in the twentieth century AD, even though he was probably a long way from that in the fourteenth century BC. King Tut took the throne in 1361 BC at about age 9 and reigned for only 11 years.

Carter first gazed by candlelight into the wonders of that tomb, unseen for more than 3,300 years. That moment has been held up ever since as the ideal archeological breakthrough — completely unlike most great discoveries, which are scratched out of the ancient dust and painstakingly pieced together.

Carter said that he stood there for a long, long time, allowing his eyes to penetrate the gloom lit only by the candle he held. His patron and partner, George Herbert, Earl of Carnarvon, stood behind him in the dark, unable to stand the suspense. "Do you see anything?" asked Carnarvon breathlessly. "Yes," replied Carter in a hushed tone. "Wonderful things."

Carter's sensational discovery made all the papers, and so did Carnarvon's untimely death. The earl died of an infected mosquito bite a few months after he helped Carter find the tomb. Naturally, somebody blamed his death on an ancient curse against anyone who disturbed the boy-king's eternal rest. (Grave robbers had been the scourge of Egypt's royalty.)

The notion of Tutankhamen's curse may have disappeared if it weren't for a 1932 horror movie called *The Mummy,* which is wrong on every point of archeology and Egyptian religion but features a compellingly subtle performance by Boris Karloff in the title role. *The Mummy* was successful enough that many remakes and variations followed, including a 1959 version with Christopher Lee as the undead Egyptian. A 1999 reimagining of *The Mummy* inspired sequels in 2001 and 2008.

Tracking the Centuries

About 4000 BC: Egyptians begin burying their dead with ritual care.

About 3300 BC: A well-equipped male traveler in the Italian Alps succumbs to an arrow wound and falls face-down into the snow.

About 1470 BC: The volcano on the island of Santorini erupts, destroying the island, wiping out villages, and probably ending a civilization.

1352 BC: Tutankhamen, young king of Egypt, dies and is mummified.

About 1250 BC: A confederation of Greek kings and warriors attack the city of Troy, in today's Turkey.

Ninth century BC: The bard Homer sings about the Trojan War.

Early fourth century BC: In Athens, the philosopher Plato writes about Atlantis, a land lost under the sea.

1870s: Heinrich Schliemann, a German commodities broker and amateur archeologist, finds Homer's Troy.

1922: Britain's Howard Carter opens Tutankhamen's perfectly preserved tomb.

1991: Hikers in the Italian Alps discover the 5,300-year-old mummy of a well-outfitted traveler. Researchers nickname him Ötzi

Mummies For Dummies

If you got a job preparing wealthy and royal Egyptians for the afterlife, how would you go about it? Here's the how-to:

1. To remove the brain, stick a long, narrow bronze probe up one nostril, breaking through the sinus bone into the cranial cavity. Wiggle the tool vigorously, breaking down the tissue until it's the consistency of raw egg. Turn the corpse over to drain the liquefied brain through the nostril. Return the body to a face-up position. Use a funnel to pour boiling-hot tree resin into the cranium to halt decomposition of remaining tissue.

2. Extract the internal organs through a slit in the abdomen wall. (You'll have to reach in with a sharp knife and feel around for them.) Wait! Leave the heart. Egyptians considered it the control center for thought and action, so they figured they'd need it in the afterlife. What to do with the other organs? Put them in jars decorated with the heads of gods or a likeness of the departed. The jars go in the tomb with the mummy.

3. Bathe the body with spices and palm wine. Cover it with *natron salts,* a sodium paste found in drying lakebeds, to retard spoilage and dry the skin. Let it sit awhile.

4. When it's good and dry, stuff rolled-up linen cloths inside where the organs were, kind of like stuffing a turkey. Try to restore the person's shape to something resembling lifelike.

5. Wrap more linen, cut into neat strips, around the outside of the body to create that creepy, bandaged look that will scare the pants off moviegoers a few millennia later.

6. Put the body in a coffin, preferably a double coffin (one inside another). If you're working on a pharaoh, put the coffin inside a stone sarcophagus inside a hidden tomb.

Chapter 3
Putting History into Perspective

• •

In This Chapter

▶ Seeing through the long lens of humanity's time on Earth

▶ Accepting the relativity of the names of eras

▶ Embracing contradictory characters

• •

In a number of places in this book, I refer to the year 1492, when the explorer Christopher Columbus, sailing under the Spanish flag, landed for the first time on a Caribbean island probably in the Bahamas. It's a big dividing point in history in that it marks the beginning of European colonialism in the Americas.

Yet according to *The New York Times,* a survey conducted in 2008 showed that less than one-half of teenagers in the United States could correctly pick the date of Columbus's discovery from a multiple-choice list. One-quarter of those asked thought the landmark voyage happened sometime after 1750.

The educational advocacy group that sponsored the survey used these findings and others like them to support its campaign for school improvements. I mention them here because they also illustrate the difficulty that many people — not just students — have in putting history and its events into perspective. The history of the world is such a huge topic; it covers so many eras, cultures, events, conflicts, ideas, and beliefs that it's easy to get mixed up. Three common problems that many people have in putting history into perspective are

✔ Sorting out such terms as *ancient, recent,* and *modern* when they're used by historians and other scholars and connecting them with the stretches of time since people have lived on the planet.

✔ Getting comfortable with the labels such as *Classical* and *Victorian* that historians use to refer to eras and periods. Often these can seem more cryptic than helpful.

✔ Understanding the often contradictory reasons certain exceptional people are judged to be worthy of historical study.

In all three cases I suggest that you relax. The terminology is less important than you may think. In this chapter, you get a chance to ponder what it means to be human before you plunge into the cavalcade of civilizations that follow in Part II. If you can work up a healthy sense of awe about this remarkable species and its beginnings, you'll be better able to appreciate the broad sweep of time that people have been around. And you can see how historical language — including relative terms such as *ancient* and labels for eras such as *Classical* Greece — are somewhat flexible and may be used differently by different historians. As with any subject matter, there are different ways of looking at history and even different ways of evaluating individual historical figures. Sometimes different perspectives conflict, but more often they complement one another.

Being Human Beings

Earth formed about 4.5 billion years ago, or so the astrophysicists and cosmologists say. My mind balks at the thought of such an expanse of time.

I do better starting with recent times, the many thousands of years since people have lived on Earth. Okay, *recent* is a relative term. The modern human species — meaning people who are anatomically the same as you — is probably not much more than 100,000 years old. And archeologists say that human beings didn't start acting fully human until much more recently. Humanity turned a corner roughly 60,000–40,000 years ago. Stone tools became more sophisticated. People carved patterns into rocks, used charcoal to make exquisite cave paintings, and invented rafts to cross water; these artistic expressions and engineering tasks mark them as more like you and less like earlier models of the hominid (humanlike) family. Many scholars refer to people who lived 30,000 years ago as *fully modern.* In that usage, *modern,* like *recent,* is a relative term.

You've probably seen the familiar illustration showing successive ancestor species marching single file, ever taller and less hairy, toward modern humanity. The concept makes for a good picture, but it didn't happen that way. Evolution is rarely that neat. Different kinds of more-or-less humanlike animals lived at the same time. Most were genetic dead ends and died out. All earlier hominids are extinct — unless you buy the idea that Sasquatch (Bigfoot) and Yeti (the Abominable Snowman) are your reclusive country cousins.

As a species, modern humans are quite young, and again I'm speaking relatively. The species *Homo erectus* — if not your direct ancestor, at least a relative — was on Earth much longer than modern people have been here. *Homo erectus* lived from about 1.7 million years ago to perhaps 250,000 BC.

If you think of the entire time since the emergence of upright-walking *hominids* to present day as a single 24-hour day, *Homo erectus* lasted over 8 hours. By that scale, modern humans have been here about 15 minutes.

Nearing the Neanderthal

The nearest relative of modern humans who left much evidence of its existence is the Neanderthal, a species that lived over a wide area stretching from today's Belgium (between France and the Netherlands on the west coast of Europe), southward to Spain, and eastward around the Mediterranean Sea to where Turkey is today. This big-brained branch of the family arose about 150,000 years ago in Europe and was adapted to harsh northern conditions. The Neanderthal died out perhaps as recently as 28,000 years ago.

While the Neanderthal people were still in their prime, glaciers receded and anatomically modern folks migrated into the Neanderthal's part of the world. The two kinds of humans coexisted for thousands of years, both leaving evidence of their camps among the same hills, valleys, and caves. Nobody knows how, or if, they got along with one another. Did they fight? Did modern humans wipe out their Neanderthal cousins over centuries of brutal genocide? Or did the newcomers simply have better survival skills?

Most experts say interbreeding was impossible between two such different species, but a few say it could have happened. If so, it's nothing to worry about. Neanderthals wouldn't make such bad ancestors, despite the big brow ridges and sloping foreheads. They had big brains — maybe bigger than yours — and they did some rather modern things, such as burying their dead with flowers and *ochre,* a reddish clay used like body paint for its color. They also had stone tools, although they may have borrowed the technology from their modern neighbors.

Neanderthals lived over a wide geographical area, but nowhere near as wide as that inhabited in a relatively short time by their anatomically modern successors. This species evolved in Africa, where earlier hominids also had originated. Then they migrated on their two spindly legs not just into the Mideast and Europe, where the Neanderthals had been coping with ice ages, but over all the other continents except Antarctica, crossing land bridges (such as the ones that periodically linked Siberia and Alaska) and large bodies of water.

Talking point

Before counting devices and pictures on rocks, human beings accomplished a more remarkable feat: They talked. Other species communicate with noises, and some — birds and certain monkeys, for example — have complex vocabularies. But no other creature has anything as versatile or expressive as human language.

Scientists don't know when language happened. No one can tell if the first anatomically modern humans were able to make all the sounds that their descendants do because soft tissues such as the tongue and larynx rot away, even when bones fossilize. Yet whenever it came about, language brought huge change. Language probably started out as imitative sounds or noises expressive of emotions such as fear (a cry) or anger (a roar). But as people gave specific meanings to combinations of vocal sounds, they devised symbols in that a sound stood for a thing or an action. Not only could humans warn of predators and call the children to dinner with unprecedented eloquence, but they could also share information.

Able to exchange information, people began to amass it — not just as individuals, but as societies. They always could learn by watching and doing; now they could also understand by somebody telling them. The how-to genre was born.

Through language, early humans benefited from experiences of tribe members no longer living. After tribes built *lore* (a body of shared knowledge), they could embellish it, spinning hunting stories that did more than help successive generations find and kill large prey, for example. Within several generations, tribes surely had more fanciful folktales about heroes, creation, and gods who commanded the stars and earth. After writing developed, it was possible for cultures to leave a permanent record of events, such as great battles or the death of a king.

Herodotus the Greek, credited as the father of history, took his subject to the level of intellectual inquiry in the fifth century BC as he gathered 1,000-year-old stories from around the Mediterranean. As the body of oral and written history grew, there came a need to organize it.

Dividing Time into Eras . . . and Giving Them Names

If your history teacher told you that *medieval* means the period between the fall of Rome (476 AD) and the Renaissance (the fourteenth century), you could have thrown the author H.G. Wells at him.

Not literally, of course. (Let Mr. Wells rest in peace.) Yet it may surprise students of history and certain teachers to find out that historians disagree about when the period called *medieval* began. Wells (1866–1946) is better remembered today as a pioneering science fiction writer and author of *War of the Worlds* (1898), but he also wrote a three-volume *Outline of History* (1920). He begins the second volume of this major history of the world, called *Medieval History,* at 300 BC with the rise, not the fall, of Rome's empire.

So what, you ask? That's exactly my point. Wells's work is just one illustration of the fact that history is full of periods divided by arbitrary lines etched in the shifting sands of time.

Historians have points of view. The good ones have really well-informed points of view, but that doesn't mean they all march in intellectual lockstep.

Sorting ancient from modern

"That's ancient history, Pops." In American movies from the 1930s–1950s, a teenage character often says something like that to an adult, thus dismissing a relatively recent event as having happened too long ago to matter. *Ancient* is another relative term like *modern* and *medieval*. In general, such words mean different things depending on the context. For example, to a person born in 2009, the teenager in that 1950s movie will seem beyond ancient.

In history, *ancient* has more specific meanings. Wells defined it as "From the World Before Man to the Rise of the Roman Empire," and he considered the modern period as beginning in 1567.

Classical schmassical

Classical is another historical label that can have different meanings in different contexts. For example, the classical period in European music was about 1750–1820, but people who study the Maya civilization of the Yucatan Peninsula refer to a classical historical period of about 250–900 AD.

One of the best-known uses of the term *classical* applies to the years 479–323 BC in the southern Balkan Peninsula of Eastern Europe. That was a particularly influential era of Greek culture, Classical Greece (with a capital C).

Traditionally, many historians have hailed the Classical Greeks as founders of Western civilization's core values — rationality, freedom of debate, individuality, and democracy. These concepts did arise and gain acceptance during that time, yet the Greece of the time was hardly an ideal society. Greek cities often fought wars against each other, and in addition to enduring ideas, they also hatched some notions that sound quite peculiar today. For example, in Aristotle's time (the fourth century BC) one could argue that women were "failed men," a lesser rendering of the same biological pattern as males. I don't recommend that you try that argument today.

The Greek city-state Athens is often cited as a model for modern democracies, but there are huge differences between the Greeks' notion of democracy and today's. In Athens, maybe 30 percent of the population at most were citizens, and all citizens were men.

Historians constantly reevaluate the past. As scholars reinterpret the period, the term *Classical* may no longer be helpful to understanding the years 479–323 BC in Greece. And you know what? That's okay. You can look at the Greeks from any number of angles and they don't get any less fascinating.

As H.G. Wells said of history, "The subject is so splendid a one that no possible treatment . . . can rob it altogether of its sweeping greatness and dignity."

Bowing to the queens

Scholars also name eras and periods for notable events or people, such as Columbus's arrival in the Americas. In the Western Hemisphere, times before that event are frequently called *pre-Columbian.* A period label is often based on the reign of a monarch, such as England's Elizabeth I. Events, fashions, and literature from her reign (1558–1603, a golden age of English culture) carry the designation *Elizabethan.* A label may cover much longer periods, as when they derive from Chinese dynasties. For example, the Ming Dynasty ruled from 1368–1644.

For a cinematic depiction of England's Elizabethan era, you can check out 1998's *Elizabeth* and its 2007 sequel, *Elizabeth: The Golden Age.* Both films take liberties with the historical truth (as do all movies based on history), but they also give a vivid visual sense of England in the sixteenth century.

As with so many of the terms discussed in this chapter, the names of historical periods can lose their meaning with the passage of time. I was born and grew up in the postwar era, but as World War II fades farther into history and as more recent wars erupt, the term *postwar* is less widely understood. (Which war are you talking about, Pops?) Some labels can seem more arbitrary than others, too. For example, only sixteenth-century England under the reign of Elizabeth I wears the tag *Elizabethan.* Elizabethan doesn't describe the worlds of late-sixteenth-century China (Ming) or late-sixteenth-century Peru (ruled by the Spanish). Yet *Victorian,* a term for the period 1837–1901, when Victoria was queen of Great Britain and empress over its vast colonial holdings, applies well outside her sphere, especially to styles and cultural attitudes. For example, Victoria never ruled California, but San Francisco is recognized for its Victorian architecture. (You can see both queens in Figure 3-1.)

Figures 3-1:
Queens
who lent
their names
to eras:
Elizabeth I
(left) and
Victoria
(right).

© Circle of John the Elder Bettes/Getty Images   © After Franz Xavier Winterhalter/Getty Images

The Noteworthy and the Notorious Are Often the Same

People are contradictory creatures, each possessed of virtues and vices. That's a good thing to keep in mind when reading history. Many of the most famous people ever were as much bad as good. For example, a great military leader can also be a cruel murderer. Furthermore, the way an individual is evaluated in history can change from book to book and historian to historian, depending on the point of view of the author and the subject matter being discussed. For example, one book focusing on his private life may depict a ruler as an abusive husband, whereas another oriented toward his impact on his subjects may show that same man as a resolute champion of social reform.

A study in contradictions

King Henry VIII, who ruled England from 1509–1547, provides a particularly colorful example of the kind of contradictory character — embodying traits that range from the admirable to the horrid — that abounds throughout history.

If you're reading about the history of Christianity, you'll note Henry's role as founder of the Church of England. In military history, his attention to building a strong navy stands as an important factor leading up to the English fleet's celebrated victory over the mighty Spanish Armada in 1588. If you're interested in his personal life, you'll remember him as handsome and athletic in his youth and obese and diseased in later life. You'll certainly remember that the most famous thing about Henry is that he married six times and ordered two of his wives beheaded for treason.

Like any person, Henry changed. He contradicted himself. He had good qualities and bad. Maybe the bad overwhelmed the good as the king got older, but his life still illustrates how spectacularly multifaceted just one historical figure can be. (You can read more about King Henry VIII in Chapters 10, 14, and 22.)

It depends on the way you look at them

Some of the most fascinating characters in history are those who appear as heroes when viewed from one perspective and villains from another. An example, also from English history, is Guy Fawkes, the man who tried to blow up King James I and both houses of Parliament in 1605. Fawkes was caught red-handed before he could ignite a massive charge that would have blown apart a meeting of monarch and parliamentarians. He was executed for his crime and remains a British national villain. In the United Kingdom, people still celebrate every November 5, the anniversary of his capture, with bonfires and burning effigies.

Yet Fawkes wasn't merely a villain, not just a mad bomber. He was part of a group of Catholic activists who planned this violent act as a last-ditch effort to overcome repressive and brutal anti-Catholic persecution in officially Protestant England. Viewed from that perspective, many English Catholics of the time considered Fawkes a freedom fighter.

In a similar vein, George Washington is viewed as one of the greatest Americans ever and the Father of His Country. But events could have unfolded differently. As an American colonist, Washington was technically a subject of the British Crown. If the American Revolution of the 1770s had failed, the king would have been justified in charging Washington with treason, a hanging offense. And thus he could have gone down in history as a traitor.

When complex, self-contradictory personalities clash, history's narrative grows beyond multifaceted and becomes multidimensional, if you will. So if you want to get comfortable with history, don't try too hard to fit any individual into any single category.

Verifying virtue

History celebrates the strong — especially those who wielded military or political power. Sometimes it seems to be exclusively about those who fought — for territory, for defense, for wealth, and so on. Yet there have also been fighters for ideals. Too often, peaceful idealists are left out of history's stories. The exceptions are idealist leaders whose courage resulted in political or cultural change. Prime examples include the following two men:

- ✔ **Mohandas Karamchand Gandhi (1869–1948):** Known as the Mahatma or *great soul,* he fought racial injustice in South Africa and then fought for his native India's independence from Great Britain — without striking a literal blow. Gandhi adopted the idea of nonviolent civil disobedience espoused by American writer Henry David Thoreau (1817–1862) and, in turn, inspired American civil rights leader Dr. Martin Luther King, Jr.

- ✔ **Dr. Martin Luther King, Jr. (1929–1968):** King was inspired by Mahatma Gandhi to use nonviolent protest against racial discrimination in the U.S. in the 1950s and 1960s. He played a major role in winning popular support for the landmark Civil Rights Act of 1964, legislation that outlawed segregation by race in schools, the workplace, and at public facilities.

Gandhi and King brought about change and stirred resistance. Each was arguably good, and each sought to make the world a better place. Had their efforts been in vain, Gandhi and King may have been seen as ineffectual dreamers. As an admirer of both men, I'd like to think that their motives had more to do with serving posterity than posturing for it. (Turn to Chapter 22 for more about Gandhi and King.)

Tracking the Centuries

About 4.5 billion BC: Earth forms.

About 4 million BC: Early *hominids* (humanlike ancestors) walk on their hind legs.

About 700,000 BC: *Homo erectus* walks out of Africa.

About 40,000 BC: Human beings leave behind early examples of art.

479–323 BC: The Classical Greek era gives rise to democracy.

1605: The Gunpowder Plot against England's King James I is foiled when conspirator Guy Fawkes is caught with explosives underneath the assembly hall of Parliament.

1789: George Washington is elected president of the United States of America.

1948: An assassin kills Mahatma Gandhi.

1968: An assassin kills Dr. Martin Luther King, Jr.

Part II
Finding Strength in Numbers

The 5th Wave   By Rich Tennant

"Tell the emperor if he has any trouble with it, just try jiggling the handle a little."

In this part . . .

Many people say civilized when they mean "nice," "mannerly," or "peaceful." Yet although human civilizations achieve peace, they rarely sustain it. An often-contradictory concept, civilization started with people building together for community benefit — raising a wall for defense, erecting a tower for surveillance, or digging an irrigation ditch to water crops. It also involved people fighting together against a common foe. Civilization often proves brutally violent — even in the name of enforcing peace.

Working together eventually led to cities, nations, and groups of nations striving toward shared goals. Civilization now stretches worldwide, with no part of humanity completely cut off from society at large.

This part of the book looks at how civilization progressed from the first isolated towns and the first public works projects to the increasingly interconnected global society of today. Will global civilization eventually achieve a nice, mannerly, world at peace? That's difficult to say. Many would say that for every step forward — cooperative agreements between nations, for example — there are two steps backward. Wars erupt, terrorists attack, and dictatorial and repressive regimes abuse their people. Yet in the word "civilization," idealists continue to see the prospect of a better tomorrow.

Chapter 4

Getting Civilized

● ●

In This Chapter

▶ Touring Jericho, the world's oldest city

▶ Drawing a connection between rivers and budding civilizations

▶ Starting a written record

▶ Conquering the world with the Greeks and Alexander

● ●

Human beings lived *without* cities — with none of what people today call *civilization* — much longer than people have lived *with* cities and civilization. Archaeologists can't find evidence that anything remotely like a city existed until 11,000 years ago at most. The people of 20,000 years ago may have thought about large permanent settlements as impractical — that is, if the idea ever occurred to them — because the way to get food reliably was to remain mobile. If you wanted to eat, you went where the plants were thriving, where the shellfish clung to the river rocks, and where the herds and flocks migrated. You followed food sources season by season, and as you wandered, you took care not to merge your band of wanderers with other bands. It wasn't a good idea to have too many mouths to feed.

But when the practice of farming got people to settle down, permanent communities followed. By 10,000 years ago, residents of the town of Jericho, in today's Palestinian West Bank, were either welcoming travelers who happened by their oasis or chasing them away with rocks and spears thrown down from the town's protective walls and tower.

Although they don't always agree, archaeologists know quite a bit about early civilizations, especially those that rose along major rivers in Iraq and Egypt. It helps that Iraq and Egypt are also where people first invented writing. When the written record began, prehistory turned into history.

Cities grew not just in the Middle East but also in Pakistan, India, and China, where great civilizations have risen and receded as they interacted with the rest of the world over three or four thousand years. Cities also arose in the Americas, where European invaders wiped out advanced native societies in the sixteenth century AD.

Across the world, early civilizations experienced common needs for order, justice, and understanding. Forms of law, religion, and philosophy developed and led, by a long, circuitous path, to modern ways of thinking and governing. The world that you know started to take shape in those first urban societies, which this chapter examines.

Building Jericho's Walls for Mutual Defense

The Bible says that Joshua and the Israelites raised a ruckus that brought down the walls of Jericho, a city in Canaan. Jericho may be the world's oldest city — at least the oldest one found — predating even the early civilizations along the Tigris and Euphrates Rivers in modern-day Iraq. What the Bible doesn't say is that Jericho's walls of perhaps 3,200 years ago were built on top of walls that were built on top of walls. (Maybe that's why Jericho's walls toppled so easily when Joshua and his posse arrived.) Scientists date the settlement's earliest buildings as early as 9000 BC, which is about 11,000 years ago. True, Jericho was abandoned and rebuilt maybe 20 times, but when you're talking about thousands of years, what's 20 do-overs?

What kind of town was Jericho? Scientists know how it was built and that the living quarters were first round and then rectangular. Researchers can speculate about the residents' lifestyle based on the stuff found lying around. For example, human skulls fitted with realistic plaster faces may have been creepy reconstructions of dead loved ones or slain enemies.

Most significantly, the walls and tall stone tower of Jericho tell a story. They show researchers that residents worked together for a common goal: to build civic structures that provided community defense. Working together in such an organized way — whether voluntarily or under the orders of a hard-handed ruler — is a sign of civilization.

Unfortunately, archaeologists don't know the names and stories that passed from generation to generation by word of mouth in Jericho. Jericho came to be too early for writing and recorded history. Civilization didn't wait for a way to write things down so that later generations could read all about its beginnings.

Planting Cities along Rivers

Although Jericho grew at a desert oasis (a prehistoric pit stop, if you will), the best-known early large-scale civilizations formed along rivers in Mesopotamia (today's Iraq), Egypt, India, and China.

River floods spread rich, silt-laden mud. Besides being fun to squish around in, this mud, over eons, built up and enriched the soil of the valleys where organized human society would first take hold on a large scale. Good soil and readily available water enabled primitive farmers to increase their annual yields and feed ever-larger populations. It follows that early cities, early legal codes, and systems of counting and writing — all elements of civilization — would also arise in these river valleys.

Settling between the Tigris and Euphrates

Mesopotamia, the land between the Tigris and Euphrates Rivers, was an inviting place for nomadic people to stop and settle. The lower rivers, as they neared the Persian Gulf, formed a great marsh with plentiful fish, birds and other wildlife. Late-Stone Age people lived there in reed huts. As hunter-gatherers and herdsman who lived around the swamp and in the hills to the north turned increasingly toward the hot new farming lifestyle (a gradual change that took thousands of years), the fertile valley to the northwest of the marshland beckoned.

By about 5000 BC, barley and flax farmers dug networks of irrigation canals from the Tigris and Euphrates Rivers and their tributaries and built villages along those canals. Their communities grew rapidly until about a dozen impressive cities became the Sumerian civilization, followed after 2000 BC by the great city-state of Babylon and its successive empires. (A *city-state* is a city that's a nation in itself — like modern-day Singapore and Monaco.)

From about 2700–2300 BC, the leading city-state in southern Mesopotamia was Ur, home to the Bible's Abraham. Like other cities in the region, Ur was built of mud bricks. Besides fertilizing the fields, the mud of the river valley proved the best building material in an area with little stone or wood.

Getting agricultural in Africa

Northern Africa, where the great Sahara Desert is today, was once fertile grassland with generous rainfall. It was a good place for animals to graze and a great place for nomadic hunters, gatherers, and herders to wander through, stop to try a little farming, and establish villages.

The switch to farming was anything but sudden. From their experience gathering edible grass seeds, tribal people knew that if there was enough rainfall, the ground where they beat or trampled seeds to remove the inedible hulls would eventually become green with new growth of that same grass. Having seen their stray seeds sprouting, over time people tried spreading some of the fattest seeds on the ground in hopes of growing more of the same.

Flooding on a mythic scale

The early cities of Mesopotamia benefitted from their proximity to the rivers and the mud that periodic floods spread over the land. Yet floodwaters could rise disastrously high. Between the ruins of one Sumerian city and the ruins of the city that came before it, twentieth-century archaeologists found a thick layer of once-oozing, now-dry river mud — evidence of a terrible flood. To the Sumerians, a flood on that scale — one that swept away cities — must have seemed the end of their world. Mud tablets (the first books) found in the ruins of the Mesopotamian city of Nineveh tell a story of how the gods decided to wipe out mankind with a flood, and how one man, Utnapishtim, his family, and his animals were saved. Is this the same story as the Bible's account of Noah and the Flood? No, but some scholars think the tale of Utnapishtim may be an earlier version of the same legend.

Farming worked only if the people stayed put or left but then came back to the same place to harvest the crop. With the promise of a regular food supply, it was easier for nomadic people to stop wandering and establish roots in agricultural villages (pun intended).

Something ironic happened in North Africa over those thousands of years when the agricultural lifestyle was taking hold. The weather slowly changed so that it rained less. Grasslands and forest gave way to sand. Over many generations, fewer seeds sprouted, fewer sprouts matured, and ultimately villages rose and fell without people being aware of what was happening to the world around them. As the climate changed, more and more folks gathered up the kids (and the goats, too, assuming they'd caught onto that crazy, new domestic-animal trend), and headed into Asia and the Middle East. In northeastern Africa, they crowded into a thin sliver of land with a terrific source of water — the Nile.

Assembling Egypt

Villages sprang up in the Nile Valley as early as 5000 BC. A thousand years later, people in the valley were burying their dead with meticulous care and ornamentation, a trend that led to big things, such as Egypt's pyramids. Villages and towns became cities that eventually came together into larger civilizations until the long river valley held just two nations: Upper Egypt and Lower Egypt. Then around 3100 BC, a great king named Menes (also known as Narmer, although that may have been the name of a slightly later king) united Egypt and built a capital at Memphis. (No, Menes never went by the name Elvis. The Egyptian was a different kind of king, and the Egyptian city was the original Memphis.)

Going up the river into Kush

Farther up the Nile (or farther down in Africa, if you're looking at a map), another culture developed in Upper Nubia, or Kush (where Sudan is today). Influenced by Egypt's culture, the Kushites built pyramid-shaped tombs in the Egyptian style. Egypt ruled the Kushites from 2000–1600 BC and again from 1500–900 BC. Later, in the eighth century BC, the Kushites turned on their northern neighbors and brought down Egypt's ruling dynasty, ruling over Egypt until about 671 BC.

Giving way as new civilizations rise

To the people of early civilizations, their cities must have seemed incredibly modern, so superior to rural villages and nomadic tribes (plenty of which still wandered the hinterlands), and also incredibly powerful and secure. Yet the early civilizations, like every civilization since, faltered, splintered, succumbed, or evolved as political and military fortunes rose and fell.

A good example of an evolving civilization is Babylon, which grew into an empire around 1894 BC as King Sumuabum conquered surrounding cities and villages. His successor, Hammurabi, extended Babylon's lands from the Persian Gulf to parts of Assyria before he died in 1750 BC. Babylon's first empire (there was another, 1,000 later, and I talk about it later in this section) lasted almost 300 years, until 1595 BC, when a fierce neighboring people, the Hittites, conquered the city of Babylon and its lands.

The Hittite Empire spread across Asia Minor, encompassing a huge area of what is today central and eastern Turkey and extending into today's Syria. Then around 1200 BC, marauders smashed and burned Hittite cities so thoroughly that eventually nobody remembered who had left carvings such as the twin lions flanking what must have been a grand ceremonial entrance shown in Figure 4-1. It took nineteenth- and twentieth-century archaeologists to rediscover these once-mighty people.

Perils of power

From the time Egypt became one nation, its increasingly powerful, ever-richer king also underwent a transformation. More than a man, the pharaoh was a living god.

Being a god wasn't as great as it sounds, though, at least not at first. Early kings of unified Egypt had to prove themselves fit to stay on top. A king who failed a rigorous annual physical challenge was considered no longer able to provide for the state and so was killed by priests in ritual sacrifice. Understandably, considering who made the rules, this practice disappeared by about 2650 BC.

Figure 4-1:
Stone lions,
carved by
the Hittites,
guard a civi-
lization that
collapsed
about
1200 BC.

The Hittites were major rivals, and later major allies, of Egypt. The two ancient superpowers pitted their armies against each other at the Battle of Kadesh in Northern Syria in 1275 BC. A few decades later they were at peace. Pharaoh Rameses II married a daughter of Hittite King Hattusilis III.

The Assyrians, a common enemy of the Hittites and Egyptians, built a great civilization as well. Centered on the upper Tigris River, Assyrians ruled much of Mesopotamia between 2600 and 612 BC. These people, or at least their rulers, appear to have been a bloodthirsty lot; for example, carvings on their palace walls feature scenes of enemies being beheaded. In Assyrian writings, kings boasted about how many captives they crucified, impaled, and skinned alive.

Babylon emerged as the center of a new empire in the late seventh century BC, after the Chaldeans, a Semitic people related to Arabs and Jews, moved into the ancient city and conquered lands stretching to the Mediterranean. This was the empire ruled by Nebuchadnezzar II (605–562 BC), whose conquest of Jerusalem you can find in Chapter 20. The empire of Babylonia fell in the Persian conquest of 539–538 BC, but the city of Babylon remained an urban center for more than 200 years (Alexander the Great died there in 323 BC).

Heading east to the Indus and Yellow Rivers

Early civilization wasn't limited to the lands around the Mediterranean. Just as the Tigris, Euphrates, and Nile Rivers gave rise to cities, so the upper Indus River (in lands now divided between Pakistan and India) and the Yellow River in China provided ideal environments for villages to grow into cities in the east.

Plumbing the mysteries of ancient Indus Valley sites

The cities on the Indus River, including sites in modern Pakistan at places such as Harappa and Moenjo-Daro, surprised archaeologists who found them for a couple of reasons. As with the Hittite cities, nobody remembered that the Indus River cities ever existed; although the city sites have been located, the identity of the people who built and lived there is still uncertain. Second, these communities were startlingly modern. For example, the communities of 2500 BC had streets laid out in a grid of rectangles, like New York City, and houses in Moenjo-Daro boasted bathrooms and toilets with drains feeding into municipal sewers. Writings found among the ruins indicate that the Indus Valley was home to a literate society that spoke what was probably an early Dravidian language related to many languages still spoken in parts of South Asia.

At its height, the Indus civilization probably covered an area bigger than Mesopotamia and Egypt put together. Moenjo-Daro was rebuilt and rebuilt again over the course of what some scientists think were centuries of geologic change that plugged up the Indus River, altered its course, and put successive layers of houses under water. Others say earthquakes and massive flooding ended the civilization around 1700 BC.

Nomadic herding tribes from the Iranian plateau arrived in northwestern India around 1700 BC and appear to have displaced the people of the Indus cities. Raiders eventually destroyed Moenjo-Daro, but by then the city appears to have been in steep decline. The newcomers brought an Indo-European language (distant ancestor of modern India's Hindi, as well as English and many other tongues) and the roots of what became Indian religion and culture.

Historians use the term *Aryan* to mean the people that displaced the Indus River civilization and gave rise to later Indian culture, but Aryan is a widely misunderstood word because of the way German Nazis misused it to refer to light-skinned Caucasians. Properly applied, Aryan refers strictly to speakers of long-ago Indo-European languages and has nothing to do with ethnicity or physical type.

Pulling prehistory from a brick pile

Harappa, perhaps the dominant city of the sophisticated Indus Valley civilization, was a mess when archaeologists started picking through it in 1920. Nineteenth-century railroad engineers had mined the site for bricks to build a roadbed. The engineers knew the bricks were old, but they couldn't have guessed that they were 4,000 years old! They left the hole in the ground, so local villagers helped themselves to the bricks, too.

In 1922, two years after the scientists at Harappa began to understand what the site had

been, an Indian archaeologist tackled another mound of brick rubble and river silt 400 miles away. He thought he'd found an abandoned Buddhist monastery. Instead, he unearthed the riches of Moenjo-Daro, a virtually untouched ruin of great villas, public baths, and dazzlingly sophisticated sculpture. Since then, archaeologists have explored more than 150 Indus Valley sites.

Separating history from myth: China's oldest dynasties

A river also runs through the beginnings of Chinese civilization — the powerful Yellow River. Around 4000 BC, people started farming (first millet and later rice) along this northernmost of China's major rivers. Chinese legends attribute the nation's origins to specific, semi-mystical individuals, including a Yellow Emperor of about 2700 BC, three sage kings (from 2350 BC), and an Hsia Dynasty that lasted until 1766 BC. Because historians have no proof that these figures are anything but legend, they credit the later house of Shang (also called Yin) as the first dynasty to bring together warring Yellow River city-states in the sixteenth century BC.

Under the Shang, the early Chinese charted the movement of the sun and stars to predict seasons, kept astronomical records to rival those of the Egyptians, and devised a nifty 12-month calendar. The Shang Dynasty lasted until 1027 BC, when it was succeeded by the Zhou Dynasty.

Isolated from Asia Minor and Africa, where the Sumerians and Egyptians invented writing, the Chinese developed their own kind of pictograph symbols. Archaeologists have found characters on Shang Dynasty artifacts that are essentially the roots of the same writing system that China uses today. China's historical writings outshine the records of any other culture in volume, detail, and continuity. For the BC period, China boasts 26 major official written dynastic histories.

Coming of Age in the Americas

By 2000 BC, good-sized communities with public buildings existed in South America, specifically in the Andes mountain range of what's now Peru. For example, archaeologists have found evidence that the people near modern Lima irrigated their farmland and built a stone pyramid at nearby El Paraiso around 1800 BC.

In Peru's northern highlands, the Chavín people started building cities around 1000 BC. Their culture thrived for 500 years, but they didn't leave many clues for the ages. The Chavín may have traded with the Olmec, who had even earlier urban centers, dating from about 1200 BC, along the southern Gulf of Mexico in today's Mexican states of Veracruz and Tabasco. The Olmec left huge stone heads that may be portraits of their kings (albeit not very flattering ones). They also seem to have passed down their culture and social structure to later, more elaborate civilizations, such as the Maya (more on them in Chapter 5).

Keeping Records on the Way to Writing and Reading

Just as the practice of farming led to the founding of villages, towns, and then cities, it also gave rise to other signs of civilization, namely record keeping and disciplines including astronomy and math.

In Egypt, for example, practical scientific and engineering methods arose as ways to keep track of planting seasons. The Nile flooded in predictable annual patterns, so farmers could calculate when the water would rise. They studied the sun and the stars, and over centuries, Egyptians developed an accurate calendar with 365 days in a year. In Mesopotamia, too, practical considerations such as keeping track of seasons, trade transactions, lawmaking, and the invention of that most-treasured aspect of modern life — large-scale government bureaucracy — gave rise to record keeping. Record keeping soon led to more general writing and reading, without which you wouldn't be doing what you're doing right now.

Planning pyramids

Measuring and math came in handy for building Egypt's pyramids, which are mind-boggling feats of engineering. Herodotus the Greek, a historian of more than 2,400 years ago, wrote that 100,000 men worked 20 years on Egypt's

Great Pyramid at Giza. That may be an exaggeration, though, because the Great Pyramid was already more than 2,000 years old when Herodotus wrote about it.

Building pyramids and keeping calendars would both be almost impossible without a way to note things. As the Sumerians had a little earlier, the Egyptians developed their own way of recording information in the form of pictures (called *pictographic writing*), which evolved into a kind of writing called *hieroglyphics* (*medu netcher* or "words of the gods" in ancient Egyptian). Then came written stories, recorded history, love poems, and (with a few steps in-between) e-mail spam.

An important way for the Egyptians to impose order on their world, hieroglyphics also became the key for much later people to find out about the Egyptians. I tell you about the Rosetta Stone, the modern world's key to deciphering hieroglyphics, in Chapter 24.

Laying down laws and love songs

In Mesopotamia, the Sumerians' pictographs (even earlier than the Egyptians') evolved into symbols that represented words, syllables, and eventually even phonetic sounds. *Cuneiform,* the Mesopotamian way of writing with the sharpened end of a reed in wet mud, spread all over the Middle East.

Also like Egyptian hieroglyphics, cuneiform writing opened up new vistas of early history in the nineteenth century AD, when European scholars figured out how to read cuneiform documents such as royal edicts and business letters. Sumerians also wrote love songs that, with the right rhythm track, could probably find a place on today's pop music charts.

Cuneiform writings include early codes of laws. Babylonian king Hammurabi in the eighteenth century BC enacted one of the best known. Here's a sample: "If the robber is not caught, the man who has been robbed shall make claim . . . and the town and its governor shall give back to him everything that he has lost."

ABCs in BC

When scribes started using symbols to represent pieces of words — first syllables and then individual sounds — alphabetic writing began. At first it was a form of shorthand even though it wasn't actually shorter, just easier to write than the pictograph style, which required a different symbol for every word. With an alphabet, scribes were able to combine fewer symbols to make many words.

Shaping the World Ever After

In just about every chapter in this book, you find references to Greeks who lived between about 479 and 323 BC. Their ideas shaped world civilization, leading to modern science, shaping influential schools of philosophy and religion, and setting precedents for democratic government.

Before I get to these Classical Greeks in this section, you need to know about their ancient world, which actually is less ancient than the earliest Mesopotamian and Egyptian civilizations.

Building the Persian Empire

By the seventh and sixth centuries BC, the Middle East had been crawling with civilizations great and small for many centuries. Before the Persians rose up and asserted themselves, they were ruled by another conqueror: the Medes. Famous for crack-shot archery, the Medes came from Media. (No, they didn't watch TV all the time.) Media (also spelled Medea) was in northern Iran.

In 512 BC, Cyrus, a young Persian king from the Achaemenid family, got tired of paying tribute to his grandfather, the king of the Medes. Cyrus gathered up his troops and turned the tables on Gramps. He then built the Achaemenid Persian Empire that ruled western Asia for two centuries, taking in an area stretching from western India to North Africa and even into Eastern Europe. Around 500 BC, one of the empire's greatest kings, Darius I, built a 1,500-mile highway from Susa in Iran to Ephesus in Turkey with stations providing fresh horses on the way for messengers (much like the Pony Express did in the nineteenth-century-AD America).

Also in Turkey, the independent-minded Ionian Greeks in coastal city-states stood up to the Persians. Originally from Greece, across the Aegean Sea, these Ionians spoke Greek, organized their society along Greek lines, and looked to Greece, not Persia, as their homeland. With support from mainland Greek cities such as Athens, they rebelled against Persian rule in 499 BC. Darius sent an army to punish Athens for helping the revolt, setting off the Persian Wars. Although the Greeks eventually won, bad feelings remained and flared up more than 150 years later, when Alexander the Great headed Greek forces.

Growing toward Greekness

Long before the Persian Empire, prehistoric cultures grew and flourished in Greece and on the islands of the Aegean Sea, developing into rich and influential societies.

The Minoans had a complex economy and government on Crete and other islands in the area until about 1450 BC, when Minoan traders suddenly disappeared from Egyptian trade accounts. (For speculation about why, see Chapter 2.) Mycenaeans living in thirteenth-century-BC Greece also had a sophisticated government and culture.

Both were predecessors and possibly ancestors of the Classical Greeks — called *Classical* not because of their taste in music (Mozart wouldn't be born for a long, long time), but because so much of what they thought, said, and wrote has survived. Classical Greek ideas, literature, and architecture — not to mention toga parties and those cool letters on the front of fraternity and sorority houses — are still around in the twenty-first century AD.

By routes direct and indirect, the Greeks — especially their philosophical approach to critically examining the world — spread all over the Mediterranean and then down through history, profoundly influencing successive cultures.

Adapting a society to the lay of the Greek land

Sea and mountains cut up the Greek homeland, separating people instead of bringing widespread populations together. Yet Greek growers gathered for trade, and from marketplaces, they built cities in mainland valleys and on isolated islands. Greek citizens gathered and lived in these independent cities, and they did something unusual for this stage of history: They talked openly about how the independent city-state (called a *polis*) should be run.

A *city-state* was an independent city, not politically part of a larger country. Many city-states, however, ruled broader lands. For example, Athens, one of the best known Greek city-states, became capital of an empire in the fifth century BC. The Greeks were great sailors who founded new city-states not just in Greece and on the Aegean islands, as shown in Figure 4-2, but eventually all over the Mediterranean Sea. They settled in places as far away as Sicily and southern Italy. These far-flung city-states were a type of colony in that they preserved and spread Greek language and culture, but they weren't colonial in the political sense. That is, the remote city-states were often as independent as the city-states back in Greece. If adventurers from the Greek city-state of Corinth founded a city-state hundreds of miles away, that new city-state wasn't necessarily a Corinthian possession.

Not only were individual city-states free, so were Greek citizens, whether in Greece, Turkey, or Italy. That is, they were *relatively* free to an extent unheard of in imperial societies such as Persia's. Most citizens were small farmers for whom freedom meant they were able to farm and market their crops without interference. Of course, *citizen* was far from a universal status; one had to be a man (never a woman) of Greek parentage and language in order to be a citizen. (Foreigners who didn't speak Greek, whose languages sounded like so much "bar bar bar" to the Greeks, were dismissed as *barbarians*.)

Yet among free Greek citizens, the custom of asking questions — about the way the city was run, about the legends of their gods, or about the way nature works — led to exciting advancements. Inquisitiveness fueled philosophy and thinking about nature. Mathematics, astronomy, physics, and even biology became issues to theorize about and problems to solve.

Finding strength in common culture

The Greek city-states built empires largely based on influence and alliance rather than conquest, and they fought each other, sometimes for ideological reasons. Sparta, famous for single-minded military ferocity, began the long, exhausting Peloponnesian War of 431–404 BC because Spartans objected to what they saw as imperialism on the part of Athens — especially under the powerful Athenian leader Pericles. Sparta brought down Athens, center of learning and beauty, and Thebes tamed Sparta. (I talk about the Greek style of fighting in Chapter 16.)

Yet the Athenians, Spartans, Thebans, and others in Greek city-states never forgot that they were Greeks; they spoke the same language, worshipped the same gods, and grew up hearing the same epic poems of Homer. (*The Iliad* and *The Odyssey* were a combination of holy scripture, *Star Wars*-type saga, and *World History For Dummies* of the time.) Different city-states also gathered for athletic competitions (the original Olympics), and when Greeks were threatened by barbarians, as in the wars against the mighty Persian kings Darius I in 490 BC and his son Xerxes I in 480 BC, the city-states worked together, if only temporarily.

The 2007 film *300*, based on a popular graphic novel, introduces elements of fantasy into its depiction of the Battle of Thermopylae in 480 BC, a landmark conflict of the Persian Wars. *300* depicts the king of Sparta and his tiny force of 300 troops standing up to the 1,000,000-strong Persian army of Xerxes I.

Making Alexander great

The Greeks' fierce, contentious independence made them vulnerable over the period between 359 and 337 BC as a king to their north, Philip of Macedon, used a combination of military force and aggressive diplomacy to muscle in on successive city-states. Macedon (today's Republic of Macedonia and the Macedonian region of modern Greece) wasn't a mighty empire like Persia, but rather a poor mountainous country. Yet the Greeks failed to unite against Philip. He conquered, coerced, and negotiated peace treaties with individual city-states until he was in position to set himself up as protector of Greece. Philip formed the city-states into a league that helped his son put together the biggest empire yet.

Ascending to the throne

Philip planned to lead the Greeks against Persia as payback for Persia's invasions of more than a century before. But he was murdered before he could mount the expedition. Some say his wife, Olympias, paid the killer to pave the way for her son, Alexander, to succeed his dad. Nineteen-year-old Alexander, well educated in war and philosophy (one of his tutors was the Athenian philosopher Aristotle), joined her in killing other candidates for the throne of Macedon.

His power at home secure, Alexander quickly disabused the Greeks of any notion that they would have an easy time resisting him, nearly destroying Thebes in the process (not to be confused with the ancient Egyptian capital also called Thebes).

Figure 4-2:
The Greeks built independent city-states all over the Aegean and well beyond.

BLACK SEA

THRACE

Mt. Olympus •

Lamnos • Troy

Iolcue •

AEGEAN SEA

ASIA MINOR

THESSALY

Leaboe

Delphi • Ecyros

Ithaca

Thebes • Chios

AECHAEA Athega •

Corinth • ATTICA

Olympia • Mycenas • Firyns

Angoe • Troezen

PELOPONNESE ARCADIA Delos

Pyloe • Sparta

Naxoa

Cythera

Rhodes

Knoeoas •

Crete

Director Oliver Stone's 2004 epic film, *Alexander,* is an ambitious attempt at tracing Alexander the Great's entire life, from his difficult relationship with Philip and his complex feelings for his mother through his greatest conquests and beyond.

Extending an empire to the farthest reaches

In a career marked by one victory after another, Alexander the Great built an empire beyond the limits of what had been the known world. By the middle of 331 BC, Alexander and his Macedonian-Greek army defeated two great Persian forces, the second led by King Darius III.

Although a brilliant, fearless, and inventive warrior, Alexander didn't do it all by force or ingenuity. The Egyptians, conquered earlier by the Persians, gladly chose Alexander as their leader instead. When the young conqueror marched into Mesopotamia, ancient cities opened their gates to him and took him as king. When Darius III was out of the way (murdered by his own men), the Persians fell down before Alexander and made him feel almost as if he were a god. He liked that, but his officers didn't.

Alexander marched on beyond the frontiers of Persia, clashing with Afghan tribes, founding cities and crossing the Himalayas. In India, his forces prevailed against the battle elephants of King Porus. Finally, his troops refused to go any farther. Returning as far as Babylon, Alexander died of a fever (perhaps malaria) at age 32 in 323 BC.

Leaving a legacy

Alexander's clout didn't die with him. Legend says that his body was preserved in honey while his followers spent more than two years building an incredibly ornate funeral wagon. When the wagon was ready, mourners loaded the imperial casket onto it and began a ponderously slow funeral procession of 1,500 miles to Macedon for burial. They never got there, however. Alexander's General Ptolemy, appointed governor of Egypt, diverted the procession to Alexandria, one of the cities the conqueror had named for himself. There, the mere possession of Alexander's corpse gave Ptolemy the status to become ruler in his own right. He founded Egypt's Ptolemaic Dynasty, which continued until his descendant Cleopatra VII killed herself with a snake in 30 BC.

One of Alexander's enduring achievements is that he spread the infectious Greek way of questioning and thinking about the world. (Proud Macedonians, by the way, take exception to the casual way Alexander is sometimes referred to as a Greek.) Alexander and his largely-Greek forces disseminated Greek attitudes. Alexandria, Egypt, was a center of *Hellenistic* culture, meaning that Greek-influenced ideas and language networked beyond the widespread Greek city-states and lasted into much later eras.

Rationality, democracy, individualism, citizenship, free debate, and the inquiry born of Greek-style philosophy percolated through other cultures. Philosophy became the cornerstone of science, and the scientific approach became the modern world's primary tool for interpreting reality. In that way, the Classical Greeks still exert a powerful influence on twenty-first-century life.

Rounding Out the World

Over the thousands of years since the first cities and civilizations rose and spread in the Middle East and Asia, many other cultures in the following areas also took significant strides:

- **Africa:** In what's now northern Nigeria, the Nok cleared tropical rainforest for farmland, using iron-bladed axes and hoes, around 600 BC. The Nok were also sculptors, making realistic figurines of terra cotta.

- **Ireland, Scotland, Denmark, France, and Spain:** Hundreds of years before the first pyramids in Egypt, people in Western Europe built communal graves out of stone and earth. Surviving examples date back to 3500 BC; some particularly good ones remain in Orkney, a group of islands off the coast of Scotland, and at Newgrange, Ireland. Europeans of the late Stone Age also left entire villages built of stone. More spectacular yet are the huge stone circles called *megaliths* (or "big rocks") that these people erected. Stonehenge, the most famous, was raised in southern England around 2800 BC.

- **Japan:** People lived in small villages on the mountainous islands that would become Japan as early as 9000 BC, mostly near the ocean and along rivers. They transitioned from a hunter-gatherer lifestyle to agriculture, first growing vegetables and millet. These people were potters, too, and their cord-pattern pots give the period its name, *Jomon*. By the end of the Jomon era, around 300 BC, Japanese potters showed a broader view of the world as they borrowed Chinese-style decorations. Another Chinese innovation, rice growing, also spread to Japan.

Tracking the Centuries

8000 BC: People live in a walled community at Jericho, a crossroads town at a spring-fed oasis near the Jordan River.

About 5000 BC: Barley and flax farmers dig networks of irrigation canals and build villages along those canals between the Tigris and Euphrates Rivers in what would become Iraq.

About 3100 BC: King Menes unites Upper Egypt and Lower Egypt into one kingdom with its capital at Memphis.

2000 BC: Egypt conquers the neighboring Kush culture to the south.

About 1700 BC: Earthquakes and sudden mass flooding may be responsible for ending the sophisticated Indus River Valley civilization.

512 BC: Cyrus, a young Persian king, leads troops against his grandfather, king of the Medes.

404 BC: Sparta defeats Athens in the 27-year Peloponnesian War.

323 BC: While staying in Babylon, Alexander the Great comes down with a sudden fever and dies.

Chapter 5

The Rise and Fall of Many Empires

The Roman city-state's origins are obscure and lost to history, if not to legend. But Rome's history, as it grew into one of the greatest empires the world has ever seen, is anything but obscure. Even in 20 books this size, I probably wouldn't be able to tell you everything that's known about the Roman Empire and its people — let alone its pervasive legacy.

Influential Rome left such a history and a lasting mark on the world that sometimes it seems as if the Roman Empire was the only great empire of the final century BC and the early centuries AD. But the Roman Empire was far from that. Powerful empires rose and fell in the Middle East and Asia. New empires arose in China and the Americas, far away and isolated from the Roman sphere. Imperial expansion dominated much of the world. You can find out about a few of these empires and other civilizations that were contemporaries of the Roman Empire later in this chapter.

As other empires rose and fell, so did Rome's. Also in this chapter, you uncover out how Rome grew from a city-state ruled by a king to a democratic empire and eventually deteriorated into a divided and crumbling political ruin.

Rome's Rise and Demise

From its legendary beginnings to its fractured demise, the Roman civilization had a certain pizzazz that has captured the imagination of not just historians but everybody fascinated by human achievement, military adventure, political intrigue, and tragedy. Shakespeare was among those drawn to its stories (see more about that in the later section "Crossing the Rubicon"), and so am I.

What's the attraction? You can look at Rome's long ascent and descent from any number of angles and wonder at the complexity and sophistication, not to mention the cruelty and corruption of this long-lived culture. In the brief glimpses that follow, you can find clues to what fascinates so many about the Roman civilization.

Forming the Roman Republic

Roman legend says that the half-god, half-mortal Romulus, a son of the Greek war god Mars, built the city of Rome on the Tiber River in 753 BC and ruled as its first king. The legend also says that a female wolf suckled baby Romulus and his twin brother Remus. Historians tend to disagree, especially about the wolf, and put the founding of Rome a bit later, around 645 BC. (For more about Romulus and Remus, see Chapter 19.)

Although he may not have ever tasted wolf's milk or murdered his smart-mouthed twin brother, the legendary Romulus is credited as the first of seven kings who ruled Rome as a city-state (not unlike the Greek city-states around the Mediterranean, which you can find out about in Chapter 4) until 509 BC. That was when King Tarquinius Superbus got on the wrong side of his advisory body of citizen-magistrates, the Roman Senate.

The Roman Senate gave Tarquinius Superbus the boot and set up a republican system of government designed to prevent a tyrant from ever misruling Rome again. Two *consuls,* elected annually, served as administrative executives under the supervision of the Roman Senate. The republic system worked, bringing the stability that Rome needed as it grew from city-state into empire. And did it grow.

Rome borrowed freely from other cultures — a pantheon of gods from the Greeks, Athenian-style democracy, and metalworking technology from an older Italian culture, the Etruscans. Yet, the Roman civilization did so much with what it borrowed that you can't begin to overestimate its impact both in its own time and ever since. How is Rome's influence felt today? In all kinds of ways. For one, the Roman language, Latin, is the foundation of not just Italian, but also of French, Spanish, Portuguese, and Romanian. Latin also left a deep impression on non-Latin languages, such as English. Even after Latin fell out of everyday use, it remained the unifying language of learning, particularly medicine and science.

Earning citizenship

Romans lived in a stratified society organized by class (see the "Roman class" sidebar for more). Opportunities and employment were strictly defined by birth — just as they were in so many other cultures dominated by privileged aristocrats. Yet Roman custom also offered ways to improve your status or that of your children.

Rome allowed foreigners and slaves to become citizens. It was a highly limited opportunity by modern standards but progressive for its time. Giving the Roman Empire's lowborn and conquered people a chance at inclusion in society helped win those people's loyalty to Rome, which added greatly to Rome's growth and resilience.

Democratic Athens, Greece, offered no such opportunities for outsiders (see more about Athens in Chapters 4 and 11). In a Greek city-state, a slave could be granted freedom, but the best he could hope for was lowly resident-alien status. He was unlikely to develop loyalty to a state that excluded him. (And I do mean *him*. Women couldn't even dream of citizenship.) When war broke out, the resident alien was unlikely to rally to the cause.

Why so exclusive? Greeks valued *Greekness*, looking down on those who didn't speak their language and worship their gods. But the exclusion was also economic. The city-states of rocky Greece were usually short of resources, especially good farmland. Granting citizenship meant increasing the number of people with a direct claim on the food supply. Making slaves citizens was too expensive and would also have meant increasing the number of voters, which may have caused unwanted power shifts.

In fertile Italy, on the other hand, food was relatively abundant, so shares weren't such an issue. Also, blocks of votes rather than individual votes determined Roman elections, so an extra vote in a block had little potential impact.

Rome offered slaves the real possibility of earning citizenship, but only in the lowest class of citizenship: *plebeian*. Plebeians, however, could hope for their children to rise to a higher class. Further, Rome united other cities to its empire by bringing conquered people into the fold. Roman officers propped up local aristocrats in newly taken provinces, making them dependent on Rome's support. The defeated country's men were enlisted in the next conflict and rewarded with part of the profits from the almost-inevitable conquest: Loyalty was lucrative.

Expanding the empire

By the third century BC, Rome had only one major rival for the position of top dog in the western Mediterranean: the city of Carthage, a big, rich trading port in North Africa.

Before 1000 BC, the Phoenicians sailed out of what is now Lebanon to expand trade opportunities, and they found Carthage, in present-day Tunisia, in 814 BC. Around 600 BC, Carthage became so rich and populous that it cast off Phoenician rule.

Roman class

Plebeian, which refers to a lowly person, is a word you may still run across. In Rome, the plebeian belonged to the second lowest of four classes in society. The lowest was the *slave,* who had no rights at all. Plebeians were a little better off in that they were free, but beyond that they had no clout. Next in the hierarchy were the *equestrians,* or riders. These were rich people — rich men, actually — of a class that rode horses when they were called to fight for Rome. They weren't rich enough to have much power, though. For that, you had to be among the *patricians,* the nobles. *Patrician* is a word that still gets used, too. Now, as back then, it's applied to people of wealthy families accustomed to having authority.

Carthage and Rome fought three Punic Wars from 264–146 BC. (*Punic* comes from *Punicus,* a Latin word for "Phoenician.") Carthage should have quit while it was ahead. In the first of these wars, Rome won the island of Sicily, its first overseas province. In the second Punic War, Carthage lost the rest of its far-flung territories and became a dependent ally of Rome. The alliance was never sweet and soured into the third Punic War, when Rome destroyed Carthage itself.

To the east, Rome fought the Hellenistic kingdoms, which were Greek-influenced nations carved out of Alexander's empire. Romans took Macedon, Greece, Asia Minor, and the eastern shore of the Mediterranean, eventually including Judah, founded by the Jewish leader Judas the Maccabee in 168 BC. The Romans sacked Jerusalem in 63 BC and made it the capital of Roman Judea.

The empire pushed north into Gaul, to the Rhine and the Danube Rivers, growing so big that administering the vast territory became too difficult for the republic, with its unwieldy and often contentious government. Turmoil created the opportunity for a military genius named Gaius Julius Caesar to step forward.

Crossing the Rubicon

Gaius Julius Caesar (better known as just Julius Caesar) was a Roman aristocrat from one of the republic's old families. As a military commander, his far-flung conquests extended Rome's growing dominion, and he was ambitious for himself as well as for his country.

In the first century BC, Rome desperately needed leadership. Decades of uneasy peace, fierce political rivalries, and widespread bitterness had followed a series of civil wars. Quarreling politicians fighting for power rendered the Roman Senate useless. In 60 BC, three leaders formed the First Triumvirate, or "rule by three," to restore order. It was actually an unofficial arrangement that was even kept secret at first, but the triumvirate dominated Roman politics for most of a decade. The three were Marcus Licinius Crassus, Gnaeus Pompeius Magnus (widely remembered as Pompey), and Julius Caesar, the youngest. Caesar was especially feared by politicians who opposed the Triumvirate, in part because he was a nephew of the late Gaius Marius, who had served seven different times as *consul,* the top administrative post in the Roman government. (A consul was a bit like a mix between prime minister and attorney general.)

Caesar's victories in the Gallic Wars (58–50 BC) pushed the empire's borders all the way to Europe's Atlantic seaboard. He also led Rome's first invasion of Britain in 55 BC. While he was away, however, Crassus died, and the First Triumvirate fell apart. Pompey sought to consolidate his own power, standing as Caesar's rival instead of his ally.

Returning home in 49 BC, Caesar started another civil war by defying a law that said Roman troops had to stay north of the Rubicon River in today's northern Italy. The law was intended to prevent a military leader from taking over the republic by force. Caesar led his troops across the stream and fought other Roman leaders for the prize of absolute power in battles that continued until 45 BC. (*Rubicon* has meant "point of no return" ever since.) His rivals defeated, Caesar took the title "Dictator for Life."

Caesar wasn't technically an emperor, but his reign marked the end of the Roman Republic and the beginning of an age of emperors. Rome's ruling families didn't take this change lightly. The dictator liked elaborate compliments and formal tributes, making his enemies think he was aiming for not just regal status but a kind of imperial divinity. Many Romans were upset at what Caesar was doing to their republic, and they still talked about Tarquinius Superbus, the last Roman king, and how the Roman Senate had kicked him out. Two senators, Brutus and Cassius, plotted Caesar's assassination and carried it out successfully.

England's William Shakespeare wrote a terrific play on the subject of Caesar's downfall 1,600 years after it happened. If you've ever said, "Beware the ides of March" or "Friends, Romans, countrymen, lend me your ears," you've quoted Shakespeare's *Julius Caesar.* Director Joseph L. Mankiewicz made a movie version of the play in 1953, with 1950s screen sensation Marlon Brando holding his own alongside Shakespearean heavyweight John Gielgud. It's not as much fun as a top-flight stage production of the play, but the movie could be a lot worse. More recent film adaptations were made in 1970 and 1979. Don't take *Julius Caesar* — the play or films — for literal truth, though. Shakespeare was a great dramatist, but he was no historian.

Many more years of civil war followed Caesar's assassination. Caesar's cousin and general, Marcus Antonius, or Mark Antony, was in position to emerge with supreme power. But Antony's formidable rival, Caesar's great-nephew and adopted son, Octavian, came out on top in 31 BC with a win over the combined forces of Antony and his wife, the Egyptian Queen Cleopatra, at Actium off the coast of Greece.

Empowering the emperor

Like his predecessor, Octavian didn't call himself King or Emperor, although that's what he was as the undisputed ruler of the Roman world. Instead he took the relatively modest title *Principate,* or "first citizen." His modesty would have seemed sincere if he hadn't also gotten the Senate to rename him *Augustus,* which means "exalted." Augustus already bore the family name Caesar. Both Augustus and Caesar became titles handed down to successive Roman emperors.

Augustus cut back the unbridled expansionism of late republican days and set territorial limits: the Rhine and Danube Rivers in Europe and the Euphrates River in Asia. The empire was stable. It annexed no territory until taking Britain in 44 AD. Then, in 106 AD, Emperor Trajan, eager to extend his territory, took Dacia (modern Romania) and Arabia.

Roaming eastward

Emperors ran Rome for hundreds of years more as dynasties and factions rose and fell and as pressure along the far-flung borders demanded vigilance. (For more on Roman defensive strategies, see Chapter 16.) Cutting back on expansion eased conflict but didn't stop incursions from the outside.

The hardest pressure was always at the frontier formed by the Rhine and Danube Rivers. Successive Roman emperors had to concentrate resources there, leading to more administrative focus toward the east. In the third century AD, the Emperor Diocletian built a new eastern capital, Nicomedia, far off in Asia Minor, where the Turkish city of Izmit is now. In 324 AD, the Emperor Constantine put his capital, Constantinople (today's Istanbul, Turkey), in the east, too. He built *New Rome,* as Constantinople was often called, at the site of the old city of Byzantium on the Bosporus, the channel that connects the Black Sea with the Mediterranean. Completing the project in 330 AD, the emperor renamed the city after himself.

Constantine became the first Christian emperor, ending a century of persecution against those who followed the new religion. Christians were relatively few until the third century and were largely ignored, but in 235 AD, the Severan Dynasty fell apart and the Roman Empire tumbled into 50 years of chaos. Emperor Decius, looking for scapegoats, began rounding up the increasingly numerous Christians and killing them. His successor, Valerian, did much the same thing. The Goths killed Decius and the Persians captured Valerian in acts the Christians saw as divine retribution. Maybe the emperors thought so, too. Romans were highly superstitious, and bad luck could convince even an emperor that supernatural forces were against him. Persecution of Christians stopped for a while, and Christianity gained many converts.

It took Diocletian, a soldier from Croatia who became emperor in 284 AD, to get the government of the Roman Empire back on line. After accomplishing that, Diocletian started persecuting the Christians again.

How did Diocletian restore order? He split the empire in half, as follows:

🖛 **The East:** Diocletian took the wealthy, healthy eastern half of the Roman Empire for himself, basing his new capital in Turkey.

🖛 **The West:** Diocletian tapped the general in charge of Gaul, Maximian, to rule the western half of the Roman Empire.

Both Diocletian and Maximian had the title *Augustus,* and two more co-rulers, Constantius and Galerius received the lesser title *Caesar.* When Constantius died, his son, Constantine, later called Constantine the Great, succeeded him and eventually won control of the whole empire. The reunification couldn't last, though, especially considering that Constantine based himself in the east, too. Diocletian's split had set a precedent.

Constantine did much more for Christians than just stopping their persecution. Starting in 331 AD, he made the Church rich by

🖛 Seizing the treasures of pagan temples and spending them on magnificent new Christian churches from Italy to Turkey to Jerusalem.

🖛 Handing out huge endowments.

🖛 Authorizing bishops to draw on imperial funds as reparation for the years of enmity.

These moves helped establish the Church as a wealthy institution for many centuries to come. In 391 AD, Constantine's successor, Theodosius I, added a final touch by prohibiting old-style Roman pagan worship.

One result of the power shift away from Rome was that the Roman Senate was sometimes relegated to the status of a city council. True, Rome was quite a city for a council to oversee, but the power was where the emperor was (or where the emperors were). Rome's western half became less and less an empire and therefore grew more and more vulnerable to invasion by the barbarian tribes from the north — Huns, Vandals, Visigoths, Ostrogoths and more.

By 400 AD, Theodosius had a senate in Constantinople and a staff of 2,000 bureaucrats. Also around this time, Roman tax collectors couldn't move about Europe without a military escort. The Visigoths sacked Rome in 410 AD.

Western empire fades into history

With its western territory overrun by barbarians and pirates, the Roman Empire was no longer anything like its former self. In 439 AD, Vandals advanced to Roman North Africa, capturing Carthage, the former Phoenician capital that had become one of the major cities of the Western Roman Empire. The once-mighty western empire was unable to defend this valuable trade center.

While the Western Roman Empire declined, the imperial government in Constantinople signaled the changing times by declaring Greek, rather than Latin, to be the official language of that capital city. Latin was the language of the west, of Rome. Greek was the language of the eastern Mediterranean, the new center of Roman ascendancy. As the Byzantine Empire, this eastern branch of the Roman Empire would persist for another 1,000 years. For more about that, check out Chapter 6.

Roman administration in the West struggled on until 476 AD, but without authority. When barbarian leaders closed in on the last emperor to sit on the Roman throne, a poor youngster named Romulus Augustus (a name recalling his great predecessors), they didn't bother to kill him. Also known by the diminutive Augustulus, he wasn't considered important enough.

Rome's legacy pervades the Mediterranean, the Middle East, Europe, the Americas, and also far-flung places culturally affected by Europeans — a broad swath that takes in the Philippines, South Africa (and most of the rest of the African continent), Australia, and arguably the whole world.

Rome and the Roman Catholic Church

After Rome was no longer an imperial capital, its name loomed so large and for so long in people's minds that it continued to invoke power and an aura of legitimacy. This was in part because the Church remained headquartered there, but the Church was in Rome because of what Rome had been at its political height — the center of the western world.

The Romans weren't the first Christians. In fact, Romans fed early Christians to the lions just for the fun of it. Yet when the Roman Empire was officially converted to Christianity, it promoted, strengthened, and spread that religion in Europe, western Asia, North Africa — everywhere the empire extended. The Church rose to wealth and power under the protection of Roman emperors.

Rome became the capital of western Christianity and remains the seat of the Roman Catholic Church. Yet ironically, by the time Christianity became the official Roman religion, the Roman Empire had shifted its energies far away from Rome.

Whatever it's called, it's still *the* Church

When talking about the Christian Church in its early years, I often refer to it simply as *the Church*. Christianity was a huge cultural force from late Roman times onward. Before the Protestant Reformation of the sixteenth century, the Catholic Church was *the* Christian church in Western Europe — virtually the only one. It was rarely called *the Catholic Church* because *catholic* was still an adjective meaning "universal" rather than the name of a religious denomination. (Spelled with a lowercase c, *catholic* still means "universal" or "wide-ranging.") After Rome banned pagan worship and as the old Norse and Celtic beliefs faded, virtually everybody was a Christian. Catholicism was the universal religion: Everybody was a Catholic, but they didn't think of themselves as Catholics because there was no such thing as a Protestant. Christians always capitalized the word *Church* when they meant the network of cathedrals, chapels, priories, and so on that looked to the pope in Rome for direction, and so do I in this chapter and in Chapters 10 and 14.

In addition to its role as root of modern Romance Languages (Italian, French, Spanish, and so on), Latin was the unifying language of the Roman Catholic Church, which to Roman and other European Christians before the sixteenth century AD was just the Church — the only church there was. (See Chapter 12 for more on early Christianity.) After the Protestant Reformation and until the middle of the twentieth century, Catholic masses worldwide were always said in Latin. (See Chapter 14 for more on the Reformation and the founding of later Christian churches.)

The Holy Roman Empire is not to be confused with the Roman Empire. The Holy Roman Empire was a much later confederation of European principalities and duchies that changed shapes and allegiances over many centuries. Yet it got its Roman name because of the regard that medieval Europeans still had for the concept of Roman power. This later empire started in 800 AD, when Pope Leo III bestowed the new title of Emperor of the West on Charlemagne, king of the Franks and the first ruler since the original Roman Empire's demise to unite most of Western Europe under a single rule. Charlemagne's empire, based where France is today, didn't long survive him, but the German king Otto I put together a new Holy Roman Empire in 962 AD, the one that hung on until the nineteenth century. (For more on the Holy Roman Empire, see Chapters 6 and 14.) Aside from the pope's blessing, this empire's nominally united German and Austrian lands had little to do with Rome. Still, the name *Roman* smacked of imperial legitimacy.

Other Roman terms endured as well, especially terms for positions of authority. The Russian title *czar* (or *tsar,* as it's often spelled) and the later German *kaiser* both came from the Roman title *caesar.* (Julius Caesar, whose name became an official Roman title, makes another appearance in Chapter 20.) The name of a powerful dynastic family, the *Romanovs,* who ruled Russia from 1613–1917, referred back to imperial Rome, too. Even in the Islamic world, the name *Qaysar* — a place name found from Afghanistan to Egypt — comes from *Caesar*.

Building Empires around the World

After Alexander the Great died of a sudden fever in 323 BC, his vast empire almost immediately disintegrated. Without Alexander, there was nothing to unite such widespread, dissimilar places as Macedonia, northern India, and Egypt — all among his territories. (Find more about Alexander the Great in Chapters 4 and 20.)

Yet the breakup of Alexander's empire brought about new empires — not as big, but impressive nonetheless. Several of them were founded by Alexander's former military governors.

Alexander was a conqueror rather than an administrator. He couldn't personally rule all the lands he won — especially not while conducting further military campaigns — so he appointed regional viceroys to govern in his name. The word *viceroy* is similar to vice-president, with the *-roy* part meaning *king*. These assistant kingships went to some of Alexander's top military commanders.

With Alexander gone, the generals were free to turn their territories, which they had been holding in trust for their boss, into personal kingdoms. (See Chapter 4 for the story of Ptolemy, Macedonian governor of conquered Egypt, who used Alexander's funeral procession to found his own Egyptian dynasty.) Although the Roman Empire, the largest and most influential empire to emerge after Alexander, arose first as a city-state, and although the Mediterranean was sprinkled with successful Greek city-states, imperial might was the model for large-scale government in the late centuries of the BC period and the early centuries of the AD period.

Ruling Persia and Parthia

Seleuces was the Macedonian general that Alexander the Great left in charge of conquered Persia (largely what's now Iran) in the 330s BC. The Persian Empire, at its height around 480 BC, was immensely powerful but in decline by the time Alexander added it to his collection of kingdoms. Still, there was a precedent for imperial government in Persia, and Seleuces took advantage of that by bringing Persian officers and Persian regional officials into his government of Macedonians and Greeks and by using his troops to keep order. He successfully transformed himself into a king, no longer a viceroy dependent on Alexander the Great's might to back him up.

Seleuces' descendants, the Seleucid Dynasty, ruled a piece of Asia that stretched from Anatolia (the Asian part of modern Turkey) to Afghanistan. Seleucid rule lasted until a powerful regional rival, the Parthians, conquered Persia in the second century BC.

The rise of the Parthians traces back to 250 BC, when the leader Arsaces, from central Asia, founded Parthia in eastern Persia. His descendant, Mithradates I, went on an empire-building campaign of his own between about 160–140 BC, assembling lands from the Persian Gulf to the Caspian Sea and eastward into India.

Mithradates' goal was to recreate the Persian Empire ruled over by Darius I more than 300 years earlier. (Chapter 4 has more about the Persian Empire.) Alexander and his successors displaced Persian culture with Greek — a change called *Hellenization* because the Greeks called themselves *Hellenes*. Mithradates reversed Hellenization and revived all things Persian. The Parthian Empire lasted until 224 AD, when a soldier called Ardashir, a member of a noble Persian family called Sassanid, rebelled against the king and killed him. Like the Parthians, the Sassanid Dynasty was Rome's major rival in the East, lasting until the Muslim Arabs conquered Persia in about 642. (For more about the Arabs, turn to Chapter 6.)

India's empires

The political borders within today's India and Pakistan shifted a few times over the centuries between 300 BC and 400 AD, a time that gave rise to both the Indian subcontinent's first united empire — the Mauryan — and India's golden age under the Gupta Dynasty.

Striking back at Alexander the Great

In 322 BC, a nobleman named Chandragupta Maurya (sometimes spelled Candra Gupta Maurya) overturned Alexander the Great's Indian conquest by leading a successful revolt against Alexander's governors in the Punjab (modern Pakistan and northwest India). He also seized Magadha, the main state in northeast India, and formed the biggest Indian political force yet, the *Mauryan Empire*. Seleucus, the general who became Persia's king after Alexander died, invaded from the west in 305 BC, but Chandragupta beat him off and won a treaty from him setting an Indian border along the high Hindu Kush Mountains. (The Hindu Kush Mountains are an extension of the Himalayan range and the same barrier that Alexander had to cross when he invaded India.)

Chandragupta's son and grandson enlarged the empire, especially to the south, but war sickened the grandson, Asoka. After early victories, he became a devout Buddhist, devoted to peace among people and nations. Instead of troops, he sent missionaries to win over Burma and Sri Lanka.

Achieving a golden age

After Asoka died in 238 BC, his successors proved less able to hold the large territory together, and the Mauryan Empire declined. An ambitious rival from the Sunga family assassinated the last Mauryan king, Birhadratha, in 185 BC, and seized power. The resultant Sunga Dynasty couldn't prevent the subcontinent from breaking up into a number of independent kingdoms and republics, something like what happened during the medieval period that Europe would soon experience.

Then another leader, another Chandragupta, united India again about 600 years after the Mauryans did. The new power grew into the *Gupta Empire,* achieving great wealth through widespread trade and intelligent government and bringing about the greatest cultural flowering ever to rock India.

Known as Chandragupta I, this conqueror started in the kingdom of Magadha in 320 AD, bringing surrounding kingdoms under his influence by force and persuasion. He revived many of Asoka's principles of humane government. Much as the Romans did, he put local leaders to work for him instead of killing or imprisoning them; he propped up regional authorities and made them dependent on his administration. This model for Indian government worked for a long time. Even the British used this model for governing India in the nineteenth century.

Chandragupta had able successors, including his son Samudragupta, who spread the Gupta territory to the north and east. Grandson Chandragupta II, a great patron of the arts, ruled from 376–415 AD, spending tax money to promote architecture, painting, and poetry. The Gupta era gave India many glorious temples and palaces, as well as sculpture, music, dance, and poetry.

The Guptas weren't without enemies. Huns from Mongolia and northern China battered the northern frontier of India in the fifth century. In the 480s AD, after the last Gupta king died, Huns took over the North. (For more about the Huns and what they were doing to Europe around the same time, turn to Chapter 6.)

Uniting China: Seven into Qin

Divided into seven warring states, China was in turmoil from 485–221 BC. Then the king of one of those states, a place known as Qin, emerged as the dominant leader. He united China for the first time by beating his rivals and consolidating their territories into greater Qin, calling himself *qin shi huangdi* or *Qin Shihuangdi,* meaning "the First Emperor of Qin," which suggests that he thought there would be more emperors after him. He was right. From Qin, which you also can spell *Chi'in,* came the name *China.*

Qin Shihuangdi got things done. He may have been inspired by the great Persian road-builder Darius I, because just as Darius built a 1,500-mile highway, Qin Shihuangdi linked the various defensive walls on China's northern border into one Great Wall. His successors continued to work on the wall until it was more than 2,500 miles long; you can see it in Figure 5-1. (Darius also inspired the Parthian empire-builder Mithradates, whom you can read about earlier in this chapter. For more on Darius, see Chapter 4.)

Qin Shihuangdi also built roads and canals with a fury, and from his northern power base, he conquered southern China. He got rid of feudalism and disarmed nobles, dividing the country into 36 military districts, each with an administrator who reported to the emperor. He was a firm believer in big government, using his clout to reform weights and measures and standardize everything from Chinese script to the length of cart axles.

The emperor looked after himself and his entourage, building a palace complex that doubled as a massive barracks sleeping many thousands. He also linked hundreds of lesser palaces by a covered road network. You may conclude from these facts that he didn't like to be alone, and perhaps this accounts for what researchers found after they opened his tomb in 1974 — 7,000 warriors sculpted of terra cotta and standing in battle formation as if to protect their king. With painted faces and uniforms, the sculptures still hold real weapons. Terra-cotta drivers man real chariots hitched to terra-cotta horses.

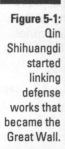

Figure 5-1:
Qin Shihuangdi started linking defense works that became the Great Wall.

© Adam Jones/Getty Images

There's nary a hint of historical authenticity in the 2008 action-horror-comedy film *The Mummy: Tomb of the Dragon Warrior.* Still, the filmmakers seem to have been inspired by Qin Shihuangdi's sculpted army. The film features Brendan Fraser battling 10,000 terra-cotta soldiers who answer to an evil, immortal ancient Chinese king. Hong Kong filmmaker Ching Siu Tung also used the pottery army as the premise for his 1990 adventure-comedy *A Terra Cotta Warrior,* about a Qin guardsman who gets turned into terra cotta but revives in the 1930s to protect the emperor from grave robbers.

The first Chinese emperor died in 210 BC, and his dynasty didn't last long, yet the family that emerged as rulers only four years later, in 206 BC, was smart enough not to undo the Qin work. Building on Qin Shihuangdi's reforms, the rulers of the *Han Dynasty* reigned until 220 AD.

Relatively late in the Han Dynasty, during a time called the Eastern Han, the Chinese invented both paper and porcelain, among other important technological advances that flourished under later dynasties such as the short-lived Sui and the succeeding Tang.

Flourishing civilizations in the Americas

During the Roman era, all the action wasn't just in Europe. Empires formed in the Americas, too.

Sharing with the Maya

The Mayan culture took shape by about 1 AD in Central America, rising to prominence around 300 AD and enjoying what historians call its Classic Period until about 900 AD, when it went into a long decline.

In the tropical rainforests on the Yucatan Peninsula, in an area spreading over what's now southern Mexico, Guatemala, northern Belize, and western Honduras, the Maya built on inventions and ideas developed by nearby cultures such as the Olmec (see Chapter 4). The Maya also shared aspects of their culture with the Toltec of northern Mexico, whose great city of Tula (about 40 miles north of present-day Mexico City) covered 13 square miles and was home to as many as 60,000 people. (The Toltec predated the Aztecs, who show up in Chapter 8.)

The Maya developed astronomy, a sophisticated calendar, and a writing technique similar to Egyptian hieroglyphics. They built terraced cities in neat rectangular grids and pyramid temples in ceremonial cities such as Copan, Palenque, and Tikal. Both the cities and temples are now ruins for archeologists to study and tourists to explore (and climb on).

An elite class of priests and nobles ruled over the majority, who tended fields cleared from the jungle. Modern experts haven't settled on why the Maya ultimately abandoned their cities, although environmental decline seems to have been a factor.

Building in Peru

Farther south, a culture called the Paracas took root as early as 750 BC on a peninsula jutting from the southern coast of Peru. What's known of the Paracas comes purely from archeological evidence. Apparently at its height from the first century BC until as late as the fourth century AD, this farming civilization built extensive canals for irrigation.

The Paracas were skilled at weaving, a fact illustrated by the beautifully embroidered textiles found wrapped around mummified bodies of their dead. Archeologists refer to a large, seaside complex of Paracas tombs as the *Paracas Necropolis,* meaning "city of the dead."

In the dry river valleys inland from the south coast of Peru, the Nazca culture appears to have risen around 200 BC, perhaps as an offshoot of the Paracas. As with the Paracas, most of what's known of the Nazca comes through interpretation of surviving artifacts such as textiles and colorful pottery.

Based on such evidence, archeologists think the Nazca reached their civilization's height between 200 BC and 500 AD. Their huge-scale earthen etchings, designs that are most visible today from the air, are cited today as evidence of long-ago interplanetary visitors. Theorists say that the figures can't be seen except from the air and so they could have been landing strips for alien spaceships. Archeologists who study the Nazca point out that the figures can indeed be seen from surrounding hills and that the lines of the drawings are far more likely to have been ritual paths that were part of the Nazca religion. The scientists reject the ancient astronaut theory as nonsense.

Arising a little later than the Nazca — in the first century AD — in the fertile valleys inland from the north coast of Peru, the Moche culture may have resembled that of Classical Greece in that it seems to have consisted of politically independent city-states united by a common language and religion.

Although the Maya had hieroglyphics, the Paracas, Nazca, and Moche people left no evidence of any written language.

Rounding Out the Rest of the World

Over the long stretch of time when the Roman Empire was rising and falling, other cultures around the globe experienced their own changes.

> ✔ **The Aksum:** In northeast Africa, where Ethiopia is now, the Aksum people put together an empire that grew rich after 200 AD by trading with places as far away as India. The Aksum became Christian in the fourth century AD and spread the new religion to neighboring peoples.

✔ **The Celts:** Tribal people with sophisticated metalworking skills but no written language, the Celts kept expanding their European territory from central Europe toward the west and south. By the fifth century BC, they were dominant in Gaul (modern France), England, Ireland, much of Scotland, and parts of Spain. By the third century BC, the Celts spread through the Balkans. They made beautiful golden jewelry and harness ornaments. In some places, the Celts built large forts atop hills and fought Roman legions as the empire absorbed Europe. Later the Celts clashed with the barbarians that overran their territory through the early centuries AD.

✔ **The Japanese:** Discovering how to mine and smelt iron, the Japanese joined the Iron Age sometime in the third century AD. They buried emperors and other big shots with their weapons and other valuable possessions in mounds made of stone and earth.

Tracking the Centuries

753 BC: According to legend, this is the year when Romulus, the half-mortal son of a Greek-Roman war god, builds the city of Rome.

About 645 BC: According to historians, people from a number of small settlements in west-central Italy establish the city of Rome on a hilly site along the Tiber River.

509 BC: Romans rise up against King Tarquinius Superbus and drive him into exile. They establish a republic in place of the monarchy.

238 BC: Asoka, emperor of India, dies. His Mauryan Dynasty begins to decline.

221 BC: The First Emperor of Qin unites warring Chinese states.

140 BC: Mithradates I begins a campaign conquest to enlarge the Parthian Empire.

45 BC: Julius Caesar emerges victorious from Roman civil war and takes the title Dictator for Life.

27 BC: Octavian, great-nephew of the assassinated Julius Caesar, accepts the title *Augustus*, becoming Rome's first emperor.

324 AD: Roman Emperor Constantine builds his new capital city, Constantinople, in Turkey, far to the east of Rome.

476 AD: Barbarian invaders remove Romulus Augustus, the last Roman emperor of the West, from his throne.

Chapter 6

History's Mid-Life Crisis:
The Middle Ages

In This Chapter

▶ Flexing the Roman Empire's muscles in Constantinople

▶ Going berserk with barbarians and Vikings

▶ Following the Bantu all over Africa

▶ Uniting Arabs and building empires

▶ Bouncing back in India

*M*iddle Ages and *medieval* mean the same thing: an age between ages. The Middle Ages in Western Europe was the period between the collapse of the Western Roman Empire (officially 476 AD, although there wasn't much of the empire left to collapse by then) and the Renaissance in the fourteenth century. (You can find much more about the Renaissance in Chapter 13.)

Calling this period the Middle Ages doesn't mean that nothing happened in Western Europe between the fifth and fourteenth centuries. There's no such thing as a 900-year span when nothing happened. What it means is that the Middle Ages were sandwiched between two more monumental-seeming eras — the Roman Empire and the Renaissance.

As I explain in this chapter, in today's Turkey and a huge surrounding region, history wasn't between two great ages during the Middle Ages but rather smack in the middle of one great age: that of the Byzantine Empire. Other empires peaked in those centuries, too, as India flowered and the Arabs conquered vast lands, inspired by their new religion, Islam.

In what used to be the Western Roman Empire, however, what civil authority there was became decentralized. Cities weren't as important as they once were, and the economy became more agricultural and local than commercial and trade-based. Authority followed the complicated rules of feudal loyalty, so that instead of depending on imperial hierarchy, local vassals served local lords in return for favor and protection. (The exception was the monolithic Church, extremely powerful and still based in Rome. You can read more about the power of Europe's medieval Church in Chapters 13 and 14.)

The Middle Ages reflected the people who brought them on, the many barbarian groups — Huns, Goths, Avars, and others — whose migrations into Europe and constant raids brought down Rome. The barbarians' descendants remained in post-Roman Europe, blending and clashing among themselves and with the descendants of earlier Europeans. These descendants formed the beginnings of modern nations by standing up to new waves of raiders from the north — the Vikings — and conquerors from the east and south, the Arabs and Moors. Local lords became more willing to join forces, pledging allegiance to a strong king who could bring them together to fend off attackers.

As the barbarians moved out of Asia, other populations continued to move — and not just into Europe. Wave after wave of a people called the Bantu transformed the African continent over a millennium of southern migrations.

The world that emerged at the end of the Middle Ages was vastly different from what it was when Rome fell. So, maybe the Middle Ages should be called the Transitional Ages. . . .

Building (And Maintaining) the Byzantine Empire

Roman Emperor Constantine the Great modeled his eastern branch of the Roman Empire (which eventually became the Byzantine Empire) on old Imperial Rome — except that the eastern branch was a Christian power rather than a pagan one and people spoke Greek instead of Latin.

Constantine chose the city of Byzantium for his new capital, rebuilding it to fit his concept of a great city and renaming it Constantinople in 330 AD. By the time the western part of the Roman Empire fell apart in the fifth century, Constantinople (today's Istanbul, Turkey) was a seat of power that rivaled old Rome at its height. The Byzantine emperor had even more power than most of his western predecessors, and the Byzantine senate evolved as a sprawling, intricate (and notoriously corrupt) bureaucracy.

As a center of government, the Byzantine capital was remarkably stable. It was an urban seat of vast power, boasting a high level of literacy and wealth as the result of a commercial economy and extensive lands. Although its boundaries changed many times, the empire was always vast.

Before he died in 565 AD, Justinian, who became emperor in 537 AD, ruled lands on the north and south shores of the Mediterranean Sea, stretching from southern Spain all the way east to Persia. Trying to reunite east and west into one Christian Empire, Justinian sent his armies to retake many formerly Roman lands in Europe and North Africa. He even recaptured Italy, establishing a western Byzantine capital at Ravenna. But no matter how hard he tried, Justinian couldn't reconcile the eastern and western branches of the Church, which were bitterly divided. (For more about the early Christian Church, see Chapter 12.)

To last so long as a power center, Constantinople had to endure physically, too. The city's location on the Bosporus (the channel that links the Mediterranean with the Black Sea) and its heavily fortified walls helped it resist invasion. Although Constantinople took a beating, the Arabs' four-year siege that finally ended in 678 AD failed. (You can read more about Constantinople's strategic advantages in Chapter 17. See the later section "Emerging Islamic Fervor" for more about the Arabs, who quickly became a force to be reckoned with.)

Sharing and Imposing Culture

The so-called Middle Ages were an unsettled time in much of the world as different populations migrated, clashed, and intermingled. Europe continued to feel the influence of the barbarian peoples that had come west from Asia during the late centuries of the Western Roman Empire. Meanwhile in Africa, the Bantu people spread their languages and cultures southward as subgroups of Bantu migrated down the continent for century upon century. Later in the period, from the eighth to eleventh centuries, seafaring raiders called Vikings plagued, conquered, and settled parts of Europe.

At the same time, cultural influences from China and India began penetrating westward into the Byzantine Empire (Turkey and the eastern Mediterranean), not through population migrations, but through growing trade along an overland route, the *Silk Road*.

Bearing with barbarians

The hordes of barbarians battering away at the Roman frontiers for centuries brought cultural crosscurrents, although destructive ones. In a way, the barbarians created the Middle Ages, so it pays to understand who they were. It's amazing how many peoples came out of the east and how far and fast they came without gas-electric hybrids or interstates.

Revealing obscure origins

To the Romans, a *barbarian* was an outsider who didn't speak Latin. The term most often applied, however, to members of tribes such as the Goths and Vandals. Seeking lands to settle and eager for plunder, these migrating, warlike folks were a force in northern Europe for a very long time before Rome fell and after.

Many barbarians came from northern parts of Asia, in the steppes region, and most were nomadic herders before they turned to raiding. The Vandals and Alans wandered north of the Black Sea before they came west, as did some of the other barbarians, although they moved so much that it's difficult to pin down where they started. Once in Europe they sometimes settled in a specific region — the Huns in Hungary, for example, and the Vandals in Denmark. That didn't mean, however, that the groups stayed put. The Vandals also built Vandalusia, a kingdom in what is now Spain. (Over time, the "V" fell off and the region is known today as Andalusia.)

When Vandals arrived in Denmark in Roman times, they met, fought, and eventually mingled with people who had been hunting and farming in Scandinavia for thousands of years. The Greek adventurer Pythias of Marseilles, visiting Britain in about 350 BC, wrote that he traveled across water (perhaps the North Sea) to a place he called Thule (maybe Norway). There he visited friendly, blond people who threshed their grain indoors to save it from the damp, cold climate. Whether Pythias's courteous hosts were direct ancestors of later invaders is difficult to say, but it's possible.

Before 500 BC, a prolonged warm spell pervaded the far north of Europe. Archeological evidence seems to show that for a while the ancient Scandinavians didn't even have to bother with much clothing. But a gradually cooling climate and difficulty raising food provided the northern tribes with the incentive to come south and prey on Celts and Romans who were enjoying the continent's warmer climes. The barbarian incursions went on for centuries, and tracing them to a colder Scandinavia gives only a small picture (and maybe a distorted one) of the population movements that defined those hundreds of years.

Related to the Mongols who made China their own, the Huns hailed from Mongolia. Huns rode into Europe in the fourth century AD and settled along the River Danube. From there, their leader Attila launched fifth-century attacks on Gaul (modern France) and Italy.

Seeking a better life

Until about 550 AD, entire populations were constantly migrating, some for thousands of miles — and not just around Europe. Migration is a response to economic hardship and climate changes. When people move, they run into other people. If the ones on the move are warlike and desperate, the encounters get ugly.

Many barbarians were poor and looking for a better life. If plunder was a way to a better life, they went for it. No doubt they felt pressures similar to those that fed the much smaller scale migration of Oklahomans out of the drought-ravaged dust bowl of the United States in the 1930s.

Traversing Africa with the Bantu

The barbarians weren't the only populations on the move. Bantu people flowed out of today's Nigeria and north-central Africa, beginning in the last century BC and continuing through the first millennium AD. The Bantu, a group of related peoples who spoke Bantu languages (the largest group of African languages today), were grain farmers and metalworkers who mastered iron-smelting technology long before the rest of Africa.

The Bantu success led to population growth that in turn forced them to seek new lands. So they took their languages and their metalworking technology with them and overwhelmed indigenous populations all the way to the southern tip of the African continent. Most of the people in Africa today are descendants of the Bantu.

Also like the barbarians of Europe, new waves of Bantu continued to move south over successive centuries, overwhelming descendants of earlier waves of Bantu immigrants. In the twelfth century, the Bantu founded the powerful Mwenumatapa civilization (in today's Zimbabwe), centered in the city of Great Zimbabwe.

Sailing and settling with the Vikings

In Europe, another wave of invasions from the north, beginning around the year 800 AD, profoundly marked the Middle Ages. The people of Norway, Denmark, and Sweden, thriving through agriculture and sea trade, started running out of good farmland. Like northern and eastern people before them, they decided to make new opportunities for themselves. One way to do this was to *go a viking* — adventuring and raiding as far as their sturdy ships could take them, which was very far indeed. With the advantage of good longboats and experienced navigators, the Vikings raided the coasts of Britain, Ireland, France, Spain, Morocco, and Italy.

The Vikings were opportunists and traders as well as warriors. Like the earlier barbarians, Vikings settled in places they raided. They founded Dublin and Limerick in Ireland, and the Shetland Islands off Scotland remained a Norwegian possession for centuries. In northeast England, the city of York was once a Viking settlement called Yorvig. Viking dynasties also set up Norse kingdoms in diverse parts of Europe from Sicily to Russia to Normandy, which is a part of France named for the Northmen who came to raid and stayed to settle.

Invading England's former invaders

The Anglo-Saxon rulers of England fought wave after wave of invading Vikings, yet Anglo-Saxons were invaders in their own time. Angles, Saxons, and Jutes were among the tribal northerners that the Romans called barbarians. (For an explanation of why the name of the Germanic tribe called the Angles becomes Anglo in the Anglo-Saxon, see the sidebar in this chapter called "Angling for a nation's name.")

From northern Europe (Denmark and Germany), some Germanic tribes had settled in Britain in the fourth century AD. It wasn't until much later, however, after the Romans left the island to its own defenses in the early fifth century that Angles, Saxons, and Jutes poured into Britain in significant numbers. These newcomers overwhelmed the indigenous Celts, or Britons, and drove some of them west to Cornwall and Wales, north to Scotland, and across the water to Brittany (now part of France).

The invaders' medieval descendants were *Anglo-Saxons,* as are their descendants today. For short, and because of the way Saxon leaders exercised power, the Anglo-Saxons of the ninth–eleventh centuries are frequently referred to as just *Saxons* — especially the Saxon kings, who controlled pieces of Britain for hundreds of years. For a time, Vikings challenged Saxon control and ruled all of northern England, including Yorkshire. But Saxons gained the upper hand in 878 AD when the king of Wessex (or the West Saxon land), Alfred, defeated the Viking ruler Guthrum. He let Guthrum keep the north, called the Danelaw, but Alfred made the Vikings pay him tribute. Saxons ruled England for most of the next 200 years, although Vikings reasserted control for a time in the early eleventh century. Alfred is the only English king to be called "the Great."

Carrying on through generations

As with the earlier waves of population movement in Europe, the Vikings' prolonged and successive impact echoed across the continent in interesting ways. For example, the Viking leader Hrolfr (or in French, the much-easier-to-pronounce Rollo) founded the dynasty of Norman kings in the duchy (like a kingdom) of Normandy (now part of France) when he conquered that land in 911 AD.

William the Conqueror was Hrolfr's descendant. Yet when he invaded England and claimed the English throne in 1066, he battled a kingdom that had only recently been under the rule of Vikings from Denmark. Edward the Confessor, of Saxon lineage, nominated William's rival, Harold II, for the English throne. Edward, however, gained the throne in 1042 only after a king called Hardicanute, a Dane, failed to leave a successor. Hardicanute's father Canute (or Cnut) ruled over England, Denmark, and Norway simultaneously. His father, Danish ruler Sweyn Forkbeard, had conquered England with Viking raiders in 1013.

Finding and losing the New World

One place Vikings had little impact was North America. Norwegians from Greenland landed in Canada around 1000 AD, but after a few years they lost interest in the new land. The first Norseman to see North America, the trader Bjarni Herjolffson, was trying to get from Iceland (colonized by the Norse in the 860s AD) to recently settled Greenland in the summer of 986 AD. Losing his way in the fog, Herjolffson came to a shoreline, probably that of Labrador, which obviously wasn't where he wanted to go, so he turned around without exploring. About 15 years later, brawny, young Leif Eriksson (son of Erik the Red, who had discovered Greenland) bought Herjolffson's boat, rounded up a crew, and set out from Greenland to find the new land.

For a short while, parties of Norse explored and even tried settling in the place they called Vinland (today's northeastern Newfoundland). They fought with some natives, but unlike the Spanish explorers who came to North America 500 years later in the south, the Vikings had no firearms, so they had no huge advantage in battle. As well as fighting them, the newcomers also traded with the indigenous people. Some Norsemen (and Norse women, too) built houses and stayed for a while, but they fought among themselves, undermining their chances to thrive. The voyages west from Greenland soon stopped, and the Vinland settlements faded into memory.

The Norse are bad guys in the 2007 adventure-drama film *Pathfinder*. The movie is about a 12-year-old Viking boy who gets left behind in North America, where a native tribe takes him in and trains him as a warrior. When the bloodthirsty villains from over the sea return years later, the boy, now a man, fights his former comrades.

Even if the Norse had taken a keener interest in North America, their discovery was marred by a number of factors.

- ✔ **The climate changed.** After 1200, the North Atlantic experienced a mini ice age, which ice-locked ports and closed off Viking settlements in Greenland. No more settlers came, and many left.

- ✔ **Trade was less lucrative.** Russian furs flooded the European market, and craftsmen clamored for elephant ivory, considered superior to the walrus tusks that the Greenlanders could offer.

- ✔ **Bubonic plague, also known as the Black Death, destroyed Norse Greenland.** When the plague arrived in Greenland in the fourteenth century, it wiped out the small remaining Norse population. Norway and Iceland, both hard-hit by the epidemic, no longer had a reason to send ships so far west.

Traveling the Silk Road

Around the second century AD, traveling merchants began moving increasing amounts of trade goods both eastward and westward along the *Silk Road*, a caravan route that followed the Great Wall of China and then wound along a natural corridor through the Pamir Mountains and Tajikistan, across Afghanistan and south of the Caspian Sea to the eastern Mediterranean. By the sixth century AD, the Silk Road had reached Constantinople.

A single caravan was unlikely to make the entire journey. Rather, traders operated an improvised relay system, with regional merchants buying and shipping over selected distances along the Silk Road. Wool and precious metals were traded eastward while coveted Chinese silk, the luxurious fabric that gave the road its name, was the primary trade good going west. See Chapter 7 for more about how centuries of trade in silk and spices changed Western tastes and contributed to European-ruled, worldwide empires.

Planting the Seeds of European Nations

In the Middle Ages, the European map looked very little like what you see in a modern atlas. There was no France, no Germany, and no Spain. For the sake of convenience, I sometimes refer to these areas by the national names they bear now, but the concept of nationhood was lost on Europe for quite a while after the Roman Empire collapsed.

Yet in the Middle Ages, people and regions began to join together and to take on identities that would lead to modern nations such as France. The catalyst for this unity came partly from the inside, as feudal leaders sought more power. But it got its biggest push from the outside, from the very raids and invasions that I cover throughout this chapter.

For example, when people in Ireland tired of Viking raids, they looked to a king strong enough to bring together regional lords to mount a defense. In France (then called Gaul), the people known as Franks feared invasion by Arabs and by fierce Magyar raiders from Hungary. The Franks, like the Irish and other Europeans, looked to someone to unite them.

Repelling the raiders

Alfred the Great was the leader who brought Saxons (and Angles and Jutes) together in Britain (you can read more about him in the "Invading England's former invaders" sidebar).

In Ireland, a warrior named Brian Boru seized power as *high king* (a king who ruled over lesser kings) and gathered forces strong enough to conquer the Vikings at Clontarf, near Dublin in 1014. Brian died in that battle, but the Irish won, and for the first time united under an Irish leader, Ireland no longer belonged to the Norse.

Uniting Western Europe: Charlemagne pulls it together

The Franks gave rise to the strongest of the new kings, the only one to forge an empire anything like old Rome's. A Germanic people from the Rhine region, the Franks settled in Gaul (roughly identified with modern France) around 400 AD, and in 451 AD they helped the Romans repel Attila the Hun at Châlons. By 481 AD, the Romans in Gaul no longer had a Roman Empire to back them up. The king of the Franks, Clovis, overthrew the Romans and took possession of all the land between the Somme and Loire Rivers. Clovis's dynasty, called the *Merovingians,* gave way to a new Frankish dynasty called the *Carolingians* in the middle of the eighth century.

Angling for a nation's name

England's Anglo-Saxon rulers were called *Anglo-Saxon,* just like Anglo-Saxons today, because they descended from Germanic tribes, chief among them the Angles and the Saxons. In fact, *England* means the "Angles' Land," and regions within England also got their names from these people. That's why there's a Wessex (West Saxon Land), Sussex (South Saxon Land), Essex (East Saxon Land), and East Anglia.

People say "Anglo-Saxon" rather than "Angle-Saxon" because of the influence of Latin on the English language. *Anglo* is a Latinized version of *Angle,* applied when the word (today often used to mean "English" or even "British") is put together with the name of another ethnic or national group, as in an *Anglo-Danish* business venture or the *Anglo-Japanese* Alliance of 1902.

French becomes *Franco* in such combinations, as in a *Franco-American* trade agreement. It gets even crazier when you're talking about the Chinese, because political scientists, historians, and even some journalists cling to an old Greek word for Chinese and then put the Latin ending on it. That's why you might read about a *Sino-Japanese* economic conference.

Modern Americans use "Anglo" without linking it to another word but usually use it to refer to Americans who are of majority-white background and speak English, as opposed to Americans of other ethnic backgrounds and those who speak Spanish.

The Arab Empire came out of the Middle East in the seventh century, conquering most of North Africa and then extending northward into Spain. (There's more about the Arabs in the later section "Emerging Islamic Fervor.") In Spain, the Arabs, who were Muslim (meaning followers of the Islamic faith) and their North African comrades the Moors beat Visigoth rulers in 711 AD, taking over most of the Iberian Peninsula. The Visigoths were among the many groups of barbarians who brought down the Roman Empire. (I cover barbarians earlier in this chapter.) From their stronghold in Spain, these Moors (as all Spanish Muslims soon were called) pummeled southern Gaul, gaining a foothold just as the Carolingians came to power later in the eighth century.

In 732 AD, Islamic forces tried to conquer Gaul. The Carolingian king, Charles Martel, stood up to them and turned them away. If he hadn't, historians say that Western Europe could have turned out Islamic. This would have upset Charles Martel's grandson, Charlemagne, a devout Christian. Charlemagne (the name means "Charles the Great") became king of the western Franks in 768 AD and then ruled all the Franks after his brother Carloman died in 771 AD.

Charlemagne wasn't the kind of Christian who thought that the meek inherit the earth. To get the Saxons of Germany (yes, they were related to the Saxons of England) converted to the faith, he fought and subjugated them. Instead of waiting for the Moors to try another invasion, he plunged his forces into Spain and attacked the Amir of Cordoba. He also smashed the kingdom of Lombardy in northern Italy, among many other conquests that brought most of Western Europe under his rule. The extent of Charlemagne's empire at his death is shown in Figure 6-1.

Pope Leo III liked Charlemagne's efforts to conquer and convert, especially the part about getting rid of the pesky Lombards, who had been a threat to the Papal States (an area ruled directly by the Pope). The pope crowned Charlemagne as Carolus Augustus, Emperor of the Romans (or Holy Roman Emperor) in 800 AD, beginning the strange-yet-enduring European entity, the Holy Roman Empire.

Charlemagne mellowed in his later years. He built churches and promoted education and the arts, along with Christianity, and he sponsored improved agriculture and manufacturing. His stable reign fostered a kind of mini-renaissance, hundreds of years before the big Renaissance. But after Charlemagne died in 814 AD, his empire deteriorated quickly.

Keeping fledgling nations together

Although strong kings rose to patch together diverse, small *principalities* and *duchies* (ruled over by princes and dukes, respectively), consolidated power was difficult to keep. The title of king or even emperor didn't guarantee that lesser lords of the feudal system would remain loyal. For example, Otto I (or Otto the Great) of Germany, who became Holy Roman Emperor in 936 AD, also gained the title King of the Lombards in 951 AD after he rescued Lombardy's Queen Adelaide (imprisoned by a neighboring prince) and married her. Lombardy is in north central Italy, and Otto's empire (supposedly Roman even though it was based in Germany) included other Italian lands. Yet even after getting Pope John XII to give him an official coronation as emperor in 962 AD, the German king never won Italian support. Italian princes who were officially his *vassals* (meaning they had to pay Otto tribute) fought him at every turn.

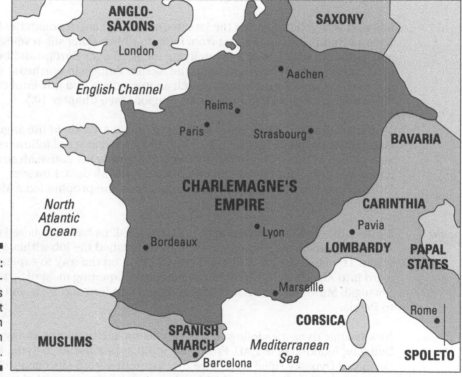

Figure 6-1:
Charlemagne's empire as it was when he died in 814 AD.

Emerging Islamic Fervor

The Arabs are a Semitic people, related to the Hebrews and the ancient Assyrians and Mesopotamians. Like the Hebrews, they consider themselves descendants of the Biblical patriarch Abraham. Originally farmers in the then-fertile region of what is now Yemen and also nomads and traders throughout Arabia, they get little mention in history up until the seventh century. Arab states rose and fell. Trade flourished and wealth grew, largely because the Arabs had two substances: frankincense and myrrh, aromatic gum resins refined from the sap of trees (frankincense) and bushes (myrrh). Highly prized for their scent, frankincense and myrrh were as valuable as gold. Think about that next time the clerk at the perfume counter offers you a sample spritz.

The Arabs followed a number of religions, including Greek-style paganism. Judaism gained a foothold, and Christianity won many converts. But that was before an Arab merchant, a fellow called Mohammed, gave up his business so that he could devote himself to contemplating Allah, or the One True God. Things in Mohammed's part of the world would never be the same.

Religion was volatile during the late Roman period and through the Middle Ages as Buddhism spread east from India to China along silk-trading routes and as Christianity became the unifying focus all over Europe and beyond. (The Christian faith even spread to the Aksum Empire in northeast Africa.) But perhaps no religion ever had such an immediate and powerful effect as Mohammed's Islam. (For more about religions, see Chapter 10.)

Mohammed said the new religion came to him in a vision of the angel Gabriel. Mohammed became a prophet, but as he gathered followers, he also gained authority in earthly matters. Leaders in his native Mecca saw his power grow and kicked him out. In the city of Medina, however, Mohammed became a lawgiver and judge. Soon the prophet led a Muslim army out of Medina to conquer Mecca.

By the time Mohammed died in 632 AD, the Muslims had conquered most of Arabia. His immediate successor, Abu Bakr, finished the job within a couple of years. Then the Muslim Arabs conquered Egypt on the way to expanding westward into Algeria in North Africa, eventually conquering most of Spain and Portugal. Muslims pushed north from Arabia into Iraq and Syria and then west to Persia.

New Islamic dynasties followed this expansion, including the Omayyad Dynasty, founded in 661 AD. From its capital at Damascus, in Syria, the Omayyad Dynasty ruled an empire that stretched from Morocco to India. Although factionalism arose within Islam and disagreements led to power struggles and war, there was remarkable continuity in the Arab world. The Abbasid Dynasty, descended from Mohammed's uncle, succeeded the Omayyads. It moved the capital to Baghdad and ruled for 500 years.

Rebounding Guptas in India

Islamic armies surged eastward as well as westward, and new national and ethnic identities formed around the faith and variations within it. Muslims from Afghanistan conquered much of India in 1100.

Yet before Muslims got there, India experienced another flowering similar to the Mauryan Dynasty of the fourth to second centuries BC. In Chapter 5, I talk about both the Mauryans, the first dynasty to unite most of India, and the Gupta Dynasty, whose stable rule brought an Indian golden age in the arts, architecture, and religion in the mid-fourth to mid-sixth centuries AD.

Hun attacks on India's northern borders eventually caused the Gupta Empire to collapse, just as a western contingent of Huns were among the barbarian people whose attacks brought down Roman authority in Europe, beginning the Middle Ages. As decades passed, the Huns of India became more Indian, adopting local customs and habits.

Assimilating into the general population diffused the Huns' power and helped a Gupta leader named Harsha, descended from the great Gupta kings, reestablish an Indian Empire in 606 AD. Equally good at conquest and administration, and an art lover like his ancestor Chandragupta II of the Gupta Dynasty, Harsha built a glorious capital city, Kanauj, famous for its magnificent buildings, on the Ganges River. Indian culture, thus fortified, spread to Burma, Cambodia, and Sri Lanka. Indian influence over the region continued as the Chola of southeast India conquered much of the country after 880 AD. Savvy merchants and businesspeople, the Chola built up prosperous trade routes with the Arabs to the west and the Chinese to the east. The Chola governmental style continued the Gupta tradition of allowing local control.

Rounding Out the World

Through the miracle of time-space travel, here's a sampling of happenings elsewhere during Europe's Middle Ages:

- ✔ **The Japanese:** Japan was deeply influenced by China beginning sometime around the fourth century. By 538 AD, that influence took the form of religious conversion as the Japanese court adopted Buddhism and replaced old temples with new ones. The cultural pendulum began to swing the other way only in the eighth century when the Chinese-influenced Japanese emperors lost power to a rising warrior class. The warrior leaders, or *samurai,* were organized by clans and fought among themselves, plunging the island into civil war in the twelfth century and giving rise to the imperial office of *shogun.* Minamoto Yoritomo became shogun in 1192 and used his samurai retainers to impose law and order. Japan was governed this way for centuries.

- ✔ **The Khmer:** In Southeast Asia, the Khmer people of Cambodia broke away from foreign influence (Chinese and Indian) as they established their first state, called Funan, on the Mekong River. The later Angkorian Dynasty grew into an empire that built a capital at Angkor and ruled until the fourteenth century.

✔ **The Maya:** In Central America, the Maya civilization lasted from 300 BC–1500 AD, although what was left after 900 AD was only a shadow of what had been. Great Mayan cities (actually independent city-states) boasted temples, ball courts, and community housing. And Mayans grew much more than corn; they also harvested beans, chiles, other vegetables, cocoa, and tobacco. They domesticated bees as well as ducks and turkeys. More importantly, the Maya were the first people in the Western Hemisphere to use an advanced form of picture writing. Good at mathematics and astronomy, the Maya developed a 365-day calendar. (Find more on the Maya in Chapter 5.)

Mel Gibson directed the 2006 drama *Apocalypto* about a young native who's captured by Mayan soldiers and almost becomes a human sacrifice to Mayan gods before escaping and fighting his way back to his family.

✔ **The Polynesians:** Between 400 and 800 AD, Polynesian people originally from Southeast Asia spread across thousands of miles of ocean to virtually every island in the Pacific — Hawaii, Tahiti, and Easter Island among them — proving themselves some of the most skillful and courageous navigators in the world. Around 1000, when Leif Erikson was checking out the east coast of Canada, a group of Polynesians made it to New Zealand, where they developed the Maori culture.

✔ **The Toltecs:** Farther north than the Maya, the nomadic Toltecs settled down and farmed central Mexico long before the Aztecs rose in the same region. The Toltecs built the city of Tula. Covering 13 square miles, Tula may have been home to as many as 60,000 people.

Tracking the Centuries

330 AD: Roman Emperor Constantine renames his eastern capital, Byzantium (in today's Turkey), making it Constantinople.

538 AD: The Japanese adopt Chinese Buddhism.

565 AD: Justinian, the Byzantine emperor, rules vast lands stretching west from his capital in Constantinople (today's Istanbul) to encompass much of formerly Roman North Africa and part of Spain and east to Persia.

632 AD: Mohammed, founder of a vigorous new religion called Islam, dies after conquering most of Arabia.

661 AD: The Omayyad Dynasty comes to power over Arab lands, ruling from its capital at Damascus, Syria.

800 AD: Pope Leo III crowns the Frankish king, Charlemagne, with a new (if anachronistic) title, Emperor of the Romans. This is the beginning of the Holy Roman Empire.

878 AD: King Alfred of Wessex and his Anglo-Saxon followers defeat the Viking ruler Guthrum, who must then pay tribute to Alfred (later referred to as Alfred the Great).

911 AD: Viking leader Hrolfr (or Rollo) founds a dynasty of Norman kings in Normandy, later a part of France.

1000: Leif Eriksson and a party of sailors from Norse Greenland land on the coast of Canada.

1014: Brian Boru, the first high king of Ireland, leads Irish warriors to defeat the Vikings at Clontarf, near Dublin.

1343: Bubonic plague begins its march across Europe, killing one-third of the inhabitants.

Chapter 7

The Struggle for World Domination

● ●

In This Chapter

▶ Grabbing a huge swath of Asia in the name of Allah

▶ Expanding trade with the Chinese

▶ Pitting European invaders against Mid-East rulers: The Crusades

▶ Following Columbus to Asia via the Americas

● ●

*I*f you had been living around the year 1000 AD and had been asked which culture you thought would end up dominating most of the globe nine centuries later, you probably wouldn't have picked Western Europe. With its feudal power struggles, confusing divisions between secular and spiritual authority, vulnerability to Viking raids, and backward agricultural practices, the region and its culture had a lot of growing to do.

Your other options would have been the Arabs, who transformed a huge part of the world with amazing zeal and ingenuity in the seventh and eighth centuries; and the Chinese, the most technologically advanced and best-governed civilization on earth. But both of these eastern cultures had their own character flaws, just like Western Europe. The Chinese leaders of 1,000 years ago were justly proud but complacent, sure that no other country had anything they wanted. And the original Arab Empire fractured into competing sects and contending emirates, united in their Islamic faith but less and less united in international goals.

In this chapter, you get to know these major world players — the Arab Empire, the Far East (especially China), and the countries and cultures of Western Europe — and how each approached global exploration and trade efforts up until the fifteenth century. I also talk about what made Europe eager and able to assert itself in the end.

Extending the Arab Empire and Spreading Islam

The Arabs rose to power with incredible swiftness and force in the seventh and early eighth centuries (you can read more about that rise in Chapter 6). The empire was inspired by a new religion, Islam, which gave its people not only warrior-like intensity but also brought education and intellectual advances.

Taking education and literacy to new heights

The Abbasid Caliphate, the Muslim dynasty that ruled most of the central Middle East from 750–1258 AD, achieved more widespread literacy than any other culture on earth at the time. Mohammed, founder of Islam, left his followers a book, the *Koran* (or *Qur'an*), as the holy centerpiece of their faith and the guide to proper living. (You can find out more about the roots of Islam in Chapter 10 and read why the Koran is one of the most important documents in Chapter 24.) Unlike Christians of the Middle Ages, who left the reading of scripture to priests and monks, Muslims stressed that everybody could and should read the Koran. And so good Muslims had to learn to read. With this holy book as a primer, the Islamic world became a culture of learning and scholarship.

Making advances in science and technology

The Arabs ruled much of what had once been the Hellenized, or Greek-dominated, world and held onto much of ancient Greek literature, including the Greeks' philosophical, scientific, and mathematical foundations. They embraced Roman engineering, which had spread to the Middle East and served the mighty Byzantine Empire of the Middle Ages. Building on those foundations, the Arabs adapted and refined Roman advances in architecture, such as the dome, to which they added the delicately distinctive Islamic minaret. You can see examples of these tall towers that adorn or adjoin mosques and from which people are called to prayer in Figure 7-1.

Great astronomers and mathematicians in their own right, the Arabs weren't content to tend the flame of Greek and Roman learning. For example, they adopted useful new notions such as the number system (from

India) and passed it down as Arabic numerals — 1, 2, 3, and so on. That the words "zero" and "algebra" come to English by way of Arabic is no coincidence, either.

Figure 7-1: The Blue Mosque boasts the distinctive Middle Eastern minarets (towers).

© Murat Taner/Getty Images

The Arabs also were way ahead of the rest of the world in medicine. For centuries, European medical textbooks were actually Persian collections of Arabic knowledge.

Mastering the Indian Ocean

Although from the desert, some Arabs took to the sea and became innovative sailors. Arabs figured out the trade winds and mastered the Indian Ocean before anybody else.

Although no Arab made the voyage to test the theory, the great Muslim scientist Al-Biruni speculated as early as the year 1000 AD that there must be a sea route south of Africa. When Portuguese explorer Vasco da Gama found such a route and arrived in northeastern India's port city of Kozhikode in 1498, becoming the first European to get to India by sea, he did it with Arab help. (You can find out more about da Gama in Chapter 8.) Arab sailors were especially familiar with the arm of the Indian Ocean called the Arabian Sea, which was notoriously difficult to navigate and virtually unknown to Europeans. Da Gama used the best European navigational science of the time to sail around the tip of Africa, but he may not have made it the rest of the way without the help of the greatest Arab navigator, Ibn Majid, author of the best Arab nautical directory. (You can find out more about Ibn Majid in Chapter 21.)

Assembling and disassembling an empire

The late seventh century proved a good time for the Arabs to amass their empire, but they weren't able to hold it together in the ninth and tenth centuries.

Taking advantage of circumstances

Muslim Arabs built on the success of founding prophet Mohammed after his death in 632 AD by completing the conquest of the Arabian Peninsula, and then turning their attention to other nearby lands. Circumstances favored the Arab advances: Older Middle Eastern powers — the Byzantine (Syria) and Sassanid (Persia) Empires — were busy fighting each other and fending off barbarian invasions. The Sassanids had to worry about Huns hammering away at their frontiers, while marauding Avars and Berbers bedeviled the Byzantines. (The Berbers hadn't yet become Islamic themselves, but would later.)

The fact that plenty of Byzantine subjects, such as the Egyptians, were fed up with taking orders from Constantinople didn't hurt the Arabs' efforts in growing their empire either. (See Chapter 6 and the section "Excelling in East Asia" later in this chapter to find out more about barbarian invasions.)

Growing apart

Islam remained an extremely important religious, cultural, and political force as the eleventh century began, but the Arabs' imperial ascendancy was past its peak by that time.

Arabs fought Arabs as early as 656 AD, when an Arab civil war resulted in the capital being moved from Mohammed's power base at Medina (in today's Saudi Arabia) to Damascus (in today's Syria). In the ninth and tenth centuries, rival *caliphates,* or Islamic kingdoms, arose in Arab North Africa and Spain, breaking the empire into pieces that, although still united by faith, were no longer politically joined.

Although the empire fractured mostly over issues of power and local control, the Islamic world also broke into religious factions. The two major branches were Sunni and Shiite, and they persist to this day. Their differences trace to a disagreement over who's qualified to lead the people both spiritually and politically. The Shiites, or Shia, trace their leaders to Ali, the son-in-law of the Prophet Mohammed, and limit the title of *imam* to descendants of Mohammed's clan. Sunnis, who are by far the majority, take a less rigid approach to designating religious leaders.

Today, the Muslims of Saudi Arabia, Kuwait, Qatar, and Indonesia, among other countries, are largely Sunnis. Iran and Azerbaijan have Shia majorities, and in Iraq, Shia comprise about 60 percent of the Muslim population and Sunni the remaining 40 percent.

Too big, too diverse, and too multifaceted, Islamic civilization was unable to sweep the world again as a single, overwhelming force after it fractured in the ninth and tenth centuries.

Excelling in East Asia

Great in both area and cultural achievements, China was so far away and sounded so strange that medieval Europeans could hardly imagine it. Yet China was a wellspring of technological inventions, an economic marvel, and a cultural model for neighboring nations. China's leaders, knowing they had something special, tended to be a bit smug.

Innovating the Chinese way

The 400-year Han Dynasty (206 BC–220 AD) was a wellspring of innovation and advancement. Following are some examples:

- ✔ Chinese scientists invented the compass and the first accurate grid-based maps.

  The Chinese didn't always use their inventions in seemingly obvious ways. For example, instead of first using the compass as a navigational device, they found it to be a dandy tool for making sure that temples were built on the proper, sacred alignment.

- ✔ They put efficient rudders on ships back when Romans and barbarians still steered by sticking a big paddle in the water at the back of the boat.

- ✔ They came up with the crossbow, a serious weapons escalation for its time.

- ✔ They made the world's first paper, which may seem trivial until you consider what the world would have been like without it. (For one thing, you might be reading this book on *parchment,* which is tanned animal skin.)

Innovation didn't stop when the Han Dynasty fell in 221 AD, either. Successive dynasties originated or embraced more new ideas, including the stirrup, allowing riders much more control and stability and giving Chinese horsemen the edge in warfare — for a little while, anyway.

Under the T'ang Dynasty, which took over in 618 AD, China developed beautiful things such as porcelain and ingenious things such as moveable-type printing, which didn't make it to Europe for hundreds of years. The Chinese invented gunpowder, too, and were using it in warfare around 1000.

China's economy and agriculture excelled. During the Han dynasty, China's ability to feed its large population stood as a model of self-sufficiency. The climate, especially in the south, allowed two rice crops a year, which fed many and therefore permitted China's growth to outpace that of any other region on Earth.

By the early twentieth century, Chinese peasants were poised on the edge of starvation, but that was after a very long decline in conditions.

Traveling the Silk Road for trade and cultural exchange

Because China had so much that other parts of the world coveted, its leaders rarely cared much about the world far beyond China.

From the Han Dynasty on, the Chinese believed themselves at the center of the world — at least the part they were interested in. They certainly were at the cultural center of East Asia and had a profound influence on language, writing, government, and art from Burma to Korea to Japan.

Even if some of their rulers tended toward isolationist policies, Chinese business-people certainly traded beyond the Great Wall. From the second century onward, Chinese goods traveled west on the backs of Bactrian camels that trekked the *Silk Road* (sometimes called the *Silk Route*). The caravans followed a natural corridor from the north of China through remote central Asia, between the peaks of the Pamir Mountains and through the Taklimakan Desert to Persia (now Iran) and the Mediterranean Sea. As a result, Middle Easterners — and some people farther west, as well — experienced Chinese silk, the finest fabric in the world, along with other luxuries such as spices.

The camels carted gold back over the route to China, but the path also fostered cultural interchange. Christian missionaries from the Nestorian Church, a controversial fringe Christian sect, traveled the Silk Road to spread their faith after the Byzantine Empire exiled them in the fifth century.

Yet the Chinese hungered for little that other cultures offered. Under the early Ming Dynasty — founded by the monk-warrior Chu Yuan-chang in 1368 after he drove out the Mongol rulers of the Yuan Dynasty — China's rulers went so far as to forbid ships from leaving coastal waters. With long voyages banned, Chinese shipbuilders stopped building big, seagoing vessels.

Breaching the wall: Invading China

China endured for such a long time that you may think it was invulnerable, but sometimes the empire succumbed to invaders.

The Chinese began the Great Wall of China as a string of defensive outposts in the third century BC and then added to this barrier over the course of many hundreds of years. But some enemies got past the wall. Around 100 BC, the Xiongnu people challenged the great Han Dynasty. More than a thousand years later, in the thirteenth century, a successful Mongol invader breached the wall again. He was Genghis Khan and his grandson, Kublai Khan, founded China's Yuan dynasty.

Genghis Khan, whose name means "universal chief," joined together lands from the Pacific

Ocean west to the Black Sea. Before he died in 1227, Genghis Khan split his empire into four parts that he called *khanates.* His Chinese lands made up the easternmost khanate.

Kublai Khan was the first Chinese ruler most Europeans found out about, because the Venetian traveler Marco Polo wrote about living and working in Kublai Khan's court (there's more on Marco Polo later in this chapter). Kublai Khan finished what his grandpa began, making his Mongol capital in Khanbaligh (now Beijing) in 1267 and finally finishing off China's Song (or Sung) Dynasty 12 violent years later.

Sailing away for a spell

In the early fifteenth century, Emperor Yung Lo turned outward — an unusual posture for a Chinese ruler — and sponsored impressive voyages of exploration. Zheng He (sometimes written *Chung Ho* or *Cheng Ho*), a Muslim court eunuch who was also an accomplished sea admiral, commanded the ventures. (A *eunuch* was a male servant, generally a slave, who had been castrated, presumably to make him more docile and to ensure that he wouldn't be tempted by the master's women, or they by him.) Zheng He somehow overcame his lowly status to become an important member of Yung's court.

Zheng sailed seven large, well-financed expeditions. His ships landed in India, navigated the Persian Gulf, and anchored off East Africa. His vessels were larger and faster than Arab and European ships of the time and equipped with sophisticated *bulkheads* (walls between sections of the ship's hold), so that if one part of the ship sprung a leak or caught fire, the damage could be contained and the ship wouldn't sink.

After Emperor Yung Lo died, the expeditions stopped and nothing much came of Zheng's voyages — no expanded trade, no extended political influence, and no broadened military influence. But the idea had never been to subdue other parts of the world anyway. In Chinese thinking, China was not just the best state; it was the *only* sovereign state. The ships were, in part, a peaceful effort to broadcast the message of Chinese superiority. But to Yung Lo's successors, the rest of the world apparently still wasn't worth the trouble, seeing as they didn't continue exploration efforts.

Europe Develops a Taste for Eastern Goods

Like the Arabs and many other cultures of the thirteenth through eighteenth centuries, Europeans fought amongst themselves, but their competition also took the form of a race for far-flung riches. They knew that vast wealth could be found in trade, especially trade with China. Several factors enhanced the European craving for more eastern trade; here's a sampling:

- ✔ Some Europeans got a tantalizing preview of Asian luxuries — including fine silks and spices not tasted in the West — thanks to the Crusades, which were hundreds of years of Christian military expeditions that began against Seljuk Turk-controlled Palestine in the eleventh century. (If you think spices are no big deal, imagine what European food tasted like before they had any.)

- ✔ The Moors in Spain, with their eastern ties, had trade-route access to Chinese delights. And a vast, Euro-Asian Mongol Empire from the Black Sea to China opened northern trade routes, bringing eastern goods west into the German states.

- ✔ *The Travels of Marco Polo,* a book about China written by a thirteenth-century commercial traveler from the Italian city-state of Venice, drummed up interest in the Far East, a place that sounded too incredible to be real.

- ✔ Oddly enough, a terrible plague in the fourteenth century helped create a market for exotic eastern goods.

These factors added up to terrific advertising for trade between Europe and the Far East. This section examines the influence of trade-leader Venice and its native son Marco Polo and Europe's efforts to circumvent the Ottoman Empire in order to create its own trade route east. Because of their massive scale and impact on so much more than just eastern trade, I address the Crusades in the later section "Mounting the Crusades."

Before they could supply the growing market and interest in eastern products, the Europeans needed to get around some serious geographic obstacles. Europeans needed to find ways to bring cargo from faraway India and China. The Byzantine Empire and competing Turkish realms (Seljuk and later the powerful Ottomans) controlled land routes east, and besides, only sailing ships could carry the volume of merchandise that European dreamers had in mind. The problem was nobody in Europe knew how to reach East Asia by sea. The Europeans needed sea routes, and the search for those routes brought about a world crisscrossed by new cultural interconnections.

Orienting Venice

Venice was a city-state of ambitious traders that started out as an island refuge from barbarians in the fifth century AD. It was part of the Byzantine Empire until the ninth century, and even later, as an independent city-state, the Venetians enjoyed favored trading status with the Byzantines. This eastern connection gave Venice an economic advantage that its rulers used to build up a neat little Mediterranean empire, including the Italian cities of Padua, Verona, and Vicenza, along with the strategically placed eastern Mediterranean islands of Crete and Cypress.

Economically and militarily, Venice was oriented toward Constantinople and Asia. The word *orient* means "east" or "to face eastward."

Although another seafaring Italian city-state, Genoa, gave Venice some stiff competition, Venice dominated Mediterranean trading. The wealth Venetians enjoyed because of their access to the East made the rest of Europe sit up and take notice.

Writing the first best-selling travel book

Over the Silk Road to China, shippers and wholesalers customarily traded goods only to the next trader down the way, so that no one trader or camel driver covered the entire, exhausting route. Thirteenth century-traveler Marco Polo's father and uncle were more ambitious than most other traders in Venice: They traveled all the way from Italy to China in their quest for lucrative deals.

Marco's elders were on their second trip to the Far East when they invited the young man (probably about 19 at the time) to tag along. The trio arrived in Beijing in 1275. According to the book that Marco Polo later wrote, he entered Emperor Kublai Khan's diplomatic service and traveled to other Mongol capitals on official business. (Kublai Khan, though China's emperor, was a Mongol.)

Almost two decades went by. Young Polo, not quite so young anymore, finally left China in 1292 and returned to Venice. But the rival city-states were at war, and Marco Polo was captured. He was in a Genoa prison when he wrote, or rather dictated to a fellow prisoner, the story of his fantastic years abroad, *The Travels of Marco Polo*.

Many of Marco Polo's contemporaries thought he lied in his book, and some modern scholars think they were right and that Polo at least exaggerated his story. But that doesn't undercut the impact of his descriptions. Polo's book was about such a faraway place, and to Europeans at the turn of the fourteenth century, it was like a dispatch from outer space. At the very least, Polo's stories spread and fed the perception that China was the trader's mother lode. *The Travels of Marco Polo* was the most influential book of its time.

Fighting for economic advantage

Venice's trade success fueled military conflicts both with the rival city-state Genoa and with more remote competitors. Venice was in there swinging when European Christendom launched the Crusades (see the section "Mounting the Crusades" later in this chapter for details).

Any military campaign against those who controlled access to the Silk Road — whether Turks or Byzantine Christians (western Crusaders sacked Constantinople in 1204) — interested the Venetians. They were first in line among Europeans who wanted unimpeded access to the profitable thoroughfare.

Venice declined as the major trading power in the Mediterranean only after 1571's naval Battle of Lepanto against the Ottoman Turks (successors to the Byzantines). In that conflict, the Venetians were allied with Rome and Spain in the *Holy League,* created by the pope. Venice won the Battle of Lepanto but lost its colony Cyprus, a crucial trade outpost, and Venice's power slipped.

Ottomans control trade routes between Europe and the East

Turkish empire-building reached its height in the fifteenth century, when another Islamic Turkish clan, the Ottoman Turks, assembled a humongous collection of lands into the Ottoman Empire. Ottoman power lasted until the twentieth century. In its heyday, the empire made significant inroads into Eastern Europe. (Animosity between modern Islamic Bosnians and Christian Serbs is rooted in long-ago Ottoman incursions west.)

European traders who lusted after eastern riches had to take the Ottomans into account because these Turks blocked land trade routes east. Coupled with Venice's and Genoa's dominance in the Mediterranean, the Turkish presence made other Europeans wonder if they could find their own Silk Roads, perhaps by sea. One sailing ship could carry more cargo than camels could, anyway. The problem was that no one knew how to get from Europe to East Asia by sea.

Necessity, as the saying goes, became the mother of invention. Or maybe it was greed more than necessity. Either way, this hunger to find a new way to get the treasure of the East gave birth to a new age of European empires.

The Portuguese, Dutch, Spanish, and English wanted a piece of the Asian market and began exploring as never before. The first to risk a bold western course toward Asia, Christopher Columbus, didn't find what he was looking for, but he did bump into the Americas, which were soon a lucrative market for slaves used to raise valuable commodities such as tobacco and sugar. (For more about Columbus, skip ahead to the section "Seeking a Way East and Finding Things to the West.")

Mounting the Crusades

It may seem that civilization has arrived at its current global interconnectedness because of air travel and the electronics revolution of the last several decades. Yet today's worldwide connections, as you can tell by skimming through almost any section in this chapter, really started taking shape many centuries back.

The Crusades are perhaps the earliest events that pointed forcefully toward today's world, which is still so deeply marked by the European empires of the sixteenth to twentieth centuries. In a nutshell, the Crusades were hundreds of years of sporadic Christian military campaigns. (For more about the marks left on today's world by Europe's second millennium empires, see the sidebar "Putting cultural dominance in perspective" in this chapter. Don't worry. It's not as stuffy as that title makes it sound.)

Meeting the main players

The Crusades began in 1095, when diverse Europeans, answering a call from the pope and united in religious zeal (or so they said), tried to free the Holy Land, Palestine, from Turk rulers. They weren't the Ottoman Turks, whose great empire would supplant the Byzantine Empire in the fifteenth century, but rather their predecessors in Middle Eastern empire-building, the Seljuk Turks.

The Seljuk Turks were a nomadic and marauding population of barbarians from wild north central Asia. Barbarians show up in Chapters 5 and 6 as well as in this chapter because they kept showing up in successive centuries — riding into lands as diverse and far-flung as China and Spain.

Like the China-conquering Mongols, the Turks called their chiefs by the title *khan*. In the early centuries of the first millennium, Turks were a subject people, paying tribute (sort of like taxation without representation) to another barbarian group, the Juan-Juan. But as the Arab conquests of the seventh and eighth centuries spread the religion Islam, the Turks converted and adopted the Arab fervor for empire-building.

The Seljuk ascendancy (conquering Asia Minor in the eleventh century and beating the armies of the Byzantine Empire) alarmed Christendom (the Christian world) all the way back to Rome, where the last straw for Pope Urban II was the Seljuk takeover of Palestine. Western Christians felt possessive about this land — today's Israel and the Palestinian territories — because Jesus of Nazareth had lived and died there and it contained the holiest shrines of Christianity. Meanwhile, nobody asked the people living in Palestine if they wanted to be freed from Turkish rule.

The pope was also angered by reports that Turks were messing with pilgrims on their way to shrines in the Holy Land. As Muslims, the Seljuk rulers had little reason to protect these Christian travelers who were easy pickings for robbers. The pope got so ticked off that in 1095 he called for a war to make Jerusalem safe for Christians again. The Crusades, the answer to his call, may have started out as idealistic religious adventures, but they descended into brutal wars of hatred and greedy opportunism.

Seljuk Turks, like the Mongols, were superior horsemen; Seljuk warriors could fire accurate arrows at full gallop while standing in their stirrups. This skill helped them wreak havoc on established powers as they swept through Afghanistan and Persia in the eleventh century, taking over Jerusalem on their way to Baghdad, a declining capital of an earlier Muslim empire founded by Arabs, to conquer the Middle East.

Looking at the misguided zeal of specific Crusades

Sadly, the thousands of ordinary Europeans who set out for Palestine full of Christian fervor were the crusaders least likely to survive. They were ignorant and in no way ready for what they'd face. But well-armed nobles and skilled warriors went east, too. Here's a rundown of some of the Crusades:

✔ **First Crusade:** In 1099, the first official European force to reach Jerusalem massacred most of the people there before setting up European-ruled Latin Kingdoms, notably the Kingdom of Jerusalem, along the eastern shore of the Mediterranean.

- **People's Crusade:** The People's Crusade was a ragtag part of the First Crusade led by an itinerant preacher from France, a monk called Peter the Hermit. His followers walked into a Seljuk slaughter. (For more about Peter the Hermit and his colleague Walter the Penniless, see Chapter 20.)

- **Second Crusade:** The Second Crusade began in 1147 when crusaders surging eastward stopped along the way to slaughter Jews living in Germany's Rhine Valley.

- **Third Crusade:** In 1189, the expeditionary force of the Third Crusade ventured eastward to attack the Kurdish leader Saladin, who had united Syrian and Egyptian Muslim forces and captured the city of Jerusalem from its Christian rulers in 1187. Crusaders in this force included King Richard I (the Lionheart) of England, Emperor Frederick I (Barbarossa) of the Holy Roman Empire, and King Philip II of France. The emperor drowned crossing a stream.

Set during the Third Crusade of the late twelfth century, director Ridley Scott's 2005 film *Kingdom of Heaven* tells a fictional story concerning the Christian Kingdom of Jerusalem. If you find the movie on DVD, I have it on good authority that the 194-minute director's cut is superior to the shorter version made for theatrical release.

- **Fourth Crusade:** The Fourth Crusade of 1202–1204 may have been the ugliest of all. Christian Crusaders sacked Constantinople, a Christian city, and then briefly based another Latin Kingdom there (as if the split between the Roman Catholic and Eastern Orthodox churches wasn't already wide enough).

- **Children's Crusade:** The Children's Crusade of 1212 was the most pitiful Crusade. About 50,000 poor kids, and some poor adults, too, walked southward from France and Germany under the delusion that they could restore Palestine to Christian control yet again. Most of the tots who made it as far as Italy's seaports succeeded only in sailing straight into the Muslim slave markets of North Africa and the Middle East. Few were ever heard from again. Some people say the story about the Pied Piper of Hamelin is based on the Children's Crusade.

Setting a precedent for conquest

Where did Europeans of the sixteenth through the nineteenth centuries get the nerve to sail all over the world claiming chunks of other continents for their kings back home? You could argue that their attitude hearkens back to Rome's imperial habits, or that the Europeans, many of barbarian stock (and thus perhaps Asian as much as European), were born to rapacious conquest.

You could argue that, but your argument would be a stretch. More accurately, you could reach back to the Middle Ages, the need to fight off Viking invaders, and how that need prompted feudal vassals to rally around strong leaders. This trend began to build nations such as Saxon England as it took shape under Alfred the Great. But nation building was a slow process, and Europeans didn't think in terms of a political state based on national identity. (For more on the emergence of strong kings, such as Alfred and Charlemagne, and the beginnings of nation building, see Chapter 6.)

The Crusades shaped a European, Christian outlook on the rest of the world and taught Westerners to assert themselves beyond Europe. Rulers put their resources toward an imperial venture in a systematic way, setting a precedent for the exercise of power. Christendom became militant, confident of its ability to stomp other parts of the globe. Militant confidence served Europe's nations well several centuries later, after navigators arrived at a reasonably accurate idea of what the globe looked like.

Growing Trade between East and West

Early in the thirteenth century, Genghis Khan and his Mongol clan conquered a huge swath of Asia stretching from the Pacific Ocean all the way to northeastern Europe above the Black Sea. For part of that century, these lands were under one rule, and even after Genghis Khan died in 1227, they remained a loose affiliation of allied Mongol powers.

The Mongol Empire cleared northern trade routes between East and West, some of them using the Volga and Dnieper Rivers that feed into the Black Sea and the Caspian Sea of the Middle East. These routes were used for centuries by Vikings and Slavs, and thanks to the Mongols, northern Europeans could take advantage of an eastern trade pipeline that flowed more freely than ever before.

As new goods filtered into northern Europe, towns grew fat. Hamburg flourished on the Elbe River, as did Lubeck on the Baltic Sea. But merchants had a problem: There was no reliable, unified German government and no source of widely recognized order to defend their shipping routes from robbers and pirates.

In 1241, businesspeople in Hamburg and Lubeck formed a *hansa,* an association for their mutual protection. Early in the next century, that association grew into the *Hanseatic League,* a commercial confederation of some 70 towns stretching from Flanders (today Belgium and part of Northern France) to Russia. Its interests were purely commercial, but the league performed some governmental functions, too. It even went to war in the middle of the fourteenth century when Danish king Waldemar IV tried to mess with its trading. In the end, Waldemar proved no match for King Commerce.

Putting cultural dominance in perspective

Europeans spent several centuries of the second millennium AD venturing out to other parts of the world, subjugating the locals and building empires. The world as you know it — with people speaking English in South Africa and Portuguese in Brazil — still bears innumerable cultural and economic marks (many people call them scars) of these adventures.

Some people, including some historians (although none recently), treat this European ascendancy as if it were inevitable, even right. This short-sighted view is called *Eurocentrism,* and you may think you smell it in this book. A reason for this is that European dominance has been so recent, relatively speaking, and that it continues — with the spread of Western clothing styles, the English language, Western-style economic systems, and American movies. It continues despite backlash from certain quarters, such as Islamic extremists who reject Western values. This book is partly an account of how civilization came to this particular point, so it must include the story of how Europeans (and their heirs, such as the United States) accomplished what they did.

Throughout this book, I relate how one culture or another always seems to be coming to the forefront, dominating for centuries, even a millennium, and asserting itself as superior. I also point out how great civilizations can disappear so thoroughly that nobody remembers them. (For an example, see information on the Hittites in Chapter 4.) The disappearance of today's worldwide civilization seems inconceivable in an age of satellites and computers and the other snazzy gizmos that have transformed commerce and daily life, but any study of history shows that civilizations not only rise; they also inevitably fall.

Surviving the Black Death

Europeans in the fourteenth century were looking at the world in a new way, seeing far-off places as desirable, worth finding out about, and maybe even worth acquiring. Yet before Europeans really got out and started taking over that world, there had to be enough personal wealth back home to make a decent-sized market for foreign luxuries. Oddly, it took a horrible disease and death on a massive scale for that market to find a foothold.

The *Black Death* (also called the *Black Plague*) was a devastating epidemic of bubonic plague and its variants that probably started in the foothills of Asia's Himalayan Mountain range. But in the fourteenth century something happened to make disease spread, and many have speculated that the culprit was the rise of trade. The disease lived in fleas carried by rats, and where people go, especially people carrying food, so go rats and their parasites.

When a rat died, the fleas jumped to another rat. When no other rat was handy, the fleas tried less desirable hosts. When those hosts were human, the people got terribly sick and most of them died quickly. The blackish bruises that appeared beneath their skin were called *buboes,* which is where the name bubonic plague comes from. (Think of that next time you hear a child call a bruise a "boo-boo.") An even deadlier version of the disease, pneumonic plague, spread through the air from person to person.

Killing relentlessly

In 1333, the plague killed thousands of Chinese and spread west. By 1347, it reached Constantinople, where it was called the *Great Dying,* and it continued rapidly west through the Balkans, Italy, France, and Spain. Then year by year, the disease advanced northward. Within a few years the Black Death reached Russia, Scandinavia, and beyond, following the Viking trade routes to Iceland and completely wiping out Norse settlements in Greenland. (For more about the Norse in Greenland, refer to Chapter 6.)

As many as 25 million people died of the Black Plague in Europe. Maybe a third of the people in England fell. Periodic outbreaks followed for centuries after, but the Black Death had an impact even beyond the horror and sorrow it inspired. (And don't forget the morbid fascination: Many examples of art from this time focus on disease and death.)

Doing the math: Fewer folks, more wealth

The Black Plague so drastically reduced Europe's population that a smaller labor pool changed the economy. Ironically, this turn of events improved many Europeans' lives by creating disposable income, which in turn spurred a demand for eastern luxuries and even eastern ideas. The intellectual and cultural result of this reduction in population and eastward focus was called the *Renaissance.* You can find out about the Renaissance in Chapter 13.

With so many dead, fewer people were left to work the land. A few workers had the spunk to stand up to the nobles and landowners and point out that they weren't about to work more for the same money — not when the supply of workers had become smaller and thus more valuable. The most famous of these uprisings was led by Wat Tyler, an English rabble-rouser who got himself killed for his trouble in 1381.

Post-plague economics forced some large landholders to split their estates into smaller plots. Instead of remaining mere sharecroppers who turned over the bulk of what they grew to the landlord, some laborers actually began earning pay for their work.

Though there were fewer people overall, more people had land, income, and the potential to buy goods. This condition stimulated a rise in merchants, craftspeople, and skilled traders who could supply goods. Up until that time, you were either rich or poor — usually poor. The plague created a middle class.

Seeking a Way East and Finding Things to the West

European nations' hunger for the luxuries possessed by China, India, Japan, Indonesia, and other eastern cultures and for the wealth that came to anyone who could import such coveted goods as silk cloth and rare spices led many adventurous sea captains of the fifteenth and sixteenth centuries in search of navigable sea routes to East Asian ports. You can read more about some of these seafarers' journeys and their results in Chapter 8. One particular navigator stands out from the rest, however, because he was the first to sail westward in search of the lands that lay far to the east of Europe. This was Christopher Columbus.

Columbus didn't find what he sought, but he changed world history in a fundamental way by landing upon populated islands in the Caribbean Sea and later on the mainland of South America.

Meeting the Americans who met Columbus

The Arawak and the Carib tribes both came to the islands later called the West Indies from northern South America. Before 500 AD, some Arawak migrated to the islands and farmed peacefully for hundreds of years before the Carib followed.

The Carib weren't much for farming. Warriors and cannibals, the Carib tortured, killed, and ate the men of the tribes they conquered and turned the women into slave wives. Or so the historical record reads. Some people, including descendants of these Native Americans, take exception to this depiction, claiming Columbus and his successors made up the whole cannibalism business as an excuse for Spaniards to enslave these people.

Around the year 1000 AD, the Carib set out on their own sea journeys from Venezuela or Guyana to the islands. Raiding Arawak villages, the Carib almost wiped out the farmers on some of the islands.

Arriving in the Indies, Columbus probably met some Arawak first and then the more hostile Carib. Full of hope that he was off the coast of Asia, Columbus called them all *Indians,* and the name stuck.

Falling down

Folklorists dismiss the idea, but many people think the children's rhyme "Ring around the Rosie" may be much older, and much more morbid, than most parents realize. They hear in it an echo of plague times, when the "rosie" was a rash that appeared as victims first came down with the disease. "Pocket full of posies" might then refer to the erroneous belief that flower petals were a defense against sickness, or at least against the overwhelming smell of death. "Ashes, ashes" is from the funereal "ashes to ashes, dust to dust." And the final line, "all fall down" may originally have carried the understanding that few, if any, would get back up again. People who study oral traditions say it's not so because there's no written evidence that the rhyme had those particular words until more recent centuries.

Some celebrate discovery, others rue it

Christopher Columbus's discovery of the Americas, a part of the world unknown to his European contemporaries, opened the way for colonization and trade, bringing great wealth to Spain, the nation that sponsored his four voyages to the Caribbean Sea, and to other imperial European powers. His discovery also began centuries of death and destruction to native populations and their cultures. Although many people, including traditional historians, have celebrated Columbus as a hero, other, less glowing evaluations take into account all the negatives — slavery, slaughter, disease, and displacement — that followed Columbus's discovery in 1492.

Training and experience shaped Columbus

For his part, Columbus never sought to discover a new world and went to his grave in 1506 without admitting that he had done so.

Genoa-born in 1471 and reared at sea, Columbus read the ancient Greeks, particularly the second-century-AD astronomer Ptolemy. A Greek who lived in Alexandria, Egypt, Ptolemy envisioned the world as a globe. His influential writings were preserved by the literate Arab culture that later ruled Egypt, and they came to Europe through Arabic translations.

As a seafarer, Columbus compiled an impressive résumé of voyages, once sailing as far as Iceland, which is a long way from both Italy and Lisbon, Portugal, the port city where he made his home.

Portugal was a good base for a seafarer because it was the location of Europe's foremost school for navigation, astronomy, and mapmaking (established by Prince Henry the Navigator in the fifteenth century). Graduates explored Africa's west coast searching for a way around the continent to the Indies. (You can read more about Portuguese explorers' discovery of a sea route from Europe to India in Chapter 8. Henry the Navigator appears in Chapter 21.)

Stumbling upon the West Indies

While working for the Spanish monarchs, Columbus sought a sea-lane linking Europe and India and sailed west instead of east, the direction that would have occurred to most European sailors. This crack navigator boasted a commonsensical grasp of Earth's general shape — even if he did seriously underestimate its circumference. But Columbus never sought new continents and doggedly refused to face up to the fact that he did, indeed, find one, the one later called South America.

After his first voyage to the Caribbean, he kept going back there (it was later named after the Carib), not because he loved piña coladas and that calypso rhythm but because he couldn't admit that what he'd found was someplace entirely new — to European navigators anyway.

Columbus wanted America to be East Asia, telling himself and anybody who would listen that these islands were just some obscure part of Indonesia, the *Indies*. If Cuba wasn't part of mainland Asia, which he made his officers swear it was, then he wanted Cuba to be Japan. Who wanted a New World when an old one — China — was the sea trader's big prize?

Smokin'

Among the most puzzling things that Columbus brought back from the West Indies were pungent leaves and seeds of a plant that the Caribbean natives prized. Dried leaves of this kind were among the first presents Native Americans offered the European visitors, who didn't know what to do with them and threw them away. Better for the sailors' lungs that they did, because the leaves were tobacco.

A couple of Columbus's colleagues, Rodrigo de Jerez and Luis de Torres, saw natives in Cuba forming the leaves into the shape of a musket with a palm or corn shuck wrapper, lighting one end on fire, putting the other to their mouths, and *drinking* the smoke. Jerez tried it, got hooked, and took the habit back to Spain. The smoke billowing from his mouth and nose frightened his neighbors, and they reported him to the Spanish Inquisition. Jerez spent seven years in prison. And some people think today's antismoking laws are extreme.

Tracking the Centuries

618 AD: The Tang Dynasty takes control of China, beginning a period of technological innovation that includes the invention of printing and gunpowder.

About 1000 AD: Members of the Carib tribe sail from Venezuela to islands in the Caribbean (as it would later be named). Carib people are still there when Columbus arrives 500 years later.

1071: Seljuk Turks defeat the Byzantine Empire's army at the battle of Manzikert, capturing Emperor Romanus IV Diogenes.

1147: Christian Crusaders, on their way eastward to liberate Jerusalem from Muslim rule, pause in Germany's Rhine Valley to massacre resident Jews.

1211: Mongol chieftain Genghis Khan invades China, adding Chinese territory to his vast Euro-Asian empire.

1212: About 50,000 poor people, most of them children, walk from France and Germany toward Italy's seaports. These Crusaders believe they can free the Holy Land from Muslim rule. Those who don't collapse along the way are sold in the slave markets of North Africa.

1241: Two northern European trading cities, Hamburg and Lubeck, form a hansa that eventually grows into the Hanseatic League, a commercial and quasi-governmental confederation of some 70 towns.

1275: Marco Polo, a teenage Venetian, arrives in Beijing and takes a job in the diplomatic service of the Chinese emperor.

1347: The Black Death (bubonic plague) reaches Constantinople on its march across Asia to Europe. The Byzantines call the epidemic the Great Dying.

1381: In England, Wat Tyler leads peasants in a revolt against landowners. He dies in the conflict, but the rebellion brings agrarian reforms.

1571: The commercial city-state Venice loses its island colony Cyprus to the Ottoman Empire. Without this Adriatic outpost, Venetian trade and influence begins a steep and permanent decline.

Chapter 8

Grabbing the Globe

• •

In This Chapter

▶ Jostling for trading bases in East India

▶ Struggling to hold on to native civilizations in the Americas

▶ Attempting to crack the trade market in Asia

▶ Profiting from the worldwide slave trade

▶ Threatening the old order with Enlightenment ideas

▶ Breaking out with revolutionary Americans and French

• •

*W*hen European sailors set out looking for new sea routes in the fifteenth and sixteenth centuries, they were in it for the money. Riches beckoned. Some sailors whose voyages changed the circumference of the world include

> ✔ **Christopher Columbus:** A Genoese (from the Italian city-state of Genoa) sailing for Spain, he discovered America in 1492 because he was trying to get to Asia, a source of lucrative trade goods.
>
> ✔ **Vasco da Gama:** A Portuguese captain who was also looking for a sea route to Asia as he rounded Africa and sailed east, he successfully reached India in 1498.
>
> ✔ **Ferdinand Magellan:** Another Portuguese, but sailing on behalf of Spain, he set out for Asia's Spice Islands (today's Indonesia) by a different route from da Gama's in 1519.

Magellan, although he died on the voyage, proved that it was possible to get from Europe to Asia by sailing west, as Columbus claimed. (You just had to steer south of the South American mainland first.) Magellan also proved that Europeans could circle the globe. The one surviving ship of his original five rounded Africa from the east and sailed into San Lucar de Barrameda, Spain, in 1522.

Magellan's achievement was a huge step in navigation, but it was also a symbolic triumph. Europeans could circle the world — by sailing, and soon thereafter, by trade and military conquest. Also in the early sixteenth century, two Spanish generals conquered the two greatest civilizations in the Americas:

- ✔ Hernan Cortés defeated the Aztecs of Mexico in 1521.
- ✔ Francisco Pizarro brought down the Inca Empire of Peru in 1533.

Europeans spoke of a New World, meaning the Americas, but in a sense the entire world was new because it was suddenly within reach — a ripe plum ready to be picked. The Spanish and Portuguese, soon joined by other Europeans such as the Dutch, English, and French, picked the plum by trading with, conquering, exploiting, and enslaving the people of the New World.

Between 1500 and 1900, European sea powers brought most of the globe under their influence, but at a price. Almost as soon as Europeans subdued other peoples, those subjects began fighting to break free. This age of empires became an age of revolutions, and not just in the Americas and other colonial lands. The freedom fever spread, and revolution came to Europe, as well.

Sailing South to Get East

For Europeans, 1498 was an even more monumental year than 1492, when "Columbus sailed the ocean blue." Columbus was trying to reach the rich ports of Asia by sea, a major goal for traders and navigators. Vasco da Gama, sailing for King Manuel I (Manuel the Fortunate) of Portugal, actually did what Columbus failed to do: Find a sea route to the East.

Da Gama found a route by sailing south around the tip of Africa, up that continent's east coast, through the treacherous waters between the big island of Madagascar and the African mainland, and then, with the help of an Arab navigator, across the Indian Ocean. The greatest seafaring venture yet, da Gama's journey made good on its promise of an economic payoff, whereas Columbus's mistaken discovery of bewilderingly wild islands had yet to prove economically rewarding.

Getting a foothold in Indian trade

Vasco da Gama crossed the Arabian Sea and arrived on India's southwest coast in 1498. He docked at the port city of Kozhikode (then called Calicut, but not to be confused with Calcutta). He was eager for Asian spices but hadn't come well prepared. By custom, the proper way to honor the Hindu ruler of Kozhikode, called the *zamorin,* especially if you wanted a favor, was to shower the zamorin with gifts. But the Indians weren't impressed by da Gama's offer of wash basins, bolts of cloth, hats, beads, and lumps of sugar.

These went over well on the coast of western Africa, but they were laughable in trade-rich Kozhikode.

Da Gama had to work hard to win a trade agreement from the zamorin, but after three months of appeals, he received approval. Da Gama was able to buy enough spices to impress the folks back home in Lisbon.

Demanding respect

Vasco da Gama's first voyage to India in 1498 seemed to point the way toward peaceful trade. Before he returned to Kozhikode, however, the tone of East-West relations turned ugly.

Just two of da Gama's four ships and 55 of his original crew of 177 survived the first trip to India and back. Those were considered reasonable losses for the time, especially for such a great breakthrough. King Manuel of Portugal was pleased. He sponsored a second expedition led by Pedro Cabral in 1500. On his way down the coast of Africa, Cabral veered so far west that he discovered Brazil. Cabral claimed it for Portugal, giving King Manuel a piece of the New World in addition to the route to Asia.

Cabral proceeded to round Africa and continue to Kozhikode, where he built on da Gama's work of winning trade privileges by negotiating a full commercial treaty with the zamorin. When he left India, Cabral left a small group of Portuguese traders to represent King Manuel's interests. Although these traders had the zamorin's permission to stay, their presence angered Muslim merchants in the port city. They saw the Europeans as cutting into their import-export business. A group of these Muslim businessmen decided to fight back and attacked and killed the Portuguese.

When word of the murders reached Portugal, an enraged King Manuel faulted the zamorin for failing to protect his ambassadors. Determined to show his displeasure, he sent da Gama on yet another voyage to India in 1502. This time, the navigator commanded a well-armed flotilla of ships.

Crossing the Arabian Sea toward India, da Gama intercepted a ship carrying Muslims home from their pilgrimage to Mecca. Demonstrating a new, militant attitude, da Gama demanded all the treasure onboard. After gathering the passengers' money and goods, the Portuguese burned the Arab ship and the hundreds of people onboard, including women and children.

When he reached Kozhikode, da Gama demanded that the zamorin surrender and that Muslims, whom he blamed for the killings of the Portuguese representatives, be banned from the city. The zamorin refused. Da Gama responded by bombarding the port. He also ordered the slaughter of 38 traders and fishermen who had sailed out in their small boats to greet da Gama's ships. These victims weren't Muslim but Hindu, like the zamorin. When da

Gama finally left on his return voyage to Lisbon, he left five ships behind to enforce Portuguese rule.

"Discovering" America

Columbus didn't think of himself as a discoverer, and perhaps you shouldn't either. The whole notion of *discovery* is insulting to the people who already lived in the Americas and had no inkling that they were undiscovered.

Many different kinds of people lived in the Americas before Columbus arrived. Columbus called the people he encountered on Caribbean Islands *Indians* because he thought he was in Asia, so the original people of the Americas have been lumped together under that label ever since (although some prefer to be called *Native Americans* or *Amerindians*). No matter what you call them, these Americans were never a single culture. They lived in widely differing climates, made their livings in different ways, spoke different languages, and wore different clothes. Even their origins were probably different.

Until late in the twentieth century, many scholars thought that all the pre-Columbian Americans crossed a land bridge that linked Asia with Alaska between 20,000 and 10,000 years ago. Then archaeological finds began to suggest that at least some people were living in the Americas much earlier and that different groups arrived at different times.

By the time Europeans came, the Americas had seen civilizations rise and fall. The Spanish arrived in time to see the great Mayan civilization of Mexico and the Yucatan, although its impressive cities were in deep decline by the sixteenth century.

To the north of the Mayan cities in the highlands of central Mexico, the Spanish military commander Hernan Cortés found a great city in 1519 that was at its peak: the Aztec capital of Tenochtitlán. Spanish soldiers said that Tenochtitlán, with its brightly painted pyramids and broad causeways linking the island city to the mainland, was as magnificent as Rome or Constantinople. The Spaniards went on to wreck it, of course, but nobody ever said conquest is pretty.

Although pre-Columbian civilizations boasted many accomplishments, they lacked some key advantages that the Spanish invaders enjoyed:

- **Gunpowder:** This technology had spread all the way from China to Europe but didn't touch the Americas until the Spaniards arrived.

- **Iron:** Although several American cultures achieved splendid metalworking by the sixteenth century, none had learned to make harder, more durable iron weapons.

> ✔ **The horse:** There were no horses in the Americas. (See Chapter 17 for more on the horse's role in warfare.)
>
> ✔ **Immunities:** Europeans brought diseases that hadn't crossed the ocean before. The Indians had no biological defenses against them.

How the Aztecs rose and fell

Before the Aztecs of Mexico rose to power, they were a conquered people, essentially slaves. Legend says they followed a prophecy that told them to build their capital, the city of Tenochtitlán, where they saw an eagle sitting on a cactus (ouch!) eating a snake. The cactus happened to be on an island in a big lake (now covered over by Mexico City). More credible accounts say the Aztecs chose the island as a defensive position and hideout from their former masters.

Mexico adopted the image of the eagle, snake, and cactus in its national flag, the detail of which is shown in Figure 8-1.

Figure 8-1: The Mexican flag commemorates a legend about the Aztecs.

Becoming masters

The Aztecs (also called the *Mexica*) founded Tenochtitlán in about 1345 and began developing military skills so that other people could no longer enslave them. They built temples, roads, an aqueduct, and causeways over the lake. There they established a hierarchical society in which commoners, although allowed to own land, were expected to pay tribute to and serve nobles, who were believed to have descended from the god Quetzalcoatl. Family lineage determined a person's place within town-like communities called *calpolli*. These communities were grouped into territorial states called *altepetl*, which were ruled by local chiefs or kings. The Aztec Empire took shape as key altepetl joined in an ever-broader alliance.

By the fifteenth century, the Aztecs were strong enough to turn the tables on tribes that had been their former masters. Aztec Kings Itzacoatl and Montezuma I (or Moctezuma) waged wars of conquest throughout the Valley of Mexico and beyond.

Why fight? They believed that the Aztec war god, Huitzilopochtli, demanded sacrificial victims. The Aztec religion included the belief that Huitzilopochtli especially relished fresh human hearts, preferably of brave victims. At the dedication of a pyramid in 1489, Aztec priests cut up 20,000 captives. Victims of the Aztecs' wars fed Huitzilopochtli.

Believing in the return of Quetzalcóatl

In the sixteenth century, things went haywire for the Aztecs. Their subject people began to revolt. King Montezuma II tried to restore order, but he was interrupted when a renegade Spanish explorer, Hernan Cortés, showed up in 1519.

Besides Huitzilopochtli, the Aztecs and their subject peoples feared the white-skinned, bearded deity Quetzalcóatl. According to a myth dating back to the Mayans, Quetzalcóatl had gone across the sea and prophesied that he would return to rule the empire. Shortly after Cortés landed on the coast of the Yucatan Peninsula, he realized that, to the locals, he fit this description. Natives thought the Spaniard and his soldiers were more than mere men. To Aztecs, who had never seen a horse, a mounted soldier looked like a two-headed beast.

When Cortés arrived at the Aztec capital, Montezuma II welcomed him — possibly believing him to be Quetzalcóatl, or possibly trying to bribe him into an alliance. Cortés suspected a trap and took Montezuma II captive. It was too late for the emperor by then, anyway, because he had bowed before the Spaniards and lost the respect of his own subjects. When Montezuma II next attempted to speak before the Aztecs, his audience turned on him and pelted him with stones and arrows. He was fatally injured. In 1521, leaderless Tenochtitlán fell to the Spaniards.

Incas grasp greatness and then fall to the Spanish

Cortés's conquest of the Aztecs in 1521 inspired another Spanish commander, Francisco Pizarro, to invade the greatest South American civilization, the Inca, a decade later. With only 200 troops to subdue an empire of over a million people, it took him only two years to capture Cuzco, the Inca capital.

Cortés's prize, the Inca Empire, was at its height. Centered in the Andes Mountains of Peru and spread over a territory from northern Chile to Ecuador, the empire encompassed a network of different tribes all subjugated and administered by one dominant culture.

Building an empire like no other

Like the Aztecs to the north, the Inca started as a subject people under the thumb of previous Peruvian empires. Incas started flexing their muscles in the twelfth century. In the 1430s, a ruler called Pachacuti repelled an invasion by a neighboring people and went on to increase the size of the Inca Empire until it encompassed parts of today's Chile, Bolivia, and Ecuador.

By the sixteenth century, Pachacuti's successors controlled more land than any South American people before them. Like the Romans (more on them in Chapter 5), the Incas brought the leadership of the people they conquered into the Inca fold, rewarding those who joined and making cooperation easier than resistance. Also like the Romans, the Incas were wonderful engineers. Inca stonemasons built fortifications of giant granite blocks fitted so perfectly together that a knife blade still won't penetrate a seam today.

Just as remarkably, the Incas maintained a 19,000-mile road system, and the government sent fleet-footed messengers along those roads, with runners stationed every 1 1/2 miles. Using this system, they could send a message 150 miles in a day.

The ruling family held everything together, a fact that proved to be the Inca's undoing. All Pizarro had to do was overcome the royals and the empire toppled. He accomplished that in 1532, by base trickery.

Accepting the invaders' invitation

In 1532, Francisco Pizarro invited the king of the Incas, Atahualpa, to a meeting at Cajamarca, a city away from his capital. When the king arrived along with his enormous royal retinue, Pizarro kidnapped him, surprised his followers, and killed several hundred of them. The victims included the king's family members. Atahualpa tried to ransom himself, but Pizarro wanted to use him as a puppet ruler. Atahualpa didn't go along with it, refusing to convert to Christianity. So Pizarro killed the king, too. Then he and his troops marched to Cuzco, Atahualpa's capital city, capturing it in 1533.

The Spanish spent about 30 years beating down revolts throughout former Inca lands (and fighting among themselves as they fought Indian rebels), but they were fully in control of the empire by the 1560s.

The 1969 film *The Royal Hunt of the Sun* is adapted from a hit British stage play and tells the story of Pizarro and Altahualpha's encounter. Unlike the play, which was revived in London in 2006, the movie wasn't a box-office success.

Circling the Planet

Like Vasco da Gama, Ferdinand Magellan was a Portuguese explorer who found a sea route to Asia. Like Christopher Columbus, Magellan was a non-Spanish commander of a Spanish flotilla that tried to reach Asia by sailing west from Europe.

Magellan's expedition was successful in spite of the fact that it lost its captain, four of its five ships, all its officers, and most of its crew on the eventful voyage that went across the Atlantic, through the straits at the southern tip of South America (ever after called the *Straits of Magellan*), across the Pacific Ocean (Magellan named it), through the coveted ports of the Spice Islands (in today's Indonesia), around Africa from the east, and home.

Although he died on the trip, Magellan (whose name in Portuguese was Fernao de Magalhaes) gets credit as the first to circle the globe. He made it as far as the Philippines, and as Magellan may have earlier sailed that far east with Portuguese expeditions, you could say he personally sailed around the world. Technically, his ship's master (like a chief petty officer on a modern ship) Juan Sebastian del Cano (or de Elcano) was the first commander to successfully circumnavigate the globe, arriving home in Spain in 1522. He took command of the expedition after Philippine natives killed Magellan.

The expedition's success gave Europeans proof that the Americas were more than just an unexplored part of Asia. The vast ocean to the west of the New World confirmed that it really was a new world — to Europeans, anyway. Further, Magellan proved it was possible to get at Asia from either direction. In 1522, when his one remaining ship and its few sick, emaciated sailors returned to Spain, Asia was still the prize that European traders and their monarchs coveted.

Ottomans ascend among Eastern empires

Although Europeans were strong and becoming stronger with their worldwide sea routes, they weren't able to immediately grab up huge parts of Asia the way Spain and Portugal claimed all of South and Central America in the late fifteenth and early sixteenth centuries. This was still a time of Asian empires, or in the case of the Ottoman Empire, of an enormous Asian, African, and European empire.

Turk clans' power grows; Ottomans amass vast lands

The Ottoman Empire arose at the end of the thirteenth century in northern Asia Minor (part of today's Turkey). Related to the Mongols and other nomads, the Turks, a loosely connected group of nomadic peoples from central Asia, were organized into dynastic clans. One such clan was the Seljuk Turks, who were powerful in the Middle East in the eleventh century. European crusaders battled the Seljuk Turks in the First Crusade of 1095.

The Ottomans, another clan of Turks, captured Constantinople in 1453, ending the Byzantine Empire. (The Ottoman Turks weren't named for a padded footstool; rather the footstool, adapted from a Middle Eastern style of low, backless chair, was named after these people.)

Like the Seljuk Turks before them as well as Arabs and other people through western Asia, the Ottoman Turks were Muslim. (See Chapter 6 for more about the rise and spread of Islam.) Also like the Arabs, the Ottoman Turks amassed a great empire that, like the Byzantine Empire before it, bridged western Asia and Eastern Europe. Besides stretching from Budapest in Hungary to Baghdad in Iraq to Aswan on the upper Nile, it also, at its height, encompassed the Mediterranean coast of Africa.

Looking eastward to other Asian empires

Another nomadic people like the Turks, the Mongols came out of Central Asia to build empires. Their greatest warrior king, Genghis Khan, controlled a huge empire across Asia to northeastern Europe in the thirteenth century. His grandson, Kublai Khan, conquered China and established a dynasty there in 1280.

The Mongol Empire fell apart in the late thirteenth century, but descendants of Genghis Khan continued to exert power. One of the most famous, the brutal Tamerlane (or Timur the Lame) came out of Turkestan to bedevil the Persians and Ottomans in the fourteenth century. His conquests ranged as far as Moscow, which his troops occupied in the late 1390s. Tamerlane's descendant Babur conquered northern India (including today's Pakistan) in 1526, founding the Mogul Dynasty; the name is a variation on "Mongol" in reference to Babur's empire-building heritage.

The Mogul Dynasty eventually claimed most of the Indian subcontinent and boasted strong rulers and remarkable stability until the eighteenth century, when struggles within the royal court weakened central authority. The empire began to crumble as provincial rulers, nominally subject to the Mogul king, claimed more power for themselves. This decline of Mogul rule eased the way in India for trade-hungry European nations. The British abolished the Mogul court in 1857.

European traders moved quickly into the East after the Portuguese opened up the sea route around Africa in 1498. After Portugal took over Kozhikode, that nation's traders seized another Indian port, Gao (now Goa Velha). Sailing on to the Spice Islands (in today's Indonesia), they also claimed Macao, a peninsula jutting from the coast of China, near Canton.

The Portuguese built fortified outposts from which they could monopolize the spice trade in the Far East. Commerce paid so well that the Dutch and British couldn't just sit by and watch while Portugal raked in the gold.

Founding East India companies

In 1599, 80 London merchants got together and formed the East India Company. Elizabeth I granted them a charter in 1600. The Dutch formed their own East India Company in 1602. The French got in on this action with their East India Company, founded in 1664.

For a short time, the Portuguese enjoyed a trading monopoly as the only European nation with the navigational charts and the trade contacts necessary to transport Asian goods by sea. How did the East India Companies get around the Portuguese monopoly? Much the way the Portuguese established that monopoly in the first place — by muscling in. After Britain established its first trading station at Surat, India, in 1612, the British moved on to other Indian ports. In 1639, the British built a fort and trading post at a fishing village called Madraspatnam, on the Bay of Bengal. It grew into the city of Madras, after which Madras plaid fabric is named. Britain's traders built a post at Bombay in 1688 and founded Calcutta as their Indian headquarters in 1690.

The Dutch captured Jakarta, a city with a fine, protected harbor on the north coast of Java (part of today's Indonesia), in 1619 and renamed it Batavia (after the Batavii, a Celtic tribe in the Netherlands in Roman times). The Dutch East India Company made Batavia its headquarters. In 1638, the Dutch got another exclusive: In an edict banning European traders from Japan's ports, that country's isolationist ruler made a single exception — the Dutch. For the right to stay, the Dutch had to promise not to preach Christianity.

Telling East from West

Why were the British, Dutch, and French trading organizations in Asia called *East* India Companies? Wasn't India to the east of Europe?

Well, yeah. But when the companies were forming, there were those other Indies in the west. When Columbus arrived in the Caribbean in 1492 (more about Columbus in Chapter 7 and earlier in this chapter), he wanted desperately for the islands he found there to be part of Asia. He imagined he was somewhere off the coast of China, perhaps in Indonesia, and so he called the Caribbean islands *Indies*.

After everybody figured out that Columbus was wrong, that the American islands to the west of Europe were different from the Asian islands to the east, they distinguished between them by saying *West* Indies and *East* Indies. For a while there, every time you headed out from port you had to specify which Indies you intended to reach.

The spice trade proved a high-risk profession. The Dutch took Amboyna, a base in the Moluccas, away from the Portuguese. Then when English merchants tried to trade there, the Dutch put the interlopers to death.

Closing the door to Japan

Japan was always a special case among Asian nations. Isolated by the sea, Japan didn't succumb to the invasions of nomadic tribes who roamed the rest of East Asia and rose to power as empire-builders (people such as the Mongols, whom I discuss in Chapter 7). Although its imperial government was structured like China's, since 1192 power in Japan was in the hands of a warrior class. Japanese authority was concentrated in the *shogun,* a warlord nominally appointed by the emperor, but in reality the shogun was far more powerful than the emperor was. The shoguns of the Tokugawa family, which ruled from 1603–1868, were essentially military dictators over all of Japan. Here's a rundown on the first three of these shoguns:

✔ **Tokugawa Ieyasu,** the first of the Tokugawa shoguns, gained office at the end of a series of messy civil wars. Tokugawa was suspicious of outsiders, especially Europeans. When Portuguese traders set up shop in Japan (before the Dutch secured a monopoly there), he worried that their influence could undermine the authority of the shogun system. As he had just restored order to the country, he was determined not to see his authority diluted.

✔ **Tokugawa Hidetada** inherited his father's distrust of European Christians. Hidetada thought that if the Christians gained too many Japanese converts, Japan's ability to defend itself against a European invasion would be weakened. The shogun persecuted Christians more and more severely; in 1622, his officials in Nagasaki crucified 55 missionaries at once.

✔ **Tokugawa Iemitsu,** the next shogun, threw all missionaries and most traders out of Japan during his reign from 1623–1651. He outlawed foreign travel for Japanese and forbade shipbuilders from building the big vessels needed for long-range voyages. Iemitsu even restricted Buddhism, preferring the Confucian emphasis on loyalty to superiors.

Japan continued to trade with China, Korea, and a small contingent of Dutch, the latter being kept off the mainland most of the time on an island in Nagasaki Bay. The Togukawa family successfully kept Japan closed off from extensive Western trade until the mid-nineteenth century.

Playing by British East India Company rules

The British, shut out of Molucca and Japan, had plenty of other ports to exploit, especially in India. From its headquarters in Calcutta, India, the British East India Company traded in textiles and expanded its influence. It oversaw the administration of trade, but it also governed British subjects in its trading ports and beyond, becoming a quasi-government.

In the mid-eighteenth century, the British East India Company expanded its role to military power, declaring war on the local Mogul ruler, or *nawab.* The nawab, Siraj-ud-Daulah, had asked the British to stop fortifying Calcutta. When they refused, he captured the city in 1756, forcing company officials to flee. The nawab's forces captured a garrison of East India Company guards and threw them into a small jail known ever after as the Black Hole of Calcutta. A British survivor claimed that 146 people were thrown into the 18-x-14-foot jail overnight and that all but 23 died. (Later scholarship showed that the number of prisoners was probably 64 to start with.) The story rallied British popular opinion against Siraj-ud-Daulah and firmed up the East India Company's resolve to fight back.

The company's soldiers responded by attacking and defeating a coalition of provincial Muslim rulers allied with the nawab and the Mogul emperor. At war's end, a British trading enterprise had transformed itself into the provincial ruler of the Bengal region of India.

The company's power and profits grew alarmingly, and so did mismanagement and corruption within it. Irresponsible speculation in company stock contributed to a banking crisis in 1772, and the British government passed a series of laws to reform the East India Company, requiring more direct government supervision of company affairs.

In 1857, Hindu and Muslim rebels massacred British soldiers, and the British responded with overwhelming weaponry and mass executions. The uprising against East India Company rule forced the government in London to re-examine colonial policies again. In 1858, Parliament passed an act requiring the East India Company to hand its powers over to the British crown.

China goes from Ming to Qing

The Ming Dynasty ruled China from 1368–1644, a period distinguished by good government, peace, artistic achievements, and prosperity. Ming emperors took an interest in the common people's welfare, going so far as to break up large estates and redistribute them among the poor. Was this some kind of prelude to the socialist government that the Chinese established in the twentieth century? Not really, but it *was* forward-thinking.

China was also fortunate that when the Ming Dynasty finally crumbled in 1644, a ruling family from the province of Manchuria took over, establishing the long-lived Qing (or Chi'ing) Dynasty, which lasted into the twentieth century. At its height, the Qing Dynasty gave China some of its ablest emperors and most stable administrations ever.

Kangxi, the Qing emperor from 1736–1796, molded himself into the image of the ideal Confucian ruler: a benevolent protector of the people (turn to Chapter 10 for more on Confucianism). Kangxi stressed loyalty, traditional morality, and hard work for the common good — especially in farming.

Adequate food production is the greatest common good in a country growing as fast as China was in the eighteenth century. By 1800, the Chinese population was 300 million, double what it was a century before. Under successive Qing emperors, the Chinese developed fast-maturing varieties of rice so that they could produce multiple harvests within a single growing season.

Using force and opium to open Chinese ports

The Qing Dynasty traded successfully, even importing foods such as corn and sweet potatoes from the Americas. (With 300,000,000 mouths to feed, why not?) But China was still suspicious of and resistant to most European business overtures, restricting foreign traders to specific ports such as Canton and Shanghai. For most transactions, the Chinese wanted hard currency such as precious metals. The British East India Company had to pay for tea and other Chinese goods with silver. The Brits felt they were getting the short end of this deal, so they looked for something else the Chinese would take in trade. By the nineteenth century they'd found it: the drug opium, from British-ruled India. More and more Chinese, especially in the south, were smoking opium and becoming addicted, to the point that they were willing to pay for it in tea, silks, and even in silver that helped to finance British India.

Opium destroyed Chinese lives and damaged the Chinese economy. For both reasons, the Qing emperor sent officials to Canton to burn 20,000 chests of British opium. This kind of thing riles a drug lord even today. The Brits were mad enough to go to war over it. And they won.

After the first Opium War, 1842's Treaty of Nanjing forced the Chinese to cede the island port of Hong Kong to Britain. Hong Kong remained a British Crown Colony through most of the twentieth century. (In 1997, Britain restored the port city and adjacent territory to China.) Another Opium War followed from 1856–1860, with a similar result. China was forced to open more ports to British and other Western traders.

Spreading the Slave Trade

Slavery is evil. You and I know that ownership of human beings by other human beings is among the worst practices ever to blight humankind. Yet much of what is called *civilization* was built on slavery. In ancient cultures including Sumer, Babylon, ancient Greece, and Rome, slavery was an economic foundation and often considered a reasonably tolerable way of life for the underprivileged — preferable to starving, anyway.

Perpetuating an evil

The Arabs had little problem with slavery, making them ideal customers for slave-dealing Vikings. Most of Sweden's seacoast is on the Baltic Sea, facing east; so Vikings from that part of Scandinavia often sailed eastward instead of to the west and south, as the Norwegian and Danish Vikings did. As these Swedish Norse adventurers explored harbors in today's Latvia, Lithuania, and Estonia, they began sailing farther eastward, up inlets and rivers into Russia. In Russia's northern, inland forests, they found a source of wealth: tribal people whom they captured to sell as slaves.

The slave markets of the Middle East weren't so difficult for Vikings to reach by water. The Vikings simply carried their cargo down a river. The Dnieper runs through today's western Russia, Ukraine, and Belarus on its way to the Black Sea. From there they could sail to Constantinople. Farther east, the Volga flows south into the Caspian Sea, which borders today's Iran. From the Caspian Sea, the Vikings could reach the lucrative slave markets of Baghdad. When Christian missionaries first ventured into Scandinavia, the Norse captured and sold some of them, too.

Arabs had long dealt in slaves and had sources besides the Viking traders for captive human beings. Since conquering much of North Africa in the sixth and seventh centuries, the Arabs took slaves from that continent. (Find more about the Arab conquests in Chapter 6.)

African wars, like wars in much of the rest of the world since prehistoric times, often involved one tribe or village capturing people from another tribe or village. As Arab traders penetrated the continent beginning in the sixth century, Africans learned that they could trade their captive enemies to these strangers for valuable goods.

The Arab slave trade created a slave economy in Africa, one that was still in force in the late fifteenth century. When Portuguese navigators began landing at West African ports, they found local slavers willing to sell them laborers. In 1482, Portuguese traders built their first slave-trading outpost in Ghana. By the early sixteenth century, the Portuguese were shipping captives to Portugal and to the Azores Islands in the Atlantic, where Portuguese settlers needed laborers. Within a few years, there was a new market for these slaves in the Americas, and the Portuguese were poised to supply that market.

Developing a new market

By the middle of the sixteenth century, Spanish settlers on the Caribbean Islands had decided they needed a new source of labor. The local Indians, whom they enslaved, had no immunity to diseases from Europe. Many were sick or weak, and too many died.

The Spaniards began importing African slaves, who were less likely to keel over from smallpox. (Smallpox — one of the deadliest diseases among Europeans and far more deadly to Caribbean Indians — was also widespread in Africa, so African slaves carried natural resistance.) The first African slaves were purchased from Portuguese ships around 1530, beginning a trade that escalated sharply through the sixteenth and seventeenth centuries and peaked in the eighteenth century.

Also in the sixteenth century, the Spanish found that slave labor made cash crops such as sugar, which they could grow on Hispaniola and other Caribbean Islands, highly profitable. And so they bought more slaves. By 1700, 4,000 slaves arrived in the Spanish-ruled islands every year.

The English, who were building their first permanent settlement in North America at Jamestown, Virginia, in 1607, didn't wait long to begin importing slaves. The English also had a labor-intensive, profitable crop — tobacco. In 1619, Virginia began using African slaves in tobacco fields.

Portugal brought slaves to Brazil in such numbers that by 1800, half the population of that big country was of African heritage.

Succeeding in the slave trade

Trafficking in slaves was one of the surest ways to get wealthy in the shipping business from 1500–1800. Europeans joined Arab traders and local African rulers who could also make fortunes in this ugly business. The Dutch, British, French, and Danish all competed with the Portuguese by building slaving stations in Africa.

In 1713, Spain granted Britain a monopoly to supply its American colonies with 4,800 slaves a year for 30 years. Nobody knows how many people were captured and sold, but they numbered perhaps 7,000,000 in the eighteenth century alone. The numbers are hard to come by partly because so many people died in transit. Appalling conditions onboard slave ships included packing chained slaves into holds a little over 3 feet high. Many died in the filth, disease, and despair of these holds, and sailors dumped the bodies unceremoniously into the sea. Those who survived were sold at auctions.

Starting Revolutions

Many Europeans who came to the Americas wanted to distance themselves from the countries they came from for one reason or another. Often that reason was economic. The New World offered land to the landless and opportunities to the poor.

Religion also played a part in making the New World a desirable destination. This was the case for Separatist Christians from England who landed in North America in 1620 — the people that Americans remember as the Pilgrims of Plymouth Colony. In Massachusetts, these immigrants could do more than worship according to their own Puritan beliefs; they could live and govern themselves by those beliefs. England was a little too far away by sailing ship for the mother country to do much hands-on supervision. Other religious refugees followed, including another sect of Puritans to Boston, Catholics to Maryland, Baptists to Rhode Island, and Quakers to Pennsylvania.

Bringing in the new

The Americas attracted people looking for something new. In the late eighteenth century, two monumental revolutions cast off the old order: the American Revolution and the French Revolution. It's not surprising that the first broke out in North America.

The American Revolution of the 1770s created the United States of America and spread the idea that colonists could break free of European rule. The French Revolution of 1789 shocked traditionalists even more deeply by revealing that the old order could be completely turned on its head, at least for a while. The French Revolution also confirmed that the old order's head — that is, King Louis XVI's head — could be chopped off and tossed into a bloody basket.

These big events, together with a couple of more peaceable agricultural and industrial revolutions, remade the world all over again.

Playing with dangerous ideas

Before the revolutions came an intellectual movement, the Enlightenment.

The American and French Revolutions grew out of economic and political issues between people and their rulers, but they also grew out of the ideas from a new crop of philosophers and scientists. The Englishman John Locke (1632–1704) was a pioneer in arguing that the authority of government comes from the governed. Locke's outlook, a major departure from tradition, was surely marked by the English Civil War of 1642–1649, a conflict between supporters of King Charles I and his opponents in Parliament, the Roundheads (named for their close-cropped haircuts). The Civil War led to the trial and execution of the English king. (Find more about Locke and the Enlightenment in Chapter 15.)

Ideas such as Locke's — that individual people are free and equal — gained ground among the educated people of Europe. In France, the writers François Voltaire and Jean-Jacques Rousseau challenged old ideas about the king representing God.

The Enlightenment also grew out of scientific thought as men such as Isaac Newton in England and Antoine Lavoisier in France theorized about, discovered, and proved natural laws such as gravity.

Beheading the monarchy in England

In 1215, dissatisfied barons forced the unpopular King John to sign the *Magna Carta* (see Chapter 24 for more about this agreement), supposedly guaranteeing English people and especially English nobles political and civil liberties. Not everybody considered the agreement binding, of course, especially not Pope Innocent III, who absolved King John from any responsibility to observe it.

The English Civil War wasn't quite the international jolt that the French Revolution was later, but it was still shocking. Despite the Renaissance and the Protestant Reformation (see Chapter 13 for the Renaissance and Chapter 14 for the Reformation), which shattered the monolithic authority of the Roman Catholic Church, most people in Europe still agreed with Pope Innocent III that nobody except God (and sometimes the pope) should be able to tell a king what to do. The Stuart kings, James I (who ruled from 1603–1625) and Charles I (king from 1625–1649), certainly believed it. Like most people and like all kings, they saw themselves as God's appointees — vice-deity in charge of earthly matters. The Magna Carta, they huffed, wasn't worth the parchment it was written on. This notion took a serious blow at the culmination of the English Civil War in 1649, when the philosopher Locke was a teenager. Protestant revolutionaries chopped off Charles I's head and set up a *Commonwealth* (a kind of republic), quickly followed by a *Protectorate* (a sort of dictatorship) led by Oliver Cromwell.

England got its monarchy back in 1660 after Cromwell died and Charles II showed up to mount the throne. (He had been bunking with friends in France.) The *royalists,* supporters of the monarchy, still hopping mad, dug up Cromwell's body and hanged it. Take that! This period is called the *Restoration,* because the monarchy was restored.

Trying to forestall unrest in France

The kings of France took some measures to prevent insurrections such as England's in 1649. First, a clever cleric, Cardinal Richelieu (1585–1642) set up governmental offices that cut into the power of the French nobles and concentrated the king's authority. Chief Minister to Louis XIII, Richelieu suited Louis XIV, who succeeded in 1643, just fine.

The English Civil War, which began the year before Louis XIV's coronation, was a clash between King Charles I and members of Parliament. Louis XIV sought to eliminate a potential forum for dissent when he stopped calling the French equivalent of Parliament, the Estates-General, into session.

Like the English Stuarts — James I and Charles I — Louis XIV believed that he, as king, was God's deputy. His spectacularly luxurious palace at Versailles, the showplace of all Europe, reflected this conviction. Louis XIV raised taxes to support his free spending and waged an expensive war with Britain from 1701–1713. The French people began to grumble and kept grumbling as succeeding kings involved France in more money-draining conflicts, including the War of Austrian Succession from 1740–1748 (France sided with Frederick the Great of Prussia) and the Seven Years' War from 1756–1763, the conflict that Americans call the French and Indian War.

Rebelling Americans

Enlightenment ideas also took hold overseas, where rational science and engineering, including practical agricultural reforms, put people in North America into a pragmatic, rational frame of mind about government. As independent-minded as many Americans always were, they had little trouble accepting the ideas that men (although still just white men, according to the ideas of the time) were inherently free and that rulers' authority flowed from the people instead of from God.

When the British government imposed a series of taxes on the American colonists to pay for the French and Indian War, colonists didn't take it kindly. "Where is our voice?" they asked. "Who represents our interests in Parliament?" The answers: Unheard, and nobody.

In one of the more creative acts of resistance, some Bostonians dressed up as Native Americans and destroyed the cargoes of several tea ships. Parliament shot back by sending troops and closing Boston harbor. New Englanders fought Old Englanders in two Massachusetts villages, Lexington and Concord, in 1775, beginning the American Revolution. A Continental Congress formed of representatives from 13 British colonies (British Canada didn't participate) declared independence from England the next year in a document, the Declaration of Independence, that rings with Enlightenment philosophy. The great shock was that the outnumbered colonists won, but they couldn't have done so without the French, who supplied money, weapons, and troops to help defeat the English.

Erupting France

Enlightenment ideas link the American and French Revolutions, but so do economics. Just as the English government bred unrest among the Americans by raising taxes to pay for the French and Indian War, so did the French government breed unrest among the French. And King Louis XVI's administration made the situation worse by stretching French finances even farther to support the American patriots.

Louis XVI's generosity toward American revolutionaries made his government all the more vulnerable to the upheaval that rocked France — eventually spilling over into much of Europe — beginning in 1789 with the French Revolution.

That was the year when Louis XVI called a meeting of the *Estates-General,* the French parliament. It was a bold move considering that the body hadn't met in more than 150 years. A well-meaning fellow and smart enough to know that things must change, Louis was trying not to lose his crown, or his head, in the process. Calling the Estates-General was an attempt to get agreement on necessary reforms.

But when he called the Estates-General to session after it had been dormant so long — essentially nonexistent since the mid-seventeenth century — Louis began something he couldn't control. The idea that the king might permit reform of any kind brought forth a flood of pent-up discontent. People were fed up with the privileged classes and high taxes.

On July 14, 1789, an angry Parisian mob stormed the Bastille prison, a symbol of arbitrary injustice, and things didn't settle down for years. Led by some of its more radical members, the Estates-General became the democratic National Assembly, which issued a Declaration of the Rights of Man abolishing the constitution and the monarchy in 1792. The revolutionary government used the guillotine — a supposedly humane means of execution — to behead Louis XVI early the next year.

Louis' beheading wasn't the end of the turmoil, however, not by a long shot. The Reign of Terror followed in 1793 and 1794. It was a period when French nobles could lose their heads for looking at somebody cross-eyed.

Within a decade, in a classic case of pendulum-swing, the neck-chopping excesses of the raging French Revolution provided an opportunity for the first guy who could restore order to step in. He wasn't exactly waiting in the wings — unless you call invading Italy and Egypt waiting in the wings — but when an opportunistic, bold, and charismatic (if physically unprepossessing) military officer called Napoleon Bonaparte returned to France, the revolutionary era gave way to an old-fashioned empire. You can read more about Napoleon's impact in the next chapter.

Writing L'Ouverture to freedom

After folks began throwing around Enlightenment ideas in revolutionary France, the ideas took on a life of their own. François-Dominic Toussaint, a slave in Haiti, was inspired by Enlightenment philosophers as well as by the news from Paris.

Calling himself Toussaint L'Ouverture, he led other slaves against the French authorities in the early 1790s. In 1795, he won control of most of the formerly French-held territory (Haiti occupies about half of the island of Hispaniola). He abolished slavery there and declared Haiti independent in 1801. Napoleon tried to put a stop to this business in 1803 when his forces retook the island nation, captured L'Ouverture, and took him to Paris where he died later that year. But the sparks of liberty aren't always that easy to extinguish. Jacques Dessaline soon led the Haitians against the French again and drove them out in 1804. (For more about L'Ouverture, see Chapter 22.)

These events in Haiti were evidence that ideas imported from Europe took root among people who would use them, over the next century or two, to shake off Europe's hold.

Tracking the Centuries

About 1345: Aztecs establish their great capital city, Tenochtitlán.

1482: Portuguese in Ghana build their first African slaving outpost.

1522: One surviving ship of Ferdinand Magellan's expedition to Asia completes the voyage around the world by returning to Spain.

1603: Tokugawa Ieyasu founds Japan's anti-Western Tokugawa Dynasty.

1619: Dutch traders capture Jakarta, Indonesia, and rename it Batavia.

1649: English Puritans execute King Charles I of England.

1776: Americans declare their independence from Britain.

1789: Angry Parisians storm the Bastille.

1801: Rebel slave Toussaint L'Ouverture declares Haitian independence.

1842: China cedes the island port of Hong Kong to Britain.

1997: Britain returns Hong Kong to China.

1999: Portugal returns Macao to China.

Chapter 9

Clashing All Around the World

● ●

In This Chapter

▶ Fighting back in the colonies

▶ Rocking Europe to the revolutionary beat

▶ Leaping forward in fields of transportation and communication

▶ Feeling the reverberations of the World Wars and the Cold War

▶ Attempting to avoid more wars: The League of Nations and the United Nations

● ●

As the nineteenth century began, the world headed in two directions at once — defiantly away from European imperialism, and headlong into the most imperialist period ever.

After two monumental revolutions — the American rebellion against British rule, and the French overthrow of monarchist order — liberation movements rose in overseas colonies such as the Spanish-ruled lands in Latin America, and on the European continent. These movements rolled on into the early twentieth century, when reform fervor turned Russia into a new kind of socialist state.

In France, revolutionary spirit faded as Napoleon Bonaparte took over, carving France's European neighbors into an empire. Britain joined with Prussia, Russia, and other allies to stop Bonaparte's land-grabs, yet Britain amassed more territory for itself at the same time. Although it lost North American colonies, Britain secured an empire that stretched around the world.

Africans, Asians, and other people intent on resisting European control or tossing out their European masters had a difficult job ahead of them — especially before Europe's powers clashed in cataclysmic twentieth-century conflicts that caught fire throughout their worldwide empires, drawing in non-European powers, too. World War I and World War II depleted the resources and resolve of colonial powers, forcing them to let go of third-world possessions. Those wars also led people worldwide to reevaluate warfare and begin international efforts intended to prevent future armed conflicts.

Managing Unprecedented Empires

Since the Portuguese sailors Magellan and da Gama pioneered sea routes around the world in the late fifteenth and early sixteenth centuries (see Chapter 8), a handful of nations built empires like nothing the world knew before. Russia extended its territory eastward across Asia to the Pacific Ocean, and venturing westward, descendants of Europeans in North America spread to the Pacific.

In 1915, both England and France ruled more people in overseas possessions than they did at home. Africa, much of which hadn't even been explored by Europeans before 1800, had by a century later become a crazy patchwork quilt of colonies held by Germany, Belgium, France, and other colonial powers.

Britain battles on multiple fronts

Britain should have beaten the nankeen britches off the upstart American rebels in the 1770s and 1780s. What were *nankeen britches?* Also called *breeches,* they were the khakis of their time — trousers made out of sturdy, buff-colored cotton cloth that the British East India Company bought from Chinese traders — and that's *not* as beside the point as it seems.

At the time of the American Revolution, the British were the greatest sea power of the world and one of the biggest trading powers. They were on their way to amassing an empire that, at its height, would have made Alexander the Great's eyes pop out of his handsome Macedonian head.

The American setback (although the American Revolution wasn't a setback to the colonists) could be blamed on just how far-flung and thinly spread the British had become. They were busy in other corners of the globe in the late eighteenth century. British soldiers fought French forces in West Africa and the West Indies and faced Dutch opposition in India. Spain got into the fight and blockaded the British colony at Gibraltar. Meanwhile, East India Company troops plunged into the second of four closely spaced Mysore Wars against the Muslims who ruled southwest India.

British manpower was so overstretched and its wealth so great that Britain resorted to fighting the American war with hired German mercenaries, the *Hessians.* (Hesse is a state in Germany.) Well-trained but hardly united behind the British cause, many German soldiers became Americans after the war.

In the larger scheme of world domination, Britain's setback in America — even Britain's inability to bring the Americans to their knees in the War of 1812 — amounted to not all that much. Not compared to all the victories and conquests the British made in the nineteenth century.

Progress for colonial powers amounted to blows upon many of the world's indigenous peoples. Australia, the last habitable continent to receive Europeans, was home to a British penal colony starting in 1788. Voluntary settlers followed. Many Australian Aborigines who were isolated from most of the world for many thousands of years met the same fate as natives in the Americas: widespread disease that was often fatal. Without immunities against the Europeans' diseases and no weapons to match the Europeans' guns, the entire native population of Tasmania, the large island off Australia's southern shore, died between 1803, when the British built a penal colony there, and 1876. They were wiped out in one lifetime.

"Wherever the European has trod," wrote the English biologist Charles Darwin in 1836, "death seems to pursue the aboriginal." Darwin was thinking of Australia, the Americas, Polynesia, and Africa.

By the early twentieth century, Britain's empire included some 400 million people, with only 35 million of them in the United Kingdom (which at that time still included what's now the Republic of Ireland).

Reinventing post-revolutionary France

Circumstances in Europe forced the British to take other challenges more seriously than they did the American colonists' breakaway. Another rebellion against a king, the French Revolution (see Chapter 8) changed France radically in 1789, but the governments in Paris and London remained enemies — more bitterly opposed than ever.

British/French rivalry only intensified as Napoleon Bonaparte seized power in Paris and made much of Europe his empire. Conquering Spain, Italy, and the Netherlands, Napoleon tried to overtake the entire continent in the early nineteenth century.

Napoleon was so successful in his military conquests and so powerful that some of his bitterest opponents — including Austria and Britain — agreed to fragile, short-lived peace agreements that gave economic and territorial concessions to France.

Finally, in 1812, making a serious mistake, Napoleon invaded Russia, marching a force of 500,000 men over muddy, rutted terrain. The outmatched Russians withdrew so rapidly that the French found themselves penetrating all the way to Moscow, trailed by supply wagons that couldn't keep the pace and broke down trying. Napoleon's troops were used to foraging and living off the land while on the march, but Russia — a land of poor, widely spaced farms with meager crops that had already been raided or even burned by the retreating Russians — offered too little sustenance. Napoleon conquered Moscow but then was unable to provision or shelter his troops through the coming

Russian winter, especially after a fire of disputed origin devastated the city. Thousands of starving French soldiers froze to death during a desperate trudge back west.

Anti-Bonapartist European nations — Britain, Austria, Prussia, Russia, Sweden, and more — joined in a series of alliances during Napoleon's years of power. Although these countries' leaders often distrusted each other, they distrusted Napoleon more.

After the disaster of the Russian invasion, Napoleon was vulnerable. His foes took advantage of the situation and invaded France in 1814. Armies commanded by Alexander I of Russia removed the self-made French emperor from his throne that year. Napoleon was exiled to an island, Elba, in the Mediterranean, but he didn't call it quits. Napoleon escaped Elba, seized power in Paris, and fought the allies again. Britain, Prussia, Russia, and Austria defeated Napoleon one final time at Waterloo, Belgium, on June 18, 1815.

Another Louis — number XVIII, the former king's brother — had taken the throne during the Elba exile but had to skip town when Bonaparte came back. After Waterloo, Louis donned the crown and stayed awhile.

What happened to Louis XVII? The son of Louis XVI and Marie Antoinette reportedly died in prison without even getting a style of furniture named after him. The fact that he wasn't guillotined led to rumors that he was still alive. A number of imposters claiming to be Louis XVII emerged long after the revolution. Some won small groups of followers, but little came of it.

Dividing up Africa

Europeans put their figurative foot in Africa's door in the fifteenth century. Portugal was both the first European sea power to sail around Africa and the first to establish a slaving station on the continent's west coast, dealing in human merchandise before 1500.

Other European nations followed the Portuguese into profitable slave trading. Yet it was inevitable that the empire-builders would eventually want more from Africa than just its captive labor. In the nineteenth century, territory-hungry Europeans carved the continent into colonies.

Making gradual inroads

Taking large pieces of African turf took a while for Europeans because, for hundreds of years after the Portuguese began landing at African ports, few outsiders were able to penetrate the interior. Thick jungles, forbidding deserts, and disease-ridden wetlands made overland journeys difficult. In 1760, Europeans knew no more about Africa beyond Egypt and the Mediterranean than their ancestors had known in Roman times — maybe less.

Presuming Dr. Livingstone

In the 1860s, while on an African expedition to settle a dispute about the source of the Nile (Europeans weren't sure where the river started), British explorer, medical doctor, missionary, and popular author Dr. David Livingstone disappeared.

Famous for his earlier African explorations, Livingstone intrigued British and American newspaper readers, who eagerly devoured any report about him. Lacking anything to report on the missing doctor, the *The New York Herald* hired another explorer, Henry Morton Stanley, to go after Livingstone. (Stanley had made his reputation writing dispatches from the American West and the Middle East.)

After two rough years of searching, Stanley sent back a story reporting what he said when he found the man: "Dr. Livingstone, I presume?"

Maybe because the public waited so long for news of Livingstone, or because Stanley's greeting was such an understated, civilized conclusion to such a long, difficult search, the phrase struck a nerve. As the only other white man for hundreds of miles, *of course* it was Dr. Livingstone. "Dr. Livingstone, I presume" became a catchphrase quoted over and over well into the twentieth century.

Livingstone was seriously ill when Stanley came across him and died before he could return to Britain. After finding Dr. Livingstone, Stanley led another expedition into Africa, and his 1878 book about the trip, *Through the Dark Continent,* was a bestseller.

Scotsmen James Bruce and Mungo Park began changing that limitation with their expeditions — Bruce in Ethiopia and Park in West Africa — in the late eighteenth century. As more European explorers followed, word got out about the vast resources of Africa's interior.

Europe's Industrial Revolution (see Chapter 15), which began in the eighteenth century, ate up raw materials. Nineteenth-century Europeans realized that they could mine, cut, and grow such resources in the wilds of Africa, so nations began sending armed expeditions to claim rights over one chunk after another of the big, yet-untapped continent.

By the early twentieth century, the African map was a jigsaw puzzle with pieces bearing European names such as French West Africa, Belgian Congo, German South West Africa, British East Africa (Kenya), and Anglo-Egyptian Sudan (British-controlled), as shown in Figure 9-1.

Overwhelming Africa's defenders

African peoples such as the Asante and the Zulu tried to resist the Europeans who took over their lands, but the natives were largely outgunned.

Samory (or Samir) Ture, the self-appointed emperor of Guinea in West Africa, built an Islamic nation in the region of the upper Niger River and had a large and disciplined, if poorly equipped, army at his command. From 1883, Emperor Ture fought hard to keep out Europeans, but squeezed between the French and the British, he had little chance. His army was defeated and he died in exile in Gabon in 1900.

Only one African nation successfully resisted the Europeans. Ethiopia smashed an invading Italian army of 17,000 at the Battle of Adowa in 1896. Ethiopia was the only independent native African nation left.

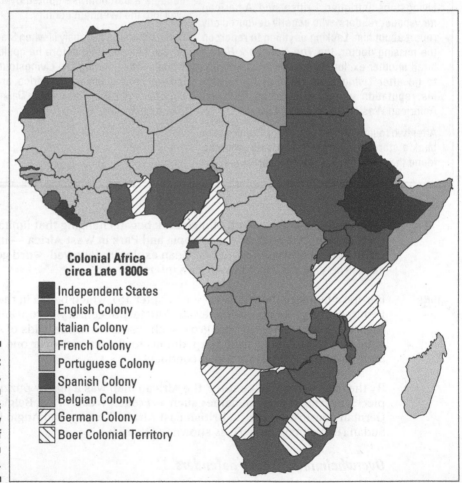

Colonial Africa circa Late 1800s

- Independent States
- English Colony
- Italian Colony
- French Colony
- Portuguese Colony
- Spanish Colony
- Belgian Colony
- German Colony
- Boer Colonial Territory

Figure 9-1:
By 1900, the African map was a jigsaw puzzle of European conquests.

Challenges Test European Dominance

By the early twentieth century, white Europeans and their descendants ruled so much of the world that it's easier to say what they *hadn't* yet grabbed than to list everything they *had*.

As I mention in the previous section, Ethiopia was a black-ruled holdout in Africa. Persia and the Ottoman Empire resisted in the Middle East — although the long-lived Ottoman Empire, based in Istanbul and ruled since the fifteenth century by an Islamic Turkish dynasty, was only a ghost of its mighty former self. In Asia, Japan stood apart. So did China, but shakily. Beyond that handful of nations, there was little that Europe (or the descendants of Europeans — as in the United States) didn't control besides poor countries no European power wanted.

Yet even the strongest colonial powers could never take their holdings for granted. They had to fight to keep their trade advantages, as when China resisted European hegemony over its ports. The colonial powers also had to fight against uprisings both by colonists and conquered indigenous people, as happened in South America and Africa. And they had to watch for new powers rising to rival them, as Japan did as it emerged from a long, self-imposed isolation.

Turning against Spanish rule in Latin America

Spain's greatest empire from the time of Christopher Columbus was in the Americas. Land claims based on explorations and conquests in the late fifteenth century brought Spanish rule to much of southern and western North America, all of Central America, and most of South America.

Yet rebels began challenging Spain's authority in South America starting in the late eighteenth century. In Peru in 1780, Jose Gabriel Condorcanqui rallied miners and factory workers — descendants of the Inca — against their Spanish bosses. They attacked Cuzco and La Paz in neighboring Bolivia.

Condorcanqui, a rich man of mixed Spanish-Inca heritage, called himself Tupac Amaru, borrowing the name of a sixteenth-century emperor. The Spanish caught and tortured him to death and finally crushed the revolt after two years. But more unrest was on the way within the Spanish empire in the Americas.

Confusing leadership in Chile

Spanish authority in the Americas really faltered after Napoleon, self-crowned emperor of France and conqueror of Spain, knocked King Ferdinand VII off the throne back in Madrid. In 1808, Napoleon gave Spain's crown to Joseph Bonaparte, his brother. Two years later in Chile, a Spanish captain-general lost his power to a *junta* (a political committee) that, in turn, was replaced by one republican leader and then another, creating continuous confusion. When Ferdinand regained his Spanish throne in 1814, royalist troops marched to restore authority in Chile, and the military leader who emerged from the republican chaos to fight them was Bernardo O'Higgins. (Now there's a historical name you ought to remember, even if you forget what he did.)

Breaking away with Bolívar

The situation in South America began to snowball as King Ferdinand VII reassumed control of Spain and its empire. Simón Bolívar, inspired by the North American patriots and the French revolutionaries, got the idea that the entire, chili pepper-shaped continent needed to break free from Spain. His revolutionaries took over Venezuela in 1816. Then Bolívar beat the Spanish in Colombia, where he became president. He went back to Venezuela when the Spanish tried to recapture it and drove them out again. Yet Bolívar was far from finished.

Hopping borders with Jose de San Martin

Down in Argentina, the Spanish-trained soldier Jose de San Martin led a revolutionary army in that country's fight for independence. Then he joined O'Higgins, who had been driven out of Chile by royalist troops. Together, they beat Spanish forces, and Chile declared independence in 1818. With O'Higgins in charge as Supreme Director (dictator), San Martin headed to the next spot on the map — Peru.

He beat the Spanish forces yet again, declaring Peru independent in 1821. He even stayed on for a bit to lead the new government in Lima. After he retired in 1822, the Peruvians got a good replacement — Simón Bolívar — who drove the remaining Spanish forces out and became dictator in 1824. But Bolívar still wasn't finished overturning Spain's colonial authorities. He moved north and founded Bolivia.

Struggling in Mexico

Mexico's struggle to break free of Spain began only a few decades after the United States had thrown off British rule, but Mexico suffered many setbacks on its way to a stable independent government. Early in the nineteenth century, Spanish authorities arrested two priests, Miguel Hidalgo y Costilla and Jose Maria Morelos y Pavon, for spreading ideas from the French Revolution (see Chapter 8). Both received the death sentence, but the revolutionary fever took hold. Augustin de Iturbide broke Mexico free of Spain in 1823, declaring a short-lived Mexican-Guatemalan Empire. The following year, Mexican patriots replaced Iturbide with a constitution based on that of the United States.

The biggest setbacks in Mexico came in quick succession from the 1830s–1860s. Still struggling to find its feet after winning independence from Spain, Mexico lost its northeastern state of Texas to a second-generation independence movement in 1836. Then Mexico lost huge territories in western North America to the U.S. in the Mexican-American War of 1846–1848.

France and some of its European allies invaded Mexico in 1861. Mexican forces defended the homeland, scoring a notably improbable and heroic victory on May 5, 1862, at the city of Puebla. The occasion is still celebrated as the holiday Cinco de Mayo. The Europeans persisted and eventually prevailed, however, and about a year later, Emperor Napoleon III offered the Mexican throne to Ferdinand Maximilian Joseph, Archduke of Austria, who belonged to the powerful Hapsburg Dynasty of Europe.

Maximilian didn't last long as emperor of Mexico. Napoleon III withdrew French troops, leaving his puppet unable to maintain authority. Mexican General Benito Juarez defeated and captured Maximilian in May 1867 and ordered the deposed emperor executed.

Reclaiming Africa for Africans

Although conquered fairly late in the game by Europeans, Africa didn't wait long to get in on the rebellion business. Although their revolt failed, the people of Zimbabwe rebelled against the British in 1896. Africans in Tanzania rose against their German government in 1905, but that movement, too, was crushed. Germany's colonial troops burned crops to create a famine and weaken the Tanzanian rebels.

The Herero and Nama people of Namibia suffered incredible losses in uprisings against the Germans. The cattle-raising Nama were reduced from a population of 20,000 to less than half that. Of the estimated 80,000 Herero living in central Namibia before the war, only 15,000 were left in 1911.

This struggle finally began to result in self-rule for African nations in the 1950s. In 1948, riots shook Ghana (then called the Gold Coast) and the British, whose home nation was impoverished by World War II, realized that they could no longer afford an empire. Other colonial powers also woke up to the same reality during WWII. The war had rocked the European empires to their foundations.

Rising Asians

In the 1820s, the Dutch rulers in Java (one of the larger islands in today's Indonesia) fought a Javanese prince, Diponegoro, who tried to liberate his island from the foreigners. The Dutch arrested and exiled him. As in so many colonial holdings, Indonesian independence had to wait until after the turmoil of the World Wars loosened the Europeans' hold.

Europe had to fight to hang onto its economic dominance in other parts of East Asia, too. The Chinese went to war against Britain from 1839–1842 and again from 1856–1860 over the issue of illegal British imports of the drug opium from India to China (see Chapter 8). Although China lost the fight and had to allow trading concessions to the British and other European powers as a result, deep-seated resentment lingered.

Japan unleashes pent-up power

In Japan, teenage Emperor Meiji inherited the throne in 1867. Simultaneously, the longstanding system of rule by a *shogun*, a warlord far more powerful than the emperor, was crumbling under pressure from nobles and others eager for the long-isolated nation to adopt Western technology. After 700 years of shogunate rule and a short civil war, the last shogun, Tokugawa Yoshinobu, gave up his powers in 1868.

Called the Meiji Restoration, this transition freed the emperor to pursue modernization and launch an ambitiously militaristic foreign policy strategy. While many empires of the era fell back or held steady, Japan gained territory from China in the 1890s and from Russia in the Russo-Japanese War of 1904–1905. The latter was a humiliating defeat for the Russians. In 1910, Japan seized control of Korea. This empire-building continued long beyond Meiji's death in 1912. In 1932, Japan turned Chinese Manchuria into the Japanese puppet state of Manchukuo.

Tom Cruise stars in the 2003 box-office hit *The Last Samurai*, a film loosely — and I mean extremely loosely — based on Japan's Meiji Restoration. Enjoy it, but don't mistake the story for fact.

Ricocheting unrest comes home to Europe

Europe didn't shake the unrest at home after the French Revolution because the ideas that fueled upheaval in 1789 didn't go away. The French saw another revolution in 1848, although this one didn't involve as much head-chopping. France replaced King Louis Phillipe, a champion of the rich, by electing Louis Napoleon, a nephew of Napoleon I, to a four-year presidency in 1850. Under a banner of law and order, the new president worked to consolidate his power and succeeded in getting the French Senate to declare him Emperor Napoleon III in 1852.

What about Napoleon II? He never got his opportunity. Born in 1811, Napoleon's son was a small child when hard-line supporters of a Napoleonic dynasty tried to prop him up as an emperor in 1815. The allies who beat his dad at Waterloo discouraged the attempt, and Junior moved to Vienna and stayed out of the way.

France had rebellious company in 1848. Many Europeans were miserable — hungry, out of work, and angry — because the changes that accompanied the agricultural and industrial revolutions didn't benefit everyone. Revolutionary movements broke out in Austria and Hungary (they finally got rid of *serfdom,* a medieval form of forced labor) and in many German and Italian states. Revolts also rocked Ireland, Switzerland, and Denmark. The revolutionaries failed to overthrow their governments, but the people made themselves heard. Change was in the air. Most of Europe — especially Western Europe — headed toward democracy, but it wasn't a smooth, easy road.

Revolting in Russia

The pressures that erupted into the 1848 revolutions in Europe were much the same as the pressures that brought about revolution in Russia a half-century later. In 1905, Russian troops fired on Russian workers marching in the streets of St. Petersburg who were trying to win higher wages and shorter hours in the factories.

Shooting at them didn't work. The surviving demonstrators went on strike, and strikes spread from St. Petersburg to other Russian cities. Then the rebellion spread to rural revolts against landlords.

Standing apart up north

Russia had long been a special case among European nations — partly because although huge, it was so remote, northern, and inland. Founded by Swedish Vikings, the Russian nation had begun forming in the ninth century. As in Poland, the indigenous population was largely Slavs, a people of obscure origin who had somehow withstood centuries of Huns, Goths, Avars, and other barbarians rumbling past on their way into Europe.

In social, economic, and technological progress, Russia lagged behind countries to the west. To a Russian, even a Russian of the highest rank, the Western European level of craftsmanship and skill in fields ranging from shipbuilding to architecture to weaponry to printing seemed remarkably advanced. Peter I (also known as Peter the Great; see Chapter 22), who became sole ruler of Russia in 1696, spent two years traveling in places such as England, France, and the German states, learning about a wide variety of industries. When he returned, he brought experts and teachers with him, because he was determined to drag Russians into the eighteenth century, kicking and screaming if necessary.

Yet despite its early modernizations, Russia still stood apart in that it was mired in the past as the nineteenth century changed the rest of Europe. For example, as many European nations abolished the old feudal system of serfdom, Russia went the other way, making even more people serfs. *Serfs* were not little blue cartoon characters from the 1980s (those are Smurfs), but rather people at the bottom rung of society who had no rights. Serfdom disappeared from England in the Middle Ages but continued in many lands on the European continent. France formally abolished the institution with its Revolution of 1789; in Austria and Hungary, serfdom endured until 1848. Russia finally freed its serfs in 1861. (Smurfdom, on the other hand, continues in TV reruns in many parts of the world.)

Rushin' toward rebellion

Perhaps it's not surprising that revolutionary unrest hit Russia hard and went to extremes in the late nineteenth and early twentieth centuries.

You'd think Russian peasants, having been freed from serfdom, would be contentedly happy, but an unfair land settlement left many without enough soil in which to grow adequate food to support themselves. Ironically, better medical care made the situation worse. Toward the close of the nineteenth century, fewer peasants died of disease, which left more mouths to feed.

High taxes also fueled unrest. Urban professionals and nobles didn't like paying for their government to build an expensive fleet of warships just to see the Japanese sink those ships during the Russo-Japanese War of 1904–1905.

Unrest locked up the country. In 1905, rebels elected representatives to the St. Petersburg Soviet of Workers' Deputies, a council to coordinate strikes and demonstrations. Other *soviets,* or councils, soon formed across Russia. In October 1905, Czar Nicholas II agreed to reforms, including the creation of a Russian parliament, the *Duma.* By giving unhappy Russians a legislative body, Nicholas hoped to provide a safety valve to ease political dissatisfaction — a place for society to air its grievances. But the Duma was doomed from the beginning. On the left, socialist groups boycotted it. On the right, reactionaries in Nicholas's court fought the Duma's efforts to reform tax and farm policies. The czar's advisors convinced Nicholas to dissolve the legislature every time they didn't like its direction. Between 1905 and 1912, he dissolved the Duma three times.

In 1917, after 5 million Russian soldiers died in World War I, Czar Nicholas faced widespread unrest. Again, he ordered a disobedient Duma to dissolve itself, but the legislators refused his order.

Taking power: The Soviet Union

After forcing Czar Nicholas to abdicate, a broad coalition of representatives — liberals, social democrats, and agrarian socialists — formed a provisional government and set up headquarters in the czar's Winter Palace. The provisional government held elections for a Constituent Assembly — a representative body to draft a constitution. But before the assembly met, extremists led by Vladimir Ilyitch Lenin seized power by force.

Lenin's followers called themselves *Bolsheviks,* which means "majority," even though they were a minority. They captured the palace in October 1917. Lenin allowed the Constituent Assembly to convene in January 1918, but then he used soldiers to break it up.

Lenin and his Red Army fought counterrevolutionaries over the next few years, but Russia — renamed the Union of Soviet Socialist Republics (USSR) or the Soviet Union, for short — became a very different beast for most of the twentieth century.

Inspired by the writings of Karl Marx, a nineteenth-century German economic philosopher, Lenin set up a government based on national ownership. Everything belonged to the government, and everybody worked for the government (or, nominally, for "the people"). For the first time ever, a great national power was run by leaders who wanted to overthrow and replace all existing society with communism's new economic model.

Not really progress for the people

As Lenin's successor, Josef Stalin, later proved, a Leninist-Marxist system could bring about rapid industrialization, turning Russia into one of the two greatest economic and military powers in the world. But on the way toward economic gains, Stalin left many millions of Russians dead. His so-called agricultural reforms caused widespread starvation.

In the 1930s, Stalin brutally eliminated any colleague he perceived as a rival for his power, staging show trials and executions of many men who had stood beside him in 1917. The USSR's most revered Bolshevik veterans were forced to confess to unlikely crimes and then were sentenced to death by firing squad or a term in a prison camp from which they would never return. From 1934–1938, hundreds of thousands of lesser officials also disappeared as victims of Stalin's purges.

Nobody knows exactly how many people Stalin killed and imprisoned, but estimates range as high as tens of millions dead.

Returning Russia

By 1991, the Soviet Union was in economic ruin, strained by Cold War military spending, and fell apart. During the first decade of the twenty-first century, the Russian Republic, successor to the USSR, reemerged as an important economic and military power with what U.S. Secretary of Defense Robert Gates characterized as an "aggressive posture" toward neighboring states.

Accelerating toward the Present: Transportation and Communication

As you get closer to modern times, you find that human civilization quickly became more tightly crisscrossed with interconnections between peoples and places than ever before. Technological innovation was a major factor in the change as people used new machines born of the Industrial Revolution (see Chapter 15) to make distances less . . . well, less distancing in terms of both transportation and communication.

Getting somewhere in a hurry

Ever since the discovery of new sea routes in the fifteenth and sixteenth centuries, oceans brought continents together as much as they separated them. Harnessing steam power in the eighteenth century meant ships covered oceanic distances quicker, or at least at a steadier, more reliable pace. After the steam engine got wheels, a land transportation revolution quickly followed.

Steaming into port

The steam engine, first used to pump water out of coal and tin mines, became a primary engine of the Industrial Revolution. This coal-fired power source was adapted to drive boats successfully early in the nineteenth century.

Robert Fulton, an American, built a functional steamship called the *Claremont* in 1807. Around the same time, England's Patrick Bell built a similar boat. At first, steam was considered useful mainly for river and canal travel, but by the 1830s, steamships were already taking trans-oceanic voyages. Shippers could keep to schedules as never before because they weren't relying on favorable winds. As a result, international commerce boomed. Steam, rather than sail, soon interlinked vast empires such as Britain's.

By the 1880s, steam engines powered virtually every kind of vessel — warship, cargo carrier, passenger liner. Steam-driven navies featured battleships that could be more heavily armed and more heavily armored than any in history. (For more about technological advances in modern warfare, see Chapter 18.)

Steam engines became so reliable that ships finally stopped carrying sails at all. The sailor's craft, which was once all about canvas, rope, and pulleys, became an occupation concerned with boilers, pistons, and coal fire.

Working on the railroads

Richard Trevithick, a British engineer, put a steam engine on wheels in 1804 and made it run on rails. (Mining wagons pulled by animals had long run on iron rails.) In 1825, England saw its first commercial railway — the Stockton and Darlington. By 1851, there were rail networks in 17 other countries. By the end of the century, Russia had built a railroad across Siberia.

In the U.S., people who had spent arduous months crossing the continent westward to California in wagons could retrace the journey in a week, rumbling along in rail passenger cars. Rail travel revolutionized commerce by opening up vast inland areas — once too isolated for large-scale settlement — to trade, commercial agriculture, and city-building as brand new communities grew up along rail lines.

Driving innovations

The steam engine uses heat from a fire to create steam in a boiler. Steam pressure then pushes a piston, which in turn powers locomotive wheels or a ship's propeller. The early success of this technology inspired some dreamers to wonder if it would be possible to build an engine containing the fire itself within the cylinder — an *internal combustion engine.* In Switzerland, Isaac de Rivaz (or Rivas) built such an engine in 1804 and used it to push a cart across a room. Rivaz's machine, however, wasn't practical. It burned a mixture of purified hydrogen and air, which had to be injected manually with every pump of the cylinder. Rivaz also had to kick open an exhaust valve every time the engine fired. Other inventors, among them Samuel Brown of England and Jean-Joseph-Etienne Lenoir, improved on Rivaz's crude design through the middle of the nineteenth century.

These new internal combustion engines were much lighter than the steam engine because they didn't require a cumbersome boiler or firebox. So, they seemed well-suited for powering vehicles light enough to travel on roads built for horse-drawn traffic rather than on the rails required for heavy steam locomotives.

In Germany in 1885, engineer Karl Benz used an internal combustion engine to power a practical motor car. (The word *car* began as a shortened version of *carriage*.) His vehicles led to one of the twentieth century's biggest and most world-changing industries.

Large-scale automobile manufacturing took off in 1908 when American Henry Ford (1863–1947) began using an assembly-line factory in Michigan to make cars affordable for the middle class. From that time on, automobiles changed people's lifestyles. Cars sparked road construction and changed the shape of cities as newly mobile workers relocated from central cities to suburban neighborhoods.

Taking to the air

Two bicycle mechanics from Ohio, Orville Wright and his brother Wilbur, flew an airplane for the first time in 1903. Commercially built aircraft followed, with passenger travel right behind. Places formerly days apart by train or car were soon separated by mere hours — and even fewer hours as passenger jets came on the scene after World War II.

Sending word

By the middle of the nineteenth century, it was possible to send messages over wires by electric current. The technological advance of the telegraph amounted to a communications revolution in itself, but it was only the beginning of a wired-up world.

Stringing cables

Samuel Finley Breese Morse, an American artist and inventor, came up with the first practical, wide-scale application for electromagnetic impulses when he invented Morse code in 1837. Seven years later he sent an instantaneous message, "What hath God wrought!" over a telegraph line strung from Baltimore to Washington, D.C.

What did he mean by that? It was a reverent expression of wonder. Soon cables crisscrossed industrialized countries in Western Europe and North America, and then they spread to more remote parts of the world.

Talking on the phone

Alexander Graham Bell (1847–1922), a speech and hearing therapist, put his interest in sound and communication together with telegraphic technology to build an experimental telephone in 1876.

Bell, a Scottish immigrant to the United States, founded the Bell Telephone Company to build and market his invention. By the early twentieth century, the phone was becoming an everyday convenience.

In 1977, the U.S. electronics company Motorola developed a wireless telephone that connected with the public telephone network through a system of short-range radio cells. In the twenty-first century, personal cellphones — which continue to get smaller and less expensive — are everywhere and threaten to replace traditional landline phones.

Sending radio waves

At the end of the nineteenth century, Italian-born inventor Gugliemo Marconi demonstrated that radio waves could be used to send signals without wires. In 1901, he successfully sent a wireless telegraph signal all the way across the Atlantic Ocean from Cornwall, England, to Newfoundland, Canada. Marconi won the Nobel Prize for physics in 1909.

By adding voice-signal technology developed for the telephone by Bell (more about him in the previous section) and by American inventor Thomas Edison (1847–1931) for his innovative phonograph, engineers turned radio communication into a voice-transmission system for ships and airplanes. Radio also became an entertainment medium as businesspeople saw it as a way to publicize their products. Advertisers began sponsoring music, news, drama, and comedy programs as affordable receivers allowed more and more people to tune in. People over vast distances joined as a common audience for this new experience.

Radio gave birth to television. In the 1920s, inventors in the U.S. came up with devices for sending electronic pictures using radio waves. Philo T. Farnsworth invented an electronic picture scanning system in 1922, and Vladimir K. Zworkin followed with the television camera and picture tube in 1923. By the middle of the twentieth century, these devices brought huge and growing audiences a form of instantaneous mass togetherness beyond any precedent in history.

Surfing the Net

In 1969, engineers working for the U.S. Department of Defense linked four computers together so that the machines could exchange information. Gradually, more computers were hooked up to this network. Around the same time, more and more government and university programmers and researchers found that sending messages from computer to computer was a good way to trade information. Data began flowing, although the use of this network was limited to people who were adept at computer programming.

As the use of new personal computers designed for people who weren't computer specialists spread, the growing network became a communications phenomenon. When American universities hooked their *supercomputers* (super-large and super-fast in their capacity to store and process data) together in the 1980s, the *Internet* began to take shape. Commercial services started offering Internet access to businesses and homes over ordinary telephone lines.

Physicist Tim Berners-Lee invented *hypertext markup language* (HTML) as a way for non-specialist Internet users to display their data in everyday language, pictures, and sound so that other computer users could access them over the Internet. In 1991, Berners-Lee put his creation, the World Wide Web, on the Internet. The World Wide Web quickly became the fastest growing part of the Internet as a place for businesses, political parties, activists, service organizations, and ordinary individuals to share information and exchange views. That led to music downloads, file sharing, social networking sites, and video sharing. As with the telegraph, radio, and the telephone (and as with the printing press of the fifteenth century), people became more tightly interconnected than ever before thanks to this new, evolving technology.

Fighting World Wars

Although steamships, railroads, and the telegraph — the advances you can find out about earlier in this chapter — bridged distances for commerce and peaceful communication, they also provided advantages for admirals and generals planning attacks and invasions around the world.

Even if you're just skimming this chapter (and by all means, feel free to skim), you may notice how European nations that had the rest of the world in a bear hug by the year 1900 seemed to fight an awful lot of wars. From ancient times onward, engaging in war was the way to build and keep empires. But with the rise of Europe's new, global empires of the nineteenth and early twentieth centuries as well as all the advances in travel and communication, wars tended more than ever to spill over from one part of the world to another.

As an early example of what was coming, the Seven Years' War had multiple fronts in India, Europe (where Prussia, Hanover, Austria, and Russia sided with Britain, and Spain sided with France), and America (the French and Indian War). The trend only got worse — lots worse. In the twentieth century, the tendency toward war and the technology to support it led to World War I and World War II.

Weapons advances, such as the more accurate, easier-to-load rifles used in the Crimean War of the mid-nineteenth century, kept right on until, by 1945, one U.S. airplane carrying one bomb would destroy a major Japanese city, Hiroshima. In one stroke, it killed 66,000 people and injured another 69,000. Even that wasn't enough, though. Soon nations had the ability to push a single button and launch a missile attack capable of wiping out all civilization on the planet.

This section focuses on the weapons and wartime advances of the World Wars. To find out more about how technology changed war in the nineteenth and twentieth centuries, turn to Chapter 18.

Redefining war: World War 1

At the time, nobody gave the *Great War* a number, because they weren't planning to have another. One was quite enough, thanks.

Later called World War I, this conflict proved uglier, bigger, longer, more widespread, and more brutal than many people realized a war could be. From 1914–1918, two lines of infantry soldiers stretching across northern France and Belgium faced each other month after month, year after year, hunkered down in muddy, rat-infested, soul-killing trenches only a few hundred yards apart.

Mechanized as no war before it had been, World War I took to the skies as airplanes dropped bombs and fought the first-ever air-to-air battles. World War I also brought about submarine warfare. German U-boats (the "u" stood for "underwater") sank enemy warships and neutralized transports without warning. Troops moved by way of trucks and armored personnel carriers. Guns were bigger, faster-firing, longer-range, and more numerous than those of any war before. And there were also so-called advances in chemical warfare, such as crippling mustard gas.

Precipitating events and attitudes

You may have learned in school that WWI started when a Serbian terrorist shot an Austro-Hungarian archduke in Sarajevo, Bosnia, in 1914. That's true, but the origins of the war are much more complicated than that.

For one thing, the Serbians were angry with the Austro-Hungarian Empire (a combination Austria and Hungary) for annexing Bosnia (even though Bosnia still technically belonged to the Ottoman Empire, which was weakened by its own internal revolt). The Austro-Hungarians worried about the Serbs potentially uniting all the Slavs in southeastern Europe, in a mountainous region called the Balkans. Such unification would have threatened the Hungarian part of their empire. Russian leaders, meanwhile, believed that the Balkans, with its largely Slavic population, rightfully belonged in the sphere of influence of the Russian Empire, also largely Slavic. Although they had no legal claim over it, the Russians felt especially protective about Slavic Serbia.

Russia didn't declare war on anyone, but it mobilized troops. That was enough provocation, though, to prompt the Germans — who were allies of the Austro-Hungarian Empire — to declare war on both Russia and its ally France. The Germans cut through neutral Belgium on the way to attack the French.

Britain had no formal quarrel with Germany, but relations between the two countries were strained by an undeclared race for naval superiority. Starting in the 1890s, Wilhelm II, the German *kaiser* (meaning "emperor"), aggressively built more and bigger ships. Britain responded by stepping up its own shipbuilding. German troops crossing into Belgium in 1914 solidified anti-German feeling in Britain because the incursion violated international law, giving the British an excuse to mobilize troops.

Adding combatants to the war

The war grew as more countries entered the fray. Here's the breakdown of the two sides:

✔ **The Entente, or Allies:** Britain, France, Russia, Japan, Serbia, Italy, Portugal, Romania, the United States, and China

The U.S. joined the Allied side in 1917 after Germany's submarine blockade of Great Britain began sinking neutral ships.

✔ **The Central Powers:** Germany, Austro-Hungary, and the Ottoman Empire

Reacting to the carnage

World War I helped create the Soviet Union, but the war changed more than Russia. Four empires — the Russian, the Ottoman, the German, and the Austro-Hungarian — collapsed in that war.

Besides rearranging the map, the Great War brought famine, collapsed economies, and demonstrated to a shocked public that war brought little more than widespread disaster. The war ground up and spit out entire towns, villages, and even countries. Even people not directly hit by WWI realized by the time it was over that maybe war wasn't so great, after all. This wasn't the heroic warfare of patriotic songs, but rather a blight.

A leader in this line of thinking was Woodrow Wilson, a former Princeton University professor turned politician. As president of the United States,

Wilson worked on the terms of peace in Europe, making sure the peace process included the *League of Nations* — an international body created expressly to prevent future wars.

The League of Nations, established by the Treaty of Versailles in 1919, helped Europe rebuild after the war. Fifty-three nations joined by 1923, including Britain, France, Italy, and Japan.

Unfortunately, the League of Nations didn't work, especially not for Wilson. The U.S. Senate refused to approve Wilson's terms or let the U.S. join the league. Wilson suffered a massive stroke while trying to drum up public support to make the senators change their minds, and he spent the rest of his term, until 1921, as an invalid.

Although Germany joined the league in 1926, it withdrew, along with ally Japan, in 1933. Italy withdrew three years later. The organization subsequently proved helpless to stop German, Japanese, and Italian expansionism. By the late 1930s, the world was in for another big one.

Nobody before him ever tried regulating international life the way President Wilson envisioned. So, maybe his brainchild was bound to fail, but the League of Nations was a step toward something new.

Returning to conflict: World War II

World War I sowed the seeds for the Second World War. In Germany after WWI, impoverished citizens and resentful leaders alike bitterly opposed the terms of the Treaty of Versailles, which included the following:

- ✔ A *war guilt clause* that blamed everything on Germany

- ✔ Lost territories — Alsace-Lorraine to France, the Rhineland turned into a demilitarized zone, and most of Germany's overseas colonial holdings going to other empires

- ✔ Cash reparations that the war-ravaged country could not pay

Adolf Hitler, the populist party boss of the National Socialists, or *Nazis,* used this national anger to take over the government of Germany. He called his administration the *Third Reich* — heir to the medieval Holy Roman Empire (the first Reich, or empire) and to the German Empire of 1871–1918.

Breaking the treaty: Hitler moves his troops

Hitler secretly rearmed the country in the 1930s and then started moving his troops in direct violation of the Versailles Treaty. He occupied the

Rhineland (so much for a demilitarized zone), annexed Austria, and headed for Czechoslovakia, a country that had been created after World War I. He considered himself within his rights there, because he worked out a deal with the governments of Italy, France, and particularly Great Britain to extend Germany's power in Czechoslovakia.

Hitler asserted that the Sudetenland region of Czechoslovakia rightly belonged to Germany, and the German-speaking residents of the region agreed. Italian dictator Benito Mussolini, whose post-WWI rise was not unlike Hitler's, arranged the meeting in Munich at which Hitler, British Prime Minister Neville Chamberlain (who was bending over backwards to avoid conflict with Germany), Mussolini, and French Prime Minister Edouard Deladier carved up Czechoslovakia, without consulting the Czechs.

Hitler also signed the Nazi-Soviet Pact with Josef Stalin, Lenin's successor in Moscow. (There's more about both Lenin and Stalin in the earlier section "Revolting in Russia.") After claiming the Sudetenland, the Nazis plunged into Poland with the idea of dividing that country with the Soviet Union.

Choosing sides

Germany's 1939 invasion of Poland proved too much even for peace-seeking Chamberlain. London didn't want another war, especially not a war against formidable Germany, but the British woke up to the reality that there was no avoiding it. Britain declared war that year.

Even more nations than in WWI took sides or were overtaken and forced into the fight that became WWII. A majority of the nations of the world participated. Here's an incomplete breakdown:

- ✔ **Axis:** Included Germany, Italy, Japan, Hungary, Slovakia, Bulgaria, Croatia, Finland, Romania, Iraq, Thailand, and many more, including vast swaths of Asia and Africa controlled by Axis nations.

  The Soviets, originally on Germany's side, were forced to switch allegiances abruptly when Hitler violated his pact with Stalin and sent an invasion toward Moscow. France was a leader of the Allies until Germany overran the country in June 1940, after which three-fifths of France became a puppet state of Germany. Many other states also shifted their allegiances during the war, often because neutral or pro-Allied governments, as in Norway, Denmark, the Netherlands, and Belgium, were overcome by invading Axis powers.

- ✔ **Allies:** Included Great Britain and the worldwide British Empire (notably British India), France (until June 1940), Vichy France (the part the Germans failed to conquer), Poland, the Soviet Union, Canada, Australia, South Africa, New Zealand, and later the United States, China, Cuba, the

Philippines, Guatemala, Nicaragua, the Dominican Republic, Honduras, Haiti, and more.

When Japan attacked the U.S. fleet in Hawaii in 1941, the U.S. was still officially neutral, although leaning toward Britain. Immediately after the attack, the Americans declared war on Japan and its Axis allies.

Assessing the war's damage

Ending in two atomic blasts, WWII killed 15 million military personnel — 2 million of them Soviet prisoners of war. About 6 million of the 35 million civilians killed were Jewish victims of the *Holocaust,* organized anti-Semite mass murders and concentration camps in Germany and Eastern Europe.

The weapons of this war grew faster, deadlier, and bigger than those in the previous war. Massive bombs devastated many European cities.

The Allied bombing of Dresden, Germany, in 1945 killed 80,000 civilians in a night. That was the work of hundreds of bombers, but later that year, on August 6, 1945, an American plane dropped a single bomb on Hiroshima, Japan, that demolished everything in a four-mile radius of where it went off. That atomic blast and a second atomic bomb dropped on Nagasaki, Japan, a few days later remain the only nuclear weapons ever used on people. The war ended soon after those atomic bombings.

Redrawing the map

World War II rearranged Europe much as World War I had done. Among the more dramatic changes after WWII, Germany emerged as two nations —West Germany, aligned with the U.S. and other Western powers; and East Germany, a satellite of the Soviet Union.

The war also brought profound changes to Asia and Africa, largely because of the way it drained power and money from the European colonial powers. Britain, on the winning side but nearly ruined, had neither resources nor will to maintain its remaining overseas holdings.

The years after WWII were big on independence movements. Britain withdrew from India in 1947, and France tried for almost two decades to hang onto Algeria before finally letting it go in 1962.

China, at war with Japan from 1937–1945 (Japan surrendered on that front, too), promptly plunged right back into a civil war between Nationalist and Communist parties. The Communists won, and under the Marxist leader Mao Ze-dong (or Tse-tung), the ancient civilization became the People's Republic of China on October 1, 1949.

Hot and Cold Running Conflicts

The years after World War II weren't peaceful, but they didn't erupt into World War III either (knock on wood). For much of the era, major world powers were preoccupied with a game of nuclear standoff.

The post-war major powers, by the way, turned out to be the U.S. and the Soviet Union. The U.S. expected to enjoy its nuclear monopoly for 20 years or more, but the Soviets surprised everyone by developing their own atomic bomb in 1949. Although they were allies on the winning side of WWII, the nations soon became bitter rivals.

Soviet foreign policy reflected Josef Stalin's viciously paranoid behavior toward any rival — real or imagined, internal or abroad (see more about Stalin in "Not really progress for the people" earlier in this chapter), and it became increasingly exclusionary and closed off. Soviet goals included maintaining control over satellite Communist states, several of which were set up in Soviet-controlled Eastern Europe in the wake of World War II, while keeping out foreign cultural and economic influences.

The U.S. emerged as leader of the West — meaning Western Europe, the Western Hemisphere, and developed nations anywhere that resisted communism and promoted (or at least permitted) the private pursuit of profit in their trade policies.

Daring each other to blink in the Cold War

With their nuclear arsenals, the Soviet Union and U.S. engaged in the *Cold War,* a diplomatic, political, and military standoff.

In diplomatic and military terms, the Cold War took the form of each side daring the other to fire the first nuclear shot. Both nations built increasingly more and increasingly bigger missiles and warheads that were capable of delivering a nuclear bomb from a Nebraska wheat field into downtown Moscow, for example. Both nations developed the ludicrously tragic ability to blow up the Earth several times over.

This madness was tempered a bit by a Nuclear Test Ban Treaty in 1963, numerous arms talks, and arms reduction agreements, but the two nations basically kept guns pointed at each other's heads until the economically ruined Soviet Union fell apart in 1991. Along the way, other countries built nuclear arsenals as well — China prominent among them.

Seeing no end to violent conflicts

Regional wars raged during the Cold War. Among them, the U.S. was embarrassed in a futile attempt to keep Vietnam, a former French colony in Southeast Asia, from going communist. During the 1980s, the Soviets failed to quash Muslim rebels in Afghanistan.

The 2007 drama *Charlie Wilson's War* is based on the true story of a Texas congressman who conspired with a CIA operative and a Houston socialite to supply weapons to Afghan rebels fighting the Soviets in Afghanistan.

When the Jewish state Israel was established in 1948 in what was British-ruled Palestine, surrounding Arab nations joined Palestinian Arabs in opposing it. The disagreement turned violent many times from the 1950s into the twenty-first century. These decades were also scarred by many terrorist bombings in the region — often motivated by support for the Palestinian cause — that killed many innocent civilians. Then in the 1990s, Iraq invaded neighboring Kuwait. A U.S.-led international force turned the Iraqis back.

On September 11, 2001, 19 extremist Muslim terrorists hijacked four American passenger jets to use as weapons. They crashed two planes into the World Trade Center in New York City, killing everyone onboard and thousands more in the twin skyscrapers, which were destroyed. A third plane crashed into the Pentagon, headquarters of the U.S. Department of Defense in Washington, D.C. All onboard that plane died, as did 125 people in the building. When they learned of the crashes in New York and D.C., passengers onboard the fourth jet attacked the hijackers flying their plane. It crashed in a field in Pennsylvania, killing all 40 people onboard.

The 2006 film *United 93* dramatizes the events onboard the United Airlines flight that crashed in Pennsylvania. It focuses on the heroism of the passengers who rebelled against the hijackers and ultimately prevented the loss of more lives by forcing the plane down in a remote area.

The U.S. responded to this slaughter — whose victims were overwhelmingly civilians — by invading Afghanistan, where a theocratic Muslim government called the *Taliban* had been harboring the terrorist organization behind the attacks, *Al Qaeda*. President George W. Bush adopted a hard-line stance against terrorism (and specifically against Islamic terrorists), and in 2003 he ordered an invasion of Iraq, although that country had not been involved in the attack on New York. In both Afghanistan and Iraq, U.S. troops ousted the reigning governments, but insurgent violence against U.S. troops and by rival groups among Afghans and Iraqis required long and costly military occupations.

After the breakup of the Soviet Union in 1991, Russia fought against an
Islamic independence movement in Chechnya, a region between the Black
and Caspian Seas. In the summer of 2008, war erupted between Russia and
the Republic of Georgia, another former part of the USSR.

Horrible violence also broke out in Africa, most shockingly in Rwanda, where
militias formed mostly of members of the Hutu majority conducted a geno-
cidal mass killing of members of the rival Tutsi tribe in 1994. Beginning in
2003 in Sudan, a government-supported militia, the Janjaweed, began a campaign of brutal attacks against farming villages, resulting in hundreds of thousands of civilians killed and many more displaced and starving.

Clearly, humanity has not come close to achieving a world without war.

Let's Get Together: The United Nations

So what happened to Woodrow Wilson's splendid, post-WWI idea of a League
of Nations (see "Reacting to the carnage" earlier) dedicated to preserving
international peace and security by promoting disarmament and intent on
preventing or quickly settling disputes?

Wilson's idea is still around. The term *United Nations* emerged during World
War II, when 26 nations pledged themselves to continue the fight against the
Axis Powers (primarily Germany, Italy, and Japan). After the war, 51 countries
signed a charter creating the United Nations (see Figure 9-2). The League of
Nations turned its functions over to the new UN.

The charter defines the UN as a world community of independent sovereign
states. It says that by preserving this community, the UN will protect international peace and will take collective action against war or against forces that
threaten war if necessary. By late 2008, the UN's membership total was up to
192 nations — many of them former colonies of European masters.

Some people see the UN as a plot to undermine the sovereignty of individual
nations. The UN has been less than effective in many of its attempts to keep
international conflicts from turning into wars, but it also has scored some
moderate successes. As it was with the League of Nations, this business of
internationalism is still new to humankind.

The UN may be beside the point as transportation and communication continue to accelerate. The world keeps shrinking, and political borders may
even blur in the future. Western European nations, for example, spent the last
decades of the twentieth century forging a unified economic force that even
shares a common currency, the *euro.* International trade agreements are
transforming global business and sparking fierce debates.

Figure 9-2:
The United
Nations
aims to
protect
international
peace.

With communications satellites and the Internet, every place is simultaneously in touch with the rest of the world. United Nations or not, national sovereignty may come to mean less and less as cultural intermingling speeds up. Civilization, whatever that funny word means, may finally become truly global. Whether or not that's a good thing remains to be seen.

Tracking the Centuries

1788: Britain establishes a penal colony in Australia.

1808: Napoleon puts his brother, Joseph Bonaparte, on Spain's throne.

1837: American Samuel Morse invents Morse code.

1848–1849: Revolutionary movements sweep Europe.

1890s: Germany's Kaiser Wilhelm II begins an aggressive shipbuilding campaign, alarming Britain, the world's top naval power.

1914: In Sarajevo, Bosnia, a Serbian terrorist assassinates the heir apparent to the Austro-Hungarian throne, triggering World War I.

1939: Germany invades Poland, beginning World War II.

1991: The government of the Union of Soviet Socialist Republics (USSR) collapses. Russia reemerges as an independent sovereign state.

2001: Islamic terrorists crash three hijacked airliners into iconic buildings in New York and Washington, D.C., killing thousands. A fourth hijacked plane crashes in Pennsylvania.

2003: The U.S. invades Iraq and deposes its ruling dictator, Saddam Hussein.

Part III
Seeking Answers

The 5th Wave   By Rich Tennant

The Reformation began in the 16th century after Martin Luther nailed his 95 Theses on the door of the Palast Church in Wittenberg Germany

©RICH TENNANT

95 Theses are nailed to the door
95 Theses are there.
If one of these Theses should happen to fall,
94 Theses are nailed to the wall.
94 Theses are nailed to the door,
94 Theses are there.
If one of these

In this part . . .

Religion and philosophy drove human societies long before the first cities arose. Religious differences sparked wars both ancient and modern. Spiritual fervor built empires. Much of history's greatest art expresses religious feeling. And the whiz-bang technological marvels that made the past 100 years so distinct from all the centuries that came before grew out of a scientific tradition founded in Greek philosophy more than 2,400 years ago; that philosophy was an effort to understand how the world's parts fit together and the place of human beings among them.

Trying to figure out reality — basic to religion and philosophy — led to writing down history. Looking back at the past is part of the impulse to make sense of it all.

Chapter 10

Religion through the Ages

• •

In This Chapter

▶ Recognizing the role of religion in history

▶ Placing gods at the center of creation — or not

▶ Seeing the world in spiritual terms

▶ Identifying the world's major religions

• •

*W*hat does religion have to do with history? Just about everything. Religious belief has both united societies and ripped them apart. Religion probably played a large and forceful role in creating civilization (see Chapter 4). Religious belief has also been a primary cause of wars, revolutions, explorations, and migrations. Some terrorists, such as those who attacked the United States on September 11, 2001, act in the name of religion. It shapes societies, because people live according to what they believe.

Civilizations were built around belief. For thousands of years, societies raised their rulers to divine status or thought of their royalty as human descendants of gods or mortal representatives of gods. Egyptians, at least as long ago as 2950 BC (that's 5,000 years ago) considered their kings to be deities. Alexander the Great (356–323 BC) declared himself a god. Rome bestowed divinity on Augustus (27 BC–14 AD), its first emperor (see Chapter 5). And in South America, the Incas of the fifteenth century AD worshipped their king as *Sapa Inca,* or Son of the Sun.

About 250 years ago, many Christians still thought that absolute monarchy was the right way for a godly society to be organized. (For more about *divine right of kings,* see Chapter 12.) They believed God wanted the world run that way.

To understand religion's impact on civilization, you need to first consider what religion is and where it may come from. In this chapter, I discuss the variety of forms a religion can take, introduce you to some major religions around the world, explain how each arose, and highlight some ways that each influenced social or political life.

Major religions have the most followers and play the biggest role in history. In this chapter, you'll find them arranged in a rough chronology.

For many people, religion is at the core of everything. It's the ultimate basis for determining right from wrong, good from evil, how to live in the world, and how to prepare for a world yet to come. If religion holds this level of importance for you, I assure you that nothing in this chapter is meant to challenge, undermine, or insult your beliefs. I try to examine each religion in this chapter objectively, which means I don't give one belief system preference over another. If the prospect of seeing your religion set side-by-side with other systems of belief and looked at as a piece of human history bothers you in any way, I encourage you to skip this chapter or any part that you suspect may offend you. If you find that I don't adequately explain the complex system of belief that is your religion, you're surely right. If I leave out your religion, you have my apologies. In either case, I mean no disrespect. I don't intend this chapter to be a complete guide to any religion or a comprehensive catalogue.

Defining Religion

No single definition could sum up the traditions, practices, and ideas lumped together under the general category *religion*. The word *religion* refers to publicly shared beliefs, privately held convictions, and ways that people express their faith. Worshipful customs such as regular churchgoing and daily prayer are part of it. So are dietary rules (as when Muslims fast for Ramadan) and modes of dress (such as an Orthodox Jew's skullcap, called a *yarmulke*). It also refers to rituals, from the simple lighting of a candle to human sacrifice. (The Aztecs, for example, used to slaughter thousands of captives at a time to feed their war god's blood lust.)

Divining the role of god (s)

Most religions are based on belief in a god or in multiple gods, but not all. Buddhism, for example, doesn't require a belief in gods, but rather concerns reincarnation and freeing the self from desire. Even where the belief in gods became a part of Buddhism, the gods aren't central to the religion.

Religions that require a belief in a god or gods — such as Judaism, Christianity, and Islam — are called *theistic* religions. Specifically, these three religions are *monotheistic,* meaning they're built on belief in a single all-powerful god. Other religions are *polytheistic* in that they embrace multiple gods. The religion of ancient Greece was polytheistic, for example. So was the Germanic-Norse religion that preceded Christianity in northern Europe.

Worshipping a supreme god

Many religions recognize a supreme god. Some polytheistic religions feature a sky god that reigns above all others. Others focus on an earth god or goddess.

In the old Germanic, or Norse, religion practiced in much of Europe before Christianity displaced it about 1,000 years ago, Odin (or Wodin) was the father god and the ruler of Valhalla (a supernatural drinking hall for dead warriors).

The Greeks' Zeus was a father god. In some later forms of Greek religion, Zeus became so supreme and powerful that he was worshipped as virtually the only god. Note that the Greek word *Zeus* resembles the Latin *Deus,* for the almighty Christian God.

Taking things a step beyond the father god ruling other gods, *monotheistic* (one-god) religions center on a single *true God,* forsaking other, false gods. The second of the Ten Commandments, central to Judaism and Christianity, is "Thou shalt have no other gods before me." The first part of the *shahada,* the Islamic profession of faith, is "There is no god but God."

Monotheistic religions often originate with, or are reinvigorated or reinvented by, an individual prophet who claims a direct relationship with God. Judaism, Christianity, and Islam all trace their roots to Abraham (also called Abram or Ibrahim). Sometime after 2000 BC, this patriarch moved his clan from the Mesopotamian city of Ur (in today's Iraq) to the promised land of Canaan (roughly today's Israel and the Palestinian territories).

Later leaders such as Moses, the lawgiver of Judaism and Christianity, and Mohammed the Prophet, founder of Islam, are in the tradition of Abraham. (See Chapter 19 for more about both men.)

Not all monotheistic visionaries fall into this Judaic-Christian-Islamic tradition, but religious ideas travel. In the fourteenth century BC, King Akhenaton of Egypt imposed monotheistic worship of the sun-disc god, Aton (or Atum), in place of traditional Egyptian polytheism. After his death, his successors went back to the old ways. Some people wonder if there was a link between this Egyptian fling with monotheism and other monotheistic movements, particularly Judaism.

Worshipping many gods

Many religions are polytheistic — the cultures that follow them worship a group of divine figures. Ancient Greek polytheism featured lustful, flawed, human-like gods such as Zeus (often depicted as a buff old guy with a big, fluffy beard) and his daughter Athena, the goddess of wisdom. Although the Greek religion arose separately from Egyptian polytheism, it adopted some Egyptian gods, such as the mysterious Isis.

The Romans adopted Greek polytheism, combining it with early Roman beliefs such as the worship of ancestors. (Many early religions required reverence for ancestors.) Rome renamed the gods, too. For example, Zeus became Jupiter, and Athena became Minerva.

Creation stories

Whether the inspiration was divine or earthly, early people told stories in an effort to understand nature's workings and explain how the world and its inhabitants came to be. Cultures everywhere have different ways of accounting for the beginning of the world. Folklorists call these stories *creation myths*. Somebody probably told the first one not long after language evolved (see Chapter 3 for the beginnings of language).

In the ancient Egyptian religion, for example, the creation story starts with a watery chaos called Nun, from which the sun god (Atum, or in his later manifestation, the hawk-headed Re) rose to bring forth air (Shu) and moisture (Tefnut), twin deities who combined to create earth (Geb) and sky (Nut). Geb and Nut also produced other gods.

Together, the characters in Greek-Roman theology are the *pantheon*. The gods in the pantheon are still widely known as literary characters. For example, they figure in the Greek poet Homer's epic poems (see Chapter 2). Because Homer told stories that were at least partly true, his poems are not just literature but also a source of rare early history about a real war between ancient Greeks and Trojans. So these gods are mixed into that early history, creating a dilemma for historians trying to winnow the facts from the myths.

Playwrights in the ancient world, poets of the European Renaissance, and later writers often based works on Greek and Roman myths and Homer's stories. Hollywood screenwriters still use these stories as inspiration. The Disney people took their shot at the pantheon in 1997's animated cartoon *Hercules,* a comic and sanitized treatment of the half-god strongman.

Projecting will on the physical world

Some thinkers wonder if the human tendency to project personalities on inanimate objects, especially among long-ago people eager to explain natural phenomena, may have brought about a form of religion called *animism*.

When my wife was a girl, her father drove a Dodge sedan that he named Brunhilde, after a Valkyrie — a mythical figure from the old Norse-Germanic religion. He called that car "she," and my wife continues to use the feminine pronoun when reminiscing about that car.

Did my wife, a science writer, and her father, a scientist, ever really think of Brunhilde as anything more than a machine? Not on a rational level, certainly. Yet human beings are often irrational. Who hasn't named a car or some other possession? Who hasn't thought or said in frustration that some inanimate object "wants" or "doesn't want" to do something? For example, a nail wants to bend rather than be pounded straight into the board, or a jar lid doesn't want to come loose. It doesn't mean you really attribute a will, let alone a soul, to the car, the nail, or the jar lid. Even if you did, you wouldn't worship these objects (unless the car is really expensive). Yet these examples illustrate the human habit of thinking about the world as if it were filled with personalities whose whims shape everyday life.

Seeking understanding through spirit

Prehistoric life was tough. The human ability to see cause and effect was a great survival tool, but it also raised questions. Early people saw patterns in herd migrations and the changing seasons. They recognized how vulnerable they were to forces beyond their control, such as floods and storms. Who wouldn't want to understand what made such things happen and take steps to appease nature and seek fate's favor?

Animism, occurring in cultures all over the world (from Native American to pre-Islamic Arab), is based on the ideas that rocks, trees, and animals have souls, and that these spirits influence events. Some late-nineteenth-century scholars — including the anthropologist Edward Taylor (1832–1917) — argued that animism was the earliest form of religion, and that other forms of religion sprang from it. More recent anthropologists reject Taylor's view as too simplistic. (That's too bad for people like me, who like to keep things simple.)

Connecting animals to deities

Simplistic or not, animism probably did give rise to the more discriminating practice of *totemism,* in which a particular animal or plant bears special significance for a clan or tribe. For example, some Australian Aborigine tribes have the kangaroo as a totem. The pioneering French sociologist Emile Durkheim (1858–1917) saw totems as a key element of primitive religions.

Ancient Egypt's religion (see Chapter 4) seems to have arisen from tribal beliefs that a certain animal represented a certain god. As Egyptian society developed, villages and regions adopted specific gods, which appear in paintings and carvings with human bodies and animal heads. The animal wasn't the god, but rather was sacred to the god. For example, the hawk was sacred to the sun god Re and the sky god Horus.

Analyzing the religious impulse

Scholarship sometimes looks at religions as purely human-made phenomena. Anthropologists, archeologists, and psychologists trace the religious impulse to the human need to understand or to the societal need for authority and an unassailable source of agreed-upon rules. Such theories rarely credit religious beliefs and customs as coming from a supernatural or transcendent truth.

Most religious people, on the other hand, would argue strongly that the god or gods they worship (or the transcendental reality they seek) existed before humans occupied the earth and will exist after humankind is gone. Religion, to most who embrace it, is a way to connect with and pay tribute to a power (or *the* power) greater than earthly existence.

Distinguishing philosophy from religion

Drawing a line between religions and philosophies (ways of explaining and coming to terms with existence; see Chapter 11) can be difficult. For example, the ancient Chinese philosopher widely known as Confucius taught a system of ethics based in responsible behavior and loyalty to family and society. He didn't advocate a religious creed, yet after his death in 479 BC, his teachings became the basis for a long-lasting religion. Sometimes Confucianism is considered a religion, and other times it's not.

Judaism

The roots of both Christianity and Islam are in early Judaism, which arose sometime after 2000 BC. The God of Abraham revealed himself to his chosen people through a series of prophets. His word is contained in the Hebrew Bible (Christians call it the Old Testament), especially in the first five books, the *Torah*. The Torah contains hundreds of commandments, including the central Ten Commandments delivered from God by the prophet Moses.

Awaiting a Messiah

Jews believe in Hebrew law, also called *Halakha*. This is the collective body of Jewish laws, including the Torah, which is contained in the first five books of the Hebrew Scriptures. They also observe Talmudic laws, which are civil and ceremonial rules arrived at long ago through discussions among high rabbis (Jewish religious scholars and teachers). Long-standing customs and traditions also come under the heading of Hebrew law. Central among Jewish beliefs are the ideas that the human condition can be improved and that a *Messiah* (Hebrew for "anointed one") will someday bring about a state of earthly paradise.

Modern Judaism contains groups that differ in the ways they interpret the Torah and the Talmud. Orthodox Jews view the Torah and its commandments as absolutely binding. Conservative Jews observe Hebrew law but allow for changes to accommodate modern life. Reform Jews concentrate mostly on the ethical content of the Torah and the Talmud rather than specific laws.

Maintaining Jewish nationalism

The tribal descendants of Abraham united under King Saul in the eleventh century BC to create the kingdom of Israel, which split in the late tenth century BC into the separate kingdoms of Israel and Judah (sometimes called Judaea). The land and its people later fell under the rule of others — notably the Seleucid Dynasty, the Syrians, the Romans, the Byzantine Empire, and the Seljuk Turks.

Throughout a long history, much of it chronicled in the Scriptures, Jews remained distinct from other people of the region, such as the Canaanites. Jews also spread to other parts of the world. In Europe, Jews were often victims of persecution by Christians. Anti-Semitism culminated in the 1930s and 1940s when the Nazi government of Germany rounded up millions of Jews — along with Roma (widely called Gypsies), homosexuals, and other "undesirables" — and shipped them to concentration camps, where they were systematically killed.

The beliefs that God promised Israel to Abraham and that God restored the homeland to Moses's followers after their slavery in Egypt have had a powerful influence on international relations, especially in the Middle East. The struggle to regain, keep, and control this homeland became part of the religion. The feast of Hanukkah, for example, commemorates the Jews' rededication of the temple at Jerusalem after a victory over the Syrians in 165 BC. The hilltop fortress Masada, where 400 Jewish revolutionaries committed suicide rather than surrender to the Romans in 73 AD, is an important symbol of Jewish solidarity.

The modern Zionist movement started in the late nineteenth century as an effort to return far-flung Jewish populations to the homeland. Beginning in 1917, Britain encouraged Jewish immigration to Palestine. After World War II, the British government referred the issue to the United Nations (see Chapter 9), which carved Israel's territory out of what was British-controlled Palestine, against the wishes of Palestinians. As a modern nation, Israel declared its independence in 1948.

By partitioning Palestine in 1948, the United Nations assured a chain of resentments and hatred between Israelis and Arabs, who in general support the cause of Palestinians displaced by the partition. That enmity brought a series of wars to the Middle East and deadly terrorist attacks on Israel and its allies, including the U.S. and Britain.

Director Otto Preminger's *Exodus,* filmed in 1960, was adapted from Leon Uris's best-selling novel about the founding of modern Israel and its first immigrants. It tells the intertwining stories of an Israeli freedom fighter and an American nurse, who meet as passengers onboard a ship called *The Exodus,* carrying Jewish survivors of the Nazi Holocaust to Palestine. The movie skips over moral issues in favor of action and romance.

Hinduism

Around 1700–1500 BC, nomads from the Iranian plateau filtered into India, bringing with them a culture and language that produced a profound and continuing effect on that part of the world.

The religion practiced by the nomads became the roots of *Hinduism.* Hindus believe that living beings are reincarnated repeatedly and that the form you take in the next life results from the quality of your actions in this life (your *karma*). Hindu sacred scriptures, the Veda, dating from about 1500 BC, contain hymns, chants, and monastic doctrine. Although Hinduism's polytheism supports numerous Hindu gods, chief among them are the trinity of Brahma the creator, Vishnu the preserver, and Shiva the destroyer. The war god Skanda, son of Shiva, is shown in Figure 10-1.

Traditional Hindu belief separates Indian society into castes, with priests, rulers, and warriors at the top and farmers and laborers at the bottom. Under the caste system, marriage outside your own caste is forbidden. Many modern Hindus have rejected the concept of caste even though it still colors social interaction among Hindus. Sects within the religion practice a wide range of rituals and hold diverse beliefs.

There are approximately 780 million followers of Hinduism worldwide; most are in India, where the religion survived many challenges. The Emperor Asoka established Buddhism as India's state religion in the third century BC, but after Asoka, Hindu beliefs rebounded and spread, withstanding the period from 1526–1857 when Muslims ruled most of India as the Mogul Empire. (Turn to Chapter 5 for more about Asoka.)

Religious disagreement often escalates into violent conflict in India, which is a diverse land of many languages and ways of life. For example, a Hindu extremist assassinated the nationalist leader Mahatma Gandhi in 1948, because Gandhi was trying to stop Hindu-Muslim conflict in the Indian state of Bengal. India's religious conflicts have grown into interregional and even international disputes. For example, the country of Pakistan was carved out of India in 1947 as a separate homeland for India's Muslim minority. Both countries now possess nuclear arms aimed at each other.

Figure 10-1:
The Hindu god Skanda is often depicted atop a peacock clutching a cobra.

Buddhism

Siddhartha Gautama, a prince from southern Nepal, achieved enlightenment in the late sixth century BC by meditation in the tradition of Hinduism. He gathered a community of monks to carry on his teachings, which are built on the law of karma, a concept adapted from Hindu belief, and on the *Four Noble Truths.*

The law of karma says that good and evil deeds result in appropriate reward or punishment in this life or in a succession of rebirths on a path toward *Nirvana,* or "the blowing out of the fires of all desires." The Four Noble Truths are as follows:

- ✔ Existence is a realm of suffering.
- ✔ Desire and belief in the importance of one's self cause suffering.
- ✔ Achievement of Nirvana ends suffering.
- ✔ Nirvana is attained only by meditation and following the righteous path in action, thought, and attitude.

Buddhism has two main traditions. The first, *Theravada,* follows the teachings of the early Buddhist writings. In the more-liberal second tradition, *Mahayana,* salvation is easier to attain. Other schools include Zen Buddhism, Lamaism, Tendai, Nichiren, and Soka Gakkai.

In the third century BC, the Indian king Asoka made Buddhism his official state religion. He adopted a policy of *dharma* (principles of right life) and stopped waging war. This is a rare instance of a religious principle overcoming dynastic ambition. Buddhism has not always had such a calming influence on the politically ambitious. The fourteenth-century AD Chinese emperor Chu Yuan-chang started out as a Buddhist monk, but he fought his way to power and used brutal violence to discourage dissent.

Christianity

Early in the first century AD, a carpenter, Jesus of Nazareth, traveled through the Roman vassal state of Judaea (today's Israel and the Palestinian territories) teaching a philosophy of mercy and God's redeeming love. His sermons and his reputed ability to heal the sick made him so popular that local leaders thought he threatened their authority and arranged to have him nailed to a wooden cross — the painful Roman method for executing criminals.

Christians believe that three days after he died, Jesus left his tomb, and after revealing himself to his followers, he rose bodily, straight into Heaven. He's considered the Messiah, as promised in the Hebrew Bible (which Christians call the Old Testament). Jesus is also seen as both God's son and God in human form — ideas hammered out in early theological debates within the Church (see Chapter 12). To Christians, his death is an act of God's love to save believers from eternal condemnation in Hell. Jesus was bestowed the title *Christ,* from the Greek for "savior."

Four of Jesus's 12 disciples, who were called the *Apostles,* told of his words and deeds in the Gospels, which make up a major part of the New Testament. The Old Testament and the New Testament together comprise the Christian Bible.

At first considered a heretic sect of Judaism, Christianity grew into one of the most powerful religious, philosophical, and political influences in history.

The Roman Catholic Church

After Jesus died, a number of his Apostles continued to preach his message and to organize converts into early Christian congregations. Paul, an early Jewish convert, was especially enthusiastic about spreading the new Christian faith to *gentiles* (non-Jews) and taught that believers didn't need to abide by Hebrew dietary restrictions and other requirements such as male circumcision.

Fantasizing on faith

In 1988's *The Last Temptation of Christ,* Jesus contemplates the lure of normal, mortal life. Willem Dafoe plays the title character in this adaptation of a novel by Nikos Kazantzakis.

The film depicts a Christ so fully human that human trivialities such as pain and sexuality threaten to distract him from his purpose. An angel shows Jesus, already on the cross,

a vision of an earthly existence as a husband and father, giving him the choice of rejecting his own godhood.

Kazantzakis's concept, interpreted by director Martin Scorsese, offended many Christians. Protesters marched outside cinemas where the movie was shown, and some theaters refused to book it.

Others among Jesus's first followers also delivered their teachings to gentiles. For example, tradition says that the Apostle James traveled to Spain and that the Apostle Peter, toward the end of his life, established a Christian congregation in Rome, where he died a martyr's death.

Historians can't confirm that Peter lived or preached on the Italian peninsula, but the Catholic Church credits him as the first bishop of Rome, which would make him the first pope. The Church came to be based in Rome, where the successive popes (from the Latin *papa,* meaning "dad") have been honored as Peter's successors and representatives of God on earth.

Becoming "the Church"

Until the Protestant Reformation (discussed later in this chapter and in Chapter 14), the Roman Catholic Church was just *the Church* — at least in Europe. Spelled with a lowercase c, *catholic* means "universal" or "wide-ranging." The Roman Catholic Church was everybody's church.

Roman Catholic doctrine (see Chapter 12) centers on the *Holy Trinity,* in which one God takes the form of three persons: God the Father, God the Son (Jesus), and God the Holy Spirit. Catholics also honor Jesus's mother, St. Mary, believed to have been a virgin when she miraculously gave birth. (*Saints* are human beings whose exemplary lives bring about God's miracles and whose virtue, as confirmed by the Church, accords them blessed status.)

Although several Roman emperors persecuted Christians, Emperor Constantine the Great did an about-face in the fourth century AD and not only ordered the toleration of Christianity but also made the Church both wealthy and powerful. (You can find more about Constantine in Chapter 5.)

Being a unifying force

After the fall of the Western Roman Empire in the fifth century AD (see Chapters 5 and 6), the Church remained the main civilizing, unifying force in Europe, which was also called *Christendom*.

Kings claimed their authority as a right granted by the Christian God. The pope was a political as well as spiritual leader. Pope Leo III (later St. Leo) crowned the Frankish king Charlemagne as Emperor of the West (or Holy Roman Emperor) in 800 AD.

Pope Urban II's clout began the Crusades when he called for the liberation of the Holy Lands (today's Israel and the Palestinian territories) from Turkish control in 1095 (see Chapter 7).

Facing dissent and departures

Not everybody agreed, however, on whether a king answered directly to God or to the pope. This debate brought on centuries of power struggles. In twelfth-century England, this disagreement led Henry II's soldiers to murder the Archbishop of Canterbury — a public relations disaster for the king. King Henry denied ordering the hit, but he had complained about the archbishop, Thomas Becket, who was also his former chancellor. The king wished aloud to be rid of the "turbulent priest."

Sometimes disputes arose about who was the rightful pope. When the Holy Roman Emperor Frederick I disagreed with the choice of Orlando (or Roland) Bandinelli to become Pope Alexander III in 1159, Fred simply appointed his own alternative. Then he appointed another and another — the *anti-popes*. Victor IV, Paschal III, Calistus III, and Innocent III all called themselves pope, but Rome denied them.

Power struggles between the Church and national rulers fueled the Protestant Reformation of the sixteenth century. The Reformation brought Protestant versus Catholic military struggles, the biggest being the Thirty Years' War. It started in 1618 when Protestants in Bohemia, part of the Holy Roman Empire, tried to appoint a Protestant king. Spain plunged into that war on the Catholic side, but as if to show that religious wars are often about things other than religion, Catholic France joined the fight on the Protestant side. (The French were nervous about the Catholic Hapsburg family, who ruled both Spain and the Holy Roman Empire, getting too powerful.)

Some nominally Protestant-Catholic conflicts raged much later. One especially bitter struggle, which frequently sparked violence over the two decades after the formation of the Provisional Irish Republican Army in 1969, centered on whether Northern Ireland, where the majority of people are Protestant, should remain a part of Great Britain or join the Republic of Ireland, a Catholic democracy.

Instigating the Inquisition

Before a German priest named Martin Luther touched off the Reformation in 1517 (see Chapter 14), Church officials tried to deal with the widespread and growing perception among Europeans that priests and monks had become corrupt, lazy, and arrogant. Some cardinals and bishops tried to root out unfit priests; reform efforts had little success, except in Spain, which faced different challenges than most of Europe and came up with a rather more rigorous solution.

The Moors, who were Muslim, ruled Spain for hundreds of years. Christians took over the last of Spain's Muslim kingdoms in 1492, the same year that Christopher Columbus set sail. Many Jews lived in Spain, too. The Moors of that time were more tolerant toward Jews than European Christians were, so Jews liked it there.

With the Moors out of power, however, and Catholicism restored as the state religion, Muslims and Jews were stuck. They could get out of the country, adopt Christianity, or risk being killed. Many converted, but they were tepid Christians at best. Most hated the Church and everything it stood for, practicing their own religions in secret.

Spanish Christians worried that these *new* Christians would revolt if Moors from North Africa or Muslim Turks from the east attacked. Church officials also worried about the new Christians' resentment undermining priestly authority. To alleviate these fears, the monarchs Ferdinand and Isabella (see Chapter 19) started the *Spanish Inquisition,* a campaign to root out, expose, and punish heresy. The Inquisition gained a reputation for thoroughness, even-handedness (commoners, nobles, and churchmen were all vulnerable), and unspeakable cruelty. Operating in secret, using anonymous informers, and making arrests by night, the Inquisition employed solitary confinement and torture to force confessions.

Sentencing was public, however; it involved a gaudy ceremony called an *auto-da-fé,* with prisoners dressed in special gowns called *sanbenitos.* Punishments ranged from fines to flogging to death. These tactics and punishments weren't unusual for the time. The Inquisition was actually less cruel than many civil courts, prohibiting torture that did permanent physical damage and requiring that a physician be present. Convicts burned at the stake had to be dead first, usually strangled.

Still, the Inquisition was feared. Foreign sailors dreaded an arrest in Spain for smuggling or piracy, certain that they would be turned over to the Inquisition. They spread stories about its horrors.

During the Inquisition, the Church in Spain tightened up its operations; lazy and corrupt priests, monks, and even bishops got the heave-ho. By the time the Reformation arrived, Spain was not fertile ground for northern ideas. The Inquisition made short work of the few people tempted by Protestantism. And just to make sure, the Inquisition kept out ideas considered dangerous by banning foreign books and prohibiting Spaniards from attending foreign universities. The restrictions worked, and Lutheran and Calvinist ideas never gained ground on the Iberian Peninsula.

Maintaining continuity

The Church remained a major civil influence in solidly Catholic countries and their territories in the sixteenth century and remains powerful in some countries today. Priests, who were among the first Spaniards in many parts of the New World, built missions and converted the Indians, establishing Catholicism as the majority religion throughout most of Latin America.

The Catholic Church still exerts political influence. Its laws have long influenced civil law, especially on moral issues such as divorce and birth control. Some dealings in political affairs, however, are contrary to Vatican policy. For example, in the twentieth century, the Roman Catholic Church rebuked South American priests for teaching liberation theology and taking part in popular political movements.

The Eastern Orthodox Church

Constantine the Great made Christianity the state religion of the Roman Empire, but he built his new Christian imperial capital far to the east of Rome, at Byzantium (today's Istanbul). This new city (renamed for its founder as Constantinople) was a center of Christianity in its own right, especially after the Western Roman Empire collapsed (see Chapter 5).

Rome's Church had less and less influence over the Eastern faithful between the fifth and the eleventh centuries. And when Roman Catholic crusaders sacked Orthodox Christian Constantinople in 1204, it showed how alienated from one another the two branches of Christianity had become. (For more about the Crusades, turn to Chapter 8.)

The Eastern Orthodox Church evolved into a communion of self-governing churches in Eastern Europe, Greece, Ukraine, Russia, Georgia, and the Middle East. To this day, practitioners honor the leadership of the patriarch of Constantinople, but they don't hold him supreme, as Roman Catholics do the pope. Orthodox doctrine looks to the scriptures as the source of Christian truth and rejects points of doctrine developed by Church fathers in Rome. Much of the estrangement between the Eastern and Roman churches began in disagreements over basic questions about the nature of God and the relationship between Jesus and God the Father. Orthodox worship places particular emphasis on the Holy Spirit within the Trinity.

The Orthodox Church suffered a serious blow in 1453 when the Ottoman Turks conquered Constantinople. The city became Islamic, and its name was changed to Istanbul. The Turks turned its magnificent domed church, Hagia Sophia, into a mosque. Now it's a museum.

Grand Prince Vladimir established the Russian Orthodox Church as part of the international community of Eastern Orthodox Christianity in 988 AD. The Russian Orthodox Church remained Russia's state religion until the Revolution of 1917 (see Chapter 9). Communist officials restricted worship and persecuted worshippers through most of the twentieth century, but the church endured and began to rebuild itself after the Soviet Union collapsed in 1991.

Relations between the Orthodox churches (which have 218 million members worldwide) and Roman Catholicism began to improve in the later decades of the twentieth century.

The Protestant churches

Protestant is a broad and imprecise term applied to a wide range of churches, most of them offshoots of the Roman Catholic Church or earlier Protestant churches. Unlike Catholics, Protestants don't look to the pope as the ultimate authority on issues of faith.

The word *Protestant* is related in meaning to *protester.* At first, *Protestant* applied to a group of sixteenth-century German princes siding with the breakaway priest Martin Luther. These princes protested efforts by other German leaders to force them and their subjects back into the Roman Church's fold.

The whole Protestant Reformation started with an individual act of protest. Luther, a university professor as well as a priest, didn't like the Archbishop of Mainz (in Germany) raising money by sending a friar around to cities and towns selling indulgences. An *indulgence* was a sort of pass that Christians could buy to get themselves into Heaven without so much suffering.

If you think that's a gross oversimplification of what an indulgence was, you're right, and you can find more about indulgences (simplified a little less grossly) in Chapter 14. The point is, however, that Luther thought the practice was wrong. He wrote down almost 100 reasons why he disagreed with the archbishop and the friar, and he stuck the paper to the door of the church in Wittenberg on October 31, 1517. The list is called the *95 Theses* (arguments), and its posting is considered the start of the Reformation.

The Reformation soon involved Frederick, the Elector of Saxony (who started the University of Wittenberg and thus was Professor Luther's protective boss) and Charles V, the Holy Roman Emperor. The Reformation would quickly touch other kings, nobles, churchmen, and commoners in ways that Luther never could have imagined. Even England, a country where the king was so fiercely anti-Lutheran that the pope named him Defender of the Faith, became Protestant as that same king (Henry VIII) named himself head of a church that no longer answered to Rome.

A few of the major Protestant denominations are

- Lutheran (of course)
- Baptist
- Church of Christ
- Church of England and affiliated Episcopalian churches
- The Reformed Church (an ideological heir to the French moral reformer John Calvin — see Chapter 14)
- Methodist
- Presbyterian
- Quaker

Many of these denominations have subgroups, such as the Southern Baptists and the Evangelical Lutheran Church in America (ELCA).

In the twenty-first century, many Protestants worship as part of what are called non-denominational congregations; they're unaffiliated with any of the denominations listed here but often are part of a widespread evangelical movement. One sense of the word *evangelical* is a synonym for *Protestant,* but the word is often reserved for fundamentalist-style Christianity.

Protestant churches are prominent social forces. In U.S. politics, for example, fundamentalist preachers have gone so far as to endorse candidates and lobby on social and moral issues. Ironically, these Protestants sometimes find that their closest ideological allies — especially on issues such as legalized abortion (which they oppose) — are Catholics.

Islam

Exploding out of Arabia in the seventh and early eighth centuries AD, *Islam* was at once a spiritual, political, and military movement. The founder of the faith was Mohammed (often written Muhammad or any of several other spellings).

He grew from a religious visionary to a lawgiver, judge, military general, and ruler before his death in 632 AD. (You can find out more about him in Chapters 6 and 19.)

The Five Pillars

Islam means "submission to God." Followers worship through the following Five Pillars:

- ✔ **The shahada, or profession of faith: "There is no god but God, and Mohammed is his Prophet."**
- ✔ **The salat, or formal prayer, performed five times a day while facing Mecca.**
- ✔ **Zakat, which is purification achieved through sharing wealth by giving alms.**
- ✔ **Saum, which is fasting during the holy month of Ramadan.**
- ✔ **Hajj, which is the pilgrimage to Mecca (Mohammed's birthplace and now the capital of the Hejaz region of Saudi Arabia).**

Going beyond Mecca and Medina

Rising out of Mecca, where Mohammed, then a merchant, received the holy vision that commanded him to preach "the true religion," Islam spread quickly during Mohammed's lifetime. When officials in Mecca threw Mohammed out, he built a power base 200 miles north in Medina. He later returned and took Mecca by force.

Mohammed's followers united most of the Arabic-speaking peoples behind this new faith in only a few decades, but there was some resistance and back-lash from Arab tribes that initially accepted and then renounced Islam. This turnaround resulted in *Jihad,* or holy struggle, to restore the faith by force.

That Jihad gathered huge momentum over the century after the prophet's death, sweeping far beyond the traditional Arab lands. Muslims believe that individuals, societies, and governments should all be obedient to the will of God set forth in the holy book, the Koran. The Muslim warriors who waged Jihad were sure that if they died honorably while fighting for Allah they would get into paradise right away and reap special heavenly rewards. Their fervor was hard to defend against, especially as the Persian and Byzantine Empires were in decline.

The conquests led to an Arab Empire that, at its height, stretched from Spain to the Indus Valley in northwest India. (See Chapter 6 for more about the Arab conquests.) However, the Arab Empire splintered into smaller Islamic kingdoms and empires. Although Arab political unity disintegrated, Islamic beliefs and law maintained a cultural common thread among Muslim countries.

Clashing cultures

Early on, Muslims were rather tolerant toward other religions, especially Judaism and Christianity, because of the kinship between the three faiths. (Muslims see Mohammed as the ultimate prophet in a line of God's prophets that began with Abraham, continued through Moses, and included Jesus.) In Syria and Egypt, the Arab conquerors let Christians and Jews keep their faiths as *dhimmi,* or protected peoples, although they had to pay a tax for the privilege.

Enmity between the Islamic, Jewish, and Christian faiths developed over centuries. The Crusades, which began in the eleventh century as European Christian attacks on the Islamic Seljuk Turk rulers of Palestine, left deep bitterness. So did territorial clashes as Christians struggled to take Spain away from its Muslim rulers, the Moors. The Ottoman Turks, also Muslim, clashed for centuries with Christians over territory in Eastern Europe.

Turks were among many non-Arab peoples who embraced Islam, which also spread among non-Arab people in Africa, East Asia, and Southeast Asia. Indonesia is the most populous of the predominantly Muslim countries today. It also has been the site of violent clashes between Muslim and Christian groups.

As Islam spread, sects arose. The two largest groups within the faith are the Sunni Muslims, who are the vast majority, and the Shiite Muslims.

- **Sunni Muslims:** The Sunnis believe that correct religious guidance derives from the *sunna* (teachings) of Mohammed. They recognize the first four *caliphs* (spiritual leaders) of the Arab Empire as Mohammed's legitimate successors. They also believe that a just government can be established on the basis of correct Islamic practice.

- **Shiite Muslims:** The Shiites, which account for about 10 percent of Muslims, believe that only descendants of Mohammed's family are the legitimate leaders of the faith. They recognize only the line of Ali, the fourth caliph and nephew and son-in-law of Mohammed, as the prophet's legitimate successors.

Among the subgroups of Shiites, the Imamis are the largest. Found in Iran, where Shiism is the state religion, the Imamis believe in 12 *imams*, charismatic leaders who were infallible sources of spiritual and worldly guidance. Because the last of these imams disappeared in the ninth century, the Imamis believe that holy men called *ayatollahs* are in charge until the twelfth *imam* returns.

Much of the fractious politics of the region called the Balkans, in southeastern Europe, results from religious differences. In one late-twentieth-century flare-up, Serbian (mostly Orthodox Christian) troops drove Albanian (mostly Sunni Muslim) civilians from their homes, killing many in the process and briefly depopulating much of the province of Kosovo.

Muslim-Jewish enmity caught fire in modern times after the United Nations carved up Palestine to create the new nation of Israel in 1948, displacing natives (both Muslim and Christian) and outraging the Arab world.

Islamic fervor also has fed rebellions against the Soviet Union in Afghanistan and against post-Soviet Russia in Chechnya. Pan-Islamic activists, who believe that Muslim identity overrides national borders, have aided these rebellions. Some of these same activists formed the terrorist organization *Al Qaeda*, which orchestrated 2001 attacks on the World Trade Center in New York and the Pentagon in Arlington, Virginia. Al Qaeda was based in post-Soviet Afghanistan, which at the time was ruled by a militia called the *Taliban* (meaning "students"). The Taliban was made up of extremist Sunni Muslims. In response to the attacks, the U.S. invaded Afghanistan and deposed the Taliban government.

Shiite revolt brought about the Iranian Revolution of 1978 and 1979. Opposed to what they saw as its Western decadence, Iranians overturned the government of their monarch, Shah Mohammad Reza Pahlavi, while he was in the U.S. for medical treatment. Demanding that the U.S. government return him to face punishment, the revolutionaries occupied the U.S. embassy in Iran and held many of its staff hostage for over a year.

Extremists — whether Shiite or Sunni — make up only an infinitesimally small, if attention-getting, fraction of the more than 1.3 billion Muslims worldwide.

Sikhism

Founded around 1500, *Sikhism* combines aspects of Hinduism and Islam into what's called the religion of the gurus. Sikhs seek union with God through worship and service.

The Guru Nanak, Hindu by birth and upbringing, was an Indian seeker of spiritual truth who gathered his followers in Kartarpur, Punjab. Nanak wanted to unite Islam with the ancient Brahmanism that was part of the Indian Hindu tradition. He also held *pantheistic* beliefs, which means he thought God and the universe are one — an idea found in Hinduism and some sects of Buddhism.

In the doctrine of Sikhism, as laid out in the *Adi-Granth,* its sacred scripture, God is the true guru. He has spoken to humanity though ten historical gurus, the first being Nanak. The last of these died in 1708, leaving the Sikh community at large to serve as guru.

Sikhs established their own kingdom in Punjab in the eighteenth century and fought fiercely in two closely spaced wars between 1845 and 1849 to prevent British conquest of the region. The Sikhs lost that struggle but maintained their devotion to the idea of a Sikh-ruled Punjab. In 1947, Punjab was partitioned between newly independent India, with its Hindu majority, and the newly created Muslim-majority country of Pakistan. Since then, activist Sikhs have continued to call for Punjab independence.

In 1984, a Sikh separatist militant group occupied the Golden Temple, Sikhism's holiest shrine, in the city of Amritsar in the Indian part of Punjab. India's prime minister, Indira Gandhi, ordered army troops to clear the shrine of the activists, resulting in an armed battle estimated to have killed hundreds of militants and as many as 3,000 others, most of them Sikh. The month after this disaster, two of Gandhi's bodyguards, both of them Sikh, assassinated the prime minister.

Tracking the Centuries

1700–1500 BC: Nomads from the Iranian plateau arrive in India, bringing with them the roots of Hindu religious belief.

Eleventh century BC: Tribes descended from the patriarch Abraham unite under King Saul to create the kingdom of Israel.

Third century BC: Asoka, king of India, makes Buddhism his official state religion. He adopts a policy of *dharma* (principles of right life) and stops conducting wars of conquest against neighboring countries.

About 33 AD: At the request of local Jewish leaders, Roman authorities arrest Jesus of Nazareth. He's sentenced to death and nailed to a cross where he hangs until pronounced dead.

313 AD: Roman co-emperors Constantine (Emperor of the West) and Licinius (Emperor of the East) jointly issue the Edict of Milan, recognizing Christianity and extending tolerance to its followers.

About 610 AD: The Prophet Mohammed begins teaching "submission to God," or Islam.

About 1500: In Kartarpur, Punjab, the Guru Nanak seeks to unite ancient brahmanism, part of the Hindu tradition, with Islam. He founds the Sikh religion.

October 31, 1517: Martin Luther, a German priest and university professor, nails his 95 Theses to a church door, protesting the clerical practice of selling indulgences.

1948: The United Nations carves a new Jewish homeland, the modern nation of Israel, out of what was British-controlled Palestine.

September 11, 2001: Muslim extremists belonging to the terrorist organization Al Qaeda hijack four American airliners and succeed in crashing three of them, passengers and all, into U.S. targets. The fourth also crashes, killing all onboard.

Chapter 11

Loving Wisdom: The Rise and Reach of Philosophy

*P*hilosophy often gets dismissed as mind games — idle speculations cooked up by eccentrics with overactive imaginations. If that's all philosophy were, you wouldn't have to take it into account when considering history. But philosophy keeps bumping into history by getting into religion, politics, and government and influencing how people conduct their lives. Therefore, any overview of world history includes looking at philosophy and where it comes from.

Traditionally, philosophy is thought to come from the ancient Greeks, although they probably picked up on earlier cultures' philosophical traditions. Wherever they got their inspiration, the Greeks — a culture of thinkers and talkers — made the most of it.

Asking the Big Questions

Philosophy can sound wild, especially when you ponder what the guys trying to practice it more than 2,500 years ago had to say. But they were doing the best they could with the knowledge and tools they had. And most of what they wrote has been lost, which makes it difficult for history to give them a fair shake.

For example, Thales, who was born about 625 BC, said the world floated on water. He also seemed to think that everything was made of water. Actually, he just could have been impressed by how much water there was.

What Thales was talking about with regard to everything being made of water isn't clear. No complete texts of philosophical works from that far back survive. However, it seems that Thales and the philosophers following him — proposing such things as air and fire and the infinite as the basis of all matter — were thinking about a reality based on observable phenomena.

What exactly do philosophers do? They tackle the big questions, which include the following:

- What is the world?
- Who am I?
- What am I doing here?
- Does reality consist of what people see and experience?
- If not, what is reality?
- What does it mean?

Founding science in philosophy

Today's scientists answer questions *empirically,* or based on physical evidence. But before modern scientific methods, scientists were philosophers: They asked questions and thought about possible answers without hard data to back them up.

In Greece almost 3,000 years ago, few tools were available for conducting scientific experiments. Thales couldn't take samples of water, marble, fingernail clippings, and olive oil and run tests that would show him that they *weren't* all forms of the same thing. So, scientist philosophers did the best they could in formulating theories that seemed to explain the world they observed.

Testing a theory but blowing the methodology

Unlike some early philosophers, Anaximenes, who came along a bit later than Thales (Anaximenes died around 500 BC), conducted experiments. They were flawed experiments, but they had an inkling of scientific method about them.

Anaximenes thought everything was made of air, which could transform into other matter by compression or expansion. He decided clouds were made of condensed air on its way to becoming more condensed. At a certain point, it would become so condensed that it would turn into water. Even more tightly compressed air, he thought, became mud, earth, and stone — in that order. Fire, he said, was extremely rarified air.

Anaximenes thought he had good evidence for his theory in that when you purse your lips and blow, a compressed stream of air comes out cold. If you open your mouth wide and breathe out, the air — now rarified rather than condensed — feels hot. Presumably, by extension, if you could open your mouth really, really wide, you could breathe out fire.

Diverging disciplines

As thinkers figured out more and better ways to test, prove, or disprove their theories about the physical world, sciences split off from philosophy. Philosophers continued to ask questions about the nature of being (called *metaphysics*), the nature of knowledge (called *epistemology*), ethics, and morals; they asked questions that couldn't be satisfactorily answered by experiments.

Yet despite this split, philosophy and science overlapped in many ways. Until the 1840s, scientists were called *natural philosophers*.

Mixing philosophy and religion

Just as philosophy and science intermingled, so did philosophy and religion — as they still do. What do I mean by *religion?* It often means much the same as philosophy — a way of understanding reality. Religion includes publicly shared beliefs, private convictions, and ways that people express faith. The Greek religion focused on a group of gods, the *pantheon,* who behaved much as human beings do, but who existed in a supernatural realm that interacted with and affected mortal affairs.

Early philosophers apparently weren't content with taking creation myths and Greek *polytheism* (the worship of many gods) at face value. However, that doesn't mean they rejected religion, as evidenced by these examples:

- ✔ One early Greek philosopher, Pythagoras (about 560–480 BC), founded a religious community and preached about the transmigration of souls. His followers said he was the son of the god Apollo and that he could appear in two places at once.

- ✔ Xenophanes, a philosopher born around 580 BC, opposed *anthropomorphic* gods (gods who look and act like people) and polytheism, yet he described a god that he called "the greatest amongst gods and men."

- ✔ Legend says that Empedocles, who thought the universe was made of four elements (fire, air, water, and earth), claimed to be a god himself. To prove it, he jumped into a live volcano.

Greeks, and later Romans, worshipped the gods of their pantheon for century after century while philosophical arguments rose, fell out of favor, and rose again. Plotinus, a Greek from Egypt who moved to Rome in 224 AD, mixed popular myths together with the ideas of Plato (discussed later in this chapter). Plato, who lived 500 years before Plotinus, said that the world as people experience it is made of imperfect, temporary reflections of perfect, eternal *Ideas,* or forms. Plotinus also stirred in bits from Aristotle, the Stoics, and the Pythagoreans and came up with *Neoplatonism,* a school of thought that flourished for a millennium and came back in new Christian forms in the four-teenth and fifteenth centuries.

Tracing Philosophy's Roots

Greeks weren't the first to ask basic questions. Supernatural creation stories (see Chapter 10) addressed some of the same things that the first philoso-phers wondered about: What is the world made of? What are the sun and the moon? What is humankind's place in nature? Philosophy arose among the Greeks less than 3,000 years ago, yet complex sophisticated civilizations existed long before that, as I explain in Chapters 2 and 4.

Some scholars argue that the Greeks built on a tradition of inquiry that came from the ancient Hindus. In the sixth century BC, an Indian philosopher known as Ajita of the Hair Blanket (catchy name, huh?) said the world con-sisted of four elements: earth, air, fire, and water. More than a century later, a Greek named Empedocles said the same thing. Usually, Empedocles gets credit for thinking up this idea, but nobody knows whether a predecessor influenced him. In the fifth century BC, the Greek Leucippus argued that the world is made up of tiny particles, or atoms. But Pakudha Kacchayana, an Indian of the sixth century BC, walked that path first.

Sumer and Babylon, both in Mesopotamia, had traditions of literacy that long predated the Greeks. So did Persia. Some scholars point to Africa as the original source of intellectual inquiry. The problem with these claims is that there's no proof. Clues, however, indicate that Greek philosophy benefited from cultural crosscurrents. For example, the first Greek philosophers didn't live in Greece.

Living on the edges of Greek society

Greeks were colonizers. As they sailed around the Aegean Sea and beyond into the wider Mediterranean, they liked to settle and establish city-states like the ones back home. Their colonies produced the Greeks' earliest hot-shot thinkers.

Pythagoras was born on an island off the coast of Turkey and moved to Italy. Thales, his student Anaximander, and the younger Anaximenes are called the *Milesians* or the *Ionians,* because they lived in Miletus, a city-state in Greek Asia. (That part of the world — in present-day Turkey — was called Ionia.) Xenophanes lived in Colophon, near present-day Izmir, Turkey.

Drawing inspiration from other cultures

You may think of the Greeks of the fifth century BC as an early culture. But they looked back on an honored past embodied in the works of their poets — especially Homer. Greeks held a traditional regard for wisdom (their word for it was *sophia*) and for skill with words. They also had a tradition of considering what is right and moral and questioning how society should function.

Greeks living on the frontiers of their culture may have found their traditions stimulated by the scholarship of other cultures. For example, Babylonians studied the stars and planets for centuries. Also, writings from Persia and probably Egypt — considerations of natural phenomena such as tides and stars and human inventions, such as mathematics — circulated among the learned in Greek society. Some modern scholars say that when the Greeks got their hands on Babylonian astronomy and started talking about the stars as natural phenomena rather than supernatural personalities, *science* began.

Traveling broadens the mind

Thales, a philosopher of the seventh century BC (who was fascinated by water), made at least one visit to Egypt and came up with a way to measure the height of the Great Pyramid. Standing next to the pyramid as the sun rose in the sky, he watched his own shadow. When his shadow exactly matched his own height, he hurried to mark the length of the pyramid's shadow. By measuring the shadow, he determined the pyramid's height. Was this novel thinking on Thales's part, or did an Egyptian surveyor teach it to him?

Living where they did, Thales and his progeny could have seen Indian poetry or accessed Sumerian texts. Could these guys have just taken older Eastern or African ways of looking at the world and talked them up among their fellow Greeks? Nobody knows for sure.

Examining Eastern Philosophies

China developed philosophical traditions around the same time that the Greeks were creating a name for themselves in the field. Chinese philosophies had a widespread impact throughout East Asia.

Confucius and Lao-tzu, China's most famous early philosophers, were roughly contemporaries of Anaximenes of Miletus (there's more about him in the earlier section "Testing a theory but blowing the methodology"). The teachings of both Chinese philosophers grew into traditions that came to be considered religious as much as philosophical.

- ✔ **Confucians stress the importance of cultural heritage, family, and society.**
- ✔ **Taoists look to the natural world and its underlying path, or** *way,* **as the route to peace.**

Also in China, the *School of Names* liked to twist concepts around and play with paradoxes. This group of philosophers theorized that if you took a stick and cut it in half every day, you would never use it all up, because half of any length, no matter how short, is still not zero. This thinking corresponded with the ideas of a fifth-century-BC Greek, Zeno of Elea, who said that to run any distance you must first run half that distance. To run that half-distance, you must first run one-quarter the total distance. But first you must run one-eighth the distance. Carried to extreme, such an argument supposedly proved that you could never run the entire distance.

Another major Chinese tradition, *legalism,* concerned a ruler's need to bring forth laws, to set out rewards and punishments, and to build the kingdom's power against its rivals — basics of a civil society then and now.

Leading to (and from) Socrates

People who study philosophy draw a line between Eastern traditions and the Greeks. Scholars also draw a line within the Greek tradition — a line that falls right at Socrates (469–399 BC). Like all such lines, it's arbitrary, but Socrates really did change things.

Socrates began something that his student Plato and Plato's student Aristotle continued: a tradition founded in a personal understanding of what is true and what is right.

Unlike the Ionians and other colonial philosophers, Socrates, shown in Figure 11-1, lived smack dab in the middle of Greek culture — in the great city-state of Athens at its cultural, economic, and military peak.

Building a tradition of seeking answers

The philosophers who came before Socrates — men such as Pythagoras, Thales, and Anaximenes — are often lumped together as the *pre-Socratics*.

Figure 11-1:
Socrates'
reputation
as a philos-
opher rests
mainly on
what Plato
wrote about
him.

© Greek School/Getty Images

You can find a few of their ideas (such as Thales's thoughts about water) at the beginning of this chapter. Many pre-Socratic ideas seem weird, even from the perspective of later Greek philosophers who wrote about them. Here are a couple of gems:

✔ Anaximander of Miletus thought that the earth was shaped like a cylinder and that gigantic, tire-shaped rings full of fire surrounded it. The firelight shone out of various holes of different sizes, which people on earth saw as stars, the moon, and the sun. Anaximander also thought that the first human embryos grew inside fish-like creatures. (He didn't eat fish.)

✔ Heraclitus, who lived in Ephesus (present-day Turkey) in the early fifth century BC, thought all things were made of fire. He also said that the soul runs around inside the human body the way a spider patrols its web.

As farfetched as their ideas seem now, the importance of the pre-Socratic philosophers was that they started a tradition of observing, thinking, and questioning that would reject Anaximander's fish embryos and Heraclitus's spiderlike soul and would hang onto their insistence on trying to understand.

Athens as the leading city-state

Greeks who lived in Miletus or other parts of Asia Minor weren't carefree, even if their theories suggest that they had too much time on their hands. They were on shaky political turf: Persian territory. The Persian Empire had controlled that part of the world since the mid-sixth century BC. Greek residents rebelled in 500 and 499 BC, but Persia's King Darius crushed the rebellion. Then he decided to teach a lesson to mainland Greeks who had supported the rebellion.

Persia attacked Greece, bringing about the Persian Wars, which lasted from 490–449 BC. Over that time, the sometimes-fractious Greek city-states pooled their resources and won. Athens emerged as the leader of a federation of city-states, including those in Ionia. Called the *Delian League,* the federation amounted to a far-flung Athenian empire.

Training in the art of persuasion

By 460 BC, a democratic Athens was the culmination of hard-won government reforms that began in the late sixth century BC. Athenians chose jurists and even magistrates by lottery. All the citizens (a class restricted to free, Athenian men as opposed to slave or foreign-born men or women) were eligible to sit in the popular Assembly, the city-state's main lawmaking body.

Thanks to the democratic proceedings in Athens, it became important for young men to learn how to speak persuasively. For that, Athens needed teachers. Itinerant instructors came to be known as *sophists,* men skilled in rhetoric and legal argument. Mostly concerned with teaching privileged youngsters how to plead their cases, sophists were criticized as more concerned with winning arguments than with truth. *Sophistry* became known as the art of constructing arguments that sound good, despite their flaws.

But some genuine philosophers emerged from among the sophists, paving the way for Socrates by engaging in thoughtful, persuasive dialogues. Still, many Athenians considered Socrates just another sophist. The comic playwright Aristophanes made fun of sophists in general and Socrates in particular in his play *The Clouds,* which depicts the philosopher walking around with his head literally in the clouds.

Living and thinking in a heady time

After the Persian wars, Athens was alive with new ideas. The thinker Anaxagoras moved from Turkey to Athens. He talked philosophy with Pericles, leader of the city-state, who became his friend and supporter.

Pericles, who built Athens into a monumental city with architecture to fit its new status as imperial capital, also hobnobbed with the new Athenian playwrights such as Sophocles and Aeschylus, men who were inventing the Western theater. The playwright Euripides also studied with Anaxagoras.

His friendship with Pericles helped make Anaxagoras a VIP around town. The philosopher's ideas also were intriguing on their own: Anaxagoras propounded a kind of proto-Big Bang theory that sounds like modern astrophysics. In his version, everything started out packed inside an infinitely small pebble-like unit that began to spin and expand, throwing out all matter into an ever-expanding universe. He also envisioned an *infinite mind* (not unlike a god) governing all matter.

Some of what Anaxagoras said was controversial, especially ideas about the sun that contradicted religious orthodoxy. Eventually the philosopher found himself banished. (Athenian citizens voted every year on whom to *ostracize,* a word that to them included physical banishment.) Before he left town, Anaxagoras may have taught Socrates.

Another war, this one pitting Athens against the Greek city-state Sparta (which had grown tired of being in Athens's shadow), lasted from 431–404 BC. Early in this conflict, called the Peloponnesian War, Pericles died of a plague. Sickness and lack of leadership in Athens helped the Spartans win (see Chapter 4), and Athens changed dramatically.

Thinking for himself: Socrates' legacy

Already in his late 30s when the Peloponnesian War broke out, Socrates served bravely in the Athenian infantry. Later in the war, he sat as a member of the Assembly when that lawmaking body judged some Athenian generals accused of abandoning warriors after a victorious sea battle. The lost warriors fell overboard in a sea so stormy that the generals decided to let the high winds blow the ships home, instead of fighting their way back to seek unlikely survivors. The generals arrived expecting to be hailed as heroes but were tossed in the clink instead.

All but one Assembly member voted for conviction. The holdout was Socrates. Why? For one thing, the law said the generals had to be tried as individuals, not in a group. Everybody else conveniently overlooked this point, but Socrates wasn't one to follow the herd.

Socrates made up his own mind and saw it as the individual's responsibility to determine virtue from vice and to act on the resulting knowledge without regard for consequences.

Glimpsing Socrates through Plato's writings

Socrates didn't write about his philosophy. His reputation rests on what other people, especially his student Plato, wrote about him.

Plato depicted Socrates as intent on convincing his fellow Athenians to reexamine their ideas about right and wrong. Plato's writings describe Socrates using a technique that has been called the *Socratic method* ever since: Socrates asks the person he's talking to for a definition of a broad concept (such as *piety* or *justice*) and then tries to get the person to contradict himself with his answer.

What Socrates seems to have believed can be summed up in a quote attributed to him: "There is only one good, knowledge, and one evil, ignorance."

Viewing Socrates as the scapegoat

Socrates lived to question and to pick apart assumptions. During the Peloponnesian War, Athenians' assumptions that they were the best among Greek city-states fell apart just like the city walls that the Spartans pulled down when they finally won the war.

When Athens went looking for a scapegoat after losing the war, its eyes fell on the man who had questioned its earlier ideas about Athenian supremacy. The state charged Socrates with *impiety* (disrespecting the state religion) and with corrupting the young.

He could have apologized. He could have promised to shut up. He could have saved his own life. But that wasn't Socrates' style. He preferred to submit to Athens's method of execution — drinking a solution prepared from the plant poison hemlock — rather than abandon his principles.

Socrates' insistence on making up his own mind based on his own understanding of what's good made him a new kind of hero — not a warrior, but a man of conviction.

Building on Socrates: Plato and Aristotle

While Socrates was alive, Athens lost its imperial greatness. But after Socrates' death, Athens rebuilt itself as a center of learning. After traveling widely, Socrates' student Plato returned to Athens to set up a school (at nearby Academia) that would train generations of thinkers.

Tracing Plato's influence

Plato developed doctrines (including a theory about the immortality of the soul) that would wield incredible influence over philosophers who followed him. The Englishman Alfred North Whitehead, who taught and wrote in the late nineteenth and early twentieth centuries, described the entire tradition of European philosophy as "footnotes to Plato."

Advancing the theory of Ideas

Perhaps the best-known tenet of Platonism is the theory of *Ideas* or Forms. Plato thought that elements of the material world, such as a table, a man, or an acorn, were imperfect reflections or *shadows* of eternal, perfect Ideas, such as the Idea of a table, a man, or an acorn.

In his book *The Republic,* Plato describes an ideal political state that brings forth philosopher kings trained in the highest levels of knowledge.

Recognizing Aristotle's advancements

Plato is often seen as the inventor of idealism, whereas Aristotle, his student, is seen as a hands-on realist. Aristotle was a naturalist, a marine biologist ahead of his time who gathered knowledge from studying the real world.

Aristotle could be down-to-earth about seemingly universal matters. When he made his famous statement, "Man is by nature a political animal," Aristotle was probably just observing that human beings are more like bees, who live in relation to one another, than like cats, who hunt alone. His ideal state, unlike that in Plato's *The Republic,* was based on the Greek city-state, with traditions such as family and even slavery intact. Aristotle wrote about ethics, morality, politics, and much more, often refining Plato's ideas, which makes sense considering Aristotle was Plato's student for 20 years. He had opinions on matters from the nature of being (the word *metaphysics* comes from the title of one of his works) to earning interest by lending money (he opposed it).

Philosophy in the Age of Alexander and After

If it weren't for Aristotle and a rather special student of his, history may have taken a very different course.

Socrates taught Plato, who taught Aristotle, who taught Alexander the Great, who conquered the world. Okay, not really the world, but Alexander conquered such a large and wide-ranging territory that it *seemed* like the whole world to the people of his time (see Chapter 4).

Alexander was never a philosopher, but he did collect samples of exotic plants and animals while on his empire-building campaigns. He sent them back to Aristotle so that his old tutor could study them. The philosopher and the emperor later grew apart, especially after Alexander proclaimed himself a god. (If you value your philosophy professor's good opinion, don't claim personal divinity.)

The philosophical schools founded by Plato and Aristotle didn't build Alexander's empire, but the thinking they nurtured was at the center of what became the dominant culture of the Mediterranean.

Spreading Hellenistic philosophies

The period after Alexander's conquests is labeled the *Hellenistic Age* (Greeks called themselves *Hellenes*) because *Hellenistic* (Greek-like) philosophies spread and remained influential through the height of the Roman Empire.

Some of these philosophies had names still recognized today — not just in the philosophy department's faculty lounge but also in everyday life. For example, you may call somebody a *cynic* or *stoic.* You may find yourself *skeptical* as you read this sentence. Perhaps you're an *epicure.* These terms applied to people behaving or thinking in certain ways emerged from the philosophies of the Hellenistic Age — from the heirs of Plato and Aristotle.

Pleasing yourself: Hedonism

The pleasure principle has been around at least since the fourth century BC, when Aristippus, who studied under Socrates, decided that the sensation of pleasure is the only good. His followers, though they practiced *hedonism,* were called *Cyrenaics* after Cyrene in Africa (Aristippus's birthplace).

Hedonism is not often clearly articulated as a philosophy — at least not by its adherents — because it's not much fun to articulate a philosophy. As a practice, hedonism sometimes figured in social movements, as with the widespread relaxation of social mores in the United States and Western Europe in the 1960s and 1970s.

Looking at original cynicism

If you think everybody's trying to con you, you may have a reputation as a cynic, but that wasn't what *cynicism* used to be. (No, I'm *not* trying to con you about this.) Antisthenes, a friend of Socrates, started cynicism with the purpose of getting back to nature, ignoring social conventions, and living simply.

Antisthenes' follower and colleague, Diogenes of Sinope, really got into *asceticism* — shunning civilization's pleasures and sleeping in a tub. Legend says he walked around Athens in broad daylight carrying a lantern and saying he was searching for an honest man. If indeed he did this, it was probably his way of commenting on the artificiality of life in the city.

Yet the idea stuck that the cynics thought honesty was hard to come by, so *cynicism* became a word for distrusting everybody and everything.

Indulging in Epicureanism

The meaning of *epicure* evolved, too. Nowadays, an epicure (or epicurean) is someone who indulges appetites. But Epicurus, who founded the movement in the early third century BC, believed in moderation.

Epicurus was concerned with logic and physics. He was an *atomist,* theorizing a universe composed of tiny particles. His name, however, became attached to his teachings about ethics and then to gross distortions of those teachings. He defined pleasure as peace of mind and freedom from pain.

Epicurus saw excessive desire as an enemy of pleasure, not something to be indulged. His ideas got mixed up with other people's grosser ideas, and the result is Epicureanism that would have appalled Epicurus. Epicureanism flourished in Rome from about 320 BC–200 AD.

Standing together in stoicism

Around 300 BC, students gathered every day where Zeno of Citium taught at the painted colonnade in Athens. A colonnade is a row of columns. The words for painted colonnade were *Stoa poikile,* so these folks came to be called the Stoics.

Zeno's students shared a vision of the world as a benevolent, organic whole. If people see evil, it's because they don't see or know the entire thing. The Stoics thought, as Socrates had, that human virtue is based in knowledge: The more you know, the more you see the good.

Like Aristotle, the Stoics saw reason as an underlying principle of nature, and they thought individuals should live in harmony with nature. The most famous part of Stoic philosophy is a bit about how pleasure, pain, and even death aren't really relevant to true happiness, and all these things should be borne with equanimity.

Stoicism spread to Rome, where it competed for followers with Epicureanism and skepticism. The Stoics believed in a brotherhood of humans, making stoicism the philosophy of Roman republicans who opposed a return to monarchy.

Doubting the world: Skepticism

A *skeptic* is someone who habitually doubts, especially someone who questions accepted assumptions. There was an element of skepticism in the way Socrates rooted out contradictions in conventional wisdom.

Skepticism as a philosophical tradition, however, goes deeper than that, casting doubt on the possibility of any human knowledge at all. Its founder, Pyrrho (360–270 BC), believed that all people are clueless and so it's best to suspend judgment and stay calm. Skepticism had adherents in Rome.

Putting philosophy to practical use

If you get the impression that Greeks after Alexander the Great didn't do anything but philosophize, remember that much of what came under the broad heading *philosophy* (Greek for "love of wisdom") would today be called *math* and *science.*

Philosophy of the time had practical applications. Geometry, for example, came in handy for surveying and building. Incredible buildings went up during the Hellenistic Age. Among them was a fantastic marble lighthouse in the harbor of Alexandria, Egypt.

Alexandria became a center of Greek-style learning. The library there held 700,000 volumes, and the librarian was a Greek named Eratosthenes, who was also a geographer. He worked out a formula for measuring the circumference of the Earth by measuring shadows in Syene, Egypt, and in Alexandria at the same time — at noon on the summer solstice. Then he took the difference between the shadows and multiplied by the distance between the two cities to calculate the planet's size.

Another Greek at Alexandria reportedly built some kind of steam engine, although nobody knew what to use it for. That thread of knowledge would be picked up in England quite a few centuries later (see Chapter 15).

Tracking the Centuries

May 28, 585 BC: The sun darkens in an eclipse accurately predicted by the philosopher Thales of Miletus.

Sixth century BC: Indian philosopher Ajita of the Hair Blanket says the world consists of four elements: earth, air, fire, and water.

500 BC: Greeks in Ionia (today's Turkey) rebel against Persian rule.

449 BC: Athens emerges victorious from the Persian Wars as leader of a federation of city-states, the Delian League.

430 BC: According to legend, the philosopher Empedocles demonstrates his own immortality by jumping into the volcanic crater atop Mount Etna.

423 BC: In his comedy *The Clouds,* playwright Aristophanes makes fun of Socrates, depicting him with his head literally in the clouds.

399 BC: Condemned to death for his teachings, the imprisoned Socrates drinks a poison hemlock potion and dies, surrounded by his followers.

387 BC: Plato returns to Athens to found a school of philosophy.

384 BC: Aristotle is born in Macedon, the son of the king's physician.

300 BC: Zeno of Citium teaches philosophy every day at the painted colonnade, or *Stoa poikile,* in central Athens.

Around 255 BC: Eratosthenes becomes librarian at Alexandria, Egypt, and is in charge of the largest storehouse of knowledge in the world.

Chapter 12

Being Christian, Thinking Greek

In This Chapter

▶ Linking everything in the Great Chain of Being

▶ Hammering out beliefs in the early Christian Church

▶ Adapting Platonic thinking

▶ Paving the way to salvation

▶ Bringing Aristotle into the fold

A t a casual glance, Christianity and the philosophies that pre-Christian Greeks developed don't seem to have much to do with each other. Jesus, after all, was a Jew. His followers saw him as the messiah promised by the Hebrew Scriptures. They consider him both the Son of God and that God in human form — a *monotheistic* God.

In contrast, the Greek philosophers came from a *polytheistic* tradition. (To find out about polytheistic religions, see Chapter 10. For more on the Greek philosophers, see Chapter 11.) They were unconnected to the Christian message, yet the Greek philosophies didn't go away after Christianity became the dominant faith of the Roman Empire and then post-Roman Europe. If anything, those old philosophies became more important than ever.

Greek thought — especially the lines of thought founded by Plato and Aristotle — worked right to the center of Christian religious contemplations and the way European society was organized. Theologians adapted Aristotelian and Platonic ideas into Church teachings through the Middle Ages and into the Renaissance. In fact, a Christian interpretation of Aristotle's philosophy shaped the attitudes that brought about the Renaissance.

All the Christian theology and philosophy mentioned in this chapter flowed from Greek ways of thinking. And at every stage through these Christian times, philosophical movements reached back to the Greeks and Romans for their ideological underpinnings.

The Great Chain of Being

One Greek idea that hung around into Christian times came to be known as the *Great Chain of Being*. This way of ordering reality owes its foundation to the tradition of Platonic thought (see Chapter 11). The Great Chain of Being was central to the way most Christians looked at the world in medieval and Renaissance times.

The Great Chain is an organizational chart of existence with the richest, most complex grade of existence at the top and the humblest at the bottom. Everything can be ranked by its relative distance from the ultimate, or ideal, reality. This Platonic notion adapted well to Christianity, which put God at the top of the chain. Everybody and everything had a station on the chain — each above and below certain other links in the chain.

The Great Chain lent itself to the certainty that kings were closer to God than lesser nobles, who were closer to God than commoners were. *Serfs,* who were essentially slaves, could be comfortably tucked at the bottom of Christian humanity without worry. Yet even serfs got to be above animals and other life forms. Worms and fleas and such were *waaay* down there. Thus, differences between levels of human society and between biological species were the same thing — part of the proper, godly order.

The Great Chain of Being was rigidly conservative. It nailed society's institutions — especially class distinctions — in place and went hand in hand with the notion of the *divine right of kings,* under which doctrine a monarch's authority came from God and a kingdom's obedience to its sovereign reflected Christendom's obedience to the Almighty. To defy the state was to defy God on high.

Kings and would-be kings disagreed all the time, of course, about who was God's rightful candidate. Sometimes churchmen — a term meaning not just priests, bishops, cardinals, and popes but also learned monks — got into these arguments, too. (You can find several of their clashes addressed in Chapters 7 and 13.) But the overarching principle of the Great Chain hung on through the Middle Ages and beyond.

Interpreting Christian Theology

Based on Jesus's teachings about God's forgiveness and on the miracle of the Resurrection of Christ (see Chapter 10), Christianity gave rise to more than 2,000 years' worth of painstaking theological interpretation and fierce, often violent, disagreements that often have grown into wars.

Divergent ideas aren't unusual in religion. Most beliefs evolve with variations on their central themes emerging and breaking off from the central religion. In the case of Christianity, circumstances contributed to early and wide-ranging interpretations.

Stacking scripture upon scripture

One reason Christianity was so open to various interpretations is that it's a religion built on another religion, embracing the writings of the original — Jewish — tradition as its own.

The Holy Scripture consists of the much-older Jewish Bible (the Old Testament) with the newer, Christian writings from the first century AD (the New Testament). From the get-go, Christians had to make decisions about how to reconcile this wealth of literature. What did these incredibly rich writings — often seemingly contradictory from one book to another and from Old to New Testaments — really mean?

By necessity, Church fathers based their teachings on interpretations — not always agreed upon among themselves — of God's will. For example, although Christians revere the Hebrew Scriptures, they never followed many Hebrew laws. Judaism's dietary restrictions and ritual circumcision weren't part of the new religion. Saint Paul, a Jewish rabbi before his conversion, brought the gospel message to many *gentiles* (non-Jews) in the first century AD. He taught that Christians who were not by birth Jews could disregard these Hebrew requirements.

Replacing Homer with the Bible

Furious interpretations and counter-interpretations marked Christianity from the beginning in part because of the places where Christianity sprang up. Christianity filtered through a world marked by *Hellenistic* (Greek-like) traditions, by the Greek teachings that followed Socrates, Plato, Aristotle, and Alexander the Great's empire.

Early centers of the Church included Alexandria, Egypt, which was a capital of Greek scholarship, and Rome, where so many Hellenistic philosophies rubbed up against one another for a long time. The New Testament was written in Greek, and Jesus came to be known by a Greek word meaning "messiah": *Christ.*

As Greek thought shifted to Christian thought, the Bible took the place of Homer's poems and the Greek-Roman pantheon as a general context for philosophical questioning. By the *Greek-Roman pantheon,* I mean the many gods, such as Zeus (the father god), Athena (goddess of wisdom), Apollo (god of the sun), and Dionysus (god of wine and celebration). Greeks worshipped these human-like, yet supernatural personalities and credited them with influencing nature and human lives. The Greek gods were characters in Homer's poems and in many other stories (today called *myths*) that all Greeks knew. Romans, who worshipped many of the same gods by different names, knew the stories, too. When pre-Christian Greeks and Romans talked about abstract concepts such as *good,* they relied on phrases such as "pleasing to the gods." They used stories about the gods to illustrate points of philosophy.

The intellectual energy from all the Greek-based philosophies of the Hellenistic Age seemed to funnel into Christian philosophy. Philosophical thought became the province of *theologians* — people trying to figure out, or at least interpret, God. In the part of the world that embraced Christianity, scholarly priests absorbed and redefined the ideas of the Greeks, channeling those ideas into beliefs about how the Church and the world should be arranged.

Establishing Jesus's Divinity

Constantine the Great and his co-emperor Licinius issued the *Edict of Milan,* which ordered toleration of Christians, in 313 AD. Only 12 years later, after Constantine had defeated and killed Licinius to become sole Roman emperor, he called together the top bishops of the newly liberated Christian Church. The churchmen met at Nicaea, a town near Constantine's new Christian capital of Constantinople, to hammer out important issues. (Chapter 6 covers Constantine's founding of Constantinople.)

At the meeting in Nicaea, the bishops wanted to work out an official policy about Jesus's divinity: Just how divine was he? In the early centuries of the Church, some priests taught that Jesus, as the Son of God, was subordinate to his father, the Hebrew God. Others thought that Jesus was essentially a mortal and God's greatest prophet, but not divine. The bishops disagreed with these ideas and drew up the *Nicene Creed,* which said that Jesus was God the Son — in essence, the same as God the Father.

The issue of Jesus's divinity wasn't settled easily, however. (It remains a point of departure for some sects even today.) Disagreement over whether Jesus and God the Father were *the same* or *similar* separated Christians in Rome from those in Constantinople. And the question of how to regard the third part of the Christian Trinity — the Holy Spirit — was a sore spot between the Western and Eastern branches of the Church and a major cause of their eventual split from one another. (You can find more about the split in Chapter 10.)

Augustine's Influence on Early Christian Thought

The most influential early interpretations of Christian thought come from Saint Augustine, a North African who followed Platonic philosophy and a religion called Manicheism before he was baptized as a Christian in 387 AD. Augustine then became a priest and was appointed the Bishop of Hippo (not the pudgy, water-loving animal, but a city in what is today Algeria).

Divining the mind of God

Some of Augustine's early writings adapted Plato's ideas to Christianity. According to Plato (turn to Chapter 11 for more on him), everything you can see and experience is an imperfect reflection of a perfect, eternal *Form* or *Idea*. In other words, there is an Idea of a table and an Idea of a woman that are apart from and superior to all actual tables and all actual women. In Augustine's version of Plato's philosophy, these eternal Ideas reside inside a mind — the mind of God.

Condoning righteous killing

Augustine's teachings affected history powerfully and directly. One example: Although some early Christians were strict pacifists and interpreted the biblical command "Thou shalt not kill" quite literally, Augustine wrote that war isn't wrong if it's conducted on divine authority. He also taught that it's okay to carry out the death penalty in accordance with the laws of the state.

According to Augustine, a just, Christian society has the authority to kill people. This opens the moral and ethical door wide, considering that there aren't many societies whose leaders would admit to being unjust.

Tracing two paths to salvation

What does the title of a television sitcom have to do with Christian philosophy? The title of *Will and Grace* (aired 1998–2006) may have been a joke on the creators' liberal arts education, but even that reflects how deeply philosophical arguments run into the workings of the world.

Will (as in free will) and grace (as in God's grace alone) are two possible paths to salvation in competing Christian philosophies. They reflect a debate that began in the writings of Saint Augustine.

Adapting Augustine's ideas

Unlike just about anybody on television these days, Augustine rejected sexual pleasure and things of the flesh. He seems to have picked up this aversion during a youthful fling with Manicheism, which was founded in Persia (today's Iran) in the third century AD.

Manicheism taught that the material world represents the powers of darkness, which have invaded the realm of light. An ascetic and puritanical religion, Manicheism seems to have marked Augustine profoundly even though he roundly denounced it when he converted to Christianity. Especially as he got older, he became firmly convinced that the whole human race had somehow taken part in the sin of Adam and Eve — an idea called *original sin*.

In the Bible story of man's creation, Adam is enticed by Eve to disobey God's order not to eat the fruit of the Tree of Knowledge. God drives Adam and Eve from the Garden of Eden for this. Here's where Augustine started interpreting: He believed that everybody descended from Adam inherited that original sin of disobedience. That's everybody — except God in human form, meaning the immaculately conceived Jesus. And so the only thing that can save any human soul is God's grace. Further, God awards that grace (and this is the tricky part) without regard for individual merit. That is, you can't earn your way into heaven. Prayer and good deeds won't do it. Salvation or damnation is decided beforehand in what's called *predestination,* and you have no free will. You can't even hope to understand grace. God is beyond understanding.

As you may imagine, Augustine's theory of predestination proved controversial. (And yes, that's a monumental understatement.) Many who rejected his doctrine preferred the view that God gave human beings *free will* — a mind and the ability to make up that mind — and that with that freedom comes the responsibility to embrace God.

Predestination has been interpreted and argued about in endless ways since Augustine. Some versions embrace *fatalism,* the idea that the future is just as unchangeable as the past. Not all versions of predestination go that far, nor are all versions restricted to Christian thought. For example, in Islam, a person can't oppose God's will but can accept or reject God. If you reject God, you face dire consequences. Much of Christianity took philosophical routes not far from this one.

Promoting other views on predestination

Some leaders of the Protestant Reformation embraced predestination (find more on this movement in Chapter 14). The Frenchman John Calvin, a major force in shaping Protestantism, was especially Augustinian. His version of predestination, called *theological determinism,* asserts that people can't influence God in the matter of who is saved and who isn't.

In most branches of Christianity that preach a form of predestation, believers are supposed to be good — that is, to do God's will — out of faith, love, and devotion. But they're not supposed to behave virtuously just because they're angling for a heavenly payoff or out of fear of eternal punishment. Yet without the spiritual equivalent of a carrot or stick, keeping some people on the narrow path is impossible, so some moralists consider predestination a lousy motivator.

The Philosophy of Aquinas

From the way Augustine looked at religion (see the preceding section), you couldn't understand anything without first believing in God. The last thing you'd want to do would be to try to arrive at belief by way of understanding. Belief, in this medieval tradition of scholarship, was the foundation of understanding.

It was later in the Middle Ages that some Christian scholars — inspired by their reading of Plato's student, Aristotle — began to reason that if God is reflected in material reality, then the study of the world can lead to an understanding of God. Chief among these was the Italian priest and author Thomas Aquinas, whose ideas would help spark the Renaissance.

Keeping scholarship alive

The idea of medieval times as *dark ages* where everybody in Europe was sunk in ignorance fails to account for the fact that universities are a medieval invention. The University of Bologna, in Italy, was the first university, founded in the tenth century. Then there was the University of Paris in the twelfth century and Oxford in the thirteenth.

Scholasticism was the intellectual tradition at these universities. Saint Anselm, an archbishop of Canterbury (in England) at the turn of the twelfth century and a scholastic himself, described *scholasticism* as "faith seeking understanding." With that orientation, working out ideas using Greek philosophy was considered okay.

For early churchmen, Aristotle's line of reasoning caused more trouble than Plato's.

✔ In Augustine's faith-based brand of Christian Platonism, you don't have to see and touch and feel objects (things your senses perceive) in order to find out about the truth. Those things, by definition, aren't true. They may be *reflections* of the truth, but the truth is in the *Idea,* which flows from God.

✔ In Aristotle's way of looking at the world, you can work your way up to understanding, even to understanding ultimate truth, using your senses and reason. This approach puts much more responsibility on the sinful human being.

Scholasticism embraced the Aristotelian way of doing things after Thomas Aquinas (later Saint Thomas Aquinas) brought Aristotle into the Church in the thirteenth century.

Coming back to Aristotle

Aquinas wasn't the first medieval European scholar to be drawn to Aristotle. An important predecessor — not a Christian, but a Muslim — was Ibn Rushd, who became known to Latin-speaking European scholars as Averroës. He was an Islamic judge and physician of the twelfth century who lived and worked both in Moorish Spain and in North Africa.

Averroës's writings contemplating Aristotle found their way to a German with the unwieldy name Albertus, Graf von Bollstädt. (*Graf von* means "count of.") Also a churchman, he taught at the University of Paris, where he started applying Averroës's arguments to Christian faith and established the study of nature as a legitimate scholarly pursuit. Albertus (better known today as St. Albertus Magnus or St. Albert the Great) passed on his interest in Aristotle to his pupil, Thomas Aquinas.

Supporting faith with logic

Aquinas wrote the major works that hooked Aristotelian reasoning into the Church, where it eventually became official Catholic doctrine. Aquinas even used Aristotle's logic to *prove* the existence of God.

How did he do that? Here's an example of his logic:

[W]hat is in motion must be put in motion by another. If that by which it is put in motion be itself put in motion, then this also must needs be put in motion by another, and that by another again. But this cannot go on to infinity, because then there would be no first mover, and consequently, no other mover. . . . Therefore it is necessary to arrive at a first mover, put in motion by no other; and this everyone understands to be God.

Arguments such as that one fired scholastics with a passion for using their minds to get at the root of big questions. The Christian universities became places where scholars pursued logic and rhetoric and debated the nature of being (within boundaries).

Embracing Humanism and More

Embracing the human intellect as a tool to confirm faith contributed to big movements in world history, such as the Renaissance (which you can read about in Chapter 13). The focus on intellect also led to a rediscovery of Classical (that is, Greek and Roman) science, which led Europeans to scientific and navigational advances. And that, in turn, helped make possible the voyages of world exploration that I talk about in Chapter 8. The reliance on rational thought wasn't a linear path, however. Not at all. You can point to scholasticism as a root of something called *humanism,* which focuses on the relationship between God and humans. Yet humanistic thinking arose as a backlash against the scholastics; it was a reaction to the abstract concerns of medieval scholarship — all that logic and analysis and such.

Nothing secular about it

Nowadays, *humanism* usually comes after the word *secular. Secular humanism* is often criticized as an anti-religious philosophy, but late medieval and Renaissance humanism was a Christian religious movement. Humanists asked, "What is humankind's place in God's plan?"

That doesn't mean that the humanists broke with all those centuries of reaching back to Greek philosophy. Early humanism is identified with Neoplatonism (which I tell you about in Chapter 11). Humanism didn't embrace Augustine's brand of Platonism, however. Augustine mistrusted the things of the world, which he saw as false reflections of the perfect reality (God). Living in this false, material world, human beings couldn't understand God.

Humanistic Neoplatonism looked at things the other way around, seeing human beings as not just made by God but also as expressions of godliness. Giovanni, Conte Pico della Mirandola (from Mirandola, Italy) was a Renaissance philosopher who probably expressed it best. In his view, all the universe — stars, trees, dogs, sausages, and human beings, especially human beings —

reflected God. (Read more about Pico della Mirandola in Chapter 13.) Humans could be understood as perfect expressions of the ultimate truth and as a small version of God's universe — a microcosm.

A human being could not only seek God but also could *find* God within the individual soul. You could look inside your finite self and find infinity.

Tracing humanism's impact

Humanism's concept that people have the ability to find God had everything to do with what happened in Renaissance art, theology, philosophy, science, and even politics. If everything that human beings can think and create, including pre-Christian art and science, reflects God, the door to exploration opens all the way. As I explain in Chapter 13, the Renaissance brought major scientific discoveries, giving rise to the *Enlightenment,* a rational-humanist philosophical movement that, in turn, brought forth modern democratic theory.

Tracking the Centuries

325 AD: Christian bishops gather near Constantinople (in today's Turkey) to hammer out basic theological principles.

354 AD: Aurelius Augustinius, later known as Saint Augustine, is born in the Roman-ruled community of Numidia, North Africa.

387 AD: Augustine becomes a Christian, accepting baptism on Easter Sunday.

1180s: Ibn Rushd, an Islamic judge and physician in Moorish Spain, writes interpretations of the Greek philosopher Aristotle.

1273: In his book *Summa Theologica,* Thomas Aquinas shows Aristotle's thoughts to be compatible with Christian doctrine.

1879: The Roman Catholic Church adopts the writings of Saint Thomas Aquinas as official Catholic philosophy.

Chapter 13

Awakening to the Renaissance

- -

- -

To many people, the word *Renaissance* means "art," especially Italian art. If you're one of those people, good. Keep thinking art. Keep thinking Italy.

You can look at Renaissance art — the result of a creative explosion that began in Italy in the early fifteenth century — and understand not just why the artists saw and depicted the world differently than their predecessors did but also why their vision reflected the world at large.

Renaissance art embodied ideas about the place of humankind in God's universe, reflecting a significant shift in the perception of what being human means. Because of this shift, striving to make the very best of mortal minds and bodies became important. The new thinking said that you could strive to be your best, and *should* do so, while enhancing rather than imperiling your immortal soul.

Even the Protestant Reformation (see Chapter 14), when all those European Christians broke away from the Roman Catholic Church, becomes easier to grasp if you look at the paintings and sculptures of Masaccio and Michelangelo first. Never heard of Masaccio? Don't worry. I discuss him — and other Renaissance supermen — in this chapter.

Realizing the Reach of the Renaissance

By focusing on Renaissance artists, you may wonder whether you risk missing the scope of the Renaissance. Wasn't it about so much more?

Yes, it was. The Renaissance was about philosophy and religion. It was also about literature, architecture, technology, science, music, political theory, and just about everything imaginable. The Renaissance was about more than I can possibly do justice to in this chapter. So why mention art? If you're interested in history, it's convenient that the intellectual, spiritual, and even commercial trends of the Renaissance all are reflected in its creative works. A defining worldview shows up in the art, so the paintings and sculpture can help you understand what made this era tick.

The Renaissance spread beyond Italy, all over Europe. One reason it's hard to put dates on the Renaissance is that it was gradual. Different aspects of it hit different parts of Europe at different times — from the fourteenth to the sixteenth centuries and maybe beyond.

The Renaissance spread far beyond Europe as explorers, responding to the same economic and cultural influences that stimulated artists back in Italy, landed in the New World and found sea routes from Europe to Asia in the late fifteenth century.

One root of all this change was more individual wealth. More Europeans could afford to buy foreign trade goods. And (here I go oversimplifying again) that came about in part because there were fewer Europeans, at least temporarily. The bubonic plague (see Chapter 7) killed so many people that those who survived had more resources, more land, and even more money. The value of their work increased because of the scarcity of workers.

Redefining the Human Role

Chapter 12, which discusses Christian philosophies through medieval times, ends with a focus on *humanism* — a philosophy that concentrates on God's relationship with humanity. This philosophy was a big deal during the Renaissance (and has been important for most of the time since it appeared); Christian writers started to depict human beings not just as God's creations but as symbolic of God — little embodiments of divinity. Among the earliest writers to reflect this view were the Italian poets Francesco Petrarcha (1304–1374), known as Petrarch, and Giovanni Boccaccio (1313–1375).

Florence in flower

The humanist shift in thinking got a boost when the Florentine chancellor, Coluccio Salutati (1331–1406), started promoting his city-state's status as the intellectual capital of Europe. In 1396, he invited Manuel Chrysoloras, a scholar from Constantinople, to teach Greek in Florence. Many more Eastern scholars came west, bringing with them Greek learning and philosophical traditions, after Constantinople fell to the Ottoman Turks in 1453.

The status associated with scholarship wasn't lost on another Florentine leader, the financier, statesman, and philanthropist Cosimo de' Medici (1389–1464). He was a patron of Florence's Platonic Academy (founded by Salutati), where scholars such as Marsilio Ficino (1433–1499) and the philosopher Giovanni, Conte Pico della Mirandola (1463–1494) worked to reconcile Christianity with newly rediscovered ideas from Greek and Roman philosophy.

In this effort, Pico della Mirandola mixed into his Christian humanism Greek and Roman stoicism (a philosophy that saw the world as a benevolent, organic whole, as you can read about in Chapter 11); material from the Jewish Kabbalah, a philosophical and literary tradition rooted in a mystic striving to know the unknowable secrets of existence; and Islamic sources. He thought all people's intellectual and creative endeavors were part of the same thing: God.

Spreading the word

The Platonic Academy in Florence and other schools like it drew students from far away, and their influence spread humanism all over Europe.

For example, John Colet (1467–1519) came to Florence from Oxford, England. When he returned to England and became a priest, he shared Florentine teachings with prominent Englishmen and the famous Dutch scholar Desiderius Erasmus (1466–1536), who lived in England. Erasmus wrote criticisms of the Church that anticipated the Protestant Reformation, which I discuss in Chapter 14.

Promoting human potential

Why did humanism pack such a wallop? Well, Pico della Mirandola, who best expressed what the early Renaissance was about, wrote that the human being is a perfect expression of the ultimate truth. As a human, he argued, you're a tiny reflection of God's enormous universe. This concept of the human as a microcosm may seem less-than-adventurous reasoning today, but it was an enormous change from the way medieval Christians thought about themselves.

Under the influence of St. Augustine, medieval Christian thinking held that humankind was false, flawed, corrupted, forever marked by Adam's sin, and unable to play any active role in winning redemption (see Chapter 12 for details). Humanism changed that, making it okay within a Christian context to celebrate human beauty and creativity in ways that no one in Europe had dared to do since Roman times.

Reclaiming the ancients

Because the dawn of the Renaissance meant that intellect and creativity reflected God's greatness, all the Classical poets and playwrights whose works had been ignored, lost, or both through medieval times could be reclaimed and inducted into the Godliness Hall of Fame (figuratively speaking). Roman playwrights such as Seneca, who wrote comedies, became fit subjects for study and emulation.

Renaissance writers took ideas from Rome and Greece and put new life into them. The word *renaissance* means "rebirth" or "reawakening." Renaissance scholars woke up to old books that had been kept in monastery libraries — books that monks copied by hand from still older books.

Chrysoloras, the Greek who came from Constantinople to teach in Florence, encouraged his students to start collecting ancient Greek manuscripts. (There were no Pokemon cards, so they thought this would be fun.) Well-heeled Florentines even started traveling to Greece to look for books. They came back with literary treasures and began amassing the first private (rather than Church-kept) libraries since the Roman Empire.

Presenting the printing press

In Mainz, Germany, along came the right technology at a crucial time. Johann Gutenberg, who started his career as a goldsmith, devised a way to print books and pamphlets using movable type. He made a little metal cast of each letter (his metalwork skills came in handy), and then he arranged the letters, clamped them firmly into place, coated them with ink, and printed as many identical pages of type as he liked before rearranging the letters and printing copies of the second page, then the third, and on and on.

Fifteenth-century printing wasn't as easy as clicking a Print icon, but it was much easier and faster than what medieval monks were doing, which was painstakingly lettering every word on every page by hand. Until Gutenberg's advance, every book was a precious, one-of-a-kind artifact. Thanks to Gutenberg, books could be mass-produced.

Printing the Gutenberg Bible

Gutenberg and his financial backer, Johann Fust, built their press around 1450. The Gutenberg Bible, the first mass-produced book, came off that press (or a successor to it) around 1455. (Actually, Fust and his son-in-law, Peter Schöffer, completed the Gutenberg Bible after Gutenberg went bankrupt. Unable to repay a loan from Fust, the printer had to hand over his innovative press.)

Books were suddenly more numerous and cheaper, so more people could afford them. And because books were more widely available, more people learned to read.

Reading other early publications

At first, other Europeans called printing *the German art*. But technology never respects borders. A wealthy merchant named William Caxton learned the new process in Cologne and took it to England around 1473. Caxton's first publications included a history of the Trojan War and a collection of sayings of the philosophers.

In Venice, the scholar Aldo Manuzio (also known by his Latin name, Aldus Manutius) picked up Gutenberg's craft and printed easy-to-read, easy-to-carry editions of Greek and Latin classics at affordable prices. Imagine the change from going to a musty abbey and heaving open a hand-lettered volume so valuable that it was chained to the library shelf, to carrying a book in your pocket!

Having an impact on Church authority

Because the pre-Christian authors were now considered reflections of God's glory, there was a reason to read, admire, and even copy them, and doing so didn't put your faith in jeopardy. But in a subtle and gradual way, the pre-Christian books still undermined the Church's authority. Through medieval times, the Church held the monopoly on wisdom. In the Renaissance, other, older, diverse voices were influencing people throughout Europe as literacy flourished. This was one of the ways that the Renaissance led to the Reformation.

Uniting Flesh and Soul

Are you still thinking about the Renaissance as a flowering of Italian art? Good, because it's time to turn toward Michelangelo's *David,* shown in Figure 13-1; the Renaissance artist sculpted this masterpiece in Florence at the beginning of the sixteenth century. The white marble statue depicts a perfect, exquisitely rendered male form — lean, muscular, graceful, and nude. David is a sculpture of the hunkiest young man that probably anybody in Italy could imagine — sexy in the extreme but also a representation of a sacred subject: David, the great biblical war hero, Hebrew king, and earthly ancestor of Jesus.

Michelangelo's masterpiece is flesh and spirit rolled into one. Sex and scripture. Earthly and godly. Flesh, according to the philosophy of humanism, *is* spirit. Not all Christians were comfortable with this convergence, which is another factor that contributed to the Protestant Reformation.

Figure 13-1:
Michel-
angelo's
David, a
holy hunk.

© Bridgeman Art Library/Getty Images

Inspiring Michelangelo

Michelangelo (1475–1564), whose style may be considered the height of Renaissance sculpture, didn't think up his approach all by himself, of course.

Pioneers such as the painter Masaccio inspired Michelangelo. Born in Florence in 1401, the painter was born Tommaso di Giovanni di Simone Guidi but earned the nickname Masaccio, which means "clumsy Tom," for his absent-minded, careless approach to life. Focused on his art, he painted biblical scenes of unprecedented drama and sensual richness, exploring the human form in ways that would have seemed sinful a century before. His fleshy, dramatic approach changed sacred art, despite his early death at age 27.

The sculptor Donatello (in full, Donato di Betto Bardi) was another pioneer and inspiration for Michelangelo. Born around 1386 in Florence, he was the first artist since Classical times to make statues that were independent works of art rather than parts of a building. He fashioned an anatomically impressive David, too — one made of bronze.

Painting a picture of Genesis

Michelangelo is the guy you may picture lying on his back on top of a scaffold, painting the ceiling of the Sistine Chapel. The 1965 film *The Agony and the Ecstasy* features Charlton Heston as Michelangelo and Rex Harrison as the pope, who stares up at the artist while he paints the chapel ceiling. There's some good dialogue between the two, assuming you can buy Heston as the artist.

Donatello was one of the earliest Renaissance artists to rediscover mathematical perspective, along with Filippo Brunelleschi (1377–1446), who moved on from sculpture to architecture. In art, perspective is any method used to achieve the illusion of three-dimensional depth. The ancient Greeks, who were interested in geometry and optics, noticed how objects appear smaller the farther away they are from the viewer. What's mathematical about that? An artist with a feel for geometry can give the impression of distance in a drawing or painting by working as if on a grid of lines (merely imagined or marked and then painted over in the finished work) shaped like an upside-down fan. Such lines seem to project from a point of convergence on the horizon called the *vanishing point*. (Imagine staring at a straight two-lane highway that you can see all the way to the horizon on a level plain.) Brunelleschi came up with this *one-point system* around 1420.

Living in the material world

Because Renaissance thinking held that the human form was a reflection of God and that the material world was an aspect of the divine, concentrating on all the angles, curves, contours, and colors of the physical world became positively holy. Artists wanted paintings and sculpture to be lifelike and reflect reality — albeit an idealized reality.

To that end, artists branched out. Artist Leonardo da Vinci (1452–1519) was also a human anatomist, botanist, engineer, architect, writer, musician, and inventor. His knowledge of the physical world informed his art (see Figure 13-2). He and other painters and sculptors ushered in new ways of thinking about the physical world and how its pieces interact. Leonardo da Vinci even drew diagrams of flying machines, although there's no evidence he ever built one.

Figure 13-2:
In Leonardo's famous drawing, Vitruvian Man, he used geometric principles to illustrate ideal human proportions, thus blending art and science.

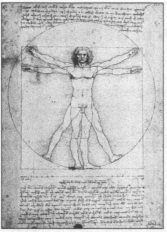

© Garry Gay/Getty Images

Leonardo's work in engineering and perspective stimulated and intersected with the work of a new breed of architects and mathematical theoreticians, some of them much more practical-minded than he was. While the artist was sketching flying machines, some other Italian engineers built on ancient mathematical disciplines to improve weapons and fortifications.

Returning to Science

The Renaissance planted the seeds of a scientific revolution that took off after 1600 with discoveries made by people such as the astronomer Galileo and the physicist Isaac Newton. (Chapter 15 has more on both men.)

Shifting the center of the universe

Copernicus, a Polish-born, Italian-educated churchman, took a big step toward the scientific revolution in 1543 when he published his theories about how the Earth and planets move in relation to the sun. Copernicus said that the sun, not the Earth, was the center around which the universe revolved.

Copernicus delayed releasing his findings, but at the urging of supporters, he published his book *The Revolution of the Heavenly Spheres* around 1543, the year of his death. His sun-centered universe, along with the notion that the earth spins on its axis, upset some other astronomers and other churchmen. To claim that God would place His creation on a spinning ball that revolved around another heavenly body struck many people as preposterous, not to mention heretical. The controversy only caught fire, however, after 1610, when physicist and astronomer Galileo Galilei of Pisa published a book about his own astronomical observations, which supported those of Copernicus. The Catholic Church banned Copernicus's book, *The Revolution of the Heavenly Spheres,* in 1616 and didn't lift the ban until 1835. (For more about Galileo, see Chapter 15.)

Studying human anatomy

Whereas Leonardo da Vinci's interest in engineering stimulated and was part of a revival of mathematical theory and Classical architecture, his anatomical studies came just as the field of medicine began to catch the Renaissance spirit.

Medieval *physic* (as doctoring was called) was based on a theory that the body contained four fluids: blood, yellow bile, black bile, and phlegm. Called the *humors,* their balance was considered essential to good health. People today still sometimes refer to *good humor,* which is rooted in this theory (although Good Humor brand ice cream treats wouldn't be nearly as appetizing if they made you think of bile).

At the turn of the fourteenth century, Pope Boniface VIII prohibited the dissection of human cadavers. The idea that human flesh reflected God meant that to cut into and study it was a kind of sacrilege. The pope's decree, however, inconveniently interrupted the work of doctors who thought that there was more to learn about the body than this humors business.

Some maverick researchers conducted dissections in secret. By 1543, this science was out in public again with the publication of *Seven Books on the Structure of the Human Body,* a breakthrough work by Andreas Vesalius, a professor of surgery and anatomy at the University of Padua (Italy). His successor there, Matteo Realdo Columbo, figured out heart-lung circulation, a phenomenon that Michael Servetus of Spain discovered independently. Their work led to the Englishman William Harvey's discovery in the following century of the circulation of the blood throughout the body.

This new focus on the body resulted in medical breakthroughs, including the following:

- ✔ Girolamo Fracastoro, who practiced medicine in Naples after 1495, came up with a theory about microscopic contagion based on his work with syphilis, typhus, and tuberculosis patients.

- ✔ In Bologna, Gaspare Tagliacozzi (1545–1599) pioneered plastic surgery in the late sixteenth century when he transplanted skin from his patients' arms to repair noses eaten away by syphilis.

Until these guys came along, surgery was the work of barbers. The anatomist and French Army surgeon Ambroise Paré (1510–1590) helped change that. Among his advances, he was the first to tie off arteries after an amputation. Until Paré, cauterizing a blood vessel with a hot iron was the accepted way to close off the vessel.

Being All That You Could Be

You could think about what happened in the Renaissance as a kind of philosophical-intellectual feedback loop.

A *feedback loop,* as anybody who was ever in a rock band knows, happens when the microphone or electric guitar picks up part of the output signal from a nearby amplifier or speaker. The mike or guitar then sends that sound back to the amp, where it's made louder, so that it creates louder interference, which is amplified again and then goes through the loop over and over — all at the speed of electric current. Within a second or two you have a shrill, incredibly loud shriek that causes everybody but really hardcore heavy metal fans to hold their hands over their ears and scream for mercy.

The noises that the Renaissance made were more pleasant and varied than that. So were the ideas and the works of art. But the Renaissance movement fed itself, and fed on itself, because humanism made it not just okay but actually *virtuous* to both contemplate and pursue human achievement.

Achievements — intellectual, artistic, and physical — amplified and gave glory to the reflection of God. The pursuit of human perfection fed an appreciation for human perfection that in turn spurred even more pursuit of human perfection.

Striving for perfection

In the Renaissance mindset, everybody had a responsibility to become as perfect as possible by developing all the powers given by God. "Be all that you can be," a recruiting slogan used by the United States Army in the twentieth century, could have been applied to the *Renaissance man*.

In pursuit of human potential, artists studied math, architecture, engineering, and even literature. Long before the world thought in terms of *interdisciplinary* work, all these subjects overlapped, each discipline informing and strengthening the others.

What a man!

One of the most wide-ranging Renaissance men was the Genoan architect Leon Battista Alberti (1404–1472). He was an artist, poet, physicist, mathematician, and philosopher, as well as one of the finest musicians of his day (he played the organ) and an astonishing athlete. Alberti claimed that he could leap, with his feet together, between the heads of two men standing shoulder-to-shoulder, without touching them. Who said white men can't jump?

Alberti's arm would have made him a fortune today as a pro baseball pitcher or football quarterback. He surprised people by throwing an apple over the highest roof in Genoa, and he could chuck the javelin farther than anyone who challenged him. He was also a crack archer.

Hate him already? Me too, especially after I read that he was always in a good mood — cheerful, unflappable, and uncomplaining, even in terrible weather.

Renaissance man sounds sexist today, and it was. There's no pretending otherwise. Although human beings — male and female — could be exalted, males were thought to have the godly gifts most worth developing.

Many people think Leonardo was the ultimate Renaissance man: engineer, artist, inventor, and so on. But there were many others, including the sculptor-architect Brunelleschi, who was also a goldsmith. The Spanish medical researcher Servetus was a theologian, and Michelangelo, a great painter and greater sculptor, was a poet, too. See the "What a man!" sidebar for another example.

Stocking up on self-help books

Because making the best of what God gave you was so important, self-improvement became a hot topic during the Renaissance.

The best-selling book of 1528, *The Courtier* by Count Baldassare Castiglione, spelled out rules for what a gentleman ought to be. Among the most desirable qualities: You should be good at everything, but you shouldn't look like you're trying too hard. Even your manners should be easy and natural — courteous, but not polished. *The Courtier* was sixteenth-century cool.

Castiglione thought that being a *courtier,* one of those nobles who hangs around the castle and waits on the prince or king, was one of the most important things anyone could do. Today, you may look back on courtiers as hangers-on and yes men, and many of them probably were. But Castiglione saw the courtier's job as both advising the prince and setting a good example for him. Even if the prince was a slobbering clod, the good manners and wisdom of exemplary courtiers were supposed to rub off on him.

Nicolo Machiavelli wrote the most notorious how-to book of the Renaissance, a little volume called *The Prince*. This 1513 publication was and remains controversial, because it seems to advocate an amoral pragmatism, a way of operating that came to be known as *Machiavellian*.

Machiavelli may be remembered as an advocate or as simply the best, most honest reporter of another aspect of all this focus on human achievement. On the more ear-punishing fringes of rock music, feedback becomes an instrument in itself. Within the Renaissance focus on humanity, sometimes the chase for human perfection turned to a selfish pursuit of human glory, personal wealth, and especially political power.

In Machiavelli's view, a ruler's end justifies his means. If a prince is successful, he is right. "Cruelties inflicted immediately to secure one's position are well inflicted (if one may speak well of ill)," he wrote. To be feared is more important than to be loved, the author claimed. As for honesty, a prince should keep his word as long as it's useful to do so.

Machiavelli's critics call him evil. His defenders say that he was telling it like it was and simply sharing what he learned as a Florentine official and diplomat. Machiavelli placed his work well within the framework of Christian humanism, as he understood it.

"God is not willing to do everything," he wrote, "and thus take away our free will and that share of glory, which belongs to us."

Writing for the Masses

With the development of the Gutenberg press and the spread of printing (refer to the earlier section "Presenting the printing press"), language changed. Regional tongues such as French, English, and Italian took on a new vitality and authority. More and more writers began using these instead of Latin to write poetry and plays (see the "Who killed Latin?" sidebar). The old prejudice that educated people shouldn't write in the *vernacular* (common) language faded.

Even before the Renaissance, the poet Dante Alighieri (1265–1321) wrote his *Divine Comedy* and other works in Italian. London's Geoffrey Chaucer (1343–1400), who traveled in Italy and read works by Boccaccio, wrote in English.

Creating new classics

Writing in the vernacular really caught on as printers realized there was a commercial market for it. William Caxton, who brought printing to England, achieved a bestseller when he published Chaucer's comic *Canterbury Tales*.

Many of the new books written in everyday language, given time, proved just as classic as the old Latin and Greek books. Here are some examples:

- Castigliano wrote *The Courtier* in Italian. (Refer to "Stocking up on self-help books" earlier in this chapter for the story behind *The Courtier*.)
- François Rabelais, a physician and humanist, wrote controversial sixteenth-century satires in French.
- In the late sixteenth and early seventeenth centuries, William Shakespeare cranked out plays for the popular theater (and the popular press) in English.
- Shakespeare's contemporary, Miguel de Cervantes, wrote *The Adventures of Don Quixote* in Spanish.

Staging dramas with Classical roots

Shakespeare brought Renaissance drama to its peak, but he built on a tradition that began in the late thirteenth century when the Italian Albertino Mussato began writing comedies in the style of Seneca, a Roman. In addition to *The Prince* and other work in political science, Machiavelli wrote stage comedies after the Classical style. The most famous to survive is called *The Mandrake,* which he wrote in 1518.

Shakespeare's plays show how thoroughly the new scholarship permeated European society. Full of references to Greek and Roman gods, his plots were sometimes drawn from Roman plays and even, as with *Julius Caesar* and *Antony and Cleopatra,* from Roman history. Even some of Shakespeare's plays set in his own time take place in Italian cities that gave rise to the Renaissance.

Packing something to read onboard a ship

Europe's growing literacy, which was rooted in a return to ancient classics and powered by the invention of printing, influenced matters much more down-to-earth than poems and plays. The ancients also wrote serious books about geography and navigation, and they drew maps that preserved what Greek and Phoenician navigators had learned about seas and landmasses. After all, Greek and Phoenician navigators were the greatest travelers of their times. (Turn to Chapter 5 for more about Phoenicians, their North African city Carthage, and their seafaring empire.) Europeans of the Renaissance read those books, too.

Fifteenth- and sixteenth-century advances in navigation and *cartography* (mapmaking), like other intellectual advances of the time, had their roots in the relevant Greek and Roman texts. Explorers such as Christopher Columbus and Vasco da Gama (more about them in Chapter 21) started with an atlas designed by the Egyptian-Greek astronomer Ptolemy (90–170 AD) and then radically redrew it. Their discoveries about the shape and size of the world went hand in hand with the theories of Copernicus (covered earlier in this chapter) and his heirs, astronomers Johannes Kepler and Galileo, both of whom I discuss in Chapter 15.

Fighting for Power in Europe

All the cross-pollination of the Renaissance — with scholars and their ideas traveling from city to city and country to country — suggests a climate of political harmony throughout Europe. It wasn't that way, however. The Renaissance was a time of many borders and lots of political powers vying for dominance.

Battling for control of Italian city-states

Italy, the heart of the Renaissance, was nothing like the modern nation it is now. Italy was a hodgepodge of city-states, kind of like ancient Greece had been (see Chapter 4).

Some of these city-states, such as intellectually rich Florence, were wealthy trade centers. Their rulers, people such as the Medicis, a family that got rich in banking, hired the sculptors, painters, architects, and writers that made their renaissance *the* Renaissance.

Italian rulers also competed with each other for influence and territory. Just as the bankers and traders who marked this age kept financial agents in other cities to look after their interests, so the rulers (some of them also bankers and traders) placed political agents to watch out for them in competing capitals. This is how both modern diplomacy and modern espionage were born.

Who killed Latin?

Latin is a dead language, but did you know that it lived long after the fall of the Roman Empire? Only when Renaissance scholars tried to *save* Latin did the language begin to ossify into the sterile tongue it has been ever since.

Latin — the language of Rome, from everyday people to government, business, and scholarship — helped hold the Roman Empire together as long as it existed. And after the Rome-based western empire declined, Latin hung on in Western Europe. (The eastern, Byzantine Empire spoke Greek.) Educated people all over Western Europe continued to communicate in Latin. All the courses and debates at medieval universities were conducted in the language; the universality of Latin was really cool if you were a professor, because whether you were from Ireland or Italy, you could be just as much at home in a German classroom as a colleague from Cologne. That applied to students, too, who didn't have to understand French to study in Paris.

As living languages do, Latin kept growing and changing. Grammatical uses shifted. Sentence structure became a little simpler here and a bit rougher there. Then in the Renaissance, scholars began reading Latin from texts that were 1,500 years old and realized how different their Latin was from the language of the great Roman rhetorician, Cicero.

With their newfound appreciation of pre-Christian classics, these scholars saw Cicero's Latin as the original, uncorrupted language: the right stuff. So they worked hard on turning the clock back on their own scholarly language, making strict rules of grammar and usage and enforcing them as an important part of a *classical education*. Schoolboys all over Christendom conjugated Latin verbs, which may have been a good tool for building disciplined young minds, but it was the beginning of the end for Latin. By losing its flexibility, Latin no longer lived the way ever-changing English, for example, lives today.

It took centuries, but Latin eventually fell out of use, even in most areas of scholarship.

The Italian states also hired mercenary soldiers, or *condottieri*. Moving as a unit, a military leader and his men provided armed support to anybody who paid. Some were foreigners. An Englishman, John Hawkwood, and his men, the White Company, were among the fiercest. Some mercenaries were also lords of Italian cities; for example, the Montefeltro family, rulers of Urbino, financed their municipal budget by hiring out as *condottieri*.

In his book *The Prince*, Machiavelli argues that a successful ruler needs to use cleverness and trickery. In heady times, Italian princes valued brainpower over brute strength, but sometimes they outsmarted themselves. In 1494, Duke Ludovico Sforza of Milan invited the French to help him defeat Naples. Because the French king, Charles VIII, had a claim on the throne of Naples (these families intermarried and seldom agreed whose turn it was to rule), the French accepted.

The French army easily routed Naples's smaller force. But then Sforza and his Italian co-conspirators, including some from the island of Sicily, turned on their northern allies and forced the French to high-tail it over the Alps. Boy, were those French angry. Sforza's trick humiliated them, and the French wanted revenge. Besides, they had just enjoyed a taste of Italian wealth, and they wanted more. After Charles VIII died, Louis XII succeeded him. Charles had been called "the Affable." Nobody called Louis affable. Also believing that he had a claim on Milan's throne, the new French king mounted another invasion force. This time, the target was Ludovico Sforza. Milan wasn't ready, so the French overwhelmed the city, captured Sforza, and threw him in prison, where he died. He wasn't so clever after all.

Things got worse for Italy — a lot worse. Remember those Sicilians who helped Sforza drive the French away in 1494? Their king was Ferdinand, who also ruled Aragon, one of the largest kingdoms in Spain, which was coming together as a united land. (His wife and joint ruler, Isabella, was queen of Castille. See Chapter 19 for more on them.) Ferdinand had a claim to Naples as well. And like the French, he had noticed how rich, and how politically divided, Italy was.

The Holy Roman Emperor, Maximilian, wanted in on the action in Italy, too. The Holy Roman Empire, as I note in other chapters, wasn't really Roman. It started out French, under Charlemagne, but for a long time it was mostly German and Austrian. Yet Maximilian had hereditary "Roman" claims on northern Italy. Since he and Ferdinand were in-laws (two of Max's kids were married to two of Ferdie's), the Emperor sided with Spain. This meant war — actually a series of wars. Spaniards and Imperialists fought to get the French out of Italy. Various Italian city-states fought on one side, then the other.

Spilling outside of Italy's borders

The Italian Wars melded into more wars that spilled out into other parts of Europe (see Chapter 13). Charles I, becoming co-ruler of Spain in 1517 (along with his mother), won election as Emperor Charles V of the Holy Roman Empire two years later. This political victory made the French nervous, because it meant they were in the middle of a Hapsburg Empire sandwich.

The election of Charles wasn't democratic, by the way. Just as the Holy Roman Empire wasn't Roman, it wasn't really an empire, either. The Holy Roman Empire was a conglomeration of states, some of which were practically kingdoms. The electors were powerful princes of seven of those states, who enjoyed the hereditary right to choose each new emperor. They elected Charles.

Being picked Holy Roman Emperor by the electors wasn't always a vote of confidence. Sometimes they chose rulers they thought they could manipulate. Charles, however, had considerable success taking charge. He wrested Milan away from his French rival, Francis I (successor to Louis VII). Charles's Spanish troops even took Francis prisoner. Charles also got Naples, and the other Italian states knew not to mess with him.

Yet that didn't settle things. The Italian Wars melded into a long fight of Hapsburg versus France that lasted until the middle of the eighteenth century.

Before he retired to a Spanish monastery in 1556, the embattled Charles found it necessary to split his empire back into two parts — Spanish and Austrian — to make it less unwieldy and easier to defend. If this reminds you of something that the Roman emperors did more than 1,000 years before Charles's time, good for you. If not, you can read about that in Chapter 5.

By the time Charles called it quits, other things in Europe had changed profoundly, partly as a result of the financial strains of prolonged wars. To start, taxes rose. Princes were forced to borrow money, enriching new generations of bankers — and sometimes bankrupting the bankers when the princes defaulted on loans. Then came this big thing called the Protestant Reformation. (I devote Chapter 14 to the Reformation.)

An irony of the Renaissance is that the place where it began, Italy, ended this era in such disarray and decline. While Spain, Portugal, England, Holland, and other powers were starting worldwide empires and becoming richer and more powerful, the once-mighty Italian city-states remained divided and dominated. Foreigners ruled several of them.

Renaissance buildings and sculptures, once symbols of a thriving movement ahead of its time, became tourist attractions, which they remain today. The symbols of a vital present and a promising future turned into artifacts of yet another glorious past.

Tracking the Centuries

1360s: Geoffrey Chaucer, an English diplomat and poet, travels to Italy and meets the writer Boccaccio.

1396: Coluccio Salutati, chancellor of Florence, invites Manuel Chrysoloras, a scholar from Constantinople, to teach Greek to Italian students eager to probe ancient writings.

About 1420: The artist Filippo Brunelleschi invents the *one-point system* for giving perspective to paintings and drawings.

1453: Constantinople falls to the Ottoman Turks. Many scholars of the Byzantine Empire flee west to Italy.

About 1455: Johann Fust and his son-in-law Peter Schöffer publish the Gutenberg Bible, the first mass-produced book. Gutenberg surrendered his revolutionary press to Fust after being unable to repay a loan to the backer.

About 1473: William Caxton returns to London from Cologne, where he learned printing, and goes into the publishing business with a book about the Trojan War and a volume of sayings of the ancient philosophers.

1519: Charles I of Spain wins election as Emperor Charles V of the Holy Roman Empire. The French, who are geographically between Spain and the Holy Roman Empire, don't find this a reassuring development.

1528: In his book *The Courtier,* Count Baldassare Castiglione spells out rules for gentlemanly behavior. He says you should be good at everything, but you shouldn't look like you're trying too hard.

1543: Andreas Vesalius, anatomy professor at the University of Padua, publishes *Seven Books on the Structure of the Human Body.*

1556: The Emperor Charles V of the Holy Roman Empire retires to a monastery in Spain.

1835: The Roman Catholic Church lifts its 219-year ban on Copernicus's book, *The Revolution of the Heavenly Spheres.*

Chapter 14

Making a Break: The Reformation

. . . .

In This Chapter

▶ Understanding the Church's loss of authority

▶ Insisting on faith: Luther's protest

▶ Spurring revolution in the name of religion

▶ Declaring divine right: Henry VIII's break from Rome

▶ Preaching predestination: Calvin's Puritanism

. . . .

*S*tarting with a disagreement over faith and turning political almost immediately, the Protestant Reformation provoked war and even revolution. It rearranged Europe's power structure. In its wake, the Holy Roman Empire was nearly ruined, and Spain, that most unshakeable of Catholic countries (see Chapter 10), fell into decline.

In this chapter, I guide you through causes and effects of this religious revolution, which spread beyond Europe and eventually around the world.

Cracks in the Catholic Monopoly

To understand how the Reformation began, it helps to consider how ready some people were to rebel against the Catholic Church, which was essentially the only Christian church in Europe. They rebelled for reasons that often had little or nothing to do with the question of how to get into heaven. As in so many conflicts, the reasons included:

✔ **Money:** Many nobles (and commoners, too) thought that the Church had too much of it and demanded too much of theirs.

✔ **Land and other property:** Regional and national rulers thought the Church possessed and controlled too much of it.

✔ **Power and autonomy:** Local rulers, especially in Germany, wanted to wrest power, especially economic control, away from the pope and the Holy Roman Emperor.

Losing authority

How vulnerable to a shake-up was the Catholic Church in the early sixteenth century? Pretty vulnerable, given that Renaissance trends undercut the Church's authority.

For one, the pre-Christian authors (those ancient Greek and Greek-style philosophers that I keep harping about) became part of Christendom during the Renaissance. These Classical authors now were seen as manifestations of God's glory, but their voices and views were diverse and contradictory. Where once there was one supreme source of wisdom — the Church — now wisdom came in a variety of flavors.

The Church even lost its monopoly on interpreting scripture. The first mass-produced book was the Bible, and printers quickly saw how newly literate Europeans wanted to read in their own languages instead of in Latin or Greek. Scholars started translating the Bible into *vernacular* (common) languages. Desiderius Erasmus, the most famous scholar of the time, was a prolific translator of scripture.

For more on the effects of the Renaissance on the Church establishment, turn to Chapter 13.

Satirizing the Church

The scholar Erasmus, who was from the Netherlands and lived in England, also wrote original works saying things that many people agreed with but that few stated as eloquently as he did. In 1509, he ridiculed silly, lazy, and incompetent churchmen in a popular satire called *The Praise of Folly*. Erasmus wasn't anti-Church, but he thought the Church could be run better.

The Catholic Church was a huge, international bureaucracy with layers upon layers of officials. (Remember that virtually every Christian in Western Europe at this time — almost everybody — belonged to one church, the one based in Rome. That's why it was called *the Church* with a capital C. The word *Catholic*, which means "universal," was part of its name, but there was no reason to say so because there were no Protestants — yet.) Like bureaucrats anywhere, some Church officials were inefficient, lazy, and dishonest. Imagine how much worse your state's Department of Motor Vehicles would be if rude, slow clerks claimed divine authority. (What's that? They already do?)

For centuries, there was a widespread feeling that churchmen had it too easy. Folks thought too many priests were hypocrites for telling the rest of society what to do while living in sin themselves. Erasmus knew about such resentment firsthand, because he started life in Rotterdam as the illegitimate son of a priest.

Some bishops, who were at a higher level of the priesthood and sworn to celibacy, kept mistresses and then used Church influence to get advantages for their out-of-wedlock offspring. Even popes had children. Pope Alexander VI, who served from 1492–1503, had many mistresses and many kids, and Pope Clement VII, who precipitated a separate branch of the Reformation in England by refusing to annul the marriage of King Henry VIII to Catherine of Aragon (coming up in this chapter in the section "Spreading Reform to England"), reportedly fathered a son.

Alexander, Clement, and Pope Leo X (who was pope when the Reformation began in 1517) were all privileged men from wealthy families who received cushy Church positions by virtue of their connections. For example, Leo began life as Giovanni de Medici, of the powerful Medici family that controlled the city-state of Florence (see Chapter 13 for more on the Medicis). Leo nearly wiped out the Vatican treasury with his extravagant lifestyle.

Pope Leo X pampered himself with the Church's money, but he also spent it on Renaissance glories. He accelerated construction of St. Peter's Basilica in Rome, a landmark of the period's architecture, and he enlarged the Vatican library. Many Christians, especially in Northern Europe, weren't impressed with these developments; they were tired of seeing their hard-earned coins carted off to Rome to pay for sculptures and painted ceilings. "What good do those things do us?" asked the Germans and the Swiss.

Don't get the impression that all priests (or monks, bishops, cardinals, and popes) were hypocritical or corrupt. Many, and probably most, led devout lives of worship, service to others, and self sacrifice. Those honest churchmen, such as German priest and university professor Martin Luther, resented the bad reputation that followed their corrupt brothers and rubbed off on the Church at large. Church officials promised reforms, and some really tried to clean things up, but abuses persisted.

Erasmus wasn't the first to mock or criticize churchmen. John Wycliffe, an English priest and theologian, had anticipated the Reformation by more than a century when, in the 1370s, he began attacking the worldliness of the Church. Wycliffe argued for limited papal authority over government matters and insisted that churchmen who fell into mortal sin forfeit their authority. But Erasmus's international prominence (he was widely read) and the timing of *The Praise of Folly* directly paved the way for a widespread public criticism of Church abuses — one that followed his book by less than a decade. It has been said that Erasmus laid the egg, and Martin Luther hatched it.

Luther Challenges the System

Many of history's great changes can be traced to a visionary, someone who did what it took to make a dream come true. Martin Luther wasn't one of those visionaries: He didn't set out to trigger religious revolt, let alone unleash international tensions, but that's what he did.

Luther — a monk, priest, and theology professor at Wittenberg University — pondered the individual's relationship to God. His thoughts on that topic interacted with other forces building in Europe in the early sixteenth century, starting a movement that profoundly changed the world even beyond Europe and North America (a continent most Europeans hadn't yet heard of when the Reformation began). Yet it all began with a rather small gesture: a one-man protest.

Luther possessed deep moral conviction, powerful faith, and incredibly stubborn resolve. But if he had known that he was going to split the Church six ways to Sunday, he might not have tacked his protest literature on the door of a Wittenberg church on October 31, 1517. The *95 Theses* (which means 95 arguments) was a list of Luther's objections to the way that Church leaders in his neck of Europe (Germany) sold indulgences, a kind of official forgiveness for sins.

Selling salvation

An *indulgence* was a grant of forgiveness, issued either to a living person or to someone who had died and whose soul was believed to be in *purgatory* (a sort of anteroom in which sinners must be cleansed before entering heaven).

You can think of an indulgence like this: Suppose you do a good deed. Your reward is that God doesn't make you suffer so much for your bad deeds, so you get into heaven a little more easily. Now, suppose you need a good deed to earn this consideration. Doesn't giving the Church money count as a good deed?

But what if your brother died before he could build up his spiritual credits? Not a problem. You, his surviving relative, can give money to the Church by purchasing an indulgence, and then transfer your credit to your bro, getting him off the hook in the afterlife.

Okay, so that's a simplistic explanation of the concept, which also involved a sort of bank account of godly merit, built up through the good works of Jesus and the saints. The important thing to remember is that the practice of selling indulgences led to an impression among common people that they could buy an express, one-way ticket to heaven.

Peddling to pay the pope

In crafting and posting his *95 Theses*, Martin Luther was ticked off in particular at a Dominican friar called Tetzel, who traveled around peddling indulgences. (The word *friar* meant "brother," and it was used for men who were members of certain religious orders, such as the Dominicans.)

Tetzel came into a village or city and gathered a crowd, much as a snake-oil salesman would in a frontier American town three centuries later. Imagine Tetzel hawking indulgences as if they were the latest things in patent medicines for your soul.

Why did he do it? Well, Tetzel was not an entrepreneur, as it may seem. He was a deputy sent out by the newly appointed Archbishop of Mainz.

Another Church practice that bred widespread skepticism was that anyone appointed to a high ecclesiastical office, such as archbishop, had to pay fees to the pope as a sort of recompense for the appointment. If that sounds like a kickback, you've got the idea. In 1514, when the Archbishop of Mainz got his job, Pope Leo X was spending a lot of money in Rome — especially on the building of St. Peter's Basilica. And so Leo set a high fee.

The new Archbishop of Mainz lacked ready cash, so he borrowed from an Augsburg family called Fugger. (No remarks, please.) Powerful banking families, another Renaissance phenomenon that started in Italy, had risen in northern Europe by this time. (The Welser family, also of Augsburg, was the other big banking force in Germany.)

The archbishop needed to repay the Fuggers. To help, the pope gave him an easy way to raise funds: He made the archbishop regional distributor for holy indulgences. Tetzel was the archbishop's sales rep.

Insisting on faith

If you wanted to rub Martin Luther the wrong way, you couldn't come up with a better method than mass-marketing indulgences. As a theology teacher, Luther had thought hard about the correct path to heaven. What did God expect of a Christian?

He decided that God was merciful. As Luther saw it, you must honestly believe. Belief, rather than good works, was the key. In some ways, Luther reflected the Renaissance philosophy of humanism (see Chapter 13) in that he saw a direct relationship between the individual mortal and God. But in other ways, Luther returned to St. Augustine's idea that good works on Earth won't earn you entrance to heaven (see Chapter 12). Instead, you had to rely on God's grace.

Luther thought that a good Christian would do good works — go to church, pray, and be kind to others — as a result of belief, not as a way to escape punishment or win reward. How much one paid to an itinerant salesman monk didn't count at all toward eternal bliss.

In his theses, Luther condemned the indulgence campaign as exploitation, and he slammed the corrupt clerical bureaucracy. But he didn't mean to raise a call for mass rebellion. As a scholar, he observed a tradition that had grown up in the medieval universities: Professors argued points of religion. Luther thought that Tetzel was wrong, so he challenged anyone who supported Tetzel to a debate. He did this on October 31, or All Hallows Eve (the night before November 1, All Souls Day), but this was no trick-or-treat prank. By pinning his theses to the door of the church, Luther issued a public challenge.

A Precarious Holy Roman Empire

Besides the writings of Erasmus and a general unhappiness with the Church, there were other reasons Europe, and especially Germany, were ready to erupt early in the sixteenth century. (Keep in mind that Germany wasn't Germany yet; that wouldn't happen for centuries. It was the Holy Roman Empire, a messy conglomeration of semi-independent states where Germany and Austria are today.)

It had been a long time since the Holy Roman Empire embodied the vision held by the pope when he crowned Charlemagne Emperor of the West in 800 AD. The emperor was supposed to serve as the pope's partner and chief protector of the Church (see Chapter 6), but popes and emperors quarreled often and bitterly.

Searching for sources of cash

When Luther posted his theses, the emperor was Maximilian I, who ruled from 1493–1519. In Chapter 13, I discuss how Max hooked up with Spain to attack the French in Italy. A big reason for that excursion was that the emperor, like everybody else in this story, needed money.

Max enjoyed spending his dough on art. He also liked hunting, flashy clothes, and armor — the perks of being the emperor. Beyond that, he had expensive plans to strengthen the empire. Even money couldn't help him there, however, as long as the individual German princes, whose land made up the empire, held power in their own hands. They were getting stronger and turning their states into little nations.

Max was so strapped for cash sometimes that he couldn't pay his soldiers, or *landsknechts*. This made it hard for him to keep an army. Sometimes the landsknechts hired themselves out as mercenary units, even to the emperor's enemies. Some even resorted to robbery and extortion.

Fighting crime and inflation

Times were hard for other Germans, too. With no strong national government to keep order, and with the line between knight and robber blurred, merchants had to pay protection money or hire their own muscle just to transport goods safely. The high cost of shipping contributed to inflation. Prices rose, not just in Germany, but all over Europe.

The situation was more complex than this (isn't everything?), but the inflation also was tied to an increase in population. A decrease in the number of people in Europe caused by the bubonic plague helped bring about the Renaissance, because plague survivors and their children had more material wealth to go around. (For more on the bubonic plague, turn to Chapter 7.)

Good times bred more people, however, and by the sixteenth century, the population burgeoned. People needed work, food, clothing, and shelter, but there wasn't enough for everybody. Things cost more despite the fact that no one had more money to pay. The price of a loaf of bread, for example, just about quadrupled between 1500 and 1600.

Cash-strapped landlords put the squeeze on peasants in order to get more work for less. People were poor, overworked, overtaxed, hungry, and nervous about both their present and future.

Setting the stage for dissent

Crises of finances, violence, and hunger all help explain why Luther's protest became more than a theological discussion. People took the 95 Theses as a rallying cry against the Church and its high-handedness. Some who agreed with the priest copied Luther's arguments, took them to printing shops, and sent copies all over Germany and beyond. Luther was suddenly famous.

Luther's action still wouldn't have had quite the impact it did, however, if rulers hadn't also been ready to challenge the Church. Some German princes were as edgy as their subjects were. They sought to limit the emperor's meddling in their kingdoms, and they were even more resistant to the pope sticking his nose where they thought it didn't belong.

Seven German princes called the *electors* got to choose the emperor (see Chapter 13). One of them — Frederick, Prince Elector of Saxony — backed Martin Luther in the religious dispute that broke out after 1517. Frederick didn't necessarily agree with Luther, but because Frederick had founded the University of Wittenberg not many years before, he had a stake in protecting his faculty member, the overnight celebrity.

Standing Up to the Emperor

When Martin Luther really needed a friend, Frederick, Prince Elector of Saxony — known as Frederick the Wise — came through for him. It happened shortly after Emperor Charles V, who succeeded his grandfather Maximilian I in 1519, tried to make Luther change what he had said about indulgences and the Church.

Charles made his challenge in 1521 at the Diet of Worms. It wasn't nearly as disgusting as it sounds. In the Holy Roman Empire, the word *diet* had nothing to do with NutriSystem. A *diet* (from the medieval Latin *dieta,* meaning "a day's work") was an all-day meeting — a day in court, or in this case, the Imperial Assembly. *Worms* referred to a city rather than a mess of tubular, dirt-dwelling animals. (Worms is on the Rhine River near Mannheim, Germany.) At the Diet of Worms, Emperor Charles V met with the empire's princes and with churchmen, including Luther. Although no one asked him to ingest squirmy, legless invertebrates, Luther gagged anyway — at the suggestion he give ground.

Oh, he thought about it. When the emperor tells you to change your tune, you have to at least think about it. Luther turned the issue over and over in his mind before he came back the next morning with his answer.

Luther faced up to the emperor, the princes, and the bishops and said, "Here I stand. I can do no other. God help me. Amen." At least, that's how the story goes. There's some doubt over whether he ever really said that, but it's too good a quote to throw away (so here I quote it; I can do no other). Whether those were his exact words or not (and, come to think of it, he didn't even speak English), they sum up what Luther meant.

In the 2003 movie *Luther,* Joseph Fiennes doesn't speak any English, either, but the DVD includes English subtitles. This German biopic takes some liberties with the facts (as all movies do), but it vividly portrays the tensions and excitement of the time. Sir Peter Ustinov, in one of his last films, plays Frederick the Wise.

Luther Gains a Following

After the Diet of Worms, Martin Luther was an outlaw, and he headed home to Wittenberg to prepare for his arrest and a probable death sentence. But on the way, he disappeared. It turned out that Prince Frederick's men kidnapped him. The prince elector locked Luther up for his own protection.

In the castle of Wartburg, Prince Freddy gave Luther a study in which to work, and work he did. Instead of taking back his theses, Luther noisily attacked other beliefs of the Church. Realizing the power of the printing press, he published his ideas — among them his claims that priests weren't the big deal they thought they were. You could get into heaven without one, Luther said. It was cut-out-the-middle-man spirituality. Luther said that Christians should read the Bible for themselves, and he translated his own user-friendly German version. He also wrote both words and music for hymns such as "A Mighty Fortress is Our God" — the theme song of the Reformation.

A pamphlet he published in 1520, *To the Christian Nobility of the German Nations,* was especially popular. Some nobles, scholars, and other people who agreed with Luther's writings began to think of themselves as his followers. Just a few years after the 95 Theses, some Christians began to call themselves *Lutherans.*

The German princes, especially the less devout among them, tended to like Luther's argument that they had a duty to put the Church back in its place. In those times of inflation, a reasoned excuse for confiscating the Church's wealth appealed to free-spending aristocrats. If a powerful noble or merchant became a Lutheran, it often meant that his followers, people who depended on him for their livings, became Lutheran, too — by persuasion or coercion.

Losing control of the Lutheran movement

Anti-Church sentiment, once unleashed, flew out of control. A bunch of knights attacked the Archbishop of Trier in 1522 in an attempt to oust him in the name of Luther. (Luther had nothing to do with it.) Other malcontents, among them former Catholic priests and self-appointed preachers, used Luther's rebellion as a jumping-off point to spread radical ideas far beyond Luther's. They said nobles and the rich should embrace the poor and share the wealth. Luther was *much* too conservative to have taught such a thing, but there was so much pent-up discontent that the extreme ideas took hold and spread.

Unrest turned to violence in 1524 as the *Peasants' War* ripped through central and southwestern Germany and into Austria. "Hey," said Luther, "this wasn't supposed to happen." (My own loose translation.) He thought people who twisted his teachings were even more wicked than churchmen who sold indulgences. On this topic, he wrote a scathing pamphlet titled, *Against the Murdering, Thieving Hordes of the Peasants.*

Luther urged the German princes to crush the rebels. The princes complied (as they would have without Luther's encouragement), calling in soldier-for-hire landsknechts. Thousands of peasants died in battle, and more were captured and put to death.

Choosing sides

After the Peasants' War nastiness was settled, the German princes tried to sort out what to do about Lutheranism. Several sided with Luther. After all, he had sided with them. More to the point, Lutheranism offered them freedom to rule with less interference from Emperor Charles and none from the pope. Some Lutheran partisans formally broke religious ties with Rome and set up their own Lutheran churches. Other princes stuck with Rome and tried to force the Lutheran princes to change their minds.

The Lutheran rulers came to be known as *Protestants,* because they protested their peers' attempts to force them back into the old Church. In 1531, they formed a mutual protection alliance, the *Schmalkald League.* Their relations with Paul III (who became pope in 1534) and Emperor Charles further deteriorated.

The Empire Strikes Back

Charles V was Holy Roman Emperor from 1519–1558. As the Protestant movement grew, Charles V's resources were strained for reasons I discuss in Chapter 13. He was fighting in Italy and taking care of his lands in Spain. He also had a major rivalry with the French. He didn't want to fight the Protestant princes. He wanted to settle the issue with diplomacy.

Finally despairing of that option, the emperor marched an army into Germany in 1546, the same year Luther died. Thus began the first of the Religious Wars of the sixteenth century.

Savoring a bitter victory

In 1547, at the Battle of Mühlberg, Emperor Charles led the loyal Catholic princes of the Holy Roman Empire against the rebel Protestant princes, who had joined together in an alliance called the Schmalkald League. Although Charles's forces defeated them handily, the Protestants wouldn't submit. In the Treaty of Passeau, which ended the war in 1552, Charles offered to make changes in the Catholic Church if they would support him. (Pope Paul III was actually working on reforms of the Counter-Reformation.) The Protestants stood fast.

Even more frustrating for the emperor: Some of the Catholic princes who had been loyal to him during the war started to worry that, with the Protestants defeated, the emperor was getting too powerful. As a result, they turned on him and drove him out of Germany.

Achieving compromise

Charles finally had little choice but to recognize Protestantism. The *Religious Peace of Augsburg* said that each prince in the empire could choose the official church in his own kingdom or duchy. The princes and the emperor signed this agreement in 1555. The Augsburg agreement wasn't a move toward a stronger or more united empire; it was really quite the opposite, but it kept the confederation from falling completely apart.

However, religious war in the Holy Roman Empire wasn't over. It would erupt again in the next century with the Thirty Years' War (see the later section "Along Comes Calvin").

Spreading Reform to England

During the Reformation, Church reform wasn't limited to the Holy Roman Empire. Kings outside Germany reformed their churches, too. For example, Lutheranism spread into the Scandinavian countries, and variants took hold throughout Northern Europe. Ultimately, the Reformation didn't create just one new church — it created many (see Chapter 10).

As in Germany, some rulers in other parts of Europe agreed with Luther's religious convictions, while others saw the growing Reformation as a great excuse to confiscate Church wealth. The king of England was one who certainly did not agree with Luther, yet he was strong-willed and took opportunities as he found them.

Creating the Church of England

In the sixteenth century, England was primed for religious reform, although perhaps not in the same way Germany had been. Papal taxes stirred widespread resentment. The dissident priest John Wycliffe had set the stage, even winning the support of England's royal family, with his arguments about Church abuses in the fourteenth century. Wycliffe also organized the first English translation of the Bible. Also, Desiderius Erasmus, author of the satire on Church abuses, *The Praise of Folly,* lived in England in the early sixteenth century. (Refer to the earlier section "Satirizing the Church" for more on Wycliffe and Erasmus.)

But after the Reformation had begun, especially when it turned violent, Erasmus rejected it. He wanted orderly reform, not revolution. Erasmus's friend Sir Thomas More represented King Henry VIII in Parliamentary arguments against Lutheranism in 1523.

Henry VIII's call for divorce

England's king was vociferously anti-Luther. Henry VIII issued writings condemning the German rebel priest, and a grateful Pope Leo X rewarded Henry with the title Defender of the Faith.

Relations between Rome and London soured, however, when Henry decided that he needed to dump his wife, Catherine of Aragon, shown in Figure 14-1. Note that she was "of Aragon" and a daughter of Ferdinand and Isabella, the Catholic monarchs whose marriage united a large chunk of Spain (see Chapter 19).

Catherine was also the aunt of Charles V, who was both Holy Roman Emperor and king of Spain (as Charles I). All these circumstances gave her a certain pull with the pope.

Henry had gotten engaged to Catherine when he was only 11 and she was the widow of his elder brother, Arthur. She bore Henry five children, but only one — a daughter, Mary — survived. Henry wanted a son to be his heir.

Until Arthur died, Henry wasn't the crown prince. He'd actually been educated to become a churchman — maybe an archbishop. So he knew a bit about religious law, and he thought he knew a lot. He decided his lack of a son was God's punishment for having married his brother's widow. Henry presented that as reason enough for the pope to rule that his marriage to Catherine had never been proper to begin with. Under Church rules, annulment was the only path to legal divorce.

Leo's successor, Pope Clement VII, didn't buy Henry's argument for annulment. Maybe the Emperor Charles, Catherine's nephew, carried more weight in Rome than Henry did. Or maybe Leo knew Henry's *other* reason for wanting a divorce: Anne Boleyn, the king's mistress.

Figure 14-1:
To be rid of wife Catherine of Aragon, Henry VIII cut England's ties with the pope.

© Roger Viollet/Getty Images

A frustrated monarch

Henry's *chancellor,* or chief advisor, was a churchman, Cardinal Thomas Wolsey. Wolsey's ambition was to become pope, so he supposedly knew his way around Church politics.

Henry gave Wolsey the specific job of getting Pope Clement to give in on the divorce question so that Henry could ditch Catherine and make Anne his queen. When Wolsey failed, the king impeached the cardinal and seized his property. Henry exiled Wolsey and then decided to execute him, but Wolsey died in 1530, before the king could get him from York to the chopping block in London.

Henry next tried to hit the pope in the pocketbook. He arranged for Parliament to pass laws cutting English fees and offerings paid to Rome. Actually, one of his advisors, a fellow called Thomas Cromwell, came up with this clever idea. If Parliament cut the payments, Cromwell told the king, Henry could pin the blame on the members.

Clement still didn't budge, so in 1533, Henry married Anne Boleyn anyway. He had an old buddy, Thomas Cranmer, Archbishop of Canterbury, perform the ceremony. (What was Cranmer going to do? Say no to the king? You could lose your head for that.)

Catherine, having never seen *The Starter Wife,* lived out her days quietly in a convent and died in 1536. Clement hadn't given permission to the king to marry again and, when the deal was done, he didn't offer forgiveness. Paul III, who became pope in 1534, held the line and excommunicated the king of England.

Breaking ties with Rome

Henry made a big move in 1534, telling Parliament to declare the king Supreme Head of the Church in England. With that, England broke away from Rome, like the duchies of those Protestant German princes Henry so eloquently disagreed with. But Henry still said he wasn't siding with the Lutherans. If a Lutheran was found in England, the king dutifully ordered the heretic burned at the stake. Henry claimed that he wasn't changing religions, just correcting the pope's boo-boo.

He did add a few Protestant touches to the Church of England, however. For example, he had English translations of the Bible installed in the churches. It was an English church, after all.

Paying the penalty for disloyalty

The converted Henry had no more mercy for Catholics than he had for Lutherans. Never mind that he had been a Catholic until recently.

Staging (then filming) a crisis of conscience

Faith and conscience prevented Sir Thomas More from endorsing Henry VIII's supremacy over the Church of England. To renounce the pope's supremacy, More believed, would be wrong in the eyes of God. More wouldn't give in to save his life.

His dramatic, tragic standoff with Henry inspired playwright Robert Bolt's stage play *A Man*

for All Seasons. It was adapted for a 1966 movie, starring Paul Scofield, Robert Shaw, and Orson Welles, that won that year's Academy Award for Best Picture. Another notable film adaptation is 1988's TV movie *A Man for All Seasons,* directed by and starring Charlton Heston.

Disloyalty wasn't tolerated. Anyone still loyal to Rome was beheaded or *drawn and quartered.* (Drawing and quartering was a gruesome form of dismemberment practiced on living individuals.) Sir Thomas More, who had helped the king attack Protestantism, became chancellor in Wolsey's place and refused to swear obedience to the king's church. Henry ordered More decapitated.

Only one English bishop, John Fisher of Rochester, publicly opposed the new church. Henry ordered Fisher executed, too. Is there any wonder more people didn't speak up?

The king stirred more opposition with his next step. On the advice of More's replacement, the crafty Thomas Cromwell, the king confiscated all the monasteries and convents.

I wouldn't want the job as Henry's chancellor, would you? Not after the last two received death sentences for crossing the boss. But apparently Cromwell was smart enough to hold his own. And Henry liked the way he thought.

Cromwell pointed out to Henry that he could present the confiscation of Church property as a reform measure. He could accuse those monks, friars, and nuns of not doing their jobs, and thus undeserving of the properties they controlled. What Henry really wanted were the monastery lands and treasures — centuries' worth of offerings that pilgrims had given the monks.

Henry sold most of the monasteries, convents, and lands because he suddenly needed a lot of money. Remember that Emperor Charles V and Francis I of France were always fighting. When the two of them made peace and started acting threateningly toward England, Henry decided to boost defense spending.

Nobles bought the former abbeys and priories from the king and turned them into private estates. Now, as any tourist can tell you, they're some of the oldest of the famous "stately homes of England."

Making the Pilgrimage of Grace

Up in northern England, especially Yorkshire, some people came to the defense of the monks. They thought Henry VIII was taking too much power for himself, so in 1536, they marched south. Called the *Pilgrimage of Grace,* it must have looked more like an invasion force.

Astoundingly, Henry was able to talk these armed marchers into going home. He blamed all the problems on Cromwell. Then he ordered his guards to overtake the homeward-bound Yorkshire rebels and kill as many of them as they could in the ugliest, most conspicuous ways possible. He ordered pieces of their hacked-apart bodies set out in all the towns where the rebels had lived to serve as warnings to anyone else who might think about marching on the king.

Realizing Henry's legacy

The Catholic Defender of the Faith had made England a capital of Protestantism, although there would be turmoil over this issue for many decades to come. And what did Henry get for it?

Well, he did get to marry Anne Boleyn, but she never gave him the son he wanted (only another daughter, who turned out to be Queen Elizabeth I). Henry had Anne beheaded and went on to four more wives, only one of whom, Jane Seymour, gave him a son, the sickly Edward VI.

Edward ruled for only a few years. As a devout Protestant, he brought some Reformation ideas into the English Church, but they were largely erased by his half-sister and successor, Mary (Catherine of Aragon's daughter), who re-instituted Catholicism during her brief reign in the 1550s. It took Henry's other daughter, Elizabeth — one of England's greatest monarchs — to bring back the Church of England and make it stick. Wouldn't her daddy have been proud?

Along Comes Calvin

Martin Luther wasn't the last word in Church reformers. Also in the sixteenth century, a young fellow from France moved to Switzerland and shared Protestant teachings that resulted in widespread changes. His name was John Calvin.

Reforming the Swiss church

The Reformation in Switzerland started about the same time it did in Germany and in much the same way. In 1518, a priest named Huldreich Zwingli opposed the selling of indulgences.

As in Germany, fighting broke out over the reform movement. Zwingli, unlike Luther, was in the thick of the violence; he died in battle near Kappel, Switzerland, in 1531. Like the Holy Roman Empire, Switzerland was a confederation of smaller states (the Swiss called them *cantons*). Protestantism eventually won official recognition, meaning that the rulers of the cantons were allowed to decide which brand of Christianity to follow.

Establishing Puritanism

Calvin was a brilliant Classics scholar at the University of Paris when the Reformation began. He was steeped in Greek and Roman philosophy as well as Christian theology. (Those Greeks keep popping up, don't they?) His thinking reached back to St. Augustine's Christian version of Platonic thought, which is built on the idea that humanity is a false and corrupt shadow of God's perfect Idea. Like Augustine, Calvin thought people are bad and have been ever since Adam and Eve sinned. But Calvin agreed with Luther that God is merciful. Instead of condemning everybody to Hell, God chooses to save some.

This type of thinking put Calvin at odds with his peers in France. University scholars in Paris had no patience for Reformation ideas, so Calvin left and headed for Switzerland. Before long, he was invited to teach reform theology in Geneva. His ideas became the basis of what's called *Calvinism* or *Puritanism*. Calvin set them down in an influential 1536 book called *Institutes of the Christian Religion*.

Calvin went much farther than Luther in embracing predestination. Although Calvin supported Luther's idea that good works alone can't win salvation, he dissented regarding the importance of faith in securing a place in heaven. Calvin thought that God decides each person's salvation or damnation at the beginning of creation. Nothing you do or believe influences whether you'll be saved or damned.

But predestination didn't mean that you could do anything you wanted, according to Calvin. He taught that in order to live a godly life, you must be vigilant and strict. It isn't to win God's favor or reap a reward, because Calvin's God doesn't bargain. But if you believe, you have the opportunity and obligation to act on that belief.

Calvin's followers had to watch for every sort of sin and be ready to cast the unworthy out of their church. Those who crossed the Reformed church could be exiled or tortured to death. Geneva, once a wide-open party town, became a place where you could be punished for singing a dirty song or even wearing clothes that were too colorful. The Puritans disapproved of feasts. They banned dancing and thought the theater sinful. They believed in hard work, thrift, and honesty. By working hard and practicing thrift, many Calvinists prospered, and some even became wealthy, which contributed to the prosperity and security of Switzerland itself. Well-heeled Puritans also shared their wealth with the Calvinist church, adding to its growth and influence.

Calvin's ideas were so strict that more-liberal Genevans initially resisted and even threw him out of town. But Calvin returned, and by the time he died in 1564, Geneva was considered Calvin's town, a Puritan town. His critics called him "the Pope of Geneva."

Puritanism soon became influential in other parts of the world as well, as the following sections illustrate.

Causing turmoil in France

Because John Calvin came from France, it seems right that his teachings returned there. Ministers from Geneva spread the word, but as had happened with the Reformation in the Holy Roman Empire and in Switzerland, some French nobles broke with Catholicism for reasons that were more political than religious. They clashed with Catholic rivals. The conflict erupted into armed violence in 1562, with intermittent fighting taking the form of nine separate French Wars of Religion over the next 36 years.

The French royal family saw the French Calvinists, or *Huguenots,* as a threat. The Huguenots suffered severe persecution. King Henry II, who came to power in 1547, wanted to kill every Protestant in France and the Netherlands. His sons Charles IV and Henry III continued this policy. Before he became king, Henry III was among the soldiers who slaughtered 50,000 Huguenots at the Massacre of St. Bartholomew in 1572.

It wasn't until Henry IV gained France's throne in 1598 that the country settled down. Henry IV had been a Calvinist, but he had to become Catholic in order to rule. He still liked the Huguenots, however, and he gave them forts from which to fend off attacks.

Sparking rebellion in Holland

Calvinism caught on in the northern Netherlands, called Holland. This development didn't sit well with the king of Spain, Phillip II, who also ruled that country (inherited from his dad, Holy Roman Emperor Charles V).

While the southern Netherlands remained Catholic and Spanish, the Calvinist north broke free in 1608 and became the United Provinces.

The Calvinist teachings of hard work and thrift helped push the Dutch to successes in navigation and trade. They excelled as merchants and colonists through the seventeenth century.

Weakening the Holy Roman Empire

By 1618, both Protestantism and Catholicism had changed. Militant Calvinism infused the Lutheran movement. Catholicism, through a reform movement called the Counter-Reformation, had managed to reinvigorate itself.

Protestants and Catholics clashed again in the last big religious war of the Reformation, the *Thirty Years' War* (1618–1648). It broke out after the Protestants in Bohemia tried to appoint a Protestant king in place of the Catholic emperor of the Holy Roman Empire.

Emperor Mathias sent forces to oppose the Bohemian Protestants. German Catholic states waded in behind the empire. Protestant states backed the Bohemians. Spain, still ruled by Hapsburg cousins of the emperor, sent soldiers to help him, and the Catholics got the upper hand.

But then in marched the Swedes on the Protestant side, commanded by King Gustavus Adolphus. The Protestants were on top until Gustavus died in battle. Then the Catholics were poised for victory — except that one more country was about to enter the war.

It was Catholic France. Did this mean the end for the Protestants? Well, not exactly. France under Louis XIII and his top government minister Cardinal Richelieu (that's right, a high official of the Roman Catholic Church) got into this conflict on the *Protestant* side. Richelieu's interest was France's security. He mobilized against the Hapsburg family — rulers of the Holy Roman Empire and Spain — to keep them from getting too powerful. (See how "religious" this war was?)

French troops helped secure the Peace of Westphalia, ending the war in 1648. After decades of fighting, Germany was an economic wreck. Spain was bankrupt; fighting the Reformation sent it into a long decline. In retrospect, it would have been better to let the Bohemians have their Protestant king.

Puritanism in England and Scotland

As Calvinist teachings caught on in England, some people there wanted to make Puritanism part of the Church of England. This movement eventually led to the English Civil War in 1642, the execution of King Charles I, and the establishment of the *Protectorate* — a government of and by the Puritans (see Chapter 8).

Scotsman John Knox (1523–1572) was a Catholic priest who became a Lutheran and came under Calvin's influence during the time that he spent in Geneva.

Knox founded the Church of Scotland in 1560. The Scottish Calvinists, called *Presbyterians,* organized their worship and religious authority after the Swiss model, but they faced a powerful critic in King James VI. He hated Puritanism and installed bishops in the Scottish Church. James VI became King James I of England in 1603 and thus the head of the Church of England (see Chapter 19).

Emigrating to America

The Pilgrims who came from England to North America onboard the *Mayflower*, landing at Cape Cod Bay, Massachusetts, in 1620, were called *Separatists*. They broke away from the Church of England so that they could freely observe their Calvinist beliefs. They were soon followed by somewhat less radical Puritans, who would have preferred to stay within the English church but make it more Calvinist. In New England, the two groups became virtually indistinguishable.

Considered founders of American society, these people adhered to a highly moralistic brand of Christianity — not unlike the rigorous Calvinism practiced in Geneva — and shaped social attitudes and civil policy for centuries.

New England Puritans earned notoriety for labeling certain women as witches and persecuting and killing them. This practice wasn't exclusive to America, Puritans, or even Protestants. Catholics burned witches throughout medieval times. The judgmental strictures of Calvinism, however, tended to encourage this kind of thing. Scottish Presbyterians were also especially strident in their witch hunts.

Tracking the Centuries

1509: Desiderius Erasmus publishes his satire on Church corruption, *The Praise of Folly*.

October 31, 1517: Martin Luther nails his *95 Theses,* a protest against Church abuses, to a church door in Wittenberg, Saxony.

1524: The Peasants' War, a rebellion of the poor against nobles, rips through central and southwestern Germany and into Austria.

1534: On the orders of Henry VIII, the English Parliament declares the king Supreme Head of the Church in England, superceding the authority of the pope.

1536: French-Swiss religious leader John Calvin publishes his influential book *Institutes of the Christian Religion,* setting down the tenets of Calvinism.

1555: The Religious Peace of Augsburg grants each prince in the Holy Roman Empire the right to decide the official church affiliation of his own kingdom or duchy.

1572: The future King Henry III of France is among soldiers who slaughter 50,000 Huguenots (French Protestants) at the Massacre of St. Bartholomew.

1608: The Protestant northern region of the Netherlands (Holland) breaks free of Catholic Spanish rule and becomes the United Provinces.

1620: English Puritans arrive in Massachusetts seeking religious freedom.

1648: The Peace of Westphalia ends the Thirty Years' War.

Chapter 15

Opening Up to Science and Enlightenment

Science and engineering shape everything in today's society — not just multimedia smartphones and global positioning systems that will fit on your keychain. I mean everything. For centuries, human beings have used scientific inquiry, method, and invention to remake the world.

Every scientific advance traces back to an idea. Yet because so much of science's incredible yield is right here where you can touch it, use it, and curse at it (especially when your laptop crashes), just how all this hardware and software owes its distant origins to philosophers is easy to overlook. Just as easy to forget: how philosophy owes huge areas of modern thought to science.

Mingling Science and Philosophy

The electric light you use to read and the computerized publishing process that produced this book are obvious examples of how science touches you. But so is your shirt. It may be made of a synthetic fiber, a product of chemistry. Even if it's made of a natural fiber such as cotton, consider that the fiber comes from a plant that was almost certainly grown by scientific methods and harvested with machines powered by internal combustion engines — more science and engineering. Then the fabric was woven mechanically on electric-powered looms and probably colored with chemical dye — yet more science.

What you eat, how you travel, what you do for a living, and the way you spend your leisure time are almost certainly all marked in some way by scientific discoveries and inventions, new and old.

Where did all this inventiveness come from — besides the marvelous human mind? People have always come up with new methods and new tools for getting things accomplished. But the scientific and engineering versatility that defines today's world stems from a tradition tracing back to the ancient Greek philosophers, a tradition of asking questions about the world and how it works. (See Chapter 11 for more about the Greek philosophers and the beginnings of science.)

Things really got cooking when the Renaissance (see Chapter 13), an economic and intellectual movement that reached back to Greek and Roman scholarship, brought forth a Scientific Revolution in the seventeenth century. And that led to the Industrial Revolution in the eighteenth century. Discoveries and inventions — and the habits of thought they inspire — have been revolving madly ever since. Science shaped technology, which shaped industry, which shaped economies, which shaped society at large.

The Scientific Revolution was born of philosophy and brought forth new ways of thinking. Rationalism and empiricism, both influential ways of thinking about the world, came out of scientific perspectives. The Enlightenment of the eighteenth century, also called the *Age of Reason,* had its roots in science. Ideas birthed during this age fueled the American and French Revolutions (find more on revolutions in Chapter 9).

The scientific and engineering applications that created the Industrial Revolution changed the way people made their livings, bringing hardship to many and fantastic rewards for a canny (or lucky) few. Social changes including child labor, slums, and newly wealthy industrialists influenced philosophy and inspired the new field of economics.

Starting a Scientific Revolution

From a sharpened stick to a campfire to those flaked stone blades that early humans taught themselves to make to silicon chip microcircuits, humans have a drive to come up with useful tools. So even without the Greek philosophers and their followers, people may have devised some of the modern wonders you take for granted every day.

But as it happened, Renaissance scholars — European guys steeped in old Greek ideas — were the ones who kick-started scientific inquiry and headed humanity toward this modern, scientific world.

Gazing at the heavens: Astronomy

Among the most influential scientists were astronomers. The Renaissance spirit (see Chapter 13), as embodied in Poland's Copernicus, brought about new theories concerning Earth's place in relation to the sun and planets. Copernicus's theories challenged the medieval beliefs (founded on the work of Aristotle and the Greek-Egyptian astronomer Ptolemy) that Earth was the center of the universe and that the stars were eternal and fixed in place.

Brahe sees a comet

Other philosophers of the sixteenth century were carefully noting the night sky. A Dane named Tycho Brahe (1546–1601) pioneered modern astronomy, even though he had no telescope, by making painstaking measurements and multiple observations.

Brahe was from a noble family in what was then Danish Sweden, and he won the sponsorship of the Danish crown, including an island (Hven) and money to build his observatory there. Brahe had the wealth, the instruments (such as navigator's sextants for measuring the positions of stars), and assistants to help him explore the skies as nobody before him had ever done.

Among his discoveries, Brahe realized in 1572 that a nova, or exploding star, was farther away than the planets. As something new in the sky, the nova wasn't supposed to be among the stars, because the stars were considered eternal. In 1577, he realized that a comet was farther away than the moon. This finding also upset conventional assumptions about how the sky was arranged. The comet's distance and movement especially clashed with a long-held idea about transparent spheres that supposedly carried the planets around Earth.

Brahe was daring enough to conclude that if the comet could move through them, perhaps the spheres didn't exist. Perhaps the planets moved independently. This theory began astronomy's shift from geometry (tracing the curves and relationships of the spheres) to physics (trying to understand the motion of independent heavenly bodies).

Brahe couldn't embrace one daring idea of Copernicus's — that Earth moves. Besides overturning Aristotle's cosmology, a moving Earth challenged the Lutheran Brahe's religious sensibility.

Brahe fell back on an old *proof* for a fixed, immobile Earth: If you shoot an arrow straight up on a windless day, it falls straight down, landing at the spot where you fired it. "If the earth rotates toward the east," he wrote, "a body thrown from it would travel toward the west; birds which fly from their nest would be carried miles away before they alighted." Remember that this was more than a century before Englishman Isaac Newton wrote about gravity and posited laws of motion.

Further, Brahe couldn't detect the *parallax,* a movement in the positions of the stars, that would show him that the ground from which he observed them was a moving platform. The idea that they were so far away that his instruments couldn't detect this movement made no sense to him. The entire universe, he thought, was only about 14,000 times as large as Earth.

These theories and disagreements illustrate how difficult it was for science to slough off old prejudices. Even Tycho Brahe, a star watcher from the time he was a teenager and the guy with the best instruments and the best information yet gathered, couldn't get past some of his essentially non-scientific ideas about how the universe must work.

Kepler charts planets

After Brahe died, his assistant and scientific heir, the German Johannes Kepler (1571–1630), took Brahe's copious data and applied it to support Copernicus's theories.

Kepler, who couldn't see well and had limited use of his hands (both the result of severe smallpox when he was a toddler), nonetheless came up with laws of planetary motion that have been the basis for study of the solar system since his time. The first of these laws is something you probably ran across in elementary school: Each planet travels an elliptical orbit with the sun at one focus.

Galileo's telescope

While Kepler worked with Brahe's data, an Italian math teacher, Galileo Galilei (1564–1642), came up with a fresh and exciting way to check out the stars by using cutting-edge technology. Only recently developed and considered a tool for gathering military intelligence, the telescope turned out to work even better for expanding scientific intelligence.

Galileo (best known by his first name) saw heavenly visions no one had seen before, such as mountains on the moon and Jupiter's own moons. In 1610, Galileo reported his findings in a book, *Sidereal Messenger. (Sidereal,* from a Latin word for "star," means "pertaining to constellations or stars.")

Galileo also saw, as nobody could before him, just how right Copernicus was: Many heavenly bodies clearly didn't orbit Earth. He published these findings in 1632, a move that got him in trouble with Church authorities. Rome's branch of the Inquisition, which wasn't as notorious as the Spanish Inquisition (covered in Chapter 10) but still fiercely conservative, forced him to recant and sentenced the then-69-year-old Galileo to live the rest of his life under house arrest.

Galileo, in true Renaissance fashion (find more on the Renaissance in Chapter 13), was much more than an astronomer. He was also an artist, musician, engineer, and mathematician.

Galileo's work in physics paved the way for England's brilliant Isaac Newton, born the year Galileo died. Perhaps the best-known physical principle that Galileo established is that weight doesn't determine the rate at which an object falls. In other words, if you discount or equalize wind resistance or any other friction, a bowling ball and a soccer ball fall at the same speed. Legend says Galileo established this principle by dropping balls off the Leaning Tower of Pisa, but that's not so. His experiment involved timing balls of equal size but unequal weights rolling down an incline. Galileo approached his work with careful observation, experimentation, and mathematics. In his wake, science came to depend increasingly on unbiased inquiry, coming at a question without prejudice in order to base any conclusion on hard evidence or a solid mathematical model.

Advancing scientific method

All kinds of discoveries came from people following Galileo's example — in physics, mathematics, anatomy, astronomy, and more.

An English nobleman, statesman, and philosopher, Francis Bacon (1561–1626) did a good job of putting his ideas into words. He argued in favor of *induction,* working from observed or demonstrated specifics to a general principle. Bacon's certainty that nature could be understood and even controlled became the orthodoxy of *natural philosophy.*

Another Englishman, the genius physicist and mathematician Isaac Newton came along a bit later (1642–1727). Newton is also cited as establishing scientific method, although he's more famous for establishing things such as the Law of Gravity (his niece began the legend that an apple falling from a tree inspired him), among other useful physical laws. He also invented calculus.

Newton applied his work with gravity to Kepler's laws of planetary motion. All the fellows mentioned in this chapter built on each other's work. Although the Internet didn't exist back then, the printing press (see Chapter 13) made keeping up with one another much easier for scholars.

Here's a sampling of other advances from this time:

- William Harvey (1678–1757), who studied at Padua, Italy, discovered the circulation of the blood.
- Carl Linne (1707–1778), who was known by his Latin name, Linnaeus, classified species of the plant and animal kingdoms for the first time.
- Robert Bakewell (1725–1795) explored scientific methods for breeding bigger, stronger farm animals.

Waking Up to the Enlightenment

In "Rules of Reasoning in Philosophy," an essay included in his 1687 book *Principia,* Isaac Newton writes, "We are to admit no more causes of natural things than such as are both true and sufficient to explain their appearances."

This approach toward exploring the world — objectively, without prejudice — was also a foundation for a branch of philosophy called *empiricism,* the idea that knowledge is based on experience and derived from the senses.

Along with *rationalism* (a contrasting way of seeking truth based in inherent reason rather than experience), empiricism signaled more than a growing openness to new ideas. These and related philosophies, together called the *Enlightenment,* rearranged conventional thinking, then politics and government, in earthshaking ways.

Experiencing empiricism

John Locke (1632–1704), an English medical doctor and philosopher, introduced empiricism in his 1689 *Essay Concerning Human Understanding.* He and his empiricist heirs — among them the Scotsman David Hume (1711–1776) — took the natural sciences as their model for all knowledge.

Locke's work was tremendously important to philosophy, but he had just as big an influence on political thought, especially with his idea that authority derives solely from the consent of the governed.

If you contrast that with older notions about the divine right of kings (see Chapter 10), you can see how Locke's idea led to political upheaval. Locke's work influenced the men who set the American Revolution in motion. Some French guys that you can read about later in this chapter were on a similar wavelength.

Living a "nasty, brutish, short" life

Not every seventeenth- and eighteenth-century philosophy rooted in scientific thinking seemed pointed toward popular revolt. Thomas Hobbes (1588–1679) was an Englishman who took an intellectual route from mathematics to political theory. The path led him to advocate absolute monarchy.

The Oxford-educated, well-traveled Hobbes became interested rather late in life in why people allowed themselves to be ruled and in what would be the best government. In 1651, he wrote his famous work *Leviathan.* (Although the word means "sea monster" and sometimes refers to a whale, Hobbes applied it to the powerful state, or commonwealth.)

Hobbes argued that each person is self-interested and thus the people collectively can't be trusted to govern society. For all his distrust of human nature, Hobbes was interested in justice and advocated that people band together so that the monarch would hear their concerns. He even coined the phrase "voice of the people."

Reasoning to rationalism

Rationalism, another seventeenth-century philosophy, chose reason rather than observation (the senses) as the basis for knowledge.

That way of thinking traces back to René Descartes (1596–1650), the French mathematician who invented analytical, or *Cartesian* (for Descartes), geometry. (Cartesian geometry uses algebra to solve geometric problems, in case you were wondering who to blame for that.)

Descartes believed reason could be based on knowledge that just exists — independent of sense-experience. (Think of the way mathematical principals seem to exist on a plane separate from everyday reality.)

Descartes decided that the only thing beyond doubt was his own thinking. This resulted in one of the most memorable quotes in all philosophy: "I think, therefore I am."

Rationalism grew into a political movement, too. Based in Paris, it was embodied in a group of writers including the poet Voltaire (1694–1778) and Swiss-born essayist Jean-Jacques Rousseau (1712–1778).

Expanding to the Encyclopedists

In the 1770s, Voltaire and other leading thinkers, led by the critic Denis Diderot (1713–1784), published *Encyclopèdie,* a collection of social and political writing that uses reason to attack France's old order, the *ancien régime.*

The Encyclopedists were intensely interested in the American Revolution, which broke out in the same decade as their collaboration. The interest was mutual. Many of America's rebels were Enlightenment thinkers — especially Thomas Jefferson, who wrote the Declaration of Independence. Signed in 1776, it contains phrases such as "We hold these truths to be self-evident" (rationalism) and "certain unalienable Rights" that sound inspired by Locke and Rousseau.

Jean-Jacques Rousseau's works — especially his 1755 *Discourse on the Origin and Foundations of Inequality Amongst Men*, which emphasized the natural goodness of human beings, and 1762's *The Social Contract* — had a big influence on political thinking of the time. *The Social Contract* introduced the slogan, "Liberty, Equality, Fraternity," the battle cry of the French Revolution in 1789 (see Chapter 8).

Engineering the Industrial Revolution

Some thinkers were more interested in solving practical problems in the material world. If physical reality was not just knowable but controllable, as Francis Bacon thought, then it fell to engineers to devise ways to control it.

One of these engineers, England's Jethro Tull (1674–1741), invented the seed drill (which hardly seems a good reason for a 1970s folk-rock band to steal his name). The seed drill (unlike the flute, the featured instrument in the Jethro Tull band) allowed crops to be planted more quickly, in neat rows that you could weed between. Crop production rose as a result.

England's Thomas Savery (1650–1715) thought along practical lines, too. In 1698, he patented a device that used steam pressure to pump water out of tin and coal mines. With the help of blacksmith Thomas Newcomen, Savery improved his device until he had a commercially feasible steam engine. Its primary use remained pumping water, but using the steam engine to turn grinding wheels, as in a flour mill, occurred to other, equally practical folks.

In the second half of the eighteenth century, Thomas Hargreaves (1774–1847), an illiterate carpenter in Nottingham, England, built a machine that put several spindles on a frame to spin several threads at once, making possible a textile production volume far beyond that of the spinning wheel. He patented his *spinning jenny* (he named it after his wife) in 1768. In the next year, Richard Arkwright came out with a similar device that was powered by a water wheel, as grindstones in mills often were.

For centuries, women had spun thread and yarn by hand and woven textiles on hand looms. These were called *cottage industries* because they were carried out in people's homes. Arkwright's machine and others were too big, too expensive, and too complex for people to use at home.

Businessmen put up large buildings where several of Arkwright's water frames could be set up in one huge room with hired laborers to operate them. This process got bigger, faster, and more powerful in 1779 when

Samuel Crompton (1753–1827) came up with the *spinning mule* (named after his brother-in-law — no, just kidding). The water-powered mule could spin up to 1,000 threads at a time and could also be rigged to a newfangled steam engine.

Large-scale industrialization was off and running. Scotland's James Watt perfected the steam engine in 1790, and more and richer investors got behind this new factory system. Mass production of goods created a need for better ways to transport them and the raw materials that manufacturing required. Industrialization led to widespread networks of canals for barge traffic. Then some bright inventors figured out how to make the steam engine mobile, which meant railroads and steamships (which I cover in Chapter 9), and, as you well know, innovations ever since.

Dealing with the social fallout

The Industrial Revolution was just as profound a change as any political upheaval. It killed cottage industries and separated home from workplace, forcing people to move to the cities for jobs. England, and then other countries, became urban as never before. And it wasn't just established cities like London that were growing like weeds; brand new towns sprang up around mills, mines, and factories.

Although they created wealth for factory owners and employment for thousands of people, these social changes caused serious problems, too. Country folk who relocated for factory jobs found themselves in small, crowded houses with inadequate ventilation and sanitation. Working-class neighborhoods rapidly deteriorated into miserable industrial slums.

Factory owners had absolute control. Remember that Europe's population had grown rapidly through the Renaissance, so labor was plentiful and cheap. Workers had no leverage and worked under conditions you wouldn't put up with: A workday was a hard 12 hours or more; factories ran six days a week, and so did workers.

Many of the new machines didn't require a man's strength. Power looms and spinning machines could be run by women and children, many of whom had little choice but to work those long hours — for less pay than men got. Figure 15-1 shows one such worker.

The Industrial Revolution created a new, urgent need for coal and iron. Coal fired the steam engines that powered the machinery, after all. In the 1850s, an engineer called Henry Bessemer (1813–1898) came up with a cheap way to make *steel,* a purified iron with hardening agents added. Steel mills rose, and mining boomed.

Figure 15-1:
Children often tended the machines of the Industrial Revolution.

© CORBIS

In the mines, even little kids did grueling physical labor, such as pulling heavy coal wagons along tracks deep underground, through tunnels too small for even a donkey to work easily. For all the work there was to do, poverty was cruel. You took the job on the factory owner's terms, or your family starved.

Such conditions inspired new lines of social philosophy — the most influential developed by the German Karl Marx, whom I discuss in the later section "Developing capitalism and Marxism."

Raging against the machines: Luddite uprising

Legend says that in 1782 (or by some accounts, 1779), a laborer in Leicestershire, England, Ned Ludd, destroyed some machinery used to make stockings. Ludd blamed the machines for putting local hand-knitters out of work.

Ludd's name came up in 1812 when workers in Nottingham rioted, attacking and destroying power looms. The rioters saw the new machinery as the source of their misery. These people were called the Ludds, or *Luddites,* after the man who supposedly inspired them. The authorities rounded them up and tried them altogether in London. Many were hanged, and others were deported to Australia.

Ever since, people who blame or fear technology have been called *Luddites.* The word saw resurgence in the late twentieth century with the dawning of the digital age and many people's resistance to using computers.

Marketing Economics

Just as philosophy gave rise to individual scientific disciplines, it also split off into other branches of philosophical thought. In the eighteenth century, economics became a discipline in itself.

Playing the money game with Adam Smith

Scotsman Adam Smith (1723–1790) used his professorships in logic and moral philosophy at Glasgow University to study how markets work and new manufacturing methods such as division of labor.

Smith traveled to Paris and met with philosophers who were transforming French political thought (and who are mentioned earlier in this chapter, in the section "Expanding to the Encyclopedists"). He found himself particularly in tune with Francois Quesnay, who opposed tariffs and other government intervention in international trade. Smith's ideas fit into the French Encyclopedists' notion of an inherent and just social order.

Smith believed that if government left the marketplace alone, individuals pursuing selfish economic ends would be led, as if by an *invisible hand*, to benefit society as a whole. Of course, it hasn't always worked out that way, especially not when you take into account the squalor and poverty that accompanied the Industrial Revolution. The worldwide economic crisis of 2008–2009 can be seen as a more recent example of Smith's invisible hand failing to do its job.

Over the long term, Smith's ideas about economic freedom, which he presented in his 1776 book *An Inquiry into the Nature and Causes of the Wealth of Nations,* were enormously influential in the development of modern economic theory and continue to be cited today.

Developing capitalism and Marxism

Adam Smith's theories support free-market capitalism, although Smith never called it that. Another classical economist (in the field of scholarship Smith founded) invented the word *capitalism* and saw *capitalists* — those who own the means of production — as oppressors.

Karl Marx was born in Trier, Germany, in 1818 and grew up seeing the effects of industrialization. He was attracted by the ideas of Georg Friederich Wilhelm Hegel (1770–1831). Hegel, an idealist, developed his own brand of *dialectic,* a philosophical technique for inquiry. Dialectic traces back to fifth-century BC Athens and the philosopher Socrates, who pretended he didn't know the answers to questions he asked as a way of using those questions to coax truths out of the people who answered him. Hegel's dialectic involves putting forth something as true (thesis), denying it (antithesis), and then combining the two (synthesis) to arrive at a greater truth.

Unlike Hegel, Marx came to believe that everything is composed exclusively of physical bits within time and space. In other words, he was a materialist. Forms of materialist philosophy go back to another Greek, Epicurus. Marx nonetheless applied Hegel's dialectic as he worked toward his own theories about economics and class struggle. (You can find out about Socrates and Epicurus in Chapter 11.)

Marx saw *capitalism* — his word for the Industrial Revolution's economic system dominated by factory and mine owners — as a primitive societal stage just above feudalism. Capitalism was a plateau on the way toward socialism and ultimately, what he thought of as an ideal arrangement, *communism*.

In his major work, 1867's *Das Kapital,* Marx describes the state as an instrument of class rule, supporting private capital and suppressing the masses. In contrast to Smith's theories about economic freedom benefiting society as a whole, Marx looks at the realities of the Industrial Revolution and argues that the need to earn a profit forces wages down to a subsistence minimum.

Marx writes that capitalist societies are unstable, defined by contradictions. Because the need for profit keeps wages down, workers can't achieve purchasing power to acquire goods that the economy produces. (He failed to anticipate the letter that starts: "Dear Mr. Marx: Congratulations! You have been pre-approved for a Citibank VISA account.")

Capitalism's inherent tendency toward booms and slumps, Marx says, will worsen until it incites a working class revolution. He argues that the working class, or *proletariat,* will grab the reins of the state and establish a people's dictatorship. Marx also argues that because an industrial economy is capable of producing enough for everybody, there's no *need* for social strata. Communal ownership will bring the abolition of social class; a classless society will lead to the withering away of the state, resulting in communism.

Marx and his collaborator, Friederich Engels (1820–1895), envisioned this change taking place in Germany and then spreading through the rest of industrialized Europe. The last place they figured their economic theories would click was the rural, economically backward empire of Russia.

Yet with a little reworking by Vladimir Lenin (more on him in Chapter 9), Russia became the starting place for an experiment in Marxism. The Union of Soviet Socialist Republics (USSR) didn't work out quite as Marx and Engels predicted. The state eventually fell away all right, in 1991, but it happened largely because the USSR was bankrupt and had lost its political credibility. The USSR was replaced by another state, today's Russia.

Still, Marxism, which also took hold in various forms adapted to China, Cuba, Vietnam, North Korea, and a few other outposts, was a major influence on the twentieth century — although Marx may not have recognized many of the interpretations of his ideas. Many nations in the twentieth century, including those of Western Europe, developed forms of democratic socialism that were influenced by Marx but not chained to his ideas.

In general, the experience of the twentieth century shows that allowing people to pursue wealth brings a more robust and resilient economy driven by incentive. Putting everything under government ownership tends to breed economic stagnation. Even China, the largest Marxist nation, reintroduced capitalist elements to its economy at the end of the twentieth century.

By contrast, however, many governments were forced to intervene in the worldwide banking industry — for example, committing public money to shore up struggling private firms — during the economic crisis of 2008. Financial firms that were once flagships of free market economics found themselves forced to seek rescue from the state. Marx may have relished the irony.

Tracking the Centuries

1543: The Polish astronomer Copernicus publishes his theory that the sun is at the center of the universe.

1560: Tycho Brahe, a teenager in Denmark, sees a partial solar eclipse and decides to devote himself to astronomy.

1564: Galileo Galilei is born in Pisa, Italy.

1610: After aiming a new invention, the telescope, at the night sky, Galileo reports his findings in his book, *Sidereal Messenger.* His most startling observation: Copernicus was right that planets don't orbit Earth.

1687: Isaac Newton's greatest book, *Principia,* establishes the basic laws of physics, including his famous third law of motion: "For every action there is an equal and opposite reaction."

1768: Thomas Hargreaves invents a machine that can spin several threads at once, the *spinning jenny.*

1770s: In Paris, Denis Diderot collects the works of his fellow thinkers and writers, including Voltaire, into *Encyclopèdie,* an anthology attacking France's old order.

1776: In *An Inquiry into the Nature and Causes of the Wealth of Nations,* Adam Smith argues that if government left the marketplace alone, individuals pursuing selfish economic ends would be led, as if by an *invisible hand,* to benefit society as a whole.

1812: Rioting workers in Nottingham, England, destroy power looms. They call themselves *Luddites,* after Ned Ludd, an earlier rebel against factory machines.

1867: In the book *Das Kapital,* Karl Marx describes the state as an instrument of class rule, supporting private capital and suppressing the masses.

1991: The Union of Soviet Socialist Republics, founded upon Marxist principles, collapses.

2008: The United States Congress approves a plan to prevent the collapse of the American economy by rescuing foundering private financial services companies using public funds.

Part IV
Fighting, Fighting, Fighting

The 5th Wave   By Rich Tennant

"We're primarily a spice company. Recently, our most popular spice has been gunpowder."

In this part . . .

Sadly, war is inseparable from human history. War and the ability and willingness to wage war drives societies and nations — a fact I chronicle throughout this book. Military might is important — often tragically important. People fight wars over boundaries, resources, ethnic differences, religious disagreements, and political alliances, among too many other causes. For example, in the twenty-first century, the United States initiated two wars in response to a terrorist attack on New York City, although it was never shown that the second of the nations invaded (Iraq) had anything to do with that attack.

In this part, you uncover the origins of war, how warfare has changed over many millennia, and how those changes shaped the world. You also get a glimpse of latter-day movements to end international aggression.

Chapter 16

Sticks and Stones: Waging War the Old-Fashioned Way

● ●

In This Chapter

▶ Reaching back to the roots of warfare

▶ Organizing armies within civilizations

▶ Battling deadly Assyrian and Persian versatility

▶ Gathering the Roman legions

▶ Standing together as Greeks: The phalanx

● ●

*W*ithout warfare, the human story would be very different, maybe unrecognizable. War stories are among the earliest and most influential folklore and literature. A prime example is *The Iliad,* which I discuss in Chapter 4. For millennia, everybody knew who fought the Trojan War and that the Greeks had won thanks to the epic poem.

Cultures in every corner of the world worshipped war gods and defined themselves by military conquest. By looking at how early wars were fought, you can get an idea of what set this violent species on the path toward smart missiles, stealth aircraft, and neutron bombs.

Fighting as an Ancient Way of Life

When outsiders first stumbled across the interior valleys of New Guinea in the 1930s, they found village after village of Stone Age farmers who looked on the people of the other villages around them as eternal enemies, or at least potential enemies. Revenge wars whose root causes were lost in time were the overwhelming rule.

We're not the only ones making war

Scientists say humankind isn't the only war-making species. What other animal indulges in such mass violence? For one, humanity's closest genetic cousin, the chimpanzee. Researchers have seen bands of male chimps from one group raid another band. If they can, they kill all the other group's males and gain mating privileges with the females.

Jane Goodall, the most famous researcher to study chimps, said, "If they had firearms and had been taught to use them, I suspect they would have used them to kill." This and other evidence causes biologists such as Michael P. Ghiglieri of the University of Northern Arizona to believe that human beings didn't invent war at all. Rather, war is a part of pre-human behavior.

In the late 1970s, anthropologist Carol Ember reported that 64 percent of remaining hunter-gatherer societies in the world at the time fought a war at least every two years. War was rare or absent in only 10 percent of groups studied. In the 1980s, another anthropologist, K.E. Otterbein, turned up even more dismaying results: Studying both hunter-gatherer and primitive farming peoples, he found that 92 percent waged war.

Archeologists note how often ancient human skulls appear to have received violent, bone-breaking blows as if from clubs or axes. The evidence suggests that ancient times were violent times and that people have always fought wars, or at least engaged in armed skirmishes.

Raising Armies

Cave people made war, but war only got organized on a large scale when civilization did. Armies arose among early civilizations in the Middle East (see Chapter 4), as did formations, such as the column and the line; and classic military strategy, such as the *flanking maneuver* (going around the side of the enemy line).

Sometime after 10,000 BC, the bow and sling both joined the warrior's arsenal. Like the earlier spear and ax, these items surely doubled as hunting tools, but they changed the way wars were fought. A wooden bow with its string of animal gut could propel a stone-tipped arrow farther than a football field is long.

Made of a leather pad with two thin straps attached, the *sling* had even more range. The slinger put a rock or a solid, baked clay projectile into the pad, swung it around his head by the straps and then let one of the straps go, sending the missile flying. The Bible hero David felled the Philistine giant Goliath with a sling. Stone carvings from the tenth century BC show Mesopotamian soldiers (from what is now Iraq) using the weapon.

Keeping out attackers

Ancient cities had defensive walls, perhaps to keep out predatory animals, but most prehistorians who study defensive walls think they were built to protect against attackers. Jericho (see Chapter 4), perhaps the oldest town that left substantial ruins, was distinguished by a defensive ditch around the community, a stone wall, and a tower with an inside stairway. Towers let you see the attacking force while it's still far away, and from the top, you can rain down projectiles on unwelcome visitors.

Another ancient ruin, the town of Catal Huyuk in central Turkey, is made up of mostly windowless, doorless houses — again, probably designed for security against attackers. Under siege, residents of the houses could pull up their ladders, drop the ladders and themselves through their rooftop hatches, close the hatches, and sit out the attack.

Defenses evolved wherever people clashed, which was just about anywhere people lived. European villagers as long as 4,000 years ago built hill forts ringed by earthen ramparts. By 220 BC, the Chinese put up the first parts of the Great Wall to protect against northern nomads. Eventually the Great Wall stretched 2,550 miles. When European explorers arrived in New Zealand in the eighteenth century, they found Maori warriors in timber forts atop steep coastal cliffs.

Escalating weapons technology: Using metal

As defenses evolved, so did weapons. A big leap came with metal blades and points. A mummified man from about 3300 BC found in the Italian Alps carried a copper ax. Copper is a soft metal, however, and that limited its usefulness as a weapon. By 3000 BC, Middle Eastern metalsmiths were mixing copper with tin to form the harder metal bronze.

Bronze made tough cutting blades and piercing points. People could also pound bronze into helmets, shields, and armor. Bronze battle-axes and swords became standard. Iron, which was even harder, followed at about 1500 BC.

Riding into battle: Hooves and wheels

Around 300 BC in Mesopotamia, armies used wheeled wagons to transport fighters. The people of Sumer, perhaps the first great urban civilization, fashioned heavy, clumsy vehicles with four solid wooden wheels that were pulled by donkeys or plodding oxen.

After about 1800 BC, armies preferred horsepower. They hitched horses to two-wheeled chariots, which were faster and lighter than the wagons but still big. Unlike the racing chariots in the 1959 movie *Ben Hur* (set in early first-century AD Rome), these earlier chariots carried several men — warriors, javelin throwers, and a driver. The Assyrians, whose civilization arose from the city-state of Assur, on the upper Tigris River, made especially good use of chariots in battle.

Awesome Assyrian Arsenals

Around the Middle East, the Sumerians, Egyptians, Babylonians, and Hittites were military powers in an ebb and flow of early martial power. But other, lesser-known peoples — Hurrians, Mitannians, Kassites, Elamites, and Amorites — fielded armed forces, too.

The Assyrians, whom I tell you more about in Chapter 4, grew particularly warlike. Perhaps Assyrian aggression began with defense. In the eleventh century BC, waves of nomadic northern invaders beat the Assyrian kingdom down to an area only 50 by 100 miles along the Tigris River in northern Mesopotamia. But at the end of the next century, Assyrian warriors began to overrun other societies until they ruled an empire 1,000 miles from border to border, stretching from Egypt to the Caucasus (between the Black Sea and the Caspian Sea).

Assembling the units

At their height, the Assyrians could field an army of 100,000. But they also relied on specialized units: quick-moving, lightly armored infantry and slower but heavily armored infantry; warriors with spears, bows, slings, pikes, and swords; and war chariots.

Perhaps most impressive, the Assyrians had engineering units. Advance corps blazed trails and laid roads for supply wagons. When the army needed to cross a river, engineers built a pontoon bridge — much as it was done for thousands of years afterward. For pontoons, they used inflated animal skins and log or reed boats lashed together to float a roadway.

Assyrians also pioneered ways to get past a city's defenses. They built *siege engines,* which were towers on wheels or sometimes on pontoons that could be moved right up next to a city's walls. Siege engines were made of timber frames covered with layers of tough cowhide that could fend off arrows. Attackers could stay inside until the engine was in place, and then climb up the inside, emerge on top, and go over the wall. Another method involved building a ramp of dirt and rubble to scale the wall.

Sometimes Assyrian engineers went down instead of up — digging under a city's wall and shoring up their tunnel with wooden beams, like a mine shaft. After they were under the wall, the engineers would set the tunnel supports on fire and then turn around and run for daylight. The supports burned up, the tunnel collapsed, and the wall above, literally undermined, crumbled. Soldiers advanced through the gap.

Wreaking havoc

Atrocities such as the wholesale slaughter of a city's residents or the mass deportation of entire populations are among the worst aspects of modern war, but slaughter and deportation are anything but modern, and the Assyrians did both. In one instance, they deported 27,000 Jews — the Lost Tribes who disappeared from history — to eastern Syria. The Assyrians used captives as forced laborers, which sometimes made taking prisoners more economical than killing everybody.

The Assyrians finally fell from power at the end of the seventh century BC, when neighboring peoples united against them, but that didn't mean Assyrian military methods were lost. The Persians built their own vast empire with war tactics inherited from the Assyrians.

Farming and Fighting Together in Greece

Like the ancient Greeks' way of governing (which you can read about in Chapter 4) and the Greek way of thinking (see Chapter 10), a Greek style of warfare grew out of the geography of mainland Greece and its agricultural economy.

Greek soldiers of the sixth and fifth centuries BC were largely small landholders, family farmers who made their livings from fields scraped out of rocky hillsides. Their landholder status made them members of a privileged middle class, the citizenry. Because these farmers were determined to maintain control of their property and their communities, they volunteered as *hoplites,* heavily armored foot soldiers. Military service for no pay was the mark of full membership in the community.

Every Greek citizen who could afford the equipment — a bronze breastplate, a helmet with a fashionable horsehair crest, a short iron sword, leg protectors called *greaves,* and the most essential item, a 9-foot-long spear — joined up. The hoplites took their name from one other piece of equipment: the heavy wooden shield they carried by its double handle. They slid one loop over the left forearm to the elbow and grasped the other loop at the rim of the shield in the left hand.

Soldiering shoulder to shoulder

The heavy hoplite weaponry fit the way Greeks fought: in a tight, porcupine-like formation called the *phalanx*. It grew out of conflicts between competing city-states.

In formal disputes, usually over farmland, the two sides decided the issue through an afternoon's worth of armored columns facing each other on cleared fields. Each side tried to bulldoze the other to a resolution.

When you hear somebody describe any group of aggressive people (say, reporters covering a big story) as a *phalanx,* remember that the original phalanxes were much deadlier (if perhaps less obnoxious than modern reporters). In battle formation, one guy's spear stuck out beyond the guy in the rank in front of him.

Hoplites fought shoulder to shoulder. They couldn't see well because of their helmets, and they couldn't move quickly because of the heavy gear. What the hoplites could do was advance behind their shields that protected the bearer's shield side and his neighbor's weapon side.

The Greek historian Xenophon put this interdependence in its agricultural context: "Farming teaches a person to help others. In fighting enemies, just as in working the earth, each person needs the help of others."

When two Greek phalanxes clashed, one would break through the other. The disrupted phalanx became ineffective because its helmet-blinded, armor-encumbered members were likely to become confused and fight each other. That happened at the Battle of Delium in 424 BC, when the Spartans broke through the Athenian line and the separated Athenians grabbed their swords and commenced hacking at anything that moved, including their comrades.

Standing up to the Persians

In time, the phalanx proved effective against other cultures' military formations, including quicker-moving light infantry (foot soldiers without such heavy gear) and even attackers on horseback.

Hoplites passed their biggest test in 490 BC, when King Darius I of Persia invaded mainland Greece. Athenian and allied hoplites, outnumbered two to one, confronted the Persians at Marathon.

Persians organized their armies along lines developed by the Assyrians (refer to the earlier section "Assembling the units"), with horses, archers, swordsmen, engineers — the whole, coordinated, multi-tiered shebang. To Darius's forces, this bunch of spear-carrying soldiers who looked like shields with stubby bronze legs promised easy pickings. But the Greeks wouldn't fall back. When a hoplite stumbled, the hoplite in the rank behind him stepped over him and shored up the advance. The Greeks pushed forward until their *flanks* — the far ends of their line — overwhelmed the most vulnerable part of the Persian forces and then folded the Persians in toward the middle. At that point, Darius's army wisely turned around and high-tailed it for their boats.

The outnumbered Greeks beat the Persians again 11 years later at Platea. The Greek phalanx made heavy infantry *the* essential force of its time. For centuries, commanders saw cavalry and archers as support for well-armored foot soldiers.

Facing Macedonian ferocity

When the Greeks finally fell to a foreign force, it wasn't the mighty Persians but a strongman king to the north of Greece, Philip of Macedon, applying his own version of the phalanx.

Imagine Clint Eastwood at his most squinty, most unmercifully flinty, in the role of Philip, a hard guy. Phil put cavalry behind his infantry, and each rider was armed with a *xyston,* a 12-foot-long lance with a foot-long iron point at both ends. The cavalry's job was twofold:

- To support the foot soldiers
- To kill any comrade among them who turned and ran

Macedon arranged its infantry in a phalanx but made crucial improvements. Philip's soldiers strapped a small, round shield that wasn't as heavy (or as protective) as the bigger hoplite shield, to the left shoulder, leaving both hands free to wield a long pike called a sarissa. The *sarissa* was like the cavalry xyston but longer, at 13–21 feet in length, with a special metal spike on its butt end. A soldier could plant the spike in the ground and then impale a charging horseman with the sword-like business end. The sarissa was so long that the tips of weapons carried by the soldiers in the fourth rank of a Macedonian phalanx often extended beyond the first rank (see Figure 16-1).

Macedon's army also took the best of Assyrian-Persian weaponry and tactics. Philip of Macedon deployed archers, javelin throwers, and slingers (experts at whipping about a leather sling to propel small-but-deadly stones at an enemy). As the Assyrians had, he absorbed conquered armies and told them to use their own weapons and formations to support his own force. Philip also employed Assyrian-style combat engineers. His inventors improved the siege engine, adding a drawbridge to the top and many platforms for archers to stand on. This new siege engine didn't have to be right up next to the target city's wall; if it came fairly close to the wall, attackers could let down the drawbridge and cross it onto the battlements.

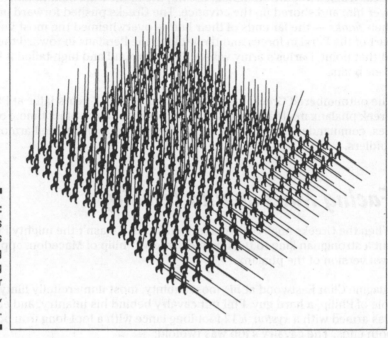

Figure 16-1:
Macedon's
phalanx was
a marching
hedgehog
of muscular
men, wood,
and metal.

Even more inventive than the improved siege engine, Macedon's engineers built a catapult that unleashed the tension of wound animal hair or sinew to hurl a large rock 1,000 feet.

Philip's approach to warfare spurred the successes of his son, Alexander the Great (I tell you about Alex in Chapters 4 and 20). Alex took the conquered Greeks with him as he turned the tables on the Persians, thoroughly defeated them, and marched through Mesopotamia and beyond to grab part of India. Alex's troops weren't even fazed by the Indians' ultimate weapon: armored battle elephants.

Making War the Roman Way

The Latins, shepherds who built a city on the Tiber River in what's now Italy, were among many Mediterranean people who admired and imitated the way the Greeks fought.

At the end of the sixth century BC, Latins organized themselves into a Greek-style phalanx and challenged their northern overlords, the Etruscans. The Latins won, and their city, Rome, became the center of a new culture built on military prowess.

Marching in three ranks

The Latin shepherds became the Romans, who soon found that the phalanx was nifty for fighting the Etruscans (another Greek-influenced people), but it wasn't perfect for fighting less-advanced neighboring tribes.

Greeks developed the phalanx on farmland — battle*fields*. The Romans' tribal neighbors weren't interested in marching formation-to-formation on a cleared hillside. Faster moving than the shield-carrying Romans, a gaggle of tribesmen could come around the flank or hide behind trees and dart out in a raid.

Even the Greeks eventually found the traditional phalanx less and less effective — especially as their armed forces evolved, in the later decades of Classical Greece, from neighborly bands of farmer-citizen-soldiers to a mix of citizens and resident aliens, some of whom were paid mercenaries. A shoulder-to-shoulder, soldier-to-soldier style didn't work so well when you weren't quite sure about the guy next to you.

Needing their own, more flexible military style, the Romans came up with the *legion* in the fourth century BC. The legion consisted of three lines of foot soldiers. Only the third line carried traditional spears. The first two lines carried a variation called a *javelin* (or *pilum*) designed for throwing and boasting a cool technological advance: The head was designed to bend and break off, making the javelin useless to the enemy after it struck its mark. The bent spearhead also tended to stick in an opponent's shield, armor, or flesh.

The Roman legion worked like this:

- **Hastati:** The first line, made up of young guys, threw their javelins, and then drew their swords and charged. If they had to fall back, they scrambled for a position behind the second rank.

- **Principes:** The more-experienced second rank also threw their javelins, and then charged. If they, too, found they had to fall back, they got behind the third rank.

- **Triarii:** The third rank of steady old hands stood fast in a solid defensive line to let the other guys retreat in safety. But Rome's battles rarely came to that.

The legion usually won, but even when Rome didn't win, the other side suffered. In 280 BC, Pyrrhus, king of Epirus, defeated troops led by the Roman Consul Laevinus (*consul* was top administrative post in the Roman republic). Both sides suffered horrible losses. After the dust cleared, 15,000 lay dead. Pyrrhus said, "If we win another battle against the Romans, we shall be completely ruined."

Like the Greek phalanx, the legion began as a citizen corps. Most soldiers came from the small landholder class, and just about every man served. Each citizen (as in Greece, women weren't citizens) between age 17 and 45 had to devote ten years to military service. A leader had to prove himself in battle before he could win political office. Failure at soldiering was failure, period.

Recruiting a standing force

Despite successes — and because of them — Roman commanders realized by the year 100 BC that they needed to change the empire's military. Battling foes from Germany to Africa to the Black Sea, the Roman Empire grew so fast that its republican legions of citizen-soldiers couldn't keep up. Troops posted far away on those frontiers couldn't come home and tend their property after a few months' campaign.

Besides that, the prosperity that came of Rome's expansions and the resulting boost in trade made the wealthy patrician class in Rome even wealthier. Rich guys were amassing big estates cultivated by slaves instead of by citizen-farmer-soldiers, the small landholders who traditionally manned the legions. And slaves were exempt from military service.

Rome struggled to fill the legions' ranks. Recruiters began conveniently overlooking the property ownership requirement for service. Commanders turned to the urban poor to fill out their rosters, but things just weren't the same. These new guys didn't have the same stake in the empire. They were harder to discipline.

Gaius Marius, a lowborn soldier who rose to the political office of consul, figured the time had arrived for Rome to ditch the old civil militia idea and officially make the army a full-time, professional gig.

The professional army worked. The military became an attractive career choice and a means of upward mobility. There was a downside, however. Instead of the citizen-soldiers' loyalty to Rome, the new pros were loyal to their commanders first. The republic became vulnerable to civil wars. A military leader whose troops were more loyal to him than to the government may have fancied himself a dictator or emperor. Rome officially became an empire (that is, ruled by an autocratic emperor) with the coronation of Augustus Caesar in 31 BC (see Chapter 19).

Diversifying the legion

The rise of Augustus wasn't the end of the citizen-soldier. Roman strategy in the later centuries of the Western Roman Empire (the Eastern Roman Empire became the Byzantine Empire) involved much defensive work. Resident defenders were important in the work of holding fortified outposts and cities against barbarian attack.

How warlike were the tribes that hammered away at Rome's borders? The Langobard people were named after their weapon: *Langobard* means "long axe." Saxons took their name not from a sexy-sounding musical instrument (not invented until the nineteenth century) but from a machete-like knife, a *sax*. Imagine a modern nation called the Thermonuclear Missiles.

In Chapter 5, I talk about the waves of people who came down through Europe, each clashing with the previous residents and some settling and becoming defenders against later waves. The Roman Empire's task of standing up to these assaults took plenty of personnel. Residents in places such as Gaul (now France) pitched in to defend their towns. The old idea that warriors fought better in defense of their own land came back.

When Attila the Hun invaded Gaul in 451, he and his fearsome allies spent months trying to break down the defenses of walled cities. They ran out of food and had no forage left for their horses. While Attila hammered away at the city of Orleans, the army of Roman General Aetius, consisting of Germanic soldiers raised mostly in Gaul, attacked and pursued the Huns to Châlons. There the Huns turned and fought, but they were too depleted to prevail. (Note, however, that it took Roman cavalry to beat Attila.) You can find more on Attila the Hun in Chapter 20.

Returning to riders

Military strategists considered cavalry secondary to infantry for centuries. But after the murderous Huns swept into Europe on horseback, terrorizing everyone with their swift fury, war strategists woke up again to the importance of speed.

By the sixth century AD, Rome no longer ruled Western Europe, but the eastern branch of its empire, based in Constantinople, endured. There, swift-riding horse units patrolled the vast borders of the Byzantine Empire (more about the Byzantine Empire in Chapter 6), backed up by lightly armored archers who could move more quickly than the heavy infantry that were the backbone of traditional Roman and Greek forces. The old-style shield-carriers now operated mostly as garrison defense.

Tracking the Centuries

About 10,000 BC: The bow and the sling are added to the warrior's arsenal.

Tenth century BC: Assyrian warriors overrun neighboring peoples, building an empire stretching from Egypt to the mountains between the Caspian and Black Seas.

424 BC: Spartans break through the Athenian line at the Battle of Delium. The disoriented troops from Athens drop their spears, grab their swords, and begin hacking indiscriminately, wounding many of their own.

409 BC: Although badly outnumbered, Athenians and their allies defeat King Darius I's invading Persian forces at Marathon.

451 AD: In Gaul (today's France), Aetius, a Roman general commanding Germanic troops, drives Attila the Hun away from his siege on Orleans. Aetius then pursues the Huns and defeats them at Châlons.

1980s: Anthropologist K.E. Otterbein discovers that 92 percent of hunter-gatherer societies and primitive farming people studied waged war.

Chapter 17

The War Machine Gets Some Upgrades

- -

In This Chapter

▶ Standing in stirrups to fight more effectively

▶ Donning metal suits to fend off arrows and lances

▶ Turning flying sparks from fireworks into firearms

▶ Bringing down the Byzantine Empire with big guns

- -

Since before the spear, warfare has always stimulated technology. Assyrian military engineers, Macedonian weapons inventors, and Roman fortification builders were the weapons techies of their respective times.

It's hard to imagine anybody coming up with a horrific substance such as *Greek fire,* a highly combustible liquid that long predated twentieth-century napalm, if not to use it as a weapon. And metalworking seems to have fed on the needs of weapons makers and armorers. But inventions spur warfare, too.

More than a millennium ago, two dandy little innovations from Asia enabled and demanded many adjustments in how wars were fought and even how war was perceived. These innovations were

- ✔ **Gunpowder:** The Chinese mixed up the first batch in the ninth century AD, although they didn't try to blow anybody up with it until a while later.

- ✔ **The stirrup:** Far less flashy than gunpowder but exceedingly practical, the low-tech stirrup — that thing that you put your foot into to climb onto and ride a horse — became part of a Chinese horse soldier's gear in the fourth century AD.

Reinventing the Cavalry

Both gunpowder and the stirrup eventually filtered west through Asia to Europe, but the simpler stirrup came first. It coincided with a reemphasis on speed and mobility that I talk about in Chapter 16. Horseback warfare gained greater importance in medieval times, and it took diverse forms ranging from the lightly armed Arab conqueror on his small, fast-turning steed to the steel-plated European knight on his ponderous, metal-clad charger.

Standing tall and staying astride with stirrups

Stirrups make it vastly easier for a rider to stay balanced while swinging a sword, aiming an arrow, and especially while wheeling around in a strategic maneuver. That stability, in turn, allows the violence-prone equestrian to wield bigger weapons with better control. Europe's armor-clad age of chivalry would have been unthinkable without stirrups. Some thirteenth- and fourteenth-century styles are shown in Figure 17-1.

Imagine a rider encased in a pounded-steel suit, bracing a long, heavy lance with one arm while trying to use his metal-shielded thighs and buttocks to grip the undulating flanks and back of a galloping steed. It wouldn't work. But give that same knight two hanging platforms, one for each foot, so he can lift and center his weight, and the heavy armor and lance become more formidable than cumbersome.

The stirrup originated either in China or in central Asia among the nomadic tribes and clans that are often labeled *barbarians*.

Figure 17-1:
Front and side views of different stirrups, a technological innovation that changed warfare.

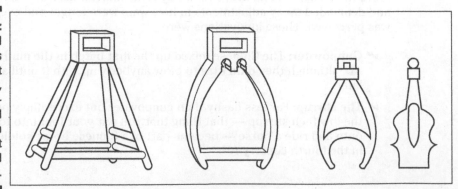

Raiding as a way of life on horseback

Chinese soldiers started using the stirrup around the fourth century AD, but the hard-riding Asian nomads called *Avars* probably had the invention as early as the first century BC. Their riders' feet were tucked into stirrups when the Avars stormed into Eastern Europe in 568 AD, taking Danube Valley lands away from the Byzantine Empire.

Avars and other barbarian peoples used the stirrup while attacking towns and cities to get what they wanted — valuable trade goods, food, money, and sometimes even control of a region or an empire. (You can find out more about barbarian raiders and conquerors in Chapters 6 and 7.) Raiding became a way of life for some nomadic tribes from interior Asia's steppes. Because these herders and hunters had little to offer in trade to settled farmers and townsfolk, such as the Chinese, they resorted to getting things they wanted by force.

Raiding is best performed quickly. You make the hit, and then put plenty of ground between yourself and your target. Horsemanship gave raiders an edge, and the stirrup sharpened it.

Guarding Byzantine borders

The rich Byzantine Empire (see Chapter 6) was a prime target of raiders, so fast horse patrols were a must to guard its borders. Stirrups, probably copied from the Avars, gave the Byzantine patrols an advantage over Western Europeans, who didn't have the technology yet. This superiority coupled with the use of a *commissariat* (a support organization that made sure cavalrymen and foot soldiers had enough to eat, even during long sieges) made the Byzantine Empire extremely difficult for outsiders to penetrate. Constantinople, the Byzantine capital, needed every advantage in the seventh and eighth centuries as its troops faced a new and persistent foe: the Arabs.

The Arabs used stirrups, too, on relatively small, quick horses. More than great riders, the Arabs focused their zeal to spread their new religion, Islam, in the seventh and eighth centuries. They gained control of the Middle East and lands eastward into India and westward across North Africa and Spain (see Chapter 6).

Yet Constantinople withstood the Arabs. The Byzantine capital (today it's Istanbul, Turkey) enjoyed a terrific strategic position, sitting on a point of high land jutting into the sea. Unable to take the capital on horseback, in the eighth century the Arabs tried ships, mounting a naval blockade that may have succeeded if not for Greek fire. A military secret, *Greek fire* may have been mostly naphtha, refined from coal oil that seeped to the surface from underground deposits. Whatever Greek fire was, it ignited on impact and floated.

The Byzantines catapulted clay pots full of Greek fire onto the decks of enemy ships, setting them aflame. Even if the pot missed, the pots' contents burned atop the water. Sometimes the Byzantines squirted Greek fire out of hand-powered pumps. After losing too many ships, the Arabs called off the blockade.

Moors challenge

Arabs may not have brought down Constantinople, but their light cavalry strategy worked just about everywhere else. (*Light cavalry* refers to lightly armored horse units with an emphasis on speed.) In 711 AD, Muslim Arabs conquered Spain, which remained in Muslim control long after the great Arab Empire broke up into regional Islamic kingdoms.

The Muslims in Spain, who advanced from North Africa, quickly came to be called *Moors*. (Find more about the Moors in Chapter 6.) Christians living a little north of them, especially the Franks, didn't like them as neighbors.

Ruling what was Gaul (now it's France and much of Germany), the *Franks* were old-style barbarian ground fighters who were also disciplined and willing to adapt. When quick-riding Moors raided his borders, the Frankish king knew he needed more speed. His solution was to build up his cavalry.

Ironically, to defeat the invading Moors at Poitiers in 732 AD, that king, Charles Martel, ordered his horsemen down on their feet. Facing the attacking riders with shields and spears, the Franks stood fast and successfully repelled the Moors.

Despite that return to infantry tactics, this battle marked the beginning of the age of chivalry, a time when the armored knight dominated European warfare.

Chivalry

The words *chivalry* and *chivalric* are related to the French *chevaux,* meaning "horse," and to other horse-based words, such as *cavalier* and the Spanish *caballero.* These words show how people of the Middle Ages associated nobility, gentility, and courage with mounted warriors. As in ancient Rome, the mounted soldier enjoyed a status denied to the foot soldier.

This era of chivalry, like so many before it and since, glorified violence. People thought of fighting skills as a mark of civilization. Jean Froissart, a fourteenth-century French chronicler, wrote, "Gentle Knights were born to fight, and war ennobles everyone who engages in it without fear or cowardice."

Ennobling or not, war costs money, and it became extremely expensive to outfit an armored, mounted knight. The Frankish king Charles Martel helped his riders pay for their gear by taking land from the medieval Church and giving it to the warrior-nobles. Under the system of feudalism (refer to Chapter 6), a landlord profited from his tenant farmers' harvests.

Charlemagne, a slightly later Frankish king and the first to unite a big piece of Europe after the Romans fell, accomplished that unification with his cavalry.

Putting on the Full Metal Jacket

A culture of chivalry lasted for hundreds of years in Europe. In movies, this armor-clad culture is associated with the legendary King Arthur, who may not have existed at all (see Chapter 19). If he did exist, Arthur probably led Celtic Britons against invading Saxons in the sixth century AD, but he certainly didn't do it in plate-metal armor. Plate armor didn't come into fashion until 800 years later, in the fourteenth century.

Interlocking metal rings: Chain mail

Before plate armor, knights wore chain mail; before chain mail, they wore scale armor, a defense against arrows since Assyrian times (in the previous chapter).

- **Scale armor,** like a lizard's scales, consisted of small metal plates sewn into overlapping rows on a leather vest.
- **Chain mail** was a bit more ingenious than scale armor. It consisted of interlocking metal rings made into a doublet, or close-fitting jacket.

The Crusaders wore mail as they rode east to liberate (in their words) the Holy Land from Muslim control (see Chapter 7). Chain mail became obsolete only as archers got better bows — bows that could shoot an arrow or a deadlier metal bolt — with enough force to pierce chain mail.

Putting more power into the archer's bow

The crossbow was yet another Chinese invention, and an ancient one at that, dating back to the fourth century BC. European archers rediscovered the crossbow's deadly power in the tenth century AD.

A short, extremely stiff bow was mounted on a stock with a mechanism for cranking back the bowstring and holding it there at a higher tension than a man could achieve by pulling the string back manually. You loosed the missile with a finger-lever, or trigger.

The crossbow usually shot short *bolts* rather than arrows. These bolts were often made of metal. They penetrated materials that an arrow from a conventional bow could not. The Normans who conquered England in 1066 used the crossbow.

Pope Urban II condemned the crossbow in 1096 as "hateful to God." In 1139, the Church banned the crossbow for use against Christians. (When it came to pagans such as the *Saracens,* a name for Turks and other Muslims, the weapon was okay.)

Charging behind the lance

Although Crusaders used the crossbow, there seemed something less than honorable about it. Chivalric values centered on personal combat. When there wasn't a war to fight, knights rode against each other in fierce and often deadly *jousts*.

The *lance,* a long, pointed weapon that a jousting knight tucked under his arm, delivered incredible force. Increasingly metal-clad riders balanced on their stirrups and braced against high-backed saddles as they used this variation on the ancient spear to try to knock each other off their horses. Heavier armor kept them from being pierced through.

Mock battles let knights win status and stay sharp for the real thing, but the mock battles were still real. At a 1241 tournament in Neuss, Germany, about 80 men and boys died in the games.

The longbow marries precision to power

The English *longbow,* a refinement of ancient Welsh technology, became the latest thing in weaponry during the fourteenth century. Both precise and powerful in the hands of a skilled archer, the longbow gave knights another reason to wear solid metal armor.

Did the Hundred Years' War really last 100 years?

The name of the Hundred Years' War suggests ten solid decades of constant battle. Actually, it wasn't one war but a series of back-and-forth conflicts from the 1330s to the 1450s.

In 1337, Philip IV of France snatched Aquitaine (today a region of southwestern France) from Edward III of England, and Edward invaded France. The next century included many battles and raids. But there were also truces, including a 28-year peace after Richard II of England married the daughter of Charles VI of France in 1396.

France eventually won, largely because England — weakened by an internal struggle, the Wars of the Roses — gave up trying to conquer its neighbor across the English Channel.

The crossbow was powerful, but its accuracy and range were limited, and it took too long to load. An English longbow could do damage at 750 feet and be reloaded rapidly. Only a skilled archer could use a longbow well, however, so England required yeomen to practice marksmanship. (*Yeomen* were small landowners, who served as soldiers when needed — as small farmers had in ancient Greece and Rome; see Chapter 16.)

In 1346, at the Battle of Crécy (in the Hundred Years' War between France and England), English archers with longbows brought down wave after wave of French opponents. France lost more than 1,500 knights that day and 10,000 foot soldiers. England lost only two knights and fewer than 200 soldiers overall.

In the short term, Crécy led the French and other European knights to strap themselves inside heavier suits of armor. No one knew then that armored knights were on the way out and guns were on the way in. A century later, firearms outshot and outpierced any bow yet invented.

Adding Firepower with Gunpowder

Between the twelfth and the eighteenth centuries, guns spread from China to western Asia, to Europe, and then around the world. They advanced from primitive experiments to precision technology. Warriors were forced to revise their strategies, sometimes adapting ancient battle formations to the new weaponry, while defenders had to find new ways to fortify outposts and cities.

Lighting the fire of discovery

Light a fire on a patch of dirt that has sulfur in it and you get a sizzling, popping reaction. Somebody whose name is lost to history noticed this a long time ago in China, and the observation led other Chinese to experiment with putting concentrated sulfur together with charcoal. By the ninth century AD, another genius added potassium nitrate crystals (saltpeter). Burn that mixture, and you get sparkly effects that made a nice backdrop to formal ceremonies. Taoist monks played with these chemicals until they had fireworks.

Over time, *pyrotechnicians* (fireworks makers) realized that their mixture of gunpowder could make stuff fly — dangerous stuff. Soldiers noticed this, too. By the twelfth century, the armies of the Sung Dynasty added metal grenades to their arsenal. China pioneered fragmentation bombs, whose casings shattered into deadly shrapnel. Within another 100 years, Chinese factories made hundreds of military rockets and bombs, some filled with poisons, such as arsenic, that released on impact. Others were packed with tar and oil and were designed to start fires. The Chinese also built early guns in the form of metal barrels packed with gunpowder that shot out rocks or metal balls.

Spreading explosive news

News of Chinese explosives spread west along the ancient trade route, the Silk Road (see Chapter 6). The Arabs got primitive firearms by the late thirteenth century. In 1267, the recipe for gunpowder turned up in Europe in the hands of English scientist Roger Bacon.

Less than a century later, European armies began using crude cannons. Archers with longbows, not their innovative comrades who were trying out noisy, stinky little *firepots,* decided the Battle of Crécy, mentioned earlier in this chapter, but the primitive cannon was a sign of things to come. The early European cannon was called a *firepot* because it was pot-shaped. It propelled an arrow (yes, an arrow) with impressive force but little reliability and no accuracy. The earliest European gunmakers were craftsmen who, until then, had made church bells. Often they melted down bells to make cannons. Soon the gunmakers found out that a tubular barrel worked better and that it should propel a metal shot. You could knock down a castle gate or level a house that way.

Bringing in the big guns

By the early sixteenth century, the Italian writer Niccolo Machiavelli observed, "No wall exists, however thick, that artillery cannot destroy in a few days."

Guns were already big, although some of the biggest didn't work so well. In the early fifteenth century some early cannon, sometimes called *bombards,* weighed 1,500 pounds and discharged balls 30 inches in diameter. How did anybody back then make a cast-metal barrel that big? At first, it wasn't cast but rather pieced together out of forged iron staves, like the curved boards used to form a pickle barrel. Iron hoops held the staves together — temporarily, anyway.

In 1445, artillerymen in Burgundy (then an independent principality and later part of France) were firing a bombard made of staves and hoops at invading Turks when a hoop burst. The crazy thing is that they fired it again. Two more hoops and a stave blew apart on the next shot. In 1460, one of King James II of Scotland's big guns exploded and killed him and many members of his royal party.

Battering down Constantinople's walls

Sometimes a big gun was just the thing. As I explain in the earlier section "Guarding Byzantine borders," the Arabs failed to capture stout Constantinople. Deciding to break out the big guns in order to breach the city, Ottoman Turkish Sultan Mehmet II hired a Hungarian gunmaker, who built him a cannon that sent a ball flying a full mile.

In 1453, the sultan fired that gun, nicknamed *Mahometta,* at the Byzantine capital's ramparts and kept firing. Like so many of these giants, the cannon cracked after the second day and became unusable after a week. But Mehmet had other big guns. After 54 days of pounding, the 1,000-year-old Byzantine Empire finally fell, a victim of technological advance.

Refining the new weaponry

Although massive bombards worked, military leaders knew there had to be less-cumbersome ways to win battles using big guns. Weapons makers went to work devising field artillery weapons that were more useful and more versatile — and that fit specific niches in the Renaissance arsenal.

Making guns lighter and more maneuverable

Eventually, artillery experts figured out that they could cast some guns in light-yet-strong bronze, rather than iron. These lighter, less-cumbersome guns could be moved into place more quickly, fired more often (some of the big ones could deliver a shot only once in two hours), and weren't so likely to explode, so they could do even more damage than the giants could.

Improving gunpowder with brandy

Guns got better, but gunpowder needed improvement because the sulfur, carbon, and saltpeter had three different weights. The saltpeter crystals settled to the bottom while the carbon came to the top.

The only way to ensure that the gunpowder worked was to mix the ingredients right before loading the weapon, which was difficult and time-consuming. Then somebody came up with a way to make the ingredients stick together by mixing the gunpowder with brandy and letting the resulting paste dry into *corns,* or *grains,* containing all three ingredients.

But what a waste of brandy. Soldiers tried substitutes, such as vinegar, which worked okay, but human urine worked even better — especially the urine from a soldier who had put that brandy to more pleasurable use. (It didn't improve the smell of gunpowder, however.)

Putting guns in soldiers' hands

Guns were first seen as replacements for the catapult and the battering ram — destructive, but not precise. As gunnery improved, however, guns gained accuracy and usefulness.

Soon, gunmakers came up with models for use on the battlefield — both as light artillery (usually a horse-drawn cannon on wagon wheels) and as weapons that soldiers could carry. *Handcannon,* as the smallest guns were called, scared the enemy's horses (and your own, for that matter) and perhaps intimidated a knight or two. But for quite a while handcannon didn't seem a practical replacement for bows and swords. How did you hold a gun, aim it, and also effectively set fire to the gunpowder charge?

In the middle of the fifteenth century, the solution was a wick soaked in alcohol and coated with saltpeter, attached to a trigger. Pulling the trigger lowered this *slow match* into the gun's touchhole to light the powder charge.

The *matchlock,* shown in Figure 17-2, freed a marksman's hands to aim a weapon, including one called a *hackbut* or *harquebus* — variations on the German *Hakenbuchse,* which meant "hook-gun." Some had a hook that you could brace on the edge of a wall when firing over it. The hook caught some of the shock from the gun's powerful recoil.

The term *musket* comes from *mosquito.* It was supposed to irritate the enemy like its namesake. But muskets were anything but mosquito-like in size. Many a musket had to be propped on a forked rest, like a crutch, to be aimed and fired. So in addition to the heavy gun, a musketeer had to lug around this cumbersome prop.

Figure 17-2:
The match-
lock added
a fuse to
ignite the
gunpowder
and free the
soldier's
hands.

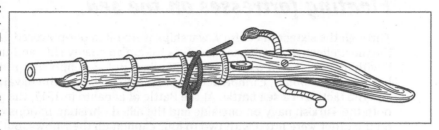

Striking sparks

Because a slow match could send off a spark that lit the charge too soon, the musket was dangerous for the musketeer. Gunsmiths came up with other ways to fire a powder charge, such as the *wheel lock,* a piece of flint held against a spring-loaded steel wheel. If you've examined the moving parts of a cigarette lighter, you have a pretty good idea of how the wheel lock struck sparks. Eventually the simpler *flintlock,* consisting of a spring-loaded hammer that struck a flint, became the dominant technology from about 1650 into the nineteenth century.

Adapting old strategies for new weapons

Until the introduction of the *breechloader* (a gun loaded from the back), a musketeer put everything — gunpowder and shot — down the barrel. He had to stand up to stuff all this material into the tube. Prince Maurice of Nassau, commander of the Netherlands troops in their religious war of independence against Spain (see Chapter 14), revived the *countermarch,* a Roman archery strategy. He put his musketeers in precise rows and had the ones in front fire all at once, and then move to the rear to reload while the next rank fired.

Under Maurice and leaders like him — Sweden's King Gustav Adolph II (1594–1632) and French Inspector General Jean Martinet (died in 1672) — armies emphasized rigid discipline more than ever. (Martinet's name became a synonym for an unbending authority figure.) Military commanders of the seventeenth and eighteenth centuries wanted soldiers to be more than fierce; they wanted them willing and able to charge into concentrated gunfire. This trait — suicidal as it often proved — became a weird new definition of manly bravery.

Floating fortresses on the sea

Through the sixteenth century, warships were often oar-powered galleys, and the most effective naval maneuver was to ram an enemy ship and then board it with fighters armed with swords and pikes. But as gunpowder redefined battlefield weaponry, cannon and firearms also redefined the naval arsenal and the tactics of a sea battle. At the Battle of Lepanto in 1517, the galleys of both the Turkish navy on one side and the allied Christian nations of Europe on the other were fitted with two to four cannon on their bows, but the Europeans won the battle by hand-to-hand combat onboard Turkish ships.

By the middle of the seventeenth century, galleys had fallen out of favor as warships, partly because guns had become the key weapon in naval battles, and vessels needed to bristle with gunports along both sides, not oars and oarsmen. Sea captains still sought to board the enemy ship but generally did so only after disabling it with cannon broadsides.

Fortifications adapt to the artillery era

Ever since the earliest walled towns, a good defensive barrier was as tall as possible. But cannonfire could topple such a wall, and so architects came up with a new way to build a fort in the mid-fifteenth century. In Genoa, Leon Battista Alberti (see Chapter 13) drew designs for star-shaped fortresses with relatively low but extremely thick walls. Figure 17-3 is a simplified depiction of Castillo San Marcos, built by sixteenth-century Spaniards in St. Augustine, Florida, where it still stands.

Jutting angles let a fort's defenders aim their cannons diagonally across the enemy lines so that a cannonball could skip down the line, wiping out more men, guns, horses, and equipment.

Figure 17-3: With thick walls and a star-shaped design, the Renaissance fort was built for cannon battles.

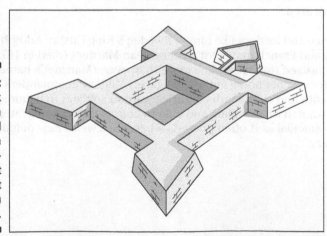

Tracking the Centuries

Fourth century AD: Chinese cavalry begin using stirrups.

568 AD: Avar horsemen, using stirrups, win battles to take Danube Valley lands from the Byzantine Empire.

732 AD: At Poitiers in Gaul, Charles Martel, king of the Franks, and his troops turn back invading Moorish horsemen from Spain.

Tenth century AD: European archers adopt the powerful crossbow.

1096: Pope Urban II condemns the crossbow as "hateful to God."

1267: England's Roger Bacon has the recipe for gunpowder.

1396: Richard II of England marries the daughter of Charles VI of France, bringing a 28-year peace in the Hundred Years' War.

1460: A Scottish military cannon explodes, killing King James II and many members of his royal retinue.

Chapter 18

Modernized Mayhem

. . . .

In This Chapter

▶ Tracking the development of modern war

▶ Enlarging the scale of armed conflict in the World Wars

▶ Turning to guerilla tactics and terrorism in the nuclear age

. . . .

Some say that modern war started with the United States Civil War in the 1860s. Or did modern war begin with the Crimean War in the 1850s? Perhaps modern war traces back several decades earlier, to when a Prussian scholar-soldier began to teach the concept *total war*.

The Crimean War has been touted as the first of the modern era's wars because it proved the wartime worth of new technologies, such as rifled muskets and telegraph lines to the front. The U.S. Civil War used such technologies and more, but it was a bigger and more devastating conflict. The U.S. Civil War seemed to personify the teachings of Karl von Clausewitz, who taught his young Prussian officers at the turn of the nineteenth century that they must conduct campaigns to do more than wipe out opposing forces — they must cripple entire regions. The Civil War's breadth and ferocity provided a glimpse of the future and previewed the global wars of the twentieth century.

Technology — from the rifle to the pilotless robot bomber jet — has fed every escalation in modern fighting styles, while backlash against the giant war-making capabilities of the post-World War II period revived age-old tactics, such as guerilla raids and terrorist sabotage.

Following Three Paths to Modern War

What's so modern about wars fought before armored tanks, airplanes, and the threat of nuclear explosions?

As I say in Chapter 3, historical terms are good only if they're useful. Maybe later in the twenty-first century, the term *modern war* will come to mean something new. Maybe a modern war will be entirely automated, waged by androids. Maybe armored vehicles with artificial intelligence programmed to think strategically will pit their microcircuits against each other. Maybe death rays beamed from satellites will play a major role. Until then, however, the term *modern war* applies to these three military milestones:

- ✔ Prussian generals, from the late eighteenth century through the nineteenth century, developed the concept of *total war* (a campaign of devastation) and *blitzkrieg* (lightning war, or a quick-strike campaign).

- ✔ The Crimean War began when England and France took on Russia in 1853, just when the armies of Western Europe were rearming with faster-firing, easier-to-load weapons and employing such innovations as the steamship and telegraph to support the fighting.

- ✔ The U.S. Civil War followed South Carolina's decision in 1860 that it didn't want to be part of the United States of America anymore. A massive death toll and the devastation wrought upon an entire region, the South, and its economy far surpassed the expectations of military commanders and civilians on either side.

Promoting devastation in Prussia

In the U.S. Civil War, which I talk about more fully in the later section "Redefining armed conflict: The U.S. Civil War," Northern troops resorted to burning crops and wiping out farmsteads so that ruined Southerners would be forced to surrender. These Northern soldiers' weary leaders were desperate to achieve peace and therefore used extreme measures — *total war* — against a determined foe.

But there were other soldiers in the emerging German state of Prussia who saw total war not as a desperation strategy but as the model for how warfare ought to be conducted. The most influential was Karl von Clausewitz (1780–1831), director of the Prussian army school. He wrote a book called *On War,* a manual for fighting an all-out campaign marked by the *scorched earth* advance.

Helmuth Graf von Moltke, commander of Prussia's army, took Clausewitz's ideas and harnessed them to new technology: needle guns, new long-range artillery, and railroads. (You'll find more on nineteenth-century weapons advances with the Crimean War in the next section.) Moltke reorganized and vastly enlarged his military. Then he used Prussia's forces to win wars against Denmark in 1864, Austria in 1866, and France in 1870.

Overwhelming in number and devastatingly efficient, the Prussians in the Franco-Prussian War advanced on Paris in a troop movement so quick it was called a *blitzkrieg,* or "lightning war." The Prussians surrounded the French Army, killed 17,000 in a rain of artillery, and took more than 100,000 prisoners, among them Emperor Napoleon III. The lightning war strategy would emerge again, especially in World War II.

Prussia's military preeminence allowed its prime minister, Otto von Bismarck, to unite Germany in 1871. Bismarck became the first chancellor of a new German Empire, which was a formidable military power through the age when total war became *world war.*

Putting technology to deadly uses: The Crimean War

Why did France and Britain declare war on Russia to start the Crimean War? Well, for one thing, Russia was nibbling away at the crumbling Ottoman Empire. That was scary because other countries didn't want any of their neighbors to be too big or powerful.

The Ottoman Empire, dating back to the Ottoman Turks' conquest of Byzantine Constantinople in 1453 (see Chapter 17), was a wreck by the mid-nineteenth century. As diplomatic friends of the Ottomans, France and Britain bristled when Russia marched troops across the Danube River into Turkish territory in Romania. Western European power players such as France and Britain didn't want Russia to control the Black Sea area and the overland trade routes to India, much less establish a seaport on the Mediterranean.

Yet France and Britain didn't really want war, either. At an 1853 conference in Vienna, France and Britain tried to get the Ottomans to compromise with the Russians, but the Turks declared war instead. Ironically, the war proceeded even after Russia gave in to Austrian demands (and the threat of the Austrian army) and withdrew from the disputed parts of Romania (Wallachia and Moldavia). Austria mobilized its troops to threaten Russia into backing down, but Austria didn't enter the Crimean War.

After Russia replied to the Turks' declaration of war by destroying the Ottoman fleet at Sinope, a seaport on the south coast of the Black Sea, Britain and France saw no alternative but to weigh in and teach the czar a lesson. Britain and France, along with the Italian principality of the Piedmont (it means "foothills"), sent forces to confront the Russians on the Crimean Peninsula in southern Ukraine (between the Black Sea and the Sea of Azov). What was at stake wasn't absolutely essential to any of the countries involved, so in some ways this was like many wars of the conflict-laden eighteenth century (see Chapter 9). But technology made this a new kind of war.

Adding accuracy and speed with new rifles

By the time of the Crimean War, the flintlock musket was old technology (refer to Chapter 17). A new device, the *percussion lock,* replaced the flintlock's old friction-spark system (see the sidebar "The clergyman's new gun"). In the percussion-lock weapon, the powder charge ignited within a reliable, easy-to-load cartridge.

What else was new about firearms? The rifled barrel was a big change. To *rifle* is to etch spiral grooves into the inside of a gun barrel. These grooves cause the shot to spin as it travels up the barrel, and that spin helps it fly straighter through the air. Think of the way a football thrown with a spin, or *spiral,* flies true, whereas one that doesn't spin develops a wobble (thus the term "wounded duck" to describe such a throw).

For the rifled barrel to be most effective, it needed ammunition that fit the barrel tightly enough to engage the groove and take its spin. That kind of shot was difficult to load through the mouth, or *muzzle,* of the barrel. If the metal slug was tight enough to engage the grooves, the slug was also tight enough to catch on the way in, blocking the barrel and making the gun useless.

The *minié* bullet — named not for its size but for its inventor, Captain Claude-étienne Minié of France — offered an early solution. Minié hollowed the bottom of a lead bullet, turning its back edge into a semi-flexible flange. When the explosive charge went off under it, the hollow expanded, pushing out the flange to fit more tightly against the sides of the barrel. The flange caught the rifling, and the bullet spun and flew true.

Then came an even better solution for getting the bullet into the barrel. With the percussion lock and its self-contained powder charge, it became practical to load the weapon from the back, or *breech end,* instead of through its muzzle. A snug fit on the way in was no longer an issue. Even better, breech-loading weapons eliminated the soldier's reliance on gravity to get the ammunition down the barrel. They no longer had to stand up when reloading; the rifleman could stay flat against the ground, presenting the minimum target.

The Prussian *needle-gun* (named for its long firing pin) came first among these breech-loaders, followed by the French chassepot and the British Snyder-Enfield. With better weapons, range more than doubled — in some cases to more than 4,000 yards. Accuracy improved tremendously, and increased rate of fire allowed a skilled rifleman with a Snyder-Enfield to get off six shots in a minute.

How much difference did new firearms make? At the Battle of Inkerman in 1854, an early landmark in the Crimean War, the allies had breech-loading rifles and the Russians did not. The score: 12,000 Russians dead to only 3,000 allies.

The clergyman's new gun

The Reverend Alexander John Forsyth of Belhelvie, Scotland, wanted to shoot birds, not soldiers, when he came up with the idea for the percussion lock — a major advance in firearms technology.

Forsyth enjoyed hunting grouse and ducks. He didn't enjoy missing a shot. Shooters missed a lot in Forsyth's time (the early nineteenth century), even if they were handy with a musket,

because the flash of a flintlock frightened the bird. Frustrated, the reverend devised a self-contained gunpowder capsule that ignited without flashing when the musket's hammer drove a firing pin into the capsule. This was the prototype for what became a self-contained bullet, in which the powder charge and slug were one package.

Transporting troops via steamship

Steam power (see Chapter 9) allowed shippers to deliver freight on time, keeping to a schedule instead of depending on the whim of the wind. The steamship did the same for military leaders.

Men, horses, and artillery transported at least part of the way to a battle site by sea have a better chance of arriving fresh rather than ground down from a long march. But a wind-powered ship sometimes stalled in becalmed waters for days or even weeks. If troops were onboard and supplies ran out, the soldiers arrived weak from hunger. With the steamship, ready troops could be shipped from England and France to Turkey and the Crimea faster and more reliably. Strategists could make plans with a reasonable certainty that the soldiers would arrive on or near the date promised.

Laying down railroad tracks to the front lines

There was no rail line handy for the British and French troops when they got to the port of Balaklava in the Crimea. So they built one to serve the inland battle headquarters. It was the first railroad built to serve a war effort. The train did on land what the steamship did on water, providing a reliable way to get troops and supplies to a battle site.

Stringing telegraph wires to the battlefield

The most modern device employed in the Crimea, the electric telegraph, allowed commanders to communicate with their troops almost instantaneously. Support troops strung wires to wherever fighters were deployed.

Previously, armies had communicated by messenger or sometimes by systems of signals, such as smoke puffs or flag code relayed by line-of-sight from station to station. With the electric telegraph, information and orders pulsed along at the speed of electric current.

Into the Valley of Death

The English of the mid-nineteenth century learned of the Light Brigade's mistaken charge through newspaper accounts. But they remembered it through verse. Lord Alfred Tennyson (1809–1892) landed the post of England's poet laureate in 1850 and was doing that job when he wrote a heroic verse that begins, "Half a league, half a league, / Half a league onward, / All in the valley of Death / Rode the six hundred." The poem caught the popular imagination as few poems ever have. There were the galloping horses and galloping cadences in the lines: "Cannon to the right of them, / Cannon to the left of them, / Cannon behind them / Volleyed and thundered."

"The Charge of the Light Brigade" is one of the few poems ever to inspire a movie, and it inspired not just one, but two of the same title. The first, made in 1936, stars Errol Flynn and Patric Knowles as brothers both in love with Olivia de Havilland. When the boys arrive in the Crimea, the audience is in for a strange interpretation of the Battle of Balaklava, which somehow involves an Indian Rajah on the Russian side. The re-created attack, however, is beautifully filmed. The 1936 film *The Charge of the Light Brigade* is better than the ill-conceived 1968 effort of the same title.

Not only were commanders and field lieutenants in touch thanks to the telegraph, but the governments in Paris and London also were connected with their armies by wire, for much of the distance, anyway. Getting a message back home no longer took weeks.

Civilians, notably the press, also could send messages quickly and easily via telegraph — presenting a new public relations problem for British officers in the Crimea. W.H. Russell, an Irish reporter working for an English paper, became the first war correspondent to file a *wire report,* as newspapers still call them. His stories in *The Times* of London told the English about the disastrous "Charge of the Light Brigade," a brave but muddleheaded British cavalry attack on Russian artillery positions during the Battle of Balaklava. Russell witnessed and wrote of the way poorly equipped allied troops suffered through the long winter siege of Russia's fort at Sebastopol in 1854 and 1855, noting that some of their commanders spent that winter onboard private yachts offshore. Outraged readers demanded reforms.

Redefining armed conflict: The U.S. Civil War

If the Crimean War changed the tools of warfare, then the U.S. Civil War changed war itself by showing how big, deadly, and devastatingly costly a modern war could be. Four million men mobilized over the course of the war, and more than 600,000 of them died in widespread battles.

More Americans died in the Civil War than died in World War I, World War II, the Korean War, and the Vietnam War combined. That's right, *combined.* And if you think of how much smaller the U.S. population was then — fewer than 31.5 million by the 1860 census compared to well over 300 million these days — you can begin to imagine the devastation.

Waging total war on Sherman's March to the Sea

For the South, the Civil War meant the wreck of an entire economy. This was the war in which a general, Ulysses S. Grant, commander of the Union Armies, first used the word *attrition* to describe his strategy. He announced his intention to pound the enemy until that enemy could do nothing but surrender. And so Grant did.

Although German theoretician Clausewitz (covered earlier in this chapter) pioneered the concept of *total war,* the U.S. Civil War was the first large-scale demonstration of his idea. Before war's end, the Union wreaked brutal and absolute devastation — military, economic, and societal. Union General William Tecumseh Sherman (see Chapter 20) wiped out virtually everything in his army's path on an 1864 march from Chattanooga, Tennessee, through Atlanta to the coastal town of Savannah, Georgia. On this campaign, known to history as Sherman's *March to the Sea,* Union troops destroyed farms, trashed machinery, spoiled any foodstuffs they didn't steal, slaughtered cattle and chickens, loosed mules, scattered slaves, sacked and burned not just Atlanta but also dozens of towns along their way, and in Sherman's words, "generally raised hell."

Sherman also gets credit for the phrase "War is hell." If he didn't actually say it, he acted it out.

Sorting through the Civil War's causes

Also called the War of the Rebellion and the War Between the States, the U.S. conflict started in 1860, although a violent prelude foreshadowed what was to come. The abolitionist John Brown (see Chapter 20), fresh from anti-slavery violence in the western territory of Kansas, came east with his men in 1859 to capture the U.S. armory at Harper's Ferry, in what would soon be the new state of West Virginia. U.S. troops commanded by Robert E. Lee captured Brown. Convicted of treason and hanged, John Brown became a martyr for the abolitionist cause.

Abolitionists wanted to abolish slavery (see Chapter 8), the labor base of the American South. This issue, intertwined with that of state self-determination versus federal oversight, led to the South's rebellion at the end of 1860.

The rebellion erupted after Abraham Lincoln of Illinois, the Kentucky-born candidate of the new, anti-slavery Republican Party, won the presidency in 1860. In December, South Carolina resigned from the Union. Ten other states said "Us, too." The following April, troops of the newly formed Confederate States of America attacked Fort Sumter, a U.S. military post in Charleston, South Carolina. Neither side was prepared for what would follow. Who could have been? Most Americans of the mid-nineteenth century had never seen war.

Exceeding each other's expectations with grim determination

In the summer of 1861, when Union troops marched south from Washington, D.C., intent on thrashing the Confederate forces camped in nearby Virginia, the capital's public treated the impending conflict as a lark. Sightseers toting picnic baskets tagged along behind the troops. Civilians and soldiers alike expected a neat victory and a quick peace.

What they got was a decisive defeat and a shock. Before the day was over, many of the 18,000 Union soldiers who met the enemy at Bull Run near Manassas, Virginia, turned and ran for their lives. The Confederate victory showed that the war wasn't going to be easy or predictable.

That early encounter is usually called the first Battle of Bull Run, after a nearby stream. Northern chroniclers of the war generally named battles after nearby waterways. Southerners called the same fight, and the one that occurred there the next year, the First and Second Battles of Manassas. Casual readers of Civil War history are sometimes confused by a single battle being known by two different names.

Believing fervently in their cause, Southerners thought that a decisive victory or two, like the first at Bull Run, would convince the Union to turn them loose. But the Union had overwhelming economic advantages — factories, railroads, and a much larger population base — that the rebels lacked. And it had a deep-seated resolve of its own. The canny, articulate Lincoln convinced the public that the Union must be saved.

The Civil War evoked the kind of popular involvement among Americans that Europe had seen in the French Revolution (see Chapter 8) and hooked the nation up to the new industrial technology. In some ways, the Civil War was a throwback to earlier ages when sacking and burning were commonplace. But as the Civil War employed the same new technologies as in the Crimean War — on a larger scale and over a longer time — it pointed toward a horrible future. Military leaders figured out, for example, that the improved range and accuracy of a rifled gun barrel added enormous risk to the infantry charge. Units learned to dig in; the spade, or *trenching tool,* came into tactical use. All this and more was a preview of the grinding, static, morale-killing style of ground fighting that would characterize WWI.

Spewing bullets from the machine gun

Ever since the cannon and musket became basic tools of warfare, inventors had struggled to find ways to load and fire guns faster. Early attempts at meeting this challenge included weapons with multiple barrels or multiple charges to be fired in succession. The first practical design was the *Gatling gun*, named after American inventor Richard Gatling. An opportunist inspired by the U.S. Civil War, he used percussion lock technology and devised a hand-crank mechanism to feed charges into his gun's chambers, fire them, and then extract the spent cartridges. Gatling claimed that this gun would fire 200 rounds a minute.

Although a Southerner, Gatling offered his invention to both sides in the war. Neither bought it. Only after the war did it become part of the U.S. arsenal. Britain, Japan, Russia, Turkey, and Spain all placed orders, too.

In the 1880s, another American inventor, Hiram Maxim, came up with an improved machine gun that required no cranking. You could hold down the trigger, and the gun would just keep firing, making this the first automatic weapon. It used the power of each charge's recoil to eject the cartridge and move the next one into the chamber. It could spit more than 600 bullets a minute. By WWI, the Maxim and imitators were a major part of just about any battle.

Tying Tactics to Technology in the Twentieth Century

In Chapter 9, I tell you how twentieth-century wars spread European-based conflicts around the world, rearranging borders and bringing down economic and political empires. WWI reset the global stage for a new era in international relations by inspiring the world's first attempt at an organization to prevent war — the League of Nations. But it did that, at least in part, by demonstrating how war had been changed by the killing trends of the nineteenth century.

WWII then added new weapon after new weapon to the increasingly technically sophisticated arsenal. Each perilous escalation in weaponry made industrialized nations better able to rain down death with an ease beyond any imagined by ancestors of even a century earlier. This so-called progress brought civilization all the way to the perilous, fiery brink of the nuclear age.

Trapping valor in a trench: World War 1

With the Maxim machine gun (see the sidebar "Spewing bullets from the machine gun") and its improved descendants so widely used in WWI, the tactic of charging enemy positions, which became more dangerous with every advance in weaponry, now became suicidal.

This lesson sank in at the first Battle of the Marne, fought in France in September 1914. After that, the front lines of the war's Western Front turned into thousands of miles of parallel trenches across Europe; the trenches were wet, rat-infested ditches in which cold, dirty, terrified men hid for days, weeks, months, and years. There they scratched at lice and warily watched the other side's trenches. On occasion, the horrible order would come, and the men would obediently climb out and fling themselves into a barrage of bullets and exploding mortar shells. Trying to break the stalemate, both sides developed new weapons, including hand grenades for lobbing into the enemy trenches, mortar shells that could be fired up and over the opposite embankment, and exploding canisters of poison mustard gas, an oily chemical that left victims blistered outside and in — especially inside their lungs — and often permanently disabled.

In 1915, a British officer came up with the idea of putting an armored casing around the kind of tractor that ran on metal chain treads. The officer thought they could mount guns on this fortified crawler and drive it toward the enemy machine gun positions. The armored tank was born and by war's end, British units were using it to cross German trenches.

Also in that war, a German engineer figured out how to time a machine gun to fire through a spinning propeller without hitting the blades. Fighter aircraft resulted. Airplanes began to drop bombs, too, although on nothing like the scale that was to come in WWII. The submarine, in the form of the German U-boat, showed its value in WWI as its crews enjoyed the advantage of underwater surprise.

Retooling the World War II arsenal

In WWII, technology in the service of mass destruction accelerated at a pace that would have astonished even General Moltke. Bazookas, aircraft carriers, anti-aircraft guns, anti-submarine depth charges, long-range fighter planes, missiles, radar, sonar, and atomic weapons all came out of that war.

What are all these things? Many of the names are self-explanatory — although *bazooka* is a weird name for anything, including bubble gum. (The so-named weapon is a small, portable anti-tank rocket launcher that an infantryman can carry and fire.) Most of the inventions — even some of the most chilling among them — are now taken for granted as part of the modern world. Some serve peaceful purposes; here are two examples:

  ✔ **Radar** (originally RADAR, an acronym for RAdio Detecting And Ranging) began as an idea based on the echo. Radar bounces radio waves off objects and then detects the pattern of the returning waves to *see* objects (especially airplanes) beyond the range of visual detection. Radar allowed Britain's outnumbered Royal Air Force to detect German bomber squads, spoiling Nazi plans to invade the British Isles. After the war, it was an invaluable tool for commercial aviation and law enforcement, because radar can tell you how fast an object (such as an automobile) is moving.

✔ **Sonar** (an acronym for SOund Navigation And Ranging) did much the same with sound waves underwater as radar did with radio waves in the air. With sonar, a ship could detect enemy submarines. Numerous postwar uses range from salvaging sunken ships to finding good fishing spots.

The U.S. dropped two atomic bombs on Japan in 1945 to end WWII. Historians, military strategists, and peace activists still argue about whether those attacks were justifiable. In any case, it's certain that those *A-bombs* and the even deadlier nuclear weapons developed after the war changed how war is perceived and fought.

Warring On Despite the Nuclear Threat

At the end of WWII, some people thought that nuclear weapons would make any further warfare unthinkable. It hasn't turned out that way.

A growing number of countries built and tested nuclear weapons (more about nuclear proliferation in Chapter 9), but in much of the world, the nuclear option remained irrelevant. This was especially so in South America, Southeast Asia, and Africa, where revolutions and civil wars raged on.

Despite the massive ability of the post-WWII superpowers (the Soviet Union, until its 1991 breakup, and the U.S.) to wreak large-scale mayhem, small-scale warriors — especially those that believed in their causes of revolution or retribution for perceived political wrongs — found ways to undermine the security of major nations. Often they reached back to pre-technological strategies such as the guerilla raid and the difficult-to-prevent terrorist strike.

Drawing strength from stealth: Guerilla tactics

Paradoxically, the nuclear age of the late twentieth century was also the era of a foot soldier treading softly in the night. *Guerilla war* is often fought by outnumbered, ill-financed bands of revolutionaries moving stealthily against better-armed powers. Guerilla units venture out under cover of darkness to conduct small-scale raids and set booby traps.

Guerilla, Spanish for "little war," first referred to the Spanish peasants who harassed Napoleon's conquering forces early in the nineteenth century. Then, as now, guerilla tactics followed precedents as old as war itself; they were the same tactics that the sneaky Italian tribes who frustrated early Rome's Greek-style phalanx in Chapter 16 probably used. Similarly, the improvisational soldiering of American revolutionaries sometimes caught Britain's infantry off-guard in the 1770s. Americans sometimes fired from cover, putting a marching formation of Brits at a disadvantage.

The British faced guerilla tactics again more than a century later in South Africa. The Boer War began in 1899 when the Boers, descendants of Dutch colonial farmers, tried to take away land controlled by Great Britain in the Transvaal. Expecting to beat down this rebellion of farmers (*Boer* means "farmer") in a few months, the British failed to consider Boer determination and toughness. The frontier-raised Boers rode horses masterfully and knew the territory intimately.

Against Britain's superior weaponry, the determined Boers resorted to hiding, raiding, and bombing. Realizing that this foe would hold on indefinitely, the British were forced to do what Grant and Sherman did in the U.S. during the Civil War: fight a war of attrition. The British burned farms and herded Dutch civilians into concentration camps.

Twentieth-century opposition forces ranging from the French Resistance in WWII to the Communist Viet Cong in 1960s Vietnam (see Figure 18-1) to the anti-Communist Contras in 1980s Nicaragua made effective use of backwoods evasiveness, quickness, mobility, and well-timed, small-scale raids against stronger foes.

Figure 18-1:
Guerilla fighters such as Vietnam's Viet Cong stage raids against stronger foes.

© Bettman/CORBIS

Wielding the weapon of fear: Terrorism

Whereas the targets of guerilla forces are generally military or at least within an area at war, terrorist violence frequently seems indiscriminate and arbitrary, as in the bombing of a shopping mall, a city bus, or a commercial airliner full of passengers.

The perpetrators of terrorism are usually minority groups who feel that violence is the only way they can advance their cause, which is often the overthrow of the established order. By definition, terrorists use terror, or fear of the next unpredictable strike, as a weapon.

The Provisional Irish Republican Army (IRA), a nationalist group that wanted to reunite British-controlled Northern Ireland with the self-ruled Irish Republic, was frequently labeled *terrorist* from the 1970s to the 1990s. Although IRA bombs were often directed at military targets, they also went off among passersby in English cities.

Although they're often labeled criminals, terrorists usually consider themselves warriors engaged in honorable acts of battle. Such is the case with the members of *Al Qaeda,* the terrorist group responsible for the notorious September 11, 2001, attacks on the U.S. Formed in the 1980s to support Muslim resistance to a Soviet incursion into Afghanistan, Al Qaeda became an international network with an increasingly antagonistic attitude toward the U.S. Its 2001 attacks on the World Trade Center in New York and the Pentagon just outside Washington, D.C., as well as a hijacked plane that went down in Pennsylvania, killed almost 3,000 people.

Terrorism is extremely difficult to defend against because its perpetrators often deliberately take their own lives so that they can kill others around them with explosives. In recent decades, Islamic terrorists in the Middle East frequently resorted to this tactic, known as *suicide bombing*. In 1983, two suicide bombers driving trucks killed 300 people — 241 of them U.S. servicepeople, mostly Marines — by driving trucks filled with explosives into two troop barracks in Beirut, Lebanon. In the years since, suicide bombers have many times struck civilian targets in Israel. Palestinian militant groups such as Hamas, which seek an end to Israeli governance, are generally credited with inciting and financing such attacks. Islamic insurgent groups have also used the tactic in Iraq, Afghanistan, Pakistan, and Sri Lanka.

Terrorist attacks also are difficult to retaliate against because the terrorists officially represent no sovereign nation. After the 2001 attacks, the U.S. attacked Afghanistan, where Al Qaeda had its headquarters, and later Iraq. American forces defeated the ruling regimes in both Islamic countries, but as I write this more than seven years later, U.S. troops have not succeeded at eliminating terrorist attacks within either country. And Osama Bin Laden, leader of Al Qaeda and supposed mastermind of the September 11 attacks, remains at large.

Tracking the Centuries

1833: Carl von Clauswitz's book *On War* teaches deliberate devastation.

1854: French and British infantrymen with new breech-loading rifles outgun Russians armed with muskets in the Crimean War.

1861: A determined Confederate force routs Union troops at the first Battle of Bull Run in Virginia.

1899: British troops fight Boer rebels in the Transvaal, South Africa.

1914–1918: Parallel trenches define the Western Front of WWI, stretching from the North Sea to Switzerland.

1945: Atomic bombs devastate the cities of Hiroshima and Nagasaki, forcing Japan's government to surrender and ending WWII.

1973: The Vietnam War nears an end as U.S. forces withdraw and North Vietnamese troops take possession of the south.

October–December 2001: The U.S. bombs and then invades Afghanistan with ground troops, overthrowing the ruling Taliban government.

2009: Newly elected U.S. President Barack Obama inherits two wars: one an eight-year effort to pacify Afghanistan and the other a nearly five-year struggle in Iraq.

Part V
Meeting the Movers and Shakers

George Washington: Father of the Country and first US President. Originator of the White House Cabinet; established Congress's right to tax US citizens and re-wrote existing boating regulations to increase the number of people allowable in a row boat from 5 to 12.

Part V

Meeting the Movers
and Shakers

In this part . . .

The historical figures who appear in this part pop up in other parts of this book, but these chapters also introduce a few historical personalities that you may be less familiar with. Each deserves a whopping fat volume that delves deeply into their personal motives and intrigues. In fact, many of the folks profiled in this part of the book have inspired full-length biographies. And there are more people — many, many more people — who could have and should have made this list if only I had unlimited space. Watch for cross-references to help you connect lives and eras.

Is this a complete list of everybody who ever made a difference in world history? Are these biographies complete? Are you kidding? The answers are "No," "No," and "You *must* be kidding."

Chapter 19

Starting Something Legendary

Societies, nations, and cultures don't just happen. Well, maybe they do, but somebody always takes credit. Or a few hundred years after the fact, somebody looks back and assigns credit for the founding of the city-state, the empire, the nation, or the culture. Sometimes it's an individual, and sometimes a group.

In Chapter 3, I talk about the way historians label eras, movements, and trends, choosing what to include and what to leave out. Trying to make sense of the hodgepodge of human experience, historians have to make choices. In this chapter, I cover only a fraction of history's founders; they're my choices based on their impact in their own times and their political and cultural legacies. (Okay, a few made the cut just because I felt like putting them in.) When you notice glaring omissions (and you will), you're free to jot them in the margins — but *please* buy the book first.

Spinning Legends

Many historical figures, even in relatively recent times, take on mythic stature. Those from long ago can be so shrouded in layers of lore that the truth about them and what they did may never be known. Did a demigod really ever found a city-state? Did a wizard's spell ever grace an enchanted age? My educated guess is no, those things didn't happen. The following legends may all have been inspired by real leaders, or they could all be make-believe:

> ✔ **Agamemnon** (legendary, but probably based on a real king of the twelfth century BC): In *The Iliad*, a Greek epic poem by Homer, King Agamemnon commands the alliance of fellow Greeks (or the pre-Greeks

called *Achaeans*) who besiege Troy. Agamemnon, the wealthy ruler of Mycenae, was the brother of Menelaus, king of Sparta. The Greeks had a bone to pick with Troy because the Trojan prince Paris stole Menelaus's beautiful wife, Helen. Because *The Iliad* is a poem laced with supernatural acts by the gods, nobody can say how much of it is literally true, but many centuries of Greeks found cultural identity in the tale. (For more about *The Iliad* and the Trojan War, see Chapter 2.)

✔ **Romulus** (probably mythical, although his legend could be based on a king of the eighth or seventh century BC): In a story about the founding of Rome, Romulus appears as one of the twin sons of Mars (the god, not the planet or the candy bar) conceived when Mars dallied with a Vestal Virgin. Abandoned as infants, Romulus and his twin brother Remus floated down the Tiber River until a she-wolf found them and suckled the babies. After they grew up, Remus cracked jokes as Romulus tried to get Rome built. (It took more than a day.) Romulus got mad and killed Remus, and later a thunderstorm blew Romulus away. How much of this is true? Probably none of it, but Romulus still gets credited as the first Roman king. (Romulus's brother is not the same as Uncle Remus, an American fictional character who told fables about talking rabbits, bears, and foxes.)

✔ **King Arthur** (perhaps sixth century AD): Maybe, just maybe, Arthur was a real person. Scholars and enthusiasts have suggested many historical figures as the real-life inspiration for the legend. Yet the history of Wales around the time when a real Arthur may have fought and ruled is exceedingly murky. Among the more intriguing possibilities is a Welsh king, Owain Ddantgwyn, who could have amassed enough strength to unite his fellow Celts against invading Germanic tribes. If so, Ddantgwyn (the name means "white teeth") may have given himself the battle name Arth-Ursus, combining the Welsh and Latin words for "bear." Welsh chronicles say Arthur died fighting in 537, a date fairly consistent with what little is known about Ddantgwyn. Other candidates for the role of King Arthur include Scots and Romans, but the most famous Arthurian tales are the fanciful inventions of Sir Thomas Malory, written 900 years after any real Arthur would have lived. Based on legends, not history, the tales are fiction.

In the 2004 film *King Arthur,* the title character is based on Lucius Artorius Castus, a real-life Roman soldier. Artorius probably fought against Picts, the fierce warrior tribes that, in the second century, occupied what later became Scotland. The real Artorius may have been Italian, but it's possible that he was of Celtic or half-Celtic descent, as in the movie. This film moves Artorius ahead 300 years, to the time when Rome was withdrawing its forces from Briton (the main British isle). This movie's Guinivere is a Woadish princess; I don't know what "Woadish" is, but in this picture the Woads are enemies of both the Romans and Saxon invaders. The character Merlin, well known from the Arthurian legends, is a Woadish king in the film. Other aspects of the

Arthurian legends, as passed down through Malory and later writers, also show up in the movie, including the character Lancelot and the famous sword Excalibur. Other movie versions of the Arthur stories include Disney's animated *The Sword and the Stone* from 1963 and the 1967 musical *Camelot*. Both are based on twentieth-century English author T.H. White's series of books, *The Once and Future King*.

Uniting for Strength

Many a founder is the one person strong enough for other leaders to rally behind. The leaders in this section made a difference through a combination of physical force and force of personality.

- **Saul** (eleventh century BC): Saul became the first king of the Israelites after Samuel, a holy man, poured oil on Saul's head. (As the greasy pompadour was not yet in style, this was not a grooming aid.) By anointing Saul, Samuel signaled that Saul was God's choice to unite a tribal confederation of Jews. Saul defeated the Philistines and ruled the Israelites from his capital at Hebron. As king, Saul took over religious ceremonial duties, angering the high priest Samuel. So Samuel began to favor David, a brave young war hero. David was best pals with Saul's son and married Saul's daughter, making him a member of the family but also making Saul jealous of all the attention paid to David. Samuel secretly anointed David as the next king. After Saul and his son Jonathan died in another battle against the Philistines, David became leader of the tribe of Judah, later reuniting the Israelites as their second king.

- **Shi Huangdi** (259–210 BC): Shi Huangdi began as Zheng, Prince of Qin, an innovative warrior who adopted iron weapons before the rest of China and told his cavalry to ditch the chariots and sit right on top of those horses, making them faster and more adaptable. Qin was just a little country whose rulers had to pay tribute to the Zhou family, which also ruled other Chinese vassal states. But then Zheng started branching out, taking neighboring provinces away from the Zheng until he could name himself Shi Huangdi, or First Emperor. As king, Shi Huangdi standardized writing and units of measure, including weights, across the lands he had conquered. This conformity helped successive dynasties rule China as a unified land. He also opposed Confucian beliefs (see Chapter 10 to find out about Confucianism), burned Confucian books, and killed scholars while surrounding himself with officials and warriors. His tomb, full of terra-cotta warriors to protect him in the afterlife, is an archeological and historical gold mine. Shi Huangdi's own Qin Dynasty survived him by only four years, until the long-lasting Han Dynasty came to power in 206 BC. Yet the name Qin (also spelled Chi'in) is the root of the name *China* (see Chapter 4 for more about early civilization in China).

- **Clovis** (about 465–511 AD): Roman officials trying to hang onto Gaul (or France) after the Western Roman Empire crumbled had to give up when Clovis, the king of the Franks, took over. After he succeeded his father, Childeric, Clovis extended his rule over everything between the Somme and the Loire Rivers by 496 AD. That year, Clovis was the first Frankish king to convert to Christianity. Credit his wife, a princess from Burgundy, for that. If Clovis ever said, "My wife is a saint," he was more right than he knew; the Catholic Church later canonized her as St. Clotilde. When Clovis converted, so did several thousand of his warriors. As Frankish leaders did in those days, Clovis had to battle Visgoths and Ostrigoths (both Germanic barbarian tribes) to stay in power.

- **Alfred the Great of England** (849–899 AD): The Danes were moving in on the Saxons when Alfred came to power as king of Wessex (the Western Saxons). Danes had their own kingdom in the north of England, and they were expanding into such Anglo-Saxon parts of Briton as Northumbria and East Anglia. Alfred put a stop to that at the Battle of Edington in 878 AD. Then he pushed back, regaining London in 886 AD. He assembled a standing army, navy, and network of forts that gave him the military advantage over his northern neighbors. Alfred got the Saxons together with other English peoples, descendants of fellow Germanic tribes such as the Angles and Jutes, so they could work together against the Danes. He emphasized Christianity (as opposed to Norse paganism) and literacy, and he codified laws. No other English king or queen is called "the Great."

- **Brian Boru** (about 926–1014 AD): Also called Brian Boroimhe (meaning "Brian of the Tribute"), this Irish warrior was a chief of the Dal Cais (a clan) and fought his way to the crown of Leinster. The fact that the Irish were tired of absorbing Viking blows helped Brian rally support. He fought regional rivals until he united Ireland. That was the beginning of a nation (although many hard centuries lay ahead). Brian's forces beat the Vikings at Clontarf, but Brian, by then too old to join the fray himself, was murdered by fleeing Viking warriors.

Vesta's girls

The Vestal Virgins waited on the Roman deity Vesta (goddess of home and hearth). Picked for the honor from a short list of suitable aristocratic girls, Vestal Virgins took a vow of chastity and served for 30 years each, cleaning Vesta's shrine and tending its fire. In return, they got a place to live — the House of the Vestals — in the Forum, downtown Rome's public square. People trusted them and gave their wills to the Vestal Virgins for safekeeping. The downside to the post was that a Vestal was buried alive if she cheated on that vow of chastity.

Playing for Power

When the going gets tough, the toughest found dynasties. The guys in this list didn't need assertiveness training; they stepped forward to shove rivals out of the way as they made themselves, and their governments, the ultimate authority. Stand aside for military strongmen and emperors.

✔ **Augustus Caesar** (63 BC–14 AD): Rome's first official emperor was Gaius Julius Caesar Octavianus, or Octavian, the son of a senator and a great nephew of *the* Julius Caesar. (See Chapter 20 for more about Julius Caesar and Chapter 5 for more on the Roman Empire.) When conspirators killed Julius Caesar, who was dictator, Octavian was a student, but he closed his books, raised an army, dealt with the assassins, and defeated his rival for power, Mark Antony. Then he forced the Senate to make him consul — the top administrative job in the Roman government. Later that year, 43 BC, Octavian made a deal with Antony and another Roman big shot, Lepidus, to form a triumvirate (or "ruling three"). Octavian's part of the bargain was Africa, Sardinia, and Sicily. Later he got the entire western half of the Roman world, and after defeating Antony and the Egyptian queen Cleopatra at Actium in 31 BC, Octavian became sole ruler. The Senate gave him the name *Augustus,* or "exalted." Under his rule, Rome saw peace, reform, and rebuilding. The Roman Senate declared him *Pater Patriae* (father of his country) in 2 BC. When he died, the Senate declared him a god.

✔ **Charlemagne** (742 AD–814 AD): The Franks, like the Romans before them, had problems with intruders. Barbarians from up north kept horning in on Gaul (today's France), and there were rumblings from those Muslims down in Spain when Charlemagne (or Charles the Great) came to power — first as king of the eastern Franks (his brother Carloman got the western bunch) and then as Great King of the Franks in 771 AD. The title *Great King* meant that he ruled over lesser kings and princes, which was the feudal style of leadership. Charlemagne brought Europe together under one rule as nobody had since the Romans, fighting Saxons, Avars, and Lombards to do it. On Christmas Day, 800 AD, Pope Leo III crowned Charlemagne as Emperor of the West or Holy Roman Emperor, starting the Holy Roman Empire (which actually had nothing to do with the original Roman Empire). Charlemagne built palaces and churches and promoted Christianity, education, agriculture, and the arts. Commerce thrived under his administration, which came to be known as the Carolingian Renaissance — a *little* awakening hundreds of years before the big awakening. The empire fell apart after he died, though, because Charlie's sons lacked his vision and authority. (For more about Charlemagne and his family, see Chapter 6.)

✔ **William the Conqueror** (about 1028–1087): When St. Edward the Confessor died, he really left a mess; as king of England, he apparently designated one noble — William, Duke of Normandy — and then another — Harold

Godwinson — to succeed him. Harold took the crown as Harold II, but William thought that Harold had promised to uphold *his* claim to the throne. William invaded, killed Harold at the Battle of Hastings, was crowned king on Christmas Day 1066, and forever after has been *the Conqueror*. He stayed in power by replacing all the leaders of the old Anglo-Saxon nobility with a new ruling class of French-speaking Normans, Bretons, and Flemings.

✔ **Genghis Khan** (around 1167–1227): Before he was Genghis Khan (see Figure 19-1), he was Temujin, who at age 13 became chief of a desperately poor clan of nomadic Mongols. Temujin was hungry, so he went to work defeating other clans, including the Naimans and the Tangut (names that nobody much remembers anymore, but they were pretty tough in their time). In 1206, after the Turkish Uigurs bowed down to him, Temujin changed his name to Genghis Khan, which means "very great ruler" or "universal king." In several campaigns starting in 1211, he overran the empire of North China and other East Asian territories. By the time of his death, the Mongol Empire stretched from the Black Sea to the Pacific.

✔ **Babur** (1483–1530): He was called Zahir-ud-din Muhammad before taking the name Babur, which means "tiger" in Arabic. The first Mogul emperor of India, Babur was born in Ferghana, Kyrgyzstan. A genius at war, he invaded India and defeated leaders of its separate kingdoms to unite an empire and found a dynasty marked by its mixed Mongol and Turkish origins and by its attitude of conciliation toward the Hindu majority. Babur was interested in architecture, music, and literature. He passed these interests down through a line of successors whose empire remained strong until the early eighteenth century but eventually fell under the domination of the British East India Company in the nineteenth century. (See Chapter 8 for more on European influence in eighteenth- and nineteenth-century Asia.)

Figure 19-1:
Genghis
Khan
assembled
a massive
empire
stretching
from Eastern
Europe to
China.

© *Bridgeman Art Library/Getty Images*

Building Bridges

The way to build something big — from a house to an empire — is to put together smaller components. As in carpentry, so in the hammering together of nations, regions, and cultures. The people in this section used means as diverse as battles and alliances to link geographic, religious, and ethnic components into new combinations. Some of them built so well that their constructions still stand.

✔ **Kublai Khan** (1214–1294): Genghis Khan's grandson established his capital where Beijing is now. As Mongol emperor of China and founder of the Yuan Dynasty, starting in 1279, he was vigorous and forceful in the way he used power, launching military campaigns against Java, Burma, Japan, and other Asian nations, although with only limited success (none at all against Japan). Kublai Khan, like many of history's most interesting people, was a study in contradictions. He was adaptable, making the Chinese style of civilization his own, yet he kept his Mongol ruling class separate from the Chinese natives and appointed many foreigners, especially Muslims, to high government offices while making Buddhism the state religion. Some accounts describe him as a cruel ruler, others as reasonable and merciful. His court is legendary for luxury and splendor.

✔ **Ferdinand** (1452–1516) and **Isabella** (1451–1504): When Ferdinand, king of Aragon (part of today's northern Spain), married Isabella, queen of Castille (also part of today's northern Spain), in 1469, their kingdoms got hitched, too, coming together as the forerunner of modern Spain. Co-ruled by this happening couple, Spain finally ousted the last of its Moorish rulers in 1492 when Ferdinand and Isabella took over the Sultanate of Granada. That same year, Isabella sponsored Christopher Columbus, leading to Spain's supremacy in the New World. In 1478, Ferdinand and Isabella began the Spanish Inquisition, a Catholic reform movement aimed at rooting out non-Christian (especially Islamic and Jewish) ideas that had dominated the Iberian Peninsula (Spain and Portugal) over centuries of rule by Moorish caliphates. (The Moors had been tolerant of Judaism.) The Inquisition also helped keep the Protestant Reformation out of Spain (see Chapter 14 for more about the Reformation). In 1512, after Isabella died, Phillip completed Spain's unification when he took over the kingdom of Navarre.

✔ **Nobunaga Oda** (1534–1582), **Hideyoshi Toyotomi** (1536–1598), and **Ieyasu Tokugawa** (1543–1616): The three great unifiers of Japan finally broke the cycle of warring feudal lords dominating the country. Noble-born Nobunaga Oda subjugated Owari Province, threw out the sitting *shogun* (a feudal big boss), occupied the capital at Kyoto in 1568, and defeated the priests at Osaka, destroying the power of the Buddhists.

Just to be sure Buddhism didn't bounce back, he briefly encouraged Christianity. When he died, he controlled half of Japan. That paved the way for his general, the lowborn Hideyoshi Toyotomi and Toyotomi's erstwhile ally, Ieyasu Tokugawa, to finally unite the country. Toyotomi banned swords for anybody but the *samurai,* or warrior class. Tokugawa eventually turned on Toyotomi and his family and established the long-lived but repressive and isolationist Tokugawa Shogunate, which lasted until the mid-nineteenth century.

✔ **James I of England/James VI of Scotland** (1566–1625): Scotland's King James didn't conquer neighboring England; he simply ascended its throne as the legitimate successor (through his English great-great-grandmother) to the childless Elizabeth I in 1603. His position unified the crowns of the two realms — the first step toward the unification of the two kingdoms (which happened in 1707 when the Act of Union created the United Kingdom). When James I became their king, the English stopped trying to annex Scotland, because there was no longer any point. James was a scholarly type who wrote pamphlets, sponsored Shakespeare's acting troupe, and commissioned an enduring and beautiful English translation of the Christian scripture, known as the *King James Bible.* He imprisoned and executed Sir Walter Raleigh — not because he hated Raleigh's newfangled habit of smoking tobacco, which he did, but for other offenses against the crown. James also hated the extreme form of Calvinist-Protestant belief called Puritanism that gained momentum in England at the beginning of the seventeenth century. (Find out more about the Puritans in Chapter 14.) James drew criticism for his habit of playing favorites and resisted Puritan pressure to purge Catholic practices from the English Church. Ironically, Catholic conspirators, not Puritans, tried and almost succeeded in blowing up the new king and Parliament in the Gunpowder Plot of 1605.

✔ **Frederick the Great** (1712–1786): As a young prince, Frederick II of Prussia studied military skills, music (he even composed some), and French literature. As king, he fought the neighboring Austrians and other Germanic states, adding Silesia (along the Oder River in east-central Europe), part of western Germany, and part of Poland to his kingdom. (Poland had, until his father's time, ruled Prussia.) Prussia doubled in size under Fred's rule and became a leading power — both militarily and economically — and the forerunner of modern Germany.

✔ **George Washington** (1732–1799): The first president of the United States of America set a remarkable precedent in 1796 when he declined to run for a third term of office. Many a new nation has stumbled over the issue of peaceful transfer of power, as the first administration balks at handing over authority to successors. Washington achieved this crucial transition gracefully. (He had turned down Congress's earlier offer to make him king.) With natural authority rather than rhetoric, Washington brought disagreeing Americans together at two critical times. In the 1770s, the self-possessed Virginia planter and British military veteran was the clear choice to lead a revolution's army. In the 1780s, his willingness to revise the Articles of Confederation (the loose agreement by which the newborn country tried to operate) led to the drafting of the U.S. Constitution. It's hard to imagine the American Revolution succeeding without him. It's even more difficult to imagine the nation succeeding without his example. For more on George Washington, check out *U.S. History For Dummies,* by Steve Wiegand (Wiley).

✔ **Nelson Mandela** (1918–): Like George Washington, Nelson Rolihlahla Mandela could be listed along with other revolutionaries in Chapter 22, but his greatest legacy lies in his commitment to reconciliation as the first post-apartheid president of South Africa. Raised to become a Thembu tribal chief, Mandela was a college student when he started working to overturn *apartheid,* the legal separation of races. As a young Johannesburg lawyer in the 1950s, he organized a black underground movement. He was arrested and convicted of conspiracy to overthrow the government and sentenced to life in prison. During 27 years in jail, Mandela became a worldwide symbol for justice. After his release in 1990, he helped negotiate the end of apartheid, shared the Nobel Peace Prize with F.W. de Klerk, and at age 75, succeeded de Klerk as president, becoming his country's first leader chosen in an all-race election. Never seeking revenge, Mandela consulted his former captors as he rebuilt South African society. When he left office in 1999, crime and poverty still plagued South Africa, but Mandela had seen the country through an extraordinary transition.

Writing Laws

Often a society's identity flows from the way it defines morality and administers justice. Consider that most modern jurisprudence is based on precedent. The way an issue was decided before becomes part of the current definition of what is legal or illegal, right or wrong. This precedence business doesn't date back just a few decades or even a few centuries; it's rooted in decisions about justice and punishment that go all the way to the foundations of human society. No wonder so many lawgivers — good and bad — are remembered in history. A small sampling follows:

✔ **Ur-Nammu** and **Shulgi** (twenty-second and twenty-first centuries BC): A ruler of the ancient Mesopotamian kingdom of Ur instituted the earliest code of laws that survives in written form. Which ruler? Researchers aren't sure, but it was either Ur-Nammu or his son and successor Shulgi. Archeologists can read only five items from *Ur-Nammu's Code,* as it's known, but it supports other evidence showing that even 4,200 years ago, civilized people had a legal system requiring testimony under oath. They had special judges who could order a guilty party to pay damages to a victim. The code also allowed for the dismissal of corrupt officials, protection for the poor, and punishment proportionate to the crime.

✔ **Moses** (fourteenth or thirteenth century BC): The Bible's book of Exodus says that God gave mankind the Ten Commandments through his servant Moses, a Hebrew reared as an Egyptian prince. Moses led the Israelites out of slavery in Egypt and on a meandering, 40-year route through the desert to Canaan. With his brother Aaron, he set up the religious community of Israel and founded its traditions through practice and writings. Moses is considered the author of the first several books of the Bible, the only source of information about the above events. (For more about Judaism and Moses, see Chapter 10.)

Moses's story has inspired some bad films. The worst may be 1975's ill-conceived epic *Moses,* with Burt Lancaster in the title role and cheesy special effects undercutting his performance. Director Cecil B. DeMille did it better in 1956 when he made *The Ten Commandments*. In that one, Charlton Heston plays Moses, heading an all-star cast speaking nonsensically shallow, pseudo-Biblical lines amidst marvelous photography. The animated musical cartoon *Prince of Egypt* from 1998 may be the best version of the Moses story on film.

✔ **Draco** (seventh century BC): Athens picked this official to write its laws, the first such written code in Greece, in about 620 BC. Draco's severe laws made the state exclusive prosecutor of those accused of crime, outlawing vigilante justice. But many offenses merited the death penalty, and the word *draconian* still refers to harsh punishment. Yet Athenians loved Draco. As Draco entered an auditorium to attend a reception in his honor, Athenians gave him the customary celebratory greeting, showering him with their hats and cloaks. He fell down and was strangely still, so they pulled all the clothing off of him and found him dead — suffocated.

✔ **Solon** (about 630 BC–about 560 BC): Solon was an Athenian statesman and reformer, not to mention a wizard at reciting verse. This Greek's breakthrough as a public figure came when he spurred Athenians to military action against the Megarians with a rousing poem. His eloquence made Solon the choice to rewrite Draco's harsh code of laws (see the previous bullet). Solon had other talents, too. He reorganized public institutions, including the senate and the popular assembly, minted coins, reformed weights and measures, and strengthened Athenian trade. The result is that his name came to be a synonym for legislator, especially in twentieth-century newspapers where *congressman* wouldn't fit in a headline.

✔ **Justinian** (482 AD–565 AD): "The things which are common to all are the air, running water, the sea, and the seashores." That's a bit of Roman law, as interpreted and set down by the Byzantine Emperor Justinian in a series of books that have been an important source for legal codes every since. The word *justice* comes from Justinian's name.

✔ **Mohammed** (about 570 AD–about 632 AD): The son of a poor Arab merchant, Mohammed was orphaned at age 6 and grew up tending sheep. As a young man, he led caravans owned by a rich widow. Later, he married her and became a merchant. But for a businessman, Mohammed (sometimes spelled Mohamet) was a bit of a loner who liked to go off and think. He was 40 when he said the Angel Gabriel commanded him in the name of God to preach the *true religion.* After a few years, Mohammed began attacking superstition and urging people to live a pious, moral life. He taught his followers to believe in an all-powerful, all-just God, or *Allah,* whose mercy could be gotten by prayer, fasting, and the giving of alms. Authorities in Mecca, alarmed by his growing popularity, threw him out in 622 AD, so he went to Medina, where he became high judge and ruler. Mohammed led a war against enemies of Islam, taking Mecca in 630. After his last pilgrimage in 632, he fell ill and died. His moral rules, set down in the Koran, remain a basis of law throughout the Islamic world. (You can find out more about Mohammed, Islam, and the Arabs in Chapters 6 and 10.)

✔ **James Madison** (1751–1836): His knowledge of history and keen ability to forge compromises served Madison well at a 1787 convention in Philadelphia. A graduate of Princeton (then called the College of New Jersey), Madison represented his native Virginia at the convention. The delegates were supposed to beef up the Articles of Confederation, governing relations between the newly independent American states. Instead, the convention threw out the articles and replaced them with the U.S. Constitution. Madison thought about governments including the democracy of ancient Athens, the Roman Republic, and European federations such as the Holy Roman Empire, and he knew that the United States needed a strong central government; he deftly managed agreements allowing the convention to hammer out a working document. Many of Madison's ideas became foundations of U.S. law, which is why he's called the Father of the Constitution. Madison's notes also contributed to the historical record, providing the most complete account of the Constitutional convention. Madison later became the fourth U.S. president.

Tracking the Centuries

About 2200 BC: The king of Ur, a Mesopotamian kingdom (today's Iraq), institutes a legal system that requires testimony under oath and authorizes judges to order a guilty party to pay damages to a victim.

About 230 BC: Shi Huangdi, self-proclaimed First Emperor of China, standardizes writing and units of measure across the lands he has conquered.

630 AD: Mohammed leads his army of Islam to capture Mecca.

1227: Genghis Khan rules a Mongol Empire stretching from the Black Sea to the Pacific Ocean.

1469: Queen Isabella of Castille and King Ferdinand of Aragon get married, forging their lands together into a forerunner of modern Spain.

1772: Frederick the Great of Prussia adds West Prussia to his kingdom in the first partition of Poland.

1787: At the Constitutional Convention in Philadelphia, James Madison's knowledge and bright ability to apply history's lessons earn him the title Father of the Constitution.

1990: Nelson Mandela walks out of jail after 27 years in the custody of the South African government.

Chapter 20

Battling Toward Immortality

- -

- -

"War is the father of all and the king of all," said Heraclitus, a Greek-Ephesian philosopher of the fifth century BC. "It proves some people gods, and some people men; it makes some people slaves, and some people free." War also makes people famous. Those in this chapter are among many more who owe their reputations to battles won or lost.

Neither complete nor absolute, my headings in this section — like any historical labels — are arbitrary. That means I made them up. What's important is that you can find examples of some of history's feistiest fighters here. Many fierce types had other distinctions, too. (You may have already discovered Genghis Khan with other founders of empires in Chapter 19.)

Towering Over Their Times

Some historical figures are so huge that . . . well, they're just *major,* that's all. Alexander the Great, Julius Caesar, Napoleon, and Hitler each changed the world profoundly and each achieved monstrous fame — or notoriety — for ambitious, world-wrenching military conquests. I could have lumped them with other empire-building fighters later in this chapter, but I decided to give them a category to themselves.

> ✔ **Alexander the Great** (356–323 BC): By the time Alexander the Great died in Babylon, everybody knew about Macedon's brilliant young prince-soldier-general-king-emperor. (Macedon was north of Greece, now split between the Macedonian region of modern Greece and the Republic of

Macedonia.) The son of Philip II, Alex thought he was descended from gods and loved the epic poems of Homer. Enjoying the best upbringing available, Alexander the Great studied under the philosopher Aristotle, his tutor (Aristotle appears in Chapter 11). As a teenager, Alexander commanded his dad's Macedonian-Greek forces, showing sharp military skills and remarkable maturity. After his dad's assassination, he took the throne as Alexander III and took the world by storm. He was handsome, charismatic, and so popular that many of the peoples he conquered welcomed his rule, but he also had a temper and lashed out at those closest to him. Alexander's brief empire stretched beyond the limits of what people of the time considered the known world (see Chapter 4).

✔ **Julius Caesar** (about 100–44 BC): Gaius Julius Caesar didn't become emperor (at least, he didn't wear that title), but his ambition helped bring down the ailing Roman Republic, and his death led to the new Roman Empire. A talented general, Caesar pushed Rome's frontier all the way to Europe's Atlantic coast in the Gallic Wars. In Egypt, he put Cleopatra VII back on the throne after her brother kicked her out. Why did Caesar help Cleopatra? The fact that she bore him a son (or at least said it was his) may be a clue. In trouble-wracked Rome, he formed a three-man ruling body, or *triumvirate,* with Pompey and Crassus, but the arrangement dissolved into a power struggle. In 49 BC, Caesar led his troops south across the Rubicon River toward Rome. This move violated a Roman law intended to protect the city against a military coup, but Caesar had come too far too turn back. His action started civil war, and the phrase *crossing the Rubicon* has meant "point of no return" ever since. He emerged with sole control, taking the title Dictator for Life. A group fed up with Caesar's airs assassinated him in 44 BC.

✔ **Napoleon Bonaparte** (1769–1821): From the Italian island of Corsica, Napoleon's father sent him to military school in France, which led the lad into that country's service at age 16. The French Revolution of 1789 proved an opportune moment for a smart, ambitious young officer, because just about every monarch in Europe declared war on the revolutionary government in Paris. Napoleon scored important victories, became a general, and in 1799 joined co-conspirators in a *coup d'état* ("stroke of state," or government takeover). Napoleon emerged as sole ruler of France and conqueror of neighboring countries; by 1807, he ruled Europe's largest empire since the Romans. His reforms improved education, banking, and the legal system. (Many countries still base their laws on his *Napoleonic Code.*) Because wife Josephine had not borne him an heir, Napoleon dumped her for Marie Louise, an Austrian princess. When their son was born, Napoleon made the baby King of Rome.

Napoleon's biggest mistake was his 1812 invasion of Russia, in which thousands of his troops froze to death or starved (see Chapter 9). The next year, Russia joined Austria, Prussia, and Sweden to crush Napoleon at Leipzig, Germany. His enemies exiled Napoleon to the Mediterranean island of Elba, where in 1814 he raised a small army and headed toward Paris. Napoleon ruled again for a famous *Hundred Days,* which ended at the Battle of Waterloo, Belgium, as English and Prussian forces delivered a defeat in 1815 from which Napoleon couldn't rebound. This time he was sent to St. Helena, an island in the south Atlantic, where he died of stomach cancer six years later.

✔ **Adolf Hitler** (1889–1945): Hitler, shown in Figure 20-1, wanted to be an artist, but the Vienna Academy turned him down. So the Austrian attended a lesser art school in Munich, Germany, and then served as an infantryman in a Bavarian regiment in World War I. After the war, he turned to right-wing politics to vent his rage at the terms of peace. As leader of the extremist National Socialist German Workers' Party, he tried to overthrow the Bavarian government in 1923 and was jailed. Over the next several years he built support for his *Nazi* party, blaming so-called outsiders, especially Jews, for weakening Germany. In 1932, Hitler won appointment as chancellor and then suspended Germany's constitution. When President Paul von Hindenburg died in 1934, Hitler became president and supreme commander — *Der Führer* (the leader). He ordered Jews, Arabs, Gypsies, homosexuals, and "mental defectives" rounded up and sent to concentration camps, where hundreds at a time were gassed. Nazis killed at least six million Jews under Hitler's leadership.

After forcefully uniting Germany with Austria, Hitler invaded Poland in 1939, starting World War II. As Germany's war strategy deteriorated under Hitler's personal direction, Colonel Claus von Stauffenberg of the German command staff led a conspiracy to assassinate Hitler. This failed attempt is the subject of the 2008 film Valkyrie, which I discuss with other movies about WWII in Chapter 9.

Figure 20-1: Adolph Hitler started World War II in 1939 when he sent German troops into Poland.

© Time & Life Pictures/Getty Images

Having escaped death, *Der Führer* purged the army of anyone he suspected of disloyalty, which weakened Germany further. As the Allies advanced on Berlin, Hitler hid in an air-raid shelter with his mistress, Eva Braun. He and Braun married and then killed themselves. After witnessing the ceremony, Nazi propaganda minister Paul Goebbels and his wife murdered all six of their children before killing themselves.

Building Empires

The conqueror's motivation wasn't just to show how tough he was. Virtually every one of history's most fearsome characters was fighting for material gain. Motives for conquest included land, of course. Conquerors sought more territory and more people to rule because of the prestige that such gains brought and also because additional territory and population brought greater trade advantages and military power. Other incentives included *booty* (goods stolen in warfare) and *tribute* (money paid to a conqueror by the conquered). The following historical figures were determined to acquire the spoils that go to the victor:

- **Nebuchadnezzar II** (about 630–562 BC): Before succeeding to the throne of Babylon, Nebuchadnezzar led his father's army to victory over Egypt. Crowned in 605 BC, Nebuchadnezzar launched campaigns against western neighbors. Babylonian forces captured Jerusalem and took thousands of Jews, including the newly crowned King Jehoiachin, back to Babylon as slaves. (Jehoiachin remained in captivity for 37 years.) Nebuchadnezzar appointed Zedekiah as his *vassal king* in Jerusalem. A vassal king's job was to govern as the deputy of an overlord or great king. After Zedekiah rebelled, Nebuchadnezzar came back and destroyed Jerusalem in 586 BC. Legend says that Jewish slaves built or helped build the fabulous Hanging Gardens of Babylon, a wonder of the ancient world. Historians know little about the gardens, which were destroyed long ago, but according to tradition they were ordered built either by Nebuchadnezzar II or his predecessor, Queen Samu-ramat. So little is known about Samu-ramat, however, that she's often referred to as "semi-legendary."

- **Wu Ti** (156–87 BC): Wu the Martial's original name was Lui Ch'e. An empire-building ruler of China's Han Dynasty, he annexed parts of Southern China, upper Vietnam, northern and central Korea, and the northern and western frontiers where the Hsuiung-nu nomads (a warlike people known elsewhere as Huns) roamed.

- **Attila the Hun** (about 406–453 AD): Known as the *Scourge of God,* Attila co-ruled the warlike, nomadic Huns with his big brother Bleda, controlling a region from the Rhine to the edge of China. In 445 AD, Attila murdered Bleda and assembled a vast horde of Huns based in Hungary. In 451, when

Attila invaded Gaul (France), Roman commander Aëtius (you can find him in the later section "Mounting a Defense") and king of the Visigoths Theodoric I resisted him. Attila pulled an end run into Italy, where Pope Leo I pleaded with Attila to spare Rome. The Hun Empire fell apart after Attila died.

✔ **Canute** (995–1035 AD): English monarchs haven't had names like Canute or Ethelred for a long time. Ethelred the Unready (it meant "ill-advised" rather than "unprepared") lost control of the kingdom to Viking invader Sweyn Forkbeard in 1013. When Sweyn died, Ethelred tried to take back his crown, but the Viking's son, Canute, was on the case. Canute ruled England from 1016, becoming king of Denmark in 1019 and adding Norway in 1028. He achieved peace throughout this far-flung realm. It's sometimes said of Canute that he thought he was such a big shot that he tried to make the waves on the sea obey him. This is a bad rap: Canute was demonstrating that he was *not* some kind of god and could *not* tell nature what to do.

✔ **Shaka** (about 1787–1828): The founder of the Zulu Empire conquered most of southern Africa with a military system that could deploy 40,000 well-trained, highly disciplined warriors. The downside was that they were equipped only with shields and short spears. A ruthless dictator, Shaka repressed his tribal rivals but died at the hands of his power-hungry half-brothers. Still, his tactics and empire survived for another half-century until the British used modern weapons to break the back of Zulu power in 1879.

Two notable films, 1964's *Zulu* and 1979's *Zulu Dawn* are treatments of the 1879 war between Britain and the Zulu Empire (after Shaka). Of the two, *Zulu Dawn* was less popular with audiences and critics, but it contains a more accurate depiction of historical events and admirably tries to show the Africans' side of the war. *Zulu* is also set in 1879, but after the events of *Zulu Dawn,* so it can be viewed as a sequel to the other film. The story of a band of Welshmen standing against the spear-thrusting warriors, *Zulu* features Michael Caine in his first starring role and was both a critical and box office hit.

Launching Attacks

No general can make do with one style of maneuver alone, but these men all made their names as audacious attackers, even though some of them lost crucial battles:

✔ **Xerxes I** (485–465 BC): Xerxes suppressed revolts all over the Persian Empire, including Babylon and Egypt. Because his dad, Darius the Great (548–486 BC), died trying to teach the Greeks a lesson, Xerxes thought he would finish the job. He burned Athens before going home to Persia, but the Greeks weren't down for long. They whipped the army that Xerxes left behind and burned the Persian fleet on the same day in 479 BC. Artabanus, his own *vizier* (captain of the guards), murdered Xerxes.

✔ **Genseric** (unknown–477 AD): Genseric was one of the barbarians who threatened the Western Roman Empire during its last years. King of the Vandals, he took over much of Spain and from there attacked North Africa. He captured Carthage from the Romans and made it his capital. He also sacked Rome but stopped short of destroying the city in 455.

✔ **Harald III Sigurdsson** (1015–1066): Being compared to a saint is not what made this Norwegian prince ruthless. His half-brother became Saint Olaf (he's listed in the section "Instigating Inspiration"), but both brothers were Viking mercenaries. Olaf, who was king first, died in 1030 while fighting Norwegian rebels allied with Denmark. Having to flee, Harald hired himself out as a warrior for the prince of Kiev Rus (an early edition of Russia, where Ukraine is now) before returning to Norway. There Harald became king in 1045, earning his nickname "The Ruthless" in wars against Denmark. He invaded England in 1066 to claim the throne after Saint Edward the Confessor died, but a fellow with a similar name, Harold II of England, killed Harald. That would have been the end of the story, but William of Normandy (see Chapter 19) succeeded where Harald failed. Had it turned out differently, Harald III of Norway would be Harald the Conqueror and this book would be in Norwegian.

✔ **Richard Lionheart** (1157–1199): Richard I was king of England for a decade, starting in 1189, but he spent only five months of that time in the country. No wonder his brother John tried to steal his throne. Called Richard *Coeur de Lion* (English rulers spoke French in those days because they *were* French), he was the third son of Henry II and an outstanding soldier. Richard was on his way back from Jerusalem and the Third Crusade when he landed in a Vienna jail. (Chapter 7 has more about the Crusades.) His mom, Eleanor of Aquitaine, paid the ransom to get him released. Richard went on to fight, and die, for England's claim to lands in what is now France.

✔ **Erwin Rommel** (1891–1944): Rommel, a German field marshal in World War II, made his name leading a mechanized division that charged through France to the English Channel in 1940. Rommel led more attacks on allied forces in North Africa, where his inventive tank warfare strategies earned him the name "Desert Fox." Nazi officials suspected Rommel of conspiracy in a plot to kill Hitler, and he was recalled from his post and forced to commit suicide by poison.

Mounting a Defense

Some fighters were at their best (or worst) when invaders came calling. Several of the people in the list that follows were just as aggressive and ambitious as any empire-builder known to history. It just so happened, however, that each of these fighters became known for an important defensive stand — whether it succeeded or not.

- ✔ **Flavius Aëtius** (about 350–454 AD): For 20 years this Roman general was in charge of keeping the barbarians at bay, which was often a losing battle. Coming from the *patrician* (or aristocratic) class, he became the empire's general-in-chief and also a consul, the top government administrator. (There's more about Roman social classes in Chapter 5.) Aëtius scored a big success at Châlons in 451 AD, when he commanded the allied forces that beat Attila the Hun. After that, Aëtius was flying high, the most popular guy in the empire, which ticked off Emperor Valentinian III. The jealous emperor stabbed Aëtius to death.

- ✔ **Charles Martel** (about 699–741 AD): The Carolingian kings of Charlemagne's family (see Chapter 19) started with Charles Martel, who ruled much of Gaul (today's France) but never got to call himself king. He was called "The Hammer," however, for his military campaigns against Saxons and Frisons and other assorted rivals through the region. He fought the Muslims and kept them from penetrating Western Europe (beyond Spain, that is) at the Battle of Poitiers in 732 AD.

- ✔ **Harold II** (about 1022–1066): The last Anglo-Saxon king of England had a short, violent, disputed reign. He fought off Harald III Sigurdsson of Norway and then turned around to take on the Duke of Normandy at the Battle of Hastings. All it got poor Harold was an arrow through the eye.

- ✔ **Shagrat al-Durr** (unknown–1259): Also known as Shajarat, she was a one-time slave girl who married two of Egypt's sultans, ran the government from behind the scenes for years, and for two months bore the title of sultan. In 1249, her first husband, Salih Ayyub, was out of town when Crusaders under Louis IX of France landed at the mouth of the Nile. Acting for the absent sultan, Shagrat organized Egypt's defense. Her hubby returned but soon died. Shagrat pretended Salih was still alive and kept acting in his name until her stepson Turan showed up and claimed his inheritance. Turan, with Shagrat's guidance, beat the Crusaders and took Louis prisoner. Egyptian army officers preferred Shagrat, a Turk like them, to Turan, so they killed Turan and installed Shagrat as sultan. But the Caliph in Baghdad said "Nope," a woman wasn't allowed to be sultan. Shagrat resigned, and then wooed and married her replacement, Aibak. She remained the power behind the throne until he decided to add a new wife to his harem, angering her. She killed Aibak in his bath, riots broke out, and harem slaves beat Shagrat with their shoes and threw her into the palace moat. Egyptians later enshrined her bones in a mosque named for her.

✔ **Robert the Bruce** (1274–1329): In 1296, the Scottish Earl of Carrick, better known as Robert the Bruce, swore loyalty to the king of England, Edward I, who was trying to establish English sovereignty over Scotland. Then Bruce changed his mind and backed William Wallace, a Scottish patriot fighting the English. After Edward tortured and beheaded Wallace in 1306, Robert the Bruce advanced his own claim on Scotland's crown by killing political rival John Comyn with a dagger. Bruce was crowned Scotland's king, and after a brief exile in Ireland (some people didn't consider this stabbing business to be fair), he came back in 1307 and thrashed the English at Loudoun Hill. Bruce and his lads trounced the English again at Bannockburn in 1314. Finally, the English signed the Treaty of Northampton (1328), agreeing that Bruce was the rightful king.

Heroic gloss and stirring cinematography bury historical perspective in Mel Gibson's 1995 film epic *Braveheart*. Gibson plays late-thirteenth-century rebel leader William Wallace in the sprawling war story, which features impressively staged wild battle scenes.

Devising Tactics

A battle's outcome often hinges on strength, as in superior numbers or better weapons. But strategy and tactics just as often make the difference between winner and loser. When two forces are evenly matched, strategic advantage comes in second only to luck in determining the result. The following fighters all used wits and innovation — although not all of them achieved success:

✔ **Hannibal** (247–182 BC): In his mid-20s, Hannibal of Carthage subdued most of southern Spain. He blindsided the Romans in the Second Punic War (refer to Chapter 5) by invading Italy from the north, over the Alps mountain range, using battle-trained elephants. (The Romans assumed Hannibal would come at them by sea from North Africa.) Ultimately, the Alps invasion failed and Hannibal went home to work on political reform. He faced stiff opposition on that front, too, and eventually exiled himself. When it looked like the Romans would capture him at last (they held grudges), Hannibal did what good soldiers did in those days — he killed himself.

✔ **William Tecumseh Sherman** (1820–1891): "War is cruelty and you cannot refine it," said Sherman. Born in Ohio and educated at West Point, Sherman resigned his U.S. Army commission in 1853 to become a California banker. The bank failed, and he became superintendent of the Louisiana Military Academy, the post he held when that state seceded from the Union. Sherman went north and rejoined the Union Army, commanding a brigade at the first Battle of Bull Run in 1861 (the North lost) and then heading up defensive forces in the border state of Kentucky. After recovering from a nervous breakdown, he led units effectively at several decisive battles. His drive to capture Atlanta, destroying and burning towns and farmsteads along the way, stands as a definitive landmark of modern war.

Instigating Inspiration

A few of history's warriors inspired others with their bravery or dedication to a cause. Some soldiers inspired those who followed them into battle. Others left legends that inspired later generations of warriors.

- ✔ **St. Olaf** (about 995–1030 AD): As a 15-year-old mercenary, Olaf joined Viking buddies in ripping down London Bridge in 1010. Three years later in Normandy, Olaf found religion. He went home to Norway, seized the throne (he was probably not yet 20), and worked to establish Christianity in place of the old Norse gods, earning posthumous sainthood. Danish-backed rebels killed King Olaf.

- ✔ **Peter the Hermit** (about 1050–about 1115): Imagine joining an army led by a monk, Peter the Hermit, and an impoverished knight, Walter the Penniless. Thousands of Christians said "I'm in!" in 1095, forming the People's Crusade, which was part of the First Crusade (see Chapter 7). Also called Peter of Amiens, Peter the Hermit was an ex-soldier who got his followers fired up about liberating the Holy Land from the Muslims. Most of Peter's followers — including co-leader Walter — died the first time they faced the Turks. Peter survived to join the better-armed branch of the First Crusade, which conquered Jerusalem in 1099. He later founded a Belgian monastery.

- ✔ **Robin Hood** (if he lived, it was sometime between the twelfth and fourteenth centuries): English ballads dating from about the fourteenth century credit the legendary Robin with protecting the poor and attacking corrupt officials. The stories may be rooted in discontent that led to the Peasants' Revolt of 1381 (see the coverage of Wat Tyler in Chapter 22). Some accounts place Robin in the twelfth century, during the rule of the unpopular King John.

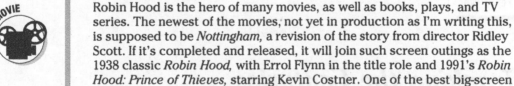

Robin Hood is the hero of many movies, as well as books, plays, and TV series. The newest of the movies, not yet in production as I'm writing this, is supposed to be *Nottingham,* a revision of the story from director Ridley Scott. If it's completed and released, it will join such screen outings as the 1938 classic *Robin Hood,* with Errol Flynn in the title role and 1991's *Robin Hood: Prince of Thieves,* starring Kevin Costner. One of the best big-screen Robins, for my money, is Sean Connery in 1976's *Robin and Marian.* Connery plays an aging Robin who arrives home from a Crusade to learn that Maid Marian, played by Audrey Hepburn, became a nun and is abbess of a priory.

✔ **Joan of Arc** (about 1412–1431): This 13-year-old girl (shown in Figure 20-2) heard the voices of saints telling her to rescue France from English domination during the Hundred Years' War. Tall order for a kid, but something about her seemed convincing. Charles VII, at that time the *dauphin,* or crown prince of France, let her lead the army against the English at Orleans. In white armor, she inspired her troops to victory and then escorted Charles to Reims for his coronation. In her next campaign, she was captured, handed over to the English, tried for sorcery and other grievous crimes against Christian sensibilities (notably wearing men's clothes), and sentenced to burn at the stake. The Catholic Church canonized her in 1920, making her St. Joan.

She hasn't been the subject of as many movies as Robin Hood, but the Maid of Orleans (as Joan of Arc is also called) has inspired several films. They include 1957's *Saint Joan,* with Jean Seberg in the title role. A 1999 return to the Joan of Arc story, *The Messenger,* turned the heroine into a victim of post-traumatic stress disorder by having her witness the (fictional) rape and murder of her sister. Many critics rank a black-and-white antique from 1928, *The Passion of Joan of Arc,* as the best cinematic version of the story. Among its admirers are actor-director Mel Gibson; as I write this, Internet rumors say Gibson is planning a remake.

Figure 20-2:
Joan of Arc led French troops to victory over the English in the Hundred Years' War.

© Getty Images

Tracking the Centuries

586 BC: Babylonian troops led by Nebuchadnezzar destroy Jerusalem and take King Zedekiah prisoner.

A tale of two — or more — bridges

St. Olaf's teen vandalism probably didn't inspire the children's song "London Bridge is Falling Down (My Fair Lady)." The wooden bridge that the Vikings demolished in 1010 was one of a series of early structures across the River Thames linking London with Southwark (now part of London).

Perhaps the most memorable London Bridge (and the likely inspiration for the song) was a 19-arch stone bridge built in the twelfth century. It included not just traffic lanes but also shops and houses along each side. Dangerously overloaded, that bridge, like its wooden predecessors, began crumbling long before it was replaced in 1831 by another stone bridge. The 1831 model was a handsome, no-nonsense, five-arch structure that stood until 1968. Then it was dismantled block by block and shipped to Lake Havasu City, Arizona, where you can see it today. Its replacement over the Thames, today's London Bridge, is rather plain.

Because the name "London Bridge" is famous, people confuse the plain replacement with Tower Bridge, modern London's best-recognized landmark. Tower Bridge, which opened in 1894, stands downriver from London Bridge and next to the Tower of London. Tower Bridge has tall, handsome towers, whereas London Bridge has none. Tower Bridge can be raised to let large ships pass beneath; London Bridge can't.

How widespread is the confusion over these two bridges? Such that when I checked an online encyclopedia for "London Bridge," I got a picture of Tower Bridge.

479 BC: Troops from Greek city-states allied against Persia both defeat King Xerxes' army and burn his fleet in a single day.

49 BC: Julius Caesar leads his troops across the Rubicon, the stream that marks the boundary of his province, beginning a Roman civil war.

445 AD: Attila the Hun murders his big brother and co-ruler, Bleda, and begins forcibly assembling a vast horde of Hun warriors in Hungary.

1028: Canute, king of England and Denmark, adds Norway to his empire.

1431: Joan of Arc is convicted of sorcery and burns to death at the stake.

1828: His power-hungry half-brothers kill Shaka, emperor of the Zulu.

1853: William Tecumseh Sherman resigns his commission in the U.S. Army to become a banker in California.

1944: Germany's Nazi Gestapo, suspecting war hero Field Marshal Erwin Rommel of conspiracy in Colonel Claus von Stauffenberg's plot to kill Hitler, recalls Rommel from his command post in northern France and forces him to commit suicide by swallowing poison.

Chapter 21

Explorers and Discoverers: Places to Go, People to See

Many people made history by traveling to new places. Sometimes they went for the sake of going, but more often they headed out for the sake of getting something they couldn't get at home, such as new territory or the glory of being first. This chapter introduces you to some of the world's greatest voyagers. You'll notice many of them are from the fifteenth to seventeenth centuries, because restless Europeans, in particular, were discovering the rest of the world during that time.

Famous Pioneers: Arriving before Their Time

Some pioneers arrived at places that were new to them before the world was quite ready for them to get there. Getting from point A to point B is always an accomplishment, but what if no cultural influence or trade links result? Some explorers, including the following, didn't even know what they had found:

✔ **Pythias** (fourth century BC): Ancient Greeks traveled and settled just about everywhere around the Mediterranean. Pythias, born in Massilia, Gaul, went farther — much farther. Around 330 BC, he sailed from Massilia (today's Marseilles, France) past Spain, out through the Strait of Gibraltar, and up the Atlantic coast of Europe, past Britain as he continued north. Remarkably adventurous for his time, Pythias reached the island of

Thule, which he said was a six-day sail from northern Britain. He probably was somewhere in Norway, but some people think he reached Iceland. Pythias's own account of the voyage is lost, but several later writers referred to it.

✔ **Leif Eriksson** (late tenth–early eleventh centuries AD): Icelandic sagas say that around the year 1000, this tall, strong, smart, and fair-dealing son of the murderous Erik the Red (see the later section "Famous Mavericks: Taking Advantage of Opportunity") set out from Greenland with a crew of 35 to explore land sighted in the west. He found Baffin Island, just north of the Hudson Strait; then he spied the coast of Labrador (calling it Markland) and camped on Newfoundland's north-eastern tip. Eriksson called that place Vinland, for the wild grapes or perhaps berries that grew there. (It's now known as L'Anse aux Meadows.) The party stayed all winter before returning to Greenland. They would have gone to Vinland again if Leif's dad, Erik, hadn't died, making Leif head of the family back in Greenland. More Viking boats did travel from Greenland to Canada carrying other members of the clan, but they fought with the native people that they called Skraelings and also among themselves. A Norse settlement never took hold. Leif also brought Christianity to Greenland.

✔ **Zheng He** (unknown–about 1433): A Muslim court eunuch (ouch!) in China's royal household, Zheng He was also an admiral, sea explorer, and ambassador. From 1405–1407, Zheng commanded a 62-ship flotilla that went all the way to India. Then he led six more expeditions into the Persian Gulf and eventually to East Africa. He brought back giraffes, ostriches, and zebras, but the Chinese never used the contacts that Zheng He established with the rulers of the countries that he visited to develop trade advantages or to wield political influence abroad. (Zheng He's name is also often written as Cheng Ho. It has to do with the different ways that Chinese names have been transcribed into Western alphabets.) Figure 21-1 shows many of Zheng He's voyages.

✔ **Christopher Columbus** (1451–1506): Some people celebrate Columbus while others vilify him for his so-called discovery of America. But the tall, red-haired, eccentric sailor died never realizing what he accomplished. Born in Genoa (then an independent Italian city-state), Columbus was a crack navigator who sailed along the Atlantic coast of Africa and probably north to Iceland. He explored the Caribbean for Spain, becoming the first European navigator to land at the Bahamas, Cuba (he thought it was Japan), Haiti, Jamaica, and Trinidad before he stumbled on the South American mainland (specifically Venezuela). Yet Columbus insisted that China, his real goal, was close by (see Chapter 7). Jealous rivals dogged his attempts to run colonial settlements. Spanish fortune hunters trumped up charges against him and hauled the Italian back to Spain in chains. Columbus's sponsors, co-rulers Ferdinand and Isabella (see Chapter 19), set him free and gave him another expedition. On his fourth trip, Columbus caught the illness that killed him. Columbus committed at least three major career errors:

- Thinking that Asia extended a lot farther east than it does
- Figuring that the Earth's radius is only three-fourths of what it really is
- Stubbornly refusing to re-evaluate the meaning of his discoveries

Columbus has inspired many movies, including some very bad ones. In 1992's *Christopher Columbus: The Discovery,* Tom Selleck plays King Ferdinand as Columbus searches for China and the screenwriters search for a plot. A 2007 Portuguese film, *Christopher Columbus, the Enigma,* is about an amateur historian in the twentieth century who's trying to prove that the navigator was really from Portugal, not Italy.

✔ **Neil Armstrong** (1930–): When he set foot on the moon in 1969, Armstrong was supposed to say, "That's one small step for *a* man, one giant leap for mankind." It came out "one small step for man," which garbled the meaning a bit ("man" without the article "a" in those pre-feminism days often meant the whole human species), but his wording didn't diminish the fact that somebody finally walked on the moon. Ohio-born Armstrong was a American fighter pilot and test pilot before training as an astronaut. After commanding the Gemini 8 orbiter in 1966, he was picked for Apollo 11, a moon-landing expedition.

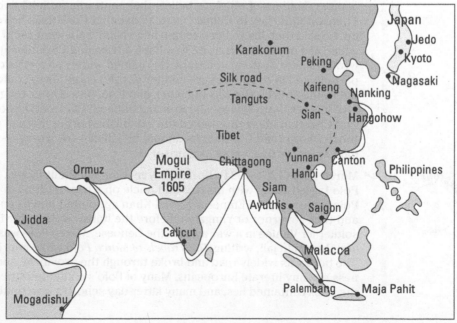

Figure 21-1:
Zheng He's voyages made China a world leader in long-range navigation.

On July 20, 1969, Armstrong climbed out of the landing module as spellbound earthlings watched on TV. Co-pilot Buzz Aldrin (1930–) was the second guy to step on moondust. Just as Columbus's landing in the New World became a monumental landmark, so may the first moon landing prove to be a great turning point — after people eventually return to the moon, probably as an international venture between the United States and other nations with space programs, or venture to other planets. So far, however, the 1969 moonwalk seems to be an achievement ahead of its time. Nobody, not even the inventive people at the National Aeronautics and Space Administration (NASA), were quite sure what to do on the moon or with the moon after they set astronauts on its surface. More American Apollo missions followed, but then moon exploration dried up in favor of space shuttles, unmanned probes of other planets in the solar system, and the International Space Station.

Notable Travelers: Carrying Messages

Some historical figures traveled to spread news. Most spread the word about where they were after they returned. Either way, travelers have always been important sources of information and even inspiration.

- ✔ **St. Paul** (about 10 AD–about 67 AD): First he was Saul, a Jew who came to Roman Judaea from his native Turkey. He became a rabbi of the strict Pharisee sect and believed in persecuting Christians, whom he saw as *heretics* (holders of religious beliefs that contradict official doctrine). Then, on a journey to Damascus to advise that Christians be rounded up, he said that Jesus came to him in a vision. Saul went blind for a while, and upon recovery, he was Paul, a traveling Christian apostle who wrote 13 New Testament letters. He roamed widely as a missionary and participated in debates over whether *gentiles* (non-Jews) could be admitted to the Church (he was in favor), and if so, how. Other religious and civil leaders, both Jewish and Roman, still held Paul's earlier opinion that Christian ideas threatened the established order. Roman policy said those who spread Christianity should be jailed — or worse — and so Paul spent his final years as a prisoner.

- ✔ **Marco Polo** (1254–1324): Born to a Venetian merchant family, Marco Polo tagged along with his dad and uncle on a trip to China in 1271. By Polo's account, the Emperor Kublai Khan appointed him as an envoy and then governor of Yangzhou before the Italian went home in 1292. A soldier for Venice in a war against the Genoese, Marco Polo was captured and thrown in jail, writing *The Travels of Marco Polo* while imprisoned. The book was widely read and broke through the provincial consciousness of many literate Europeans. Many of Polo's contemporaries thought the book contained lies, and many latter-day scholars also doubt Polo's truthfulness. They think he padded his own Chinese resume, but the book's descriptions of the East still stand as a cross-cultural milestone. (See Chapter 24 for more on Marco Polo.)

✔ **Ibn Battuta** (1304–1368): Some people call this writer the Arab Marco Polo, but that fails to do Ibn Battuta justice, because he wrote about so many places. Born in Tangiers, Morocco, he spent almost three decades (from 1325–1354) covering more than 75,000 miles. Like Polo, he visited China and was well received. He also visited all the Muslim countries, writing about Mecca (in present-day Saudi Arabia), Persia (now called Iran), Mesopotamia (now Iraq), Asia Minor, Bokhara (in present-day Uzbekistan), southern Spain, and the North African city of Timbuktu, as well as India and Sumatra. He then settled in Fez, Morocco, and dictated the story of his journeys; his book, *Rihlah,* is a memoir of cultural, social, and political observations.

✔ **Amerigo Vespucci** (1454–1512): Florentine Vespucci wrote about his 1499 voyage to Venezuela and points south. But Martin Waldseemüller (around 1470–1518), a clergyman in northeastern France, is the one who tacked the navigator's name onto the New World. In a little publication called *Cosmographiae Introductio* (or *Cosmo,* for short), Waldseemüller spread the idea that there was a fourth part of the world beyond Europe, Asia, and Africa. He called this new mainland *America,* a Latinized tribute to Vespucci. The name stuck. Other mapmakers made it South America, using Vespucci's name for North America, too.

Vespucci later became a victim of historical libel, as the charge spread that he stole credit for discovering America from Columbus or that he was the mapmaker who egotistically applied his own name to the New World. These false accusations are perhaps rooted in the irrational dislike that an American philosopher, Ralph Waldo Emerson (1803–1882), held toward Vespucci. Emerson wrote about the Italian as a "pickle vendor" and "boatswain's mate in an expedition that never sailed." It's not clear where Emerson got the impression that Vespucci never traveled to the Western Hemisphere or that Vespucci was anything but a well-born and literate sailor with solid credentials in ocean navigation. Vespucci became pilot-major of Spain, the government's top navigator, in 1505.

Trailblazing Explorers: Seeking New Routes

Many travelers left home in search of something specific — and many of these, especially in the sixteenth to the nineteenth centuries AD, were look- ing for sea routes between Europe and Asia.

✔ **Henry the Navigator** (1394–1460): Prince Henry had a singular dream of finding a sea route to India and China. To realize that vision, this member of Portugal's royal family founded a school of scientific navigation and sponsored expeditions along the west coast of Africa. In the same interest, he built Portugal's first observatory to advance the science that taught sailors how to steer by the stars. Although he died before his students sailed around Africa, the prince paved the way for his country's greatest nautical and commercial successes.

✔ **Juan Ponce de León** (1460–1521): Running a Spanish plantation on the island of Hispaniola (today's Dominican Republic and Haiti), this veteran officer (he may have been onboard Columbus's second mission to the Caribbean) heard local Indians mention another tempting island. He sailed there, subdued the locals, and became Spanish governor of Puerto Rico. Then de León was inspired to follow another Indian story that told of an island where a spring made anyone who drank from it feel young and healthy. He never found that island or its *fountain of youth,* but he did land in Florida early in 1513. He died of an arrow wound suffered on his second expedition to Florida.

✔ **Meriwether Lewis** (1774–1809) and **William Clark** (1770–1838): Better known as Lewis and Clark, these buddies crossed North America looking for the thing that so many seafarers failed to find: a northern water route between oceans. Backed by the U.S. government, Lewis and Clark wanted to find a route defined by rivers with a manageable overland stretch at the continental divide. Nobody knew how high, steep, and wide-ranging the Rocky Mountains were; the American idea of a mountain range at the time was based on the Appalachians. The Lewis and Clark expedition was supposed to reach the headwaters of the Missouri River and then *portage* (carry their canoes and supplies) to the nearby headwaters of a westward-flowing river, which would carry them to the Pacific. Such a route would have been a commercial boon to U.S. traders, who wanted to establish a Pacific trading post on the West Coast (despite the fact that the U.S. had no territorial claims on the West Coast at the time).

President Thomas Jefferson chose Lewis, his private secretary, to lead the expedition in 1804. Lewis took Clark along as co-commander of a party that journeyed by canoe, horse, and foot up the Missouri River and into the Rockies. In the Rockies, they found the mountain crossing to the Columbia River to be too long and rugged for commercial use. They traveled down the Columbia to the Pacific, wintered in Oregon, and returned east. Their observations of lands, people, plants, and wildlife were invaluable, although Lewis failed to publish their journals.

Lewis became governor of the Louisiana Territory in 1807. A troubled man, he killed himself while traveling through Tennessee. Clark went on to hold numerous government posts and negotiated several treaties with Indian tribes.

- ✔ **Sir John Franklin** (1786–1847): British Naval officer Franklin fought in the Napoleonic Wars (see Chapter 9) and served as governor of Tasmania. He set out like so many sailors before him to find the Northwest Passage — a northern sea route around North America. Franklin's expedition can't exactly be termed a success given that he and his crew all died in their icebound ship. Yet they got so close — within a few miles — of finding the channel that Franklin gets credit for discovering the passage. Nobody successfully sailed the treacherous route until the Norwegian explorer Roald Amundsen (see "Famous Firsts" later in this chapter) did it in the early twentieth century. An ice-breaking oil tanker was the first commercial vessel to use the passage, in 1969. In the twenty-first century, as Arctic ice recedes, the Northwest Passage may at long last prove an accessible route for general navigation between Atlantic and Pacific.

Notorious Conquerors: Bad Company

Not all explorers had positive motives for seeking new worlds; some visitors, such as the following fellows, just barged in and took over:

- ✔ **Vasco da Gama** (about 1469–1525): Check out Chapter 8 for the story of how da Gama went from Portugal to Kozhikode (or Calicut) on India's Malabar (southwest) coast. Born in Sines, Portugal, he was one in a series of Portuguese explorers trained and dispatched for the purpose of exploring the African coast, rounding the continent's southern tip, and establishing a trade route with the East. The first to succeed, da Gama returned to Portugal with a load of spices in 1499. Portugal followed da Gama's success with a voyage by Pedro Alvarez Cabral (about 1467–about 1520), who accidentally touched the coast of Brazil on his way south, thus establishing Portugal's claims in South America. Vasco da Gama returned in 1502 as an enforcer, establishing a pattern for brutal European colonialism in Asia. When Portuguese authority in India slipped in the 1520s, the government called da Gama out of retirement and sent him as a get-tough viceroy. He fell ill on that trip and died.

- ✔ **Francisco Pizarro** (about 1478–1541): Pizarro, a soldier from Trujillo, Spain, was crafty and brutal. He used both qualities to defeat the mighty Inca Empire of South America in the 1530s, capturing King Atahualpa by trickery and killing him. (For more about the Spanish conquest of the Inca, see Chapter 8.) Pizarro also fought with his fellow conquistador, Diego de Almagro (about 1475–1538). (*Conquistador* is the Spanish name for the conquering commanders who took lands away from American Indians.) When Almagro, the conqueror of Chile, challenged Pizarro's authority in Peru, the ailing Pizarro sent his brothers to capture and kill Almagro.

✔ **Hernan Cortés** (1485–1547): Cortés helped his commander, Diego Velázquez de Cuéllar (1465–1524), conquer Cuba. After quarreling with Velázquez, Cortés, a proud nobleman from Medellin, Spain, accelerated his planned departure from Cuba to the mainland of Mexico, founding the port city of Vera Cruz before heading inland. Making allies of natives opposed to Aztec rule, he then marched on the Aztec capital. The Aztec king, Montezuma, welcomed Cortés as a god at first, but when the Aztecs became suspicious of the Spaniard's motives, Cortés took Montezuma captive. Velázquez sent an expedition to bring Cortés back to Cuba, but Cortés convinced the party's leader to join him and even burned their ships so that he couldn't be taken back to Cuba. After an Indian rebellion, Montezuma's death at the hands of rebels, and a brief Spanish retreat, Cortés conquered Mexico in 1521. He also tried to conquer Honduras but failed.

Famous Firsts

As Jean-Luc Picard (not a historical figure but a science fiction character) once said, the explorer aims "to go where no one has gone before." (Yes, *Star Trek* fans; James T. Kirk said it first, but his gender-specific version — "where no *man* has gone" — sounds ironically dated now.) What's true in the make-believe future was certainly true in the real-world past, as explorers competed to be the first person ever to conquer a geographic barrier or to slip the bonds of geography entirely. The following people fit that description, and those who survived won the bragging rights that go with the title "first."

If you've noticed that other explorers in this chapter were first to go where no one had gone before, congratulations. That means you're paying attention. A chapter about explorers is bound to be full of *firsts*. But, as I explain in Chapter 3, the study of history is divided up into arbitrary categories — valid only if you have to pass a history test or as memory devices. The section titles in this chapter are just such arbitrary labels.

✔ **Ferdinand Magellan** (about 1480–1521): What Columbus dreamed of doing — reaching the East by sailing west — Magellan accomplished. The Portuguese captain sailing under Spain's colors traveled from Seville, Spain, around South America, and across the Pacific to the Philippines, where he died in a tribal dispute. His expedition, commanded by Juan Sebastian del Cano, continued, and a small, scurvy-weakened surviving crew completed the first trip all the way around the world. When Magellan first entered the *new* ocean west of South America, the weather stayed nice and the water calm for weeks on end, so he named the ocean the Pacific, or "peaceful." The Pacific proved at least as violent as the Atlantic when a storm hit, but the name stuck.

✔ **Robert E. Peary** (1856–1920) and **Matthew A. Henson** (1866–1955): Peary and Henson, credited as first to get to the North Pole, may not have touched the exact geographic pole in 1909. It was tough to tell, because there's no actual pole to mark the North Pole and no land either — just ice floating so swiftly that a campsite drifts miles overnight. Still, Peary's observations show that he and Henson came within 20 miles of the pole and probably closer.

A U.S. Navy officer from Pennsylvania, Peary commanded several arctic expeditions, at least four aimed at reaching the North Pole. Henson, whom Perry hired as a valet (personal servant) in 1897, was his navigator, trailbreaker, and translator. They almost lost their claim of being first to the North Pole to a former member of Peary's expedition, Frederick A. Cook (1865–1940), who claimed to have reached the pole a year earlier. But Cook, who also said he climbed Alaska's Mt. McKinley, had a habit of exaggerating. Peary's other projects included a surveying expedition in Nicaragua. Henson wrote the 1912 book *A Black Explorer at the North Pole*.

✔ **Roald Amundsen** (1872–1928): Norway's Amundsen never finished the race for the North Pole, although he was first to locate the magnetic North Pole (not the same as the geographic North Pole, a discrepancy that caused hassles for northern navigators who used compasses, which point to the magnetic pole, not the geographic pole). When he found out that Robert Peary had beat him in the northern competition, Amundsen headed for the South Pole, reaching it in December 1911. Britain's Robert F. Scott (1868–1912) arrived a month later, only to find he was too late; Scott and all his party died on the way back. Amundsen's other accomplishments included sailing the Northwest Passage (see John Franklin in the section "Trailblazing Explorers: Seeking New Routes" earlier in this chapter) and flying across the North Pole in a blimp.

✔ **Yuri Gagarin** (1934–1968): Gagarin, the first *cosmonaut* (Russian astronaut) died young, before the age of manned space exploration reached beyond its beginnings. Gagarin was a member of the Soviet air force and became the first human being to travel outside the Earth's atmosphere when he made one trip around the planet in the Vostok spaceship in 1961. He was alive to see American John Glenn achieve sustained orbit by circling the earth three times in 1963, but Gagarin died in a plane accident the year before men first walked on the moon (see the entry for Neil Armstrong in the earlier section "Famous Pioneers: Arriving before Their Time").

Name that explorer

To make remembering history easier, keep in mind that explorers often got things — cities, rivers, and lakes, for example — named after them. Here are a few notable examples:

✔ **Sir Francis Drake** (about 1540–1596): Drake was an Englishman who fought the Spanish Armada and sailed around the world. His ports of call ranged from Virginia to the Caribbean to California, where a bay north of San Francisco bears his name.

✔ **Samuel de Champlain** (1567–1635): He was France's man in Canada — explorer, diplomat, and governor. He established French alliances with several Indian tribes and founded Quebec. The British captured Quebec in 1629 and made Champlain their prisoner until 1632. When Quebec was restored to French rule, Champlain served as its governor from 1633 until his death.

Lake Champlain, which lies mostly between the states of New York and Vermont but also extends into Canada, is named for him.

✔ **Henry Hudson** (unknown–around 1611): Nothing is known about this navigator's early life, but he sailed for the Dutch and the English, making claims for both countries along the northeast coast of North America. Like France's Cartier before him, Hudson was looking for the Northwest Passage. He explored the river (in New York), the strait (in Canada), and the bay (also in Canada) that now bear his name. Late in 1610, he found himself in Hudson Bay and decided to winter there. When the ship ran short of food, Hudson's crew rebelled. The mutineers set their captain and eight other men adrift to die.

Renowned Guides

Some people just know how to get places. Out ahead of many a great explorer was a guide to show the way.

✔ **Ahmad Ibn Majid** (early 1430s–around 1500): When Portugal's Vasco da Gama (outlined earlier in this chapter and in Chapter 8) rounded the southern tip of Africa, sailing through the perilous waters between that continent's east coast and the island of Madagascar, he knew he would need help to travel all the way to India. He hoped to find an Arab ship pilot to guide him. Perhaps overqualified, the man da Gama found in Malindi was Ahmed Ibn Majid, also known as "the Lion-of-the-Sea-in-Fury." (Nobody has great nicknames like that anymore.) This greatest of Arab navigators wrote more than three dozen books about seafaring, oceanography, and geography. He specialized in the Arabian Sea, the Red Sea, and the Indian Ocean, and his knowledge was precisely what da Gama needed to open that part of the world to European sea trade. Many Arabs and other Muslims later regretted that Ibn Majid shared what he knew.

✔ **Sakagawea** (unknown–1812): A rival tribe captured the young Shoshone woman from her native village (in today's Idaho) and sold her to Toussaint Charbonneau, a Canadian fur trapper. Charbonneau married her by Indian rite and took her along when Lewis and Clark hired him as their expedition guide (refer to the earlier section "Trailblazing Explorers: Seeking New Routes" for more on Lewis and Clark). Sakagawea proved a better guide than Charbonneau, and she also served as interpreter, trader, ambassador, and quick-thinking aide, once rescuing Lewis's priceless journal from floating down a river. Pregnant when they set out, she gave birth along the way and then carried the baby boy on her back. Her name, which means "Bird Woman," has variant English spellings, including Sakajawea.

Famous Mavericks: Taking Advantage of Opportunity

Traveling well often means grabbing your chance when it presents itself — turning banishment into a chance to found a settlement, for example, or taking over the colony when you see an opening. The following voyagers are among many in history who broke a few rules on the way to discovery:

✔ **Erik the Red** (tenth century AD): The Viking leader Erik Thorvaldson was banned from his native Norway for manslaughter. He sailed west to Iceland in 982 AD, but after settling there and killing again, he was outlawed once more. Erik moved to a peninsula reaching west from Iceland and — you guessed it — he killed somebody again; this time the sentence was three-year banishment. Where could he go but farther west? He knew there was supposed to be land out there because a sailor named Gunnbjorn had reported it after being blown off-course 50 years before. So Erik sailed and found Greenland, rich with game and grassy enough to make good pasture (it was warmer then). After his banishment was up, Erik and his crew returned to Iceland and rounded up 25 ships full of Icelanders eager for life in another new land. Erik would have commanded his son Leif Eriksson's expedition to North America (see "Famous Pioneers: Arriving before Their Time" earlier in this chapter) if he hadn't been thrown from a horse just before leaving and decided it was an omen against his travel plan. He told Leif to go without him.

✔ **Vasco Núñez de Balboa** (1475–1519): Balboa came to Darién (now part of Panama) as a stowaway on a Spanish ship. He seized power during an insurrection and extended Spanish influence into nearby areas. Extending influence required traveling through low jungle and wetlands, but he found some high ground, too, and from atop a hill Balboa sighted what he called the Southern Ocean and claimed it for Spain. Later, the navigator Magellan called this ocean the Pacific. Despite Balboa's industry, Spain appointed Pedro Arias Dávila (about 1440–1531) as governor of Darién. Balboa made the best of this arrangement by leading several expeditions for Dávila. But in 1519 Dávila and Balboa clashed, and the governor had Balboa beheaded.

Tracking the Centuries

Around 330 BC: Pythias of Massilia (today's Marseilles, France) sails out through the Strait of Gibraltar and up the Atlantic coast of Europe to what may have been Norway.

First century AD: St. Paul, a former Jewish rabbi of the Pharisee sect, travels widely through southern Europe and the Middle East, spreading the new Christian faith.

1354: The scholar Ibn Battuta settles in Fez, Morocco, to dictate his book *Rihlah,* a memoir of 30 years of travels from Spain to Uzbekistan, China, and Timbuktu.

1804: Sakagawea helps American explorers Meriwether Lewis and William Clark find their way up the Missouri River toward the Great Divide.

1911: Roald Amundsen, a Norwegian explorer, arrives at the South Pole and is the first person to reach this frigid goal.

1969: Neil Armstrong, an American, steps out of his lunar landing module to become the first human being to set foot on the moon.

Chapter 22

Turning Tables: Rebels and Revolutionaries

*I*n a democracy like the United States, voters determine who leads. The transition from one administration to the next rarely involves violence — unless you consider mudslinging to be violent. Over the course of history, however, the quest for change has often involved brute force. This chapter offers a sampling of those who sought and/or achieved change — reformers, revolutionaries, and a few usurpers. These people — whether in power, wanting it, seizing it, or rejecting it — fought, plotted, and labored to usher in new eras.

Revolutionaries Who Became Rulers

The goal of any political revolution is to oust the people currently in power and replace them with new people. Usually, the leaders of the revolution become the leaders of the new political order. But forming a government and restoring order is a different job altogether from tearing down the old order.

The people in this section struggled to oust oppressors but then came up against a different set of challenges as leaders of their countries. The way in which each was changed by the transition illustrates what a tricky business it is to wield power wisely and with grace.

> ✔ **Lucius Junius Brutus** (late sixth century BC): History knows this Roman hero by an unlikely nickname that became part of his formal name and was proudly handed down to descendants (see "Fallen Rebels" later in

this chapter). In the earliest days of Rome, then a city-state ruled by a king, *brutus* meant "stupid." Lucius Junius earned this title by pretending to be an idiot so that King Lucius Tarquinius Superbus wouldn't kill him. When Brutus's rich dad died, the king confiscated his property and killed Brutus's brother. He didn't bother to kill the "stupid" one.

After the king's son, Tarquinius Sextus, raped a nobleman's wife and she committed suicide, public sentiment turned against the king. Brutus led the Romans in a revolt. They declared a republic in 509 BC. His fellow citizens elected "Stupid" to their top office, consul. But Brutus had two sons of his own who turned against him. They conspired to restore the Tarquin family (Tarquinius Superbus's clan) to the throne. With the fledgling republic at stake, Brutus ordered his boys arrested and put to death. The Roman republic survived, but Brutus didn't: He died in one-on-one combat with Tarquinius Aruns, another son of Tarquinius Superbus.

✔ **Chu Yuan-chang** (1328–1398): When he was 17, after his entire farm-laborer family died in an epidemic, Chu entered a Buddhist monastery. Eight years later, he left the monastery to lead the province of Anhwei against China's Mongol rulers. After years of struggle, Chu's forces occupied Beijing, the Mongol capital. At age 40, Chu Yuan-chang proclaimed himself the first emperor of the Ming Dynasty.

✔ **Oliver Cromwell** (1599–1658): Cromwell was a staunch Puritan (see Chapter 14), a disciplined military officer, and a persuasive member of England's Parliament during the reign of Charles I. Charles's religious and economic policies led to civil war. Cromwell originally defended the king, but then he put Charles on trial and signed his death warrant in 1649.

After the execution, Cromwell stood looking at the king's lifeless body and muttered "Cruel necessity."

Cromwell replaced the monarchy with a *commonwealth* ruled by a single-house parliament over which he presided as chairman. When this form of government proved ineffective, he took the title lord protector, a kind of Puritan dictator with king-like powers. He quashed opponents, reorganized the English church along Puritan lines, and ruthlessly put down an Irish rebellion. After Cromwell's death, his son Richard briefly succeeded him as lord protector, but the younger Cromwell was unable to withstand challenges from rivals, who removed him from office in 1659. Parliament restored the monarchy the following year. (For more on the English Civil War, see Chapter 8.)

✔ **Vladimir Ilyitch Lenin** (1870–1924): Lenin put the economic philosophy Marxism (see Chapter 15) to work in Russia. As a law student in St. Petersburg, his underground leftist activities got him sent to Siberia. He came back as leader of the far-left faction of the Russian Social Democratic Labor Party. Lenin spent much of World War I in exile. After Russia's government collapsed in 1917, Germany, enemy of the Czarist government,helped Lenin return to his native land. Lenin rallied Russians with the slogans "Peace and bread" and "All power to the soviets." (A *soviet* is a council of workers or peasants.) In October 1917, he led the Bolshevik revolution and became head of the first Soviet government.

Counterrevolutionary forces tried reversing what Lenin had done, which lead to the Russian Civil War of 1918–1921. Lenin's Communists won the war after nationalizing major industries and banks and seizing control of farms. The measures helped Lenin defeat the counterrevolutionaries, but they sent the fledgling Union of Soviet Socialist Republics hurtling toward economic collapse and famine. Lenin reacted by instituting a *New Economic Policy,* permitting private production. This retreat from all-out socialism disappointed Lenin's harder-line Communist colleagues. The new policy was too late, though, because the farm economy recovered slowly and many thousands of Russians died in the famine of 1922–1923.

✔ **Ho Chi Minh** (1892–1968): As Nguyen Tat Thanh, he was a well-educated young man from French Indochina (French-ruled Vietnam) who traveled widely and lived in England, the United States, France, and China. In Paris, he became active in France's fledgling Communist Party and then went to the newly established Soviet Union, where the government recruited him as a foreign agent and sent him to Guanzhou, in southern China. There, Ho Chi Minh (the name means "He Who Enlightens") organized Vietnamese exiles into an Indochinese Communist Party.

Touchy, touchy

Although Chu Yuan-chang had been a Buddhist monk and brought other monks into his court, he also promoted Confucian rituals and scholarship. Among the Chinese of this time, few people felt that it was important to accept only one religious tradition while rejecting all others.

The emperor wasn't as tolerant about other things as he was about religion. For example, he forbade any reference to his years in the monastery — not because of religion, but because he was sensitive about his humble origins. (You didn't dare mention that he'd grown up a peasant, either.) Once, two Confucian scholars sent Chu Yuan-chang a letter of congratulations in which they used the word *sheng,* which means "birth." The term was a little too close to the word *seng,* which means "monk." The emperor took it as a pun and had them killed.

Later, Chu got so touchy that he made it a capital crime to question his policies. When he thought the people of Nanjing didn't display proper respect to him, he slaughtered 15,000 of them.

After his party's first efforts against the French government of Indochina failed in 1940, Ho (shown in Figure 22-1) took refuge in China, only to be thrown in jail by the anticommunist Nationalist government there. Japanese forces occupied Indochina during World War II, and in 1943 Ho returned home to organize Vietminh guerilla forces to fight back. The Vietminh succeeded, and Ho proclaimed the Democratic Republic of Vietnam in 1945, only to see French colonial forces return. Ho once again fought the French. By 1954, the Vietminh ousted the French, but Ho's struggle was not won. Rival Vietnamese leaders seized control of the southern part of the country.

The Geneva Conference of 1954, officially ending the French-Indochinese War, partitioned Vietnam along the seventeenth parallel, with Ho in charge of North Vietnam. Ho remained committed to a reunited Vietnam. After a 1963 military coup left South Vietnam vulnerable to North Vietnamese takeover, the U.S. sent military assistance to South Vietnam. The resultant war — marked by U.S. escalation through the 1960s and into the 1970s — was raging when Ho died, but his side eventually won, as U.S. forces withdrew from South Vietnam in the 1970s. The former South Vietnamese capital, Saigon, was renamed Ho Chi Minh City.

Figure 22-1: North Vietnamese leader Ho Chi Minh found Communism as a young man in France.

© Getty Images

✔ **Fidel Castro** (1927–): Born into a prosperous Cuban family, Castro was a law student in Havana and a gifted baseball pitcher — some say he might have made the pros — but he became convinced that the corrupt government of dictator Fulgencia Batista (1901–1973) had to be overturned. Castro joined a revolutionary uprising in 1953, but it failed, and he was imprisoned. Granted amnesty, he fled to the U.S. and then to Mexico, where he gathered support for another assault on Batista, which started in 1956. Castro and supporters finally forced Batista to leave the island in 1959. Castro ordered many remaining Batista supporters executed, raising alarm in Cuba and abroad. Failing to negotiate diplomatic relations or a trade agreement with the U.S., Castro turned to the Soviet Union for support. In 1961, he declared a Marxist-Leninist government. His far-reaching reforms depended for decades on Soviet financing, especially because the anticommunist U.S. imposed an embargo on trade with Cuba. Yet Castro's regime survived the USSR's 1991 collapse. In 2006, his brother and longtime number two, Raúl, filled in as provisional head of state for the ailing Fidel. Although Fidel recovered, he declined another term as president and Raúl Castro officially succeeded him in February 2008. As of early 2009, Fidel Castro remained his brother's advisor and First Secretary of the Cuban Communist Party.

✔ **Robert Mugabe** (1924–): As a young teacher, Mugabe helped form democratic political organizations in Rhodesia, a British colony in southern Africa with limited, white-controlled self-rule. With Ndabaningi Sithole, Mugabe co-founded the Zimbabwe African National Union (ZANU), which sought black liberation. Convicted of "subversive speech," Mugabe spent a decade in prison; while jailed, he earned a law degree and directed a coup that ousted Sithole from ZANU leadership.

In the late 1970s, Mugabe's ZANU joined forces with rival Joshua Nkomo's (1917–1999) Zimbabwe African People's Union (ZAPU) in guerilla war against the white government. A 1979 democratic election, the nation's first, transformed Rhodesia into black-ruled Zimbabwe. Mugabe was elected prime minister in a landslide election the following year, but then he undermined democracy by establishing one-party rule in 1987. His dictatorial reign turned increasingly repressive as Mugabe's popularity waned throughout the 1990s and into the 2000s.

A contentious 2008 election resulted in what appeared to be a win for challenger Simba Makoni (1950–). Weeks passed before an official but widely disputed vote count showed neither candidate with a majority. Mugabe then "won" a run-off election. Faced with outrage over the rigged elections, civil chaos, widespread hunger, and an outrageous inflation rate that rendered the country's money worthless, Mugabe agreed to a power-sharing agreement with Makoni's party but failed to abide by it. Meanwhile, Zimbabwean water supplies failed and a cholera epidemic swept through the country. Both in Africa and worldwide, there were calls for Mugabe's resignation. Many said he should be forcibly ousted. As of early 2009, the 85-year-old Mugabe continued to defy his critics and hold tight to power.

Charismatic Rebels

Rebellion carries a certain romantic cachet. "The Leader of the Pack," as the old pop song about a gang leader puts it, boasts a defiant magnetism — whether it's the appeal of a wild-eyed idealist or gritty guerilla toughness. Many movements have charismatic leaders who attract interest and galvanize support. The following may fit that label:

✔ **Toussaint L'Ouverture** (1746–1803): François-Dominique Toussaint (nicknamed "L'Ouverture") was born to slave parents from Africa and rose up to free the blacks on the Caribbean island of Hispaniola. As a member and then leader of Haiti's French Republicans, Toussaint faced armed opposition from the Napoleonic French overlords; the British, whom he drove off the island; the Spanish, who ran the other half of the island (today's Dominican Republic); and the *mulattos,* persons of mixed black-white heritage, who were opposed to losing their place in Haiti's racial hierarchy. Napoleon's agents captured the defiant Toussaint and shipped him to Paris, where he died in jail.

✔ **Simón Bolívar** (1783–1830): Caracas-born Bolívar is a national hero in at least five countries: Venezuela, Colombia, Ecuador, Peru, and Bolivia (which is named for him). Known as "The Liberator" and "The George Washington of South America," he was instrumental in wars of independence that booted Spain from much of South America. The passionate Bolívar traveled the continent, leading campaigns of independence. Yet he clashed with other freedom fighters and, as the first president of the Republic of Colombia (today's Colombia, Venezuela, and Ecuador), struggled with dissent and even civil war. Disheartened, Bolívar was headed into exile when he died.

✔ **Sun Yixian** (1866–1925): Chinese Communists on the mainland and Chinese Nationalists on the island nation of Taiwan may not agree on much, but they both honor Sun Yixian as the founder of modern China. Also known as Sun Yat-sen, he founded China's *Tongmenghui,* or United League, in Tokyo, Japan, in 1905. Sun lived away from China during the first decade of the twentieth century because he was exiled after a failed 1895 attempt to bring down the aging Qing Dynasty. The decaying imperial government saw Sun as such a threat that its agents kidnapped him while he was visiting London during his exile. (The English negotiated his release.) The Qing were right to fear Sun, because his Tongmenghui evolved into the *Kuomintang,* or Chinese Nationalist Party, which was instrumental in bringing down the Qing in 1911 and setting up a short-lived Nationalist government. Sun was briefly president in 1912 before stepping aside in favor of another revolutionary leader, who repaid Sun by banning the Kuomintang. Sun set up a separate government in Canton in 1913 and oversaw an uneasy alliance with the newly formed Chinese Communist Party in the 1920s. He was trying to negotiate a unified government when he died. (For more about the Nationalists in China, see Mao Zedong and Jiang Jieshi, both later in this chapter.)

✔ **Che Guevara** (1928–1967): In the late 1960s, a popular poster on college dorm room walls showed the shadowy, bearded face of Ernesto Guevara de la Serna, a one-time medical student from Argentina. After helping overthrow Cuba's government in the revolution of 1956–1959, Che — as he was popularly known — served in various posts in Fidel Castro's regime (see the earlier section "Revolutionaries who Became Rulers"). He left Cuba in 1965 to lead guerillas in Bolivia. Che's shaggy good looks, jaunty beret, and especially the timing of his 1967 arrest and execution made him a martyr of the 1960s political left. His image still shows up on t-shirts today, as a retro-radical fashion statement.

For evidence of Che Guevara's enduring appeal, you can check out three movies produced well over a quarter century after his death. Director Steven Soderbergh's *Che: Part 1, the Argentine* tells of the revolutionary's involvement in the Cuban revolution. Also by Soderbergh, *Che: Part 2, Guerilla* is about Guevara's failed attempt to bring revolution to Bolivia. The two films, both released in 2008, were shown together in theatrical release. An earlier movie, 2004's *The Motorcycle Diaries,* depicts a pleasure-seeking young Che on a 1953 road trip around South America that opens his eyes to poverty and social injustices.

Two Idea Guys

Ideas start revolutions, but thinkers don't always make the best revolutionaries. The men in this section weren't just writers who synthesized the ideas that rallied supporters to their cause; they were also doers who made momentous decisions involving others' lives and destinies. Transforming an idea into a practical result isn't easy, however, especially when politics are involved. A sublime theory may bear sublime results, or it may bring tragedy. An example of each follows:

✔ **Thomas Jefferson** (1743–1826): In 1774, Jefferson wrote *A Summary View of the Rights of British America* expressing the unhappiness that led him to become a delegate to the Continental Congress in Philadelphia. Jefferson also wrote the Declaration of Independence, which was approved by that revolutionary congress in 1776. His public service included serving as U.S. president (two terms), vice president (under John Adams), secretary of state (under George Washington), Virginia governor, and ambassador to France. As president, his nervy Louisiana Purchase more than doubled the size of the United States. He also commissioned the Lewis and Clark expedition (Chapter 21 has more on the explorers), setting the precedent for U.S. expansion to the Pacific.

Jefferson was happiest in aesthetic pursuits, especially architecture. The University of Virginia and the Virginia statehouse are among his designs. His wife's death after ten years of marriage marred his private life, and four of their six children died young. In the late 1990s, DNA evidence supported the long-repeated rumor that Jefferson fathered children with a slave woman in his household, Sally Hemings.

✔ **Mao Ze-dong** (1893–1976): Also spelled Mao Tse-tung, this longtime chairman of the People's Republic of China led his party through a hard-fought struggle for power and guided his country through a tumultuous stretch of the twentieth century. Mao came from rural Hunan Province and was just out of college when he landed a job in the library of Beijing University. Marxist professors there changed his thinking.

Mao became involved in the Chinese nationalist *May Fourth Movement,* which began on May 4, 1919, with a student demonstration against a Chinese trade agreement with Japan. He attended meetings of the May Fourth group that led to the formation of the Chinese Communist Party. As a newly converted communist, he moved to Shanghai in 1923 as a political organizer for the Kuomintang, or Nationalist People's Party, which was fighting to establish a new Chinese Nationalist government in place of the Revolutionary Alliance that had ruled since 1911. When the Kuomintang decided in 1927 that it didn't want communists among its fighters, the ousted Mao formed the Jiangxi Soviet, an outlaw guerilla force that watched the Nationalists take over but finally emerged victorious from a post-WWII civil war against forces led by Nationalist President Jiang Jieshi.

On October 1, 1949, Mao proclaimed the formation of the People's Republic of China. As chairman of the new government, Mao delegated administration to others, but he occasionally emerged with dramatic and disastrous reform proposals such as the *Great Leap Forward,* which lasted from 1958–1960. A drive for industrial and agricultural expansion, it resulted in crop failures and the starvation of as many as 13 million peasants. Mao tried again in 1966 with the *Cultural Revolution.* A drive to root out Western influences from every corner of Chinese society, the Cultural Revolution brought widespread chaos and violence. A prolific poet and essayist, Mao was a much-quoted source of leftist thought in the turbulent 1960s. The plump chairman's jovial, Buddha-like portrait became especially popular.

Standing against Authority

Some people live by conscience, consequences be damned. The men in this section showed rare courage in standing up to the powerful and speaking out against injustice.

✔ **Martin Luther** (1483–1546): Chapter 14 tells the story of how Luther, a German university professor and priest, started the Protestant Reformation. He spent three years in a monastery before earning his degree. Initially, his big issue was the Church's practice of selling indulgences, which many people understood as a way to buy entry into heaven. When he started taking on the papal system, Luther moved on to other issues, including priestly celibacy. He married Katharina von Bora, a former nun, in 1525.

✔ **Mohandas Karamchand Gandhi** (1869–1948): His fellow Indians called him the *Mahatma,* or "great soul." After studying law in England, Gandhi fought to end discrimination against Indian immigrants in South Africa. After two decades there, he returned to his native India in 1914. He led the Indian National Congress, a group seeking independence from British rule. Inspired by the American writer Henry David Thoreau, Gandhi preached and practiced nonviolent noncooperation, or *civil disobedience.* The colonial government jailed him for conspiracy from 1922–1924.

Gandhi helped shape independent India's first constitution. Achieving his goal of self-rule for India in 1947, Gandhi's next challenge was to stop Hindu-Muslim violence. For that, a Hindu fanatic killed him.

✔ **Martin Luther King, Jr.** (1929–1968): Named for the German who started the Protestant Reformation, King guided the U.S. civil rights movement during its most crucial years, from 1955–1968. As a young Baptist pastor in Montgomery, Alabama, he took up the cause that Rosa Parks had started and led the 1955 boycott of that city's bus line to protest racial discrimination. Two years later, the newly formed Southern Christian Leadership Conference chose King as its leader.

King looked to India's Gandhi (see the preceding entry) for inspiration as he preached and practiced nonviolent opposition to racism. Arrested, jailed, stoned by mobs, his family threatened, his home bombed, and his privacy ravaged by a hostile FBI, King continued to lead protests. He made his famous "I Have a Dream" speech at the Lincoln Memorial in Washington, D.C., in 1963, and in 1964 he was awarded the Nobel Peace Prize. An assassin killed King in Memphis, Tennessee, where he was supporting striking garbage collectors.

Rule Changers

Sometimes change, even radical change, comes from the top. The rulers in this section weren't content with the status quo and set about shaping their domains to fit their visions.

- **Akhenaton** (fourteenth century BC): As Amenhotep IV, he became Egypt's king in 1379 BC, but after six years, he changed everything — his own name, his capital city, and the state religion. Akhenaton was devoted to a cult that discarded Egypt's traditional array of gods (more on religions in Chapter 10) in favor of just one — the sun disc god, Aton. He put the new center of government at Amarna, which he called Akhetaton, 300 miles from the established capital at Thebes. Art thrived under Akhenaton and his queen, the beautiful Nefertiti. (Many surviving sculptures depict her beauty.) But Akhenaton failed to take care of earthly business, and Egypt's commercial and military fortunes declined.

- **Asoka** (third century BC): Also spelled Ashoka, this King of India was the last ruler of the Mauryan Dynasty. Early in his reign, Asoka led armies, but he didn't like bloodshed. He swore off fighting, converted to Buddhism, and spread the religion throughout India and beyond. His policy of *dharma* (principles of right life) called for tolerance, honesty, and kindness. It was beautiful while it lasted, but after Asoka died, the empire went downhill.

- **Henry VIII** (1491–1547): Nineteenth-century novelist Charles Dickens looked back on big Henry as "a blot of blood and grease upon the history of England." You may remember this king as the fat guy who chopped off two of his six wives' heads, but he was also England's first Renaissance Prince — educated, handsome (before he packed on the pounds), witty, popular (until he closed down the monasteries), and ruthless. Henry was thought to meet the very high expectations that educated people had for a ruler during the Renaissance. I talk about the ideas of the Renaissance, including the role of a king, in Chapter 13. Chapter 14 gives you the scoop on how Henry broke England away from Catholicism and founded the Church of England.

- **Peter the Great** (1672–1725): As a kid, Peter I of Russia was a sort of co-czar with his mentally disabled half-brother. But this arrangement had their big sister Sophia calling the shots. In 1696, Peter sent Sophia to live in a convent, became sole ruler of Russia, and started changing things. He reformed the military, the economy, the bureaucracy, the schools, the Russian Orthodox Church, and even the way Russian people dressed and groomed themselves. He wanted Russia to mirror its Western European neighbors. How did he get Russians to do what he wanted? With brutality and repression, of course. Peter's many wars, especially a big victory over Sweden, made Russia a major power with a Baltic seaport where the czar built a new capital city, St. Petersburg. His wife succeeded him as Catherine I. (For more on Peter I, see Chapter 9.)

Living and Dying by the Sword

Often the person who gets power by force has it pried away by force.

✔ **Atahualpa** (unknown–1532): Atahualpa, last Incan ruler of Peru, was one of history's many sons who wanted a bigger piece of his dad's estate. Rather than being grateful for inheriting the northern half of the Inca Empire, Atahualpa overthrew the king of the southern half, who happened to be his brother. Just a few months later, Spain's Francisco Pizarro (see Chapter 19) captured Atahualpa and killed him.

✔ **Maximilien-François Marie-Isidore de Robespierre** (1758–1794): He was called "The Incorruptible" and later "The Headless." Okay, I just made up that second name, but Robespierre, who energetically employed the guillotine upon anybody he thought threatened the French Revolution (see Chapter 8), also died under the falling blade. He was a lawyer and a member of the Estates-General, an official gathering of the three estates of the French realm (the Church, the nobility, and the commons). The Estates-General had begun centuries earlier as an occasional advisory body to the king, but it had fallen into disuse a century and a half before King Louis XVI called it into session in May 1789, with the unexpected (to the king) result of precipitating the French Revolution. Led by its radical fringes, the Estates-General transformed itself into the revolutionary National Assembly. Robespierre emerged as a leader of the revolution, becoming public accuser and, two years later, a member of the notorious Committee of Public Safety, directing a steady flow of executions over the three months known as the Reign of Terror. At this point, his ruthlessness scared even his former allies. The Revolutionary Tribunal, an institution he had helped create, sent him to get a bad haircut — fatally bad.

✔ **Jean-Jacques Dessalines** (about 1758–1806): He was born in West Africa, taken as a slave, and shipped to Haiti, where he proclaimed himself emperor. In Haiti's slave insurrection of 1791, Dessalines served as a lieutenant to rebel leader Toussaint L'Ouverture (see the earlier section "Charismatic Rebels"). With British help, Dessalines chased the French out of Haiti in 1803 and assumed the post of governor general. In 1804, he had himself crowned Jacques I. As monarch, he slaughtered whites and took their land. His former political allies, Henri Christophe (1767–1820) and Alexandre Pétion (1770–1818), couldn't tolerate his self-importance, cruelty, and immorality. They arranged for Dessalines's assassination.

✔ **Bernardo O'Higgins** (1778–1842): Though born in Ireland, Ambrosio O'Higgins (about 1720–1801) fought for the Spanish and became Spain's captain-general of Chile and viceroy of Peru. His son Bernardo, however, was on the side of those Chileans who wanted to break away from Spain. (For more about the revolutions in the Spanish colonies of South America, turn to Chapter 9.) Bernardo O'Higgins planned and helped carry out the revolt that unfolded between 1810 and 1817. Then he became president of independent Chile. Yet another revolution threw O'Higgins out of office, and he was forced to flee to Peru.

✔ **Jiang Jieshi** (1887–1975): Also known as Chiang Kai-shek, Jiang was the revolutionary leader who took over the Kuomintang, or Chinese Nationalist Party, in 1926 after founder Sun Yixian died (see "Charismatic Rebels" earlier in this chapter). The Kuomintang was largely responsible for the overthrow of China's decrepit imperial government in 1911. Struggling against rival revolutionary forces, Jiang ousted Chinese communists from the Kuomintang and in 1928 established his Nationalist government at Nanjing. (Westerners used to call it Nanking.) The Kuomintang had unified most of China by 1937, but World War II provided an opportunity for the Communists, who had regrouped under Mao Ze-dong (see "Two Idea Guys" earlier in this chapter) to regain momentum. The Communists won the ensuing Chinese Civil War, forcing Jiang and his supporters into exile. In 1949, Jiang set up a government in exile on the island of Taiwan and surprised the world with that nation's dramatic economic growth.

Fallen Rebels

Many rebels die for a cause, and their failed revolutionary efforts can make a lasting impact. The people in this section never rose to be presidents or prime ministers, but they left a legacy in the causes they championed and the sacrifices they made.

✔ **Spartacus** (unknown–71 BC): Born in Thrace, a northeastern region of Greece, Spartacus was a slave and gladiator who led the most serious slave uprising that Rome ever faced. Starting in 73 BC, Spartacus assembled a huge army of slaves and dispossessed people that more than challenged the mighty Roman army; his army actually scored numerous victories. Finally, a general called Crassus (about 115–53 BC) beat the rebels and killed Spartacus. Crassus had all the rebels crucified and left hundreds of their bodies hanging along the Appian Way, the main Roman road.

✔ **Marcus Junius Brutus** (about 85–42 BC): This Roman politician's name means "stupid," but he wore it with honor. The name was handed down from a famous ancestor (see Lucius Junius Brutus in "Revolutionaries who Became Rulers" earlier in this chapter). When Pompey and Caesar fought a civil war, Brutus sided with Pompey. He then bowed to the winner, Caesar, who appointed him governor in a region of Gaul (present -day France). Because the first famous Brutus had helped drive the last Roman king out of town, Marcus Brutus fancied the idea of being a king-breaker himself. That made it easier for a fellow politician, Cassius, to enlist Brutus in a plot against Caesar in 44 BC.

After they assassinated the dictator, the conspirators fought Caesar's avengers, Antony and Octavian. Antony and Octavian defeated Brutus at Philippi. Brutus killed himself, and Octavian became Emperor Augustus Caesar, which wasn't quite the outcome Brutus had in mind.

✔ **Wat Tyler** (unknown–1381): In 1381, English peasants rebelled against working conditions in Kent. They chose Tyler to lead them. He led a march to London to see King Richard II. The meeting ended in violence, and William Walworth, Lord Mayor of London, wounded Tyler. His supporters took him to St. Bartholomew's Hospital, but Walworth had Tyler dragged out of the hospital and beheaded.

Tyler's uprising, called the Peasants' Revolt, proved to be centuries ahead of its time. Workers rebellions rarely again amounted to much in England until 1812, when a group calling itself the Luddites protested the injustices of the Industrial Revolution. The Luddite revolt also failed, but a call for workers' rights then figured in widespread revolts in several European countries in 1848. The short-lived National Labor Union, formed in the U.S. in 1866, began an era of spreading workers' rights movements in North America and Europe.

✔ **Guy Fawkes** (1570–1606): Though born in York to Protestant parents, Fawkes converted to Catholicism and served in the Spanish army, fighting Dutch Protestants. Back in England, where Catholics were an oppressed minority, he conspired with fellow activists to blow up King James I and Parliament in 1606. Fawkes was caught red-handed in a cellar full of gunpowder. He was convicted and hanged. Each November, on the anniversary of his death, the English joyfully burn him in effigy.

✔ **Emelian Ivanovich Pugachev** (1726–1775): Political opponents killed Russia's weak Czar Peter III in 1762 and installed his widow, Catherine, in his place. Catherine the Great rose to the challenge, but not without turmoil. *Cossacks,* semi-independent tribes of roving warriors in southern Russia, resented her authority.

In the 1770s, a rebellion among rank-and-file Cossacks grew into a wider revolt, joined by peasants who flocked to support the Cossack soldier Emelian Ivanovich Pugachev when he proclaimed himself to be Peter III, the empress's murdered husband. With that claim, he led a fierce mass rebellion against Catherine, promising to strike down government repression. Catherine's officers captured Pugachev in 1774 and took him to Moscow where they tortured and killed him. Long after his death, his name stood for the spirit of Russian peasant revolution.

✔ **John Brown** (1800–1859): Brown's opposition to slavery dated back to his days as a youth in Ohio, but the tradesman and occasional farmer was in his 50s (and the father of 20 children!) when he decided emancipation must be won by force. With six of his sons and a son-in-law by his side, he went to Kansas to fight slavery in that state. In retaliation for a raid on an anti-slavery town, Brown and his followers attacked the slavery stronghold of Pottawatomie Creek and killed five men. Then they headed east for the U.S. arsenal at Harpers Ferry, Virginia (later West Virginia). He took the arsenal in 1859, but U.S. Army Colonel Robert E. Lee (future commander of Confederate forces) captured Brown. Hanged for treason, Brown became a martyr for the abolitionist cause.

Tracking the Centuries

509 BC: Lucius Junius Brutus wins the top administrative post in Rome's new republican government.

71 BC: Roman General Crassus puts down a slave revolt led by the gladiator Spartacus. He executes Spartacus and hundreds of his followers by hanging them from crosses along the Appian Way.

44 BC: Marcus Junius Brutus, descendant of Lucius Junius Brutus, joins fellow conspirators in assassinating Roman dictator Julius Caesar.

1381: William Walworth, Lord Mayor of London, orders the injured peasant leader Wat Tyler dragged out of a hospital and beheaded, ending England's Peasants' Revolt.

1532: Atahualpa, ruler of the northern half of the Inca Empire, overthrows his brother, king of the southern half, to reunite Inca lands. Within months, Spanish conquerors capture and kill Atahualpa.

1775: Officers under Russian Empress Catherine the Great torture and kill the leader of a widespread Cossack uprising, Emelian Ivanovich Pugachev.

1893: Mao Ze-dong, future founder and chairman of the People's Republic of China, is born in rural Hunan Province.

1922: The British colonial government of India imprisons nationalist leader Mohandas Karamchand Gandhi, known as the Mahatma, for conspiracy.

2008: President Robert Mugabe of Zimbabwe, who came to power as a revolutionary leader in 1980, agrees to a power-sharing agreement with rival parties after critics accuse him of manipulating the results of a hotly contested election and run-off.

Part VI
The Part of Tens

The 5th Wave   By Rich Tennant

IN JAN. 1943, THE DECISION TO INVADE ITALY THROUGH SICILY WAS MADE AT THE CASABLANCA CONFERENCE.

"President Roosevelt, you know General de Gaulle, Prime Minister Churchill, Sam the piano player..."

In this part . . .

Henry VIII had six wives. By some accounts, his second wife, Anne Boleyn, had an extra finger. So, Henry had as many wives as Anne had fingers on her right hand. What does this mean? Nothing that I can think of.

History, as I remind you throughout this book, is full of arbitrary judgments made by the people who gather it. I have only ten fingers, which is as good a reason as any for making the lists in this part of the book contain ten landmarks (that, and it's a standard but fun characteristic of *For Dummies* books). History is full of big dates and important documents. Which are the very tippy-top biggest and most important? In this part, I share my choices, but remember that they aren't the *only* choices. Disagreements help make history fun.

Chapter 23

Ten Unforgettable Dates in History

• •

In This Chapter

▶ Breaking new ground with democracy in Athens

▶ Watching the Roman Empire crumble

▶ Kicking off the Crusades

▶ Starting an age of revolutions in Philadelphia

▶ Taking a turn against human bondage

▶ Opening the polling booths to women

• •

1 f a teacher ever required you to memorize dates without bothering to get you interested in *why* whatever happened that day, month, or year matters, then you know why I almost hate to mention them.

Still, dates give events context and help you remember the order in which things occurred. Many dates serve as shorthand, standing for a broad change that hinged on a particular day or year. So, even if you hate memorizing dates (as I do), the ten that are spotlighted in this chapter are worth remembering. (If you don't think these dates are such biggies, feel free to choose your own.)

460 BC: Athens Goes Democratic

The aristocratic leader Pericles achieved his goal of turning Athens into a democracy between 462–460 BC. It wasn't the first-ever participatory government, but Athens became powerful during this time, and it remains the early democracy that most inspired later ones. In fact, the founding fathers of the United States looked back to Athenian democracy as a model.

Athens's popular assembly, the principal lawmaking body, was open to any male citizen (but not to women or to slaves, who were ineligible for citizenship). In addition to the popular assembly, there was a senate made up of citizens over age 30; it operated as an executive council that drew up the government's agenda and administered law enforcement. These two bodies set a precedent for two-house legislatures in later democracies. Think of Britain's House of Commons and House of Lords and the U.S. House of Representatives and Senate.

Although Athens's democracy was rule by citizens, Athenian society hung onto some aspects of its former *oligarchy* (rule by a few) as aristocrats retained privileges won by birth or connection. The glaring example was Pericles himself, who functioned almost as a king. (I talk more about Pericles' Athens in Chapter 11.)

323 BC: Alexander the Great Dies

Born in 356 BC, Alexander the Great succeeded his dad as king of Macedon (north of Greece) in 336 BC. Those were big dates. So were the years of his victories, such as when he beat Persia's King Darius III in 334 BC. But the year of the conqueror's early death — 323 BC — is most worth remembering.

Alex's conquests probably wouldn't have ended while he lived. He was too ambitious for that. Instead, his victories stopped when a fever (probably malaria) killed him. This event was a beginning as well as an end in that it began a remarkable period when Alex's generals became kings and founded dynasties in places ranging from Macedon to Persia to Egypt. Take Egypt, for example: Alexander's general Ptolemy founded a dynasty that continued until Rome's Augustus captured Queen Cleopatra in 30 BC.

476 AD: The Roman Empire Falls

Rome wasn't built in a day, and it didn't collapse in one either. Civil wars between competing military and political leaders rocked the Roman Republic from 88–28 BC, leading to the end of the republican form of rule and the beginning of government by one strong emperor. (Check out Augustus, the first emperor, in Chapter 19.)

Yet imperial rule eventually faltered, too, as the combination of third-century AD attacks on many fronts along the Roman Empire's far-flung borders and internal revolts forced the emperor Diocletian to take an extreme measure: Diocletian split the empire in two in 286 AD, installing himself as Emperor of the East (Egypt and Asia) and his colleague Maximian as Emperor of the West (Europe and northwest Africa). Although Diocletian still held authority over both halves, this system eventually led to the East becoming a separate empire, the Byzantine Empire, while the West went into a slow decline.

Huns, Vandals, Visigoths, and Ostragoths — all enemies of the Romans — kept pouring across the Rhine in the fifth century, eroding Rome's ability to defend its lands. By 476 AD, the empire had little authority left in Europe, so it wasn't such a big a deal when barbarians removed young Emperor Romulus Augustus (also known as Augustulus, or "little Augie") from his throne that year. Yet 476 AD stands as the symbolic end and the symbolic beginning of a feudal, fractured society from which the nations of Europe would eventually grow. (Find more about that ascendancy in Chapters 7 and 8.)

1066: Normans Conquer England

Wearing polyester half-sleeve shirts, plastic pocket protectors, and tape on their glasses, a band of guys named Norman rode into London and . . . oh, wait. These Normans were *French,* and they certainly weren't sporting pocket protectors.

I don't know how Britain would have turned out if William, Duke of Normandy, hadn't won the Battle of Hastings on October 14, 1066. I do know that the effects of the Norman conquest were felt for a long time. William, crowned king of England on December 25, 1066, and his family ruled for almost a century, replacing English nobles with Normans (from Normandy, later northern France), Bretons (also from France), and Flemings (from northern France and Belgium). From 1066–1144, England and Normandy had the same government, and Normandy remained in English hands until France's Philip II wrested it away in the thirteenth century.

Royal family ties and conflicting claims kept the English and French linked — and often at war — for centuries. You can trace the Hundred Years' War of the fourteenth and fifteenth centuries back to the Norman invasion. (For more about that war, see Chapter 17.)

1095: The First Crusade Commences

The Crusades, a prelude to worldwide European empires and colonialism, sent Western Europeans surging into another part of the world — the Middle East — where they threw their weight around and acted self-righteous.

The Crusades started after Seljuk Turks took over a large part of the Middle East from Arabs and from the Byzantine Empire, which resisted. The Turks had become Muslim, like the Arabs. But unlike Arabs of the seventh to eleventh centuries, the Turks weren't tolerant toward Christians. The Byzantine emperor asked Pope Urban II, a fellow Christian, to help him resist this new

Turkish threat. Urban also worried about reports of Christian pilgrims being harassed on their way to Palestine, the Holy Land (now under Seljuk rule).

On November 26, 1095, the pope called for Christian warriors to take on the Seljuk Turks. Two kinds of warriors answered:

- ✔ Untrained, ill-armed peasants and townspeople, who headed east, getting into trouble on the way and then getting themselves killed.

- ✔ Well-armed nobles and their troops, who defeated the Seljuk army defending Jerusalem in 1099 and massacred everybody in the city.

Later Crusades — which went on for centuries — were just as bloody and wandered even farther from the goal of restoring holiness to the Holy Land. (To find out how the Crusades foreshadowed European imperialism of the sixteenth to twentieth centuries, see Chapter 7.)

1492: Columbus Sails the Ocean Blue

Even if you've never memorized another date, you know 1492. The year marked the beginning of Europe's involvement with lands and cultures that would forever after bear the mark of Spain (the country Columbus represented), Portugal (his home base for years), and other European nations.

Columbus's discovery rearranged the world — or at least the way everybody thought of the world — by feeding a growing European hunger for conquest and helping bring about an age of imperialism that lasted into the twentieth century. Columbus's voyages (he kept going back to the New World, trying to establish that it really was part of Asia) also devastated the people who already lived in the New World, the people he called *Indians*. European diseases decimated their numbers, and European immigration pushed them from their lands.

For all the changes it brought, however, Columbus's feat was disappointing at the time — especially compared to what Portugal's Vasco da Gama did by rounding Africa and reaching India, a coveted trade destination, in 1598. (For more about Columbus, da Gama, and other European explorers, see Chapter 7.)

1776: Americans Break Away

The spirit of July 4, 1776, when the Continental Congress adopted the revolutionary Declaration of Independence, brought forth what would eventually be the most powerful nation in the world. But there's another reason this date is unforgettable.

The American Revolution, which was inspired by the Enlightenment thinking of the eighteenth century (see Chapter 15), began an age of revolutions. It set the stage for the culturally shattering French Revolution of 1789 and for many successive revolts both in European colonies and in Europe.

Rebellion swept South America early in the nineteenth century, and the middle of the century (especially 1848 and 1849) saw many more revolts in places such as Bohemia and Hungary. In the twentieth century, revolutionary fervor finally ended the colonial age. Revolutions also took on Marxist rhetoric and continued to overturn the old order in places as diverse as Russia and China.

1807: Britain Bans the Slave Trade

In the eighteenth century, more and more free people in Britain and elsewhere realized how wrong slavery was. They focused on the worst abuses, especially the cruelty of the transatlantic slave trade. Denmark was first to outlaw the trade in 1803. But because of Britain's stature in trade and naval power, the British ban a few years later marked a huge international shift. Parliament took the crucial step with the Abolition Act in 1807. In 1815, after the Napoleonic Wars, Britain leaned on France, the Netherlands, Spain, and Portugal to also stop trading in slaves.

The change grew out of Enlightenment ideas (see Chapter 15), specifically notions about natural law and human rights that also fed the revolutions in America and France. Religious and political sentiment turned. England's Quakers formed a Christian abolition society in 1787. Britain's top judge, Lord Mansfield, ruled as early as 1772 that fugitive slaves became free upon entering British soil. In the 1830s, Britain ordered all slaves freed.

Although idealism drove anti-slavery sentiment, the movement got a boost from economic pragmatism. By 1807, Britain's industrial revolution was taking off. The English saw more profit in Africa's natural resources and overseas markets than in slave labor.

1893: Women Start Getting the Vote around the World

The democratic revolution is still happening. Women first won the right to vote in New Zealand (then still a British colony) in 1893, but many other nations followed. Among them Australia in 1894, Norway in 1907, and Russia in 1917. British women over age 30 gained *suffrage* (they got the vote) in 1918, and the voting age for women there was lowered to 21 in 1929.

Women in the U.S. won this right when the 19th Amendment to the Constitution was ratified in 1920, although some states had passed women's suffrage earlier. France was a relative latecomer to this party, granting women the vote in 1944. In Switzerland, women didn't gain suffrage until 1971.

The twentieth century also saw a rapid, generation-by-generation expansion of women's roles and status in many societies worldwide. In Western industrial nations, especially, women took on professions formerly reserved for men and excelled in science, medicine, law, and journalism, among many other pursuits. Women ran for and won elective offices. Major democracies — notably Britain, India, Pakistan, and Israel — all saw female prime ministers in the second half of the twentieth century. In 1997, Madeleine Albright (1937–) became the first woman to serve as U.S. secretary of state, the top post in the president's cabinet. Following this precedent, Condoleezza Rice (1954–) and former first lady Hillary Clinton (1947–) also filled this important job in the early twenty-first century. Meanwhile, women in other countries — especially some parts of the Muslim world — were just beginning to seek greater freedoms.

1945: The United States Drops the A-Bomb

On August 6, 1945, 90,000 people died in the brilliant flash and impact that demolished 75 percent of the city of Hiroshima, Japan, after an American plane dropped the first nuclear bomb ever used in war. The explosion and the fire that followed wounded another 60,000 people, many of whom later died of radiation sickness and cancer. Three days later, Americans dropped another atomic bomb on Japan, this one on Nagasaki. Another 40,000 people died instantly.

The two atomic bombs caused indescribable, indiscriminate death and destruction. World War II finally ended, and the world entered the nuclear age.

These remain the only times nuclear weapons have been used against people. I hope they remain the only times. But the very existence of these atomic bombs and the far-more-powerful thermonuclear weapons that succeeded them make 1945 a huge and fearsome turning point.

Chapter 24

Ten Essential Historical Documents

Documents give humankind its history in that they preserve history. If no one had ever invented writing or started making formal records of battles, beliefs, laws, treaties, and so on, you'd have to sift history out of oral accounts.

Did you ever play the telephone game, where you whisper something into your neighbor's ear and she whispers what she heard to the next person, continuing around the room? If you have, you know how oral history changes from person to person, even in a span of a few minutes. Over centuries of relying on oral history, people would be left with little idea of what really went down. As for contractual agreements, everybody knows that the really important stuff should be put in writing.

Documents are important, and some documents prove to be extra important, not just in preserving the past but also in shaping it. Documents set down basic tenets of understanding, societal identity, and principles of right and wrong. Rule of law is a concept crucial to modern democracies. It means no king, president, mayor, police officer, or anybody else can make up the rules on the spot. To legally take any action — whether it be to negotiate a treaty between nuclear powers, appoint a town dogcatcher, or make an arrest — public officials are supposed to go by the book. And the book is a document.

The Rosetta Stone

As much artifact as document, the Rosetta Stone is a slab of black basalt that bears an inscribed text in ancient Greek and in two forms of old Egyptian writing: formal hieroglyphics (as seen on royal tomb walls) and the more common demotic script. In 1799, during Napoleon's occupation of Egypt, some of his soldiers found this rock on the Rosetta fork of the Nile River at Raschid, near Alexandria. The stone had been carved about 2,000 years earlier, in 196 BC.

When the French soldiers recovered the stone, nobody knew how to read hieroglyphics (more on hieroglyphics in Chapter 4). Ancient Egyptian history seemed lost forever.

Scholars Thomas Young and Jean François Champollion worked long and hard to decipher the Rosetta Stone, establishing that the three texts all said the same thing in different languages. Using his knowledge of ancient Greek, Champollion was able to announce in 1822 that he could read hieroglyphics. The Rosetta Stone provided an entryway into the remote Egyptian past.

You can see the Rosetta Stone in London's British Museum.

Confucian Analects

In the Western world, people attribute the golden rule to Jesus. But 500 years before Jesus, a humble Chinese teacher, Kung Ch'iu, told his students, "Do to others what you would have them do to you."

Kung lived from around 551–479 BC. He became a government official as a teenager, in charge of grain stores and pastures at 15, and worked his way up to high office. His ideas for reform made him popular with the public but also angered some privileged people.

After enemies forced him to leave his native province, Kung traveled and spread his ideas about respect for others, reverence for ancestors, obedience, shared values, loyalty, and self-improvement. He stressed the concepts of *li* (proper behavior) and *jen* (sympathetic attitude). His students gave Kung the respectful title *Futzu,* meaning "venerated master." You can find more about Kung Futzu's teachings in Chapter 10.

Late in Kung's Futzu's life and after he died, followers gathered his sayings into the *Analects,* a tremendously influential source of Chinese thought. Confucianism (from the Latin version of Kung Futzu, *Confucius*) shaped

Chinese character, blending with other philosophical and religious schools such as Taoism, Buddhism, and Legalism. Until the twentieth century, every student training to be an official in the Chinese government had to study the *Analects*. Confucianism also influenced other Asian cultures. It was especially important in Japan during the Tokugawa, or *Edo,* period, which lasted from 1603–1867. Over most of those years, Confucian values were endorsed and enforced by a military dictatorship called the Shogunate and helped maintain a remarkable level of social stability in Japan.

The Bible

This is a package deal — a treasure chest of documents all wrapped up into one volume. Which version of the Bible you're talking about depends on which tradition you follow, but regardless of how you know the Bible, it's an indispensable document for understanding the course of many world events.

In its Christian form, the Bible includes writings that are at the heart of two major religions — Judaism and Christianity. (Chapter 10 talks about world religions.) The Bible contains the *Pentateuch,* or Jewish Priestly Law (the written Torah) and both the Ten Commandments (Old Testament) and the Christian golden rule.

Bible stories stand as an important source of history, even as many historians challenge their literal truth. The Bible's teachings have shaped the courses of great nations, including the Roman and Byzantine empires, as I discuss in Chapters 5 and 6. The Bible also figures in a huge technological change, courtesy of Johannes Gutenberg, who chose it as the first book to come off his revolutionary printing press.

The Bible played a role in important linguistic changes, too. Both the German and English languages were shaped by early major translations of the Bible into those languages. For German, it was Martin Luther's 1530 translation. For English, it was the King James edition of 1611. It may sound funny, but the way you talk right now owes a lot to a 400-year-old book full of "thee" and "thou."

The Koran

A holy book like the Bible, the Koran (also spelled Qur'an) is the foundation of not just religious practice but also daily life, formal law, and government policy in most of the Islamic world — a huge, wealthy, and powerful part of humanity more than a millennium ago and today, too.

The Koran defines Islam's place in history. Its verses spurred the Arab conquests of the seventh and eighth centuries and continue to shape the Muslim worldview today.

Muslims believe that the Koran is God's direct, infallible word, and that the angel Gabriel revealed it, as written in heaven, to the Prophet Mohammed, founder of Islam, in the seventh century AD (see Chapter 10). Muslims consider the text sacred. To touch sacred text without being ritually pure is forbidden. If you imitate its style — in which God (Allah) speaks in verse — you have committed a sacrilege.

Like other religious scripture, the Koran has been subject to conflicting interpretations. Some extremist Islamic teachers cite the book as a source of justification for acts of violence carried out by anti-Israeli, anti-American, anti-Indian, and other terrorist organizations. The vast majority of Muslims worldwide, however, see nothing in the Koran that justifies modern terrorism.

In addition to its impact on world events, the Koran is also the book from which Muslims traditionally learn to read Arabic. That makes the Koran perhaps the most widely read of all books, ever.

The Magna Carta

The idea of the divine right of kings (covered in Chapter 12) was based on the understanding that the monarch, as God's deputy, had to care for creation's lesser children. A subject, whether commoner or noble, had a duty to respect and obey the king. But the king's godly duty, in return, was to defend and protect his subjects. A certain mutual respect was implied.

Often it didn't work like that, however. John, the most unpopular of England's kings, upset his barons and they rebelled. In 1215, the barons got the upper hand, forcing King John to sign a contract, the Great Charter, or *Magna Carta* in Latin (official language of thirteenth-century Europe).

By signing, King John agreed to specific rules on respecting his subjects. The Magna Carta contained 63 clauses, most relating to King John's misuse of his financial and judicial powers. Clauses 39 and 40, the two most famous, say that

> *No freeman shall be taken or imprisoned except by the lawful judgment of his equals or by the law of the land.* [A freeman was an adult male subject of the crown who wasn't a serf or slave.]

> *To no one will we sell, to no one will we deny or delay right or justice.*

This first formal attempt at separating kingship from tyranny didn't solve all the problems between King John and the barons, but the charter set a precedent for laws regarding rights, justice, and the exercise of authority in England, the British Empire, and beyond. The Great Charter pointed toward constitutional freedoms guaranteed by the founders of republics such as the United States of America.

The Travels of Marco Polo

When thirteenth- and fourteenth-century Venetians called Marco Polo *Il Milione,* they were repeating one title of his well-read book about his travels and his life in China. (Polo's book appeared under other titles in various translations and editions.) *Il Milione* referred to the vast wealth (millions) possessed by China's emperor, Kublai Khan.

But some of Polo's fellow Europeans also used the term *Il Milione* to mean that Marco Polo told a million lies. Many couldn't believe his tales of Kublai Khan's magnificent empire. China seemed almost as remote as another planet; only a few other Western travelers of the thirteenth century had seen Beijing, including Polo's father and uncle, who took the lad along on their second journey east in 1271.

Marco Polo's knowledge of the East and its riches gained believers because he put his experiences in writing. More and more people became fascinated by his reports, and his book, known in English as *The Travels of Marco Polo,* became a fourteenth-century must-read. It fed hunger for silk, ceramics, and other exotic goods and drove the quest to find a sea route to transport those goods. As historian Daniel J. Boorstin puts it in his book *The Discoverers,* "Without Marco Polo . . . would there have been a Christopher Columbus?" You could go so far as to trace the age of European conquest and colonialism to Polo's account of travels through the Far East.

The Declaration of Independence

When in the Course of human events, it becomes necessary for one people to dissolve the political bands which have connected them with another . . . they should declare the causes which impel them to the separation.

Say what? It's my pared-down version of the opening sentence from a great document written largely by Thomas Jefferson and approved by the Continental Congress on July 4, 1776 (see the previous chapter for more on that monumental date).

The Revolutionary War was already on, so the Declaration of Independence wasn't about war as much as it was an *explanation* of why America's colonial leaders felt they had to do what they were doing. For example, it's full of specific grievances against King George III. But Jefferson — with assists from Benjamin Franklin and John Adams — also did a brilliant job of summing up some of the most compelling political and social philosophy to come out of the eighteenth century philosophical movement, the Enlightenment. Here's a perfect example:

> *We hold these truths to be self-evident, that all men are created equal, that they are endowed by their Creator with certain unalienable Rights, that among these are Life, Liberty and the pursuit of Happiness.*

The Declaration doesn't mention women and didn't apply to all men — it excluded slaves. Still, Jefferson's were powerful words. The document says that people have not just a right but a *responsibility* to stand up to government when the exercise of authority is unjust. Those words echoed through the rest of the eighteenth century, the two centuries that followed it, and into this one. (Chapter 15 has more about revolutionary philosophies.)

The Bill of Rights

Drawn up in 1789 and added to the U.S. Constitution on December 15, 1791, the first ten Constitutional amendments were powerful afterthoughts intended to limit the power of government and to guarantee certain rights — civil liberties — to everybody.

Freedom of speech, freedom of the press, and freedom of religion come from the First Amendment, which specifically guarantees those freedoms. The Second Amendment, the one that begins, "A well-regulated Militia, being necessary to the security of a free State . . . ", is the one that gun control advocates and gun-rights advocates continue to argue about more than 200 years after it was passed.

People argue all the time about the Bill of Rights. Everyday citizens, members of Congress, talk show hosts, and judges interpret and reinterpret this essential American document. Supreme Court justices spend much of their time deciding what the framers of the Constitution meant when they wrote these amendments.

Debatable but indelible, the Bill of Rights provides a permanent curb on what government can get away with. Like the Declaration of Independence, these amendments have been copied and elaborated upon by many other democracies around the world.

The Communist Manifesto

The 1848 *Communist Manifesto* and its 1869 sequel, *Das Kapital,* seem thoroughly discredited now. The biggest governments founded upon *Das Kapital*'s arguments collapsed (the Soviet Union in 1991) or made concessions to private property and individual incentive (the People's Republic of China).

Still, the worldwide impact of this economic-political treatise by Karl Marx and Friedrich Engels has been incredible. The work has incited numerous revolutions and drastically reshaped societies.

The *Communist Manifesto* attacks government, religion, and traditional culture as tools of a repressive *capitalist class,* defined as people who own factories and mines and use other people to get profit from these properties. Marx and Engels present communism — with collective ownership of industry and farms and equal distribution of resources among everybody — as the only economic system fair to everybody. In theory, their arguments struck a powerful chord among working people worldwide in the nineteenth century. In practice, no so-called communist society ever achieved anything close to its ideal of a classless society in which all are equal and none enjoy special privilege. Communist party leaders in the Soviet Union, for example, became a new aristocracy, enjoying the confiscated summer homes that had once belonged to Russian nobles.

Despite such failures, socialist ideas linked to Marx's theories are still powerful influences on workers' rights and government responsibility in virtually every developed country. Western European nations, with their national health services, generous unemployment benefits, and numerous government-run social programs, are widely understood to be socialist democracies. Even in the United States, where socialism has long been considered a dirty word, labor protection laws and programs such as Medicare and Social Security are rooted in the socialist concept of a society's responsibility to its citizens.

On the Origin of Species

Charles Darwin's theory of evolution by natural selection, set forth in his 1859 book *On the Origin of Species,* underlies the way scientists ever since Darwin approach the study of living things. Modern biology, anthropology, and paleontology are all based on the idea of evolution.

In the nineteenth century, most naturalists thought that plant and animal varieties were unchanged since God created the world. Others acknowledged change but thought that a trait acquired in life could be passed on to offspring, as in a mare with a bad hoof giving birth to a limping colt. In his 20s, Darwin (1809–1892) traveled around the world as a naturalist onboard a British naval survey ship. His observations made him doubt both theories.

The idea of species evolving by natural selection is called *Darwinism* even though Darwin recognized at least 20 other scientists who had proposed similar ideas. What Darwin did that the others didn't, though, was support his theory with boatloads of hard data from all over the world.

Darwin also wrote in plain enough language that anybody could read *On the Origin of Species.* This accessibility brought him fame but also attracted opposition. Many religious people decried any theory of life that didn't rely on direct divine intervention. Some religious conservatives were especially shocked at the Darwinist notion that humankind evolved like other animals.

Others hijacked Darwin's ideas and applied them incorrectly to human society in ways that led to some of the twentieth century's most shameful episodes. Even respected scholars and government leaders in the U.S. bought into the false idea that members of certain ethnic groups and social classes are more highly evolved than other people. This belief led to state laws that allowed doctors and judges to order involuntary sterilization of citizens judged to be "unfit" to reproduce. These victims included the mentally and physically ill but also habitual criminals, alcoholics, and even the unemployed. Germany's anti-Semitic National Socialist party used such American laws as a template when fashioning the policies that eventually led to wholesale slaughter of Jews and others deemed undesirable by dictator Adolf Hitler.

Meanwhile, scientists made legitimate use of Darwin's ideas by developing such fields of study as genetics and molecular genetics. In the late twentieth and early twenty-first centuries, the study of DNA led to an ever more detailed and complex understanding of how living things pass on genes to their offspring and how evolution actually works.

Index

BUSINESS, CAREERS & PERSONAL FINANCE

Accounting For Dummies, 4th Edition*
978-0-470-24600-9

Bookkeeping Workbook For Dummies†
978-0-470-16983-4

Commodities For Dummies
978-0-470-04928-0

Doing Business in China For Dummies
978-0-470-04929-7

E-Mail Marketing For Dummies
978-0-470-19087-6

Job Interviews For Dummies, 3rd Edition*†
978-0-470-17748-8

Personal Finance Workbook For Dummies*†
978-0-470-09933-9

Real Estate License Exams For Dummies
978-0-7645-7623-2

Six Sigma For Dummies
978-0-7645-6798-8

**Small Business Kit For Dummies,
2nd Edition*†**
978-0-7645-5984-6

Telephone Sales For Dummies
978-0-470-16836-3

BUSINESS PRODUCTIVITY & MICROSOFT OFFICE

Access 2007 For Dummies
978-0-470-03649-5

Excel 2007 For Dummies
978-0-470-03737-9

Office 2007 For Dummies
978-0-470-00923-9

Outlook 2007 For Dummies
978-0-470-03830-7

PowerPoint 2007 For Dummies
978-0-470-04059-1

Project 2007 For Dummies
978-0-470-03651-8

QuickBooks 2008 For Dummies
978-0-470-18470-7

Quicken 2008 For Dummies
978-0-470-17473-9

**Salesforce.com For Dummies,
2nd Edition**
978-0-470-04893-1

Word 2007 For Dummies
978-0-470-03658-7

EDUCATION, HISTORY, REFERENCE & TEST PREPARATION

African American History For Dummies
978-0-7645-5469-8

Algebra For Dummies
978-0-7645-5325-7

Algebra Workbook For Dummies
978-0-7645-8467-1

Art History For Dummies
978-0-470-09910-0

ASVAB For Dummies, 2nd Edition
978-0-470-10671-6

British Military History For Dummies
978-0-470-03213-8

Calculus For Dummies
978-0-7645-2498-1

Canadian History For Dummies, 2nd Edition
978-0-470-83656-9

Geometry Workbook For Dummies
978-0-471-79940-5

The SAT I For Dummies, 6th Edition
978-0-7645-7193-0

Series 7 Exam For Dummies
978-0-470-09932-2

World History For Dummies
978-0-7645-5242-7

FOOD, GARDEN, HOBBIES & HOME

Bridge For Dummies, 2nd Edition
978-0-471-92426-5

Coin Collecting For Dummies, 2nd Edition
978-0-470-22275-1

Cooking Basics For Dummies, 3rd Edition
978-0-7645-7206-7

Drawing For Dummies
978-0-7645-5476-6

Etiquette For Dummies, 2nd Edition
978-0-470-10672-3

Gardening Basics For Dummies*†
978-0-470-03749-2

Knitting Patterns For Dummies
978-0-470-04556-5

Living Gluten-Free For Dummies†
978-0-471-77383-2

Painting Do-It-Yourself For Dummies
978-0-470-17533-0

HEALTH, SELF HELP, PARENTING & PETS

Anger Management For Dummies
978-0-470-03715-7

**Anxiety & Depression Workbook
For Dummies**
978-0-7645-9793-0

Dieting For Dummies, 2nd Edition
978-0-7645-4149-0

Dog Training For Dummies, 2nd Edition
978-0-7645-8418-3

Horseback Riding For Dummies
978-0-470-09719-9

Infertility For Dummies†
978-0-470-11518-3

**Meditation For Dummies with CD-ROM,
2nd Edition**
978-0-471-77774-8

Post-Traumatic Stress Disorder For Dummies
978-0-470-04922-8

Puppies For Dummies, 2nd Edition
978-0-470-03717-1

Thyroid For Dummies, 2nd Edition†
978-0-471-78755-6

Type 1 Diabetes For Dummies*†
978-0-470-17811-9

* Separate Canadian edition also available
* Separate U.K. edition also available

Available wherever books are sold. For more information or to order direct: U.S. customers visit www.dummies.com or call 1-877-762-2974.
U.K. customers visit www.wileyeurope.com or call (0) 1243 843291. Canadian customers visit www.wiley.ca or call 1-800-567-4797.

INTERNET & DIGITAL MEDIA

AdWords For Dummies
978-0-470-15252-2

Blogging For Dummies, 2nd Edition
978-0-470-23017-6

Digital Photography All-in-One Desk Reference For Dummies, 3rd Edition
978-0-470-03743-0

Digital Photography For Dummies, 5th Edition
978-0-7645-9802-9

Digital SLR Cameras & Photography For Dummies, 2nd Edition
978-0-470-14927-0

eBay Business All-in-One Desk Reference For Dummies
978-0-7645-8438-1

eBay For Dummies, 5th Edition*
978-0-470-04529-9

eBay Listings That Sell For Dummies
978-0-471-78912-3

Facebook For Dummies
978-0-470-26273-3

The Internet For Dummies, 11th Edition
978-0-470-12174-0

Investing Online For Dummies, 5th Edition
978-0-7645-8456-5

iPod & iTunes For Dummies, 5th Edition
978-0-470-17474-6

MySpace For Dummies
978-0-470-09529-4

Podcasting For Dummies
978-0-471-74898-4

Search Engine Optimization For Dummies, 2nd Edition
978-0-471-97998-2

Second Life For Dummies
978-0-470-18025-9

Starting an eBay Business For Dummies, 3rd Edition†
978-0-470-14924-9

GRAPHICS, DESIGN & WEB DEVELOPMENT

Adobe Creative Suite 3 Design Premium All-in-One Desk Reference For Dummies
978-0-470-11724-8

Adobe Web Suite CS3 All-in-One Desk Reference For Dummies
978-0-470-12099-6

AutoCAD 2008 For Dummies
978-0-470-11650-0

Building a Web Site For Dummies, 3rd Edition
978-0-470-14928-7

Creating Web Pages All-in-One Desk Reference For Dummies, 3rd Edition
978-0-470-09629-1

Creating Web Pages For Dummies, 8th Edition
978-0-470-08030-6

Dreamweaver CS3 For Dummies
978-0-470-11490-2

Flash CS3 For Dummies
978-0-470-12100-9

Google SketchUp For Dummies
978-0-470-13744-4

InDesign CS3 For Dummies
978-0-470-11865-8

Photoshop CS3 All-in-One Desk Reference For Dummies
978-0-470-11195-6

Photoshop CS3 For Dummies
978-0-470-11193-2

Photoshop Elements 5 For Dummies
978-0-470-09810-3

SolidWorks For Dummies
978-0-7645-9555-4

Visio 2007 For Dummies
978-0-470-08983-5

Web Design For Dummies, 2nd Edition
978-0-471-78117-2

Web Sites Do-It-Yourself For Dummies
978-0-470-16903-2

Web Stores Do-It-Yourself For Dummies
978-0-470-17443-2

LANGUAGES, RELIGION & SPIRITUALITY

Arabic For Dummies
978-0-471-77270-5

Chinese For Dummies, Audio Set
978-0-470-12766-7

French For Dummies
978-0-7645-5193-2

German For Dummies
978-0-7645-5195-6

Hebrew For Dummies
978-0-7645-5489-6

Ingles Para Dummies
978-0-7645-5427-8

Italian For Dummies, Audio Set
978-0-470-09586-7

Italian Verbs For Dummies
978-0-471-77389-4

Japanese For Dummies
978-0-7645-5429-2

Latin For Dummies
978-0-7645-5431-5

Portuguese For Dummies
978-0-471-78738-9

Russian For Dummies
978-0-471-78001-4

Spanish Phrases For Dummies
978-0-7645-7204-3

Spanish For Dummies
978-0-7645-5194-9

Spanish For Dummies, Audio Set
978-0-470-09585-0

The Bible For Dummies
978-0-7645-5296-0

Catholicism For Dummies
978-0-7645-5391-2

The Historical Jesus For Dummies
978-0-470-16785-4

Islam For Dummies
978-0-7645-5503-9

Spirituality For Dummies, 2nd Edition
978-0-470-19142-2

NETWORKING AND PROGRAMMING

ASP.NET 3.5 For Dummies
978-0-470-19592-5

C# 2008 For Dummies
978-0-470-19109-5

Hacking For Dummies, 2nd Edition
978-0-470-05235-8

Home Networking For Dummies, 4th Edition
978-0-470-11806-1

Java For Dummies, 4th Edition
978-0-470-08716-9

Microsoft® SQL Server™ 2008 All-in-One Desk Reference For Dummies
978-0-470-17954-3

Networking All-in-One Desk Reference For Dummies, 2nd Edition
978-0-7645-9939-2

Networking For Dummies, 8th Edition
978-0-470-05620-2

SharePoint 2007 For Dummies
978-0-470-09941-4

Wireless Home Networking For Dummies, 2nd Edition
978-0-471-74940-0